MW01275121

The Laws and the Land

PATRONS OF THE OSGOODE SOCIETY

Professor Constance Backhouse, University of Ottawa
Chernos, Flaherty, Svonkin LLP
Gowlings WLG
Hull & Hull LLP
Mr. Wayne Kerr
McCarthy Tetrault LLP
Osler, Hoskin & Harcourt LLP
Paliare Roland Rosenberg Rothstein LLP
Pape Chaudhury LLP
The Hon. Robert J. Sharpe
Torys LLP
WeirFoulds LLP

The Osgoode Society is supported by a grant from
the Law Foundation of Ontario

The Society also thanks the Law Society of Ontario
for its continued support.

LAW AND SOCIETY SERIES
W. Wesley Pue, Founding Editor

The Law and Society Series explores law as a socially embedded
phenomenon. It is premised on the understanding that the conventional
division of law from society creates false dichotomies in thinking, scholarship,
educational practice, and social life. Books in the series treat law and society
as mutually constitutive and seek to bridge scholarship emerging from
interdisciplinary engagement of law with disciplines such as politics,
social theory, history, political economy, and gender studies.

For a list of the titles in this series, see the UBC Press website,
www.ubcpress.ca.

The Laws
and the Land

The Settler Colonial Invasion of Kahnawà:ke in Nineteenth-Century Canada

DANIEL RÜCK

PUBLISHED BY UBC PRESS FOR
THE OSGOODE SOCIETY
FOR CANADIAN LEGAL HISTORY

© UBC Press 2021

All rights reserved. No part of this publication may be reproduced, stored in a retrieval system, or transmitted, in any form or by any means, without prior written permission of the publisher, or, in Canada, in the case of photocopying or other reprographic copying, a licence from Access Copyright, www.accesscopyright.ca.

30 29 28 27 26 25 24 23 22 21   5 4 3 2 1

Printed in Canada on paper that is processed chlorine- and acid-free, with vegetable-based inks.

Library and Archives Canada Cataloguing in Publication

Title: The laws and the land : the settler colonial invasion of Kahnawà:ke in nineteenth-century Canada / Daniel Rück.
Names: Rück, Daniel (Professor), author.
Series: Law and society series (Vancouver, B.C.)
Description: Series statement: Law and society | Co-published by the Osgoode Society for Canadian Legal History. | Includes bibliographical references.
Identifiers: Canadiana (print) 20210247886 | Canadiana (ebook) 20210256516 | ISBN 9780774867436 (hardcover) | ISBN 9780774867450 (PDF) | ISBN 9780774867467 (EPUB)
Subjects: LCSH: Indigenous peoples – Land tenure – Québec (Province) – Kahnawake. | LCSH: Land tenure – Québec (Province) – Kahnawake – History. | LCSH: Canada. Indian Act. | LCSH: Kahnawake (Québec) – Race relations – History. | LCSH: Kahnawake (Québec) – Ethnic relations – History. | LCSH: Kahnawake (Québec) – History – 19th century. | LCSH: Settler colonialism – Canada. | CSH: First Nations – Legal status, laws, etc. – Québec (Province) – Kahnawake. | CSH: First Nations – Québec (Province) – Kahnawake – Government relations.
Classification: LCC KIC5532.7 .R83 2021 | LCC KF8228.M8 R83 2021 kfmod | DDC 342.7108/72–dc23

Canada

UBC Press gratefully acknowledges the financial support for our publishing program of the Government of Canada (through the Canada Book Fund), the Canada Council for the Arts, and the British Columbia Arts Council.

This book has been published with the help of a grant from the Canadian Federation for the Humanities and Social Sciences, through the Awards to Scholarly Publications Program, using funds provided by the Social Sciences and Humanities Research Council of Canada.

UBC Press
The University of British Columbia
2029 West Mall
Vancouver, BC V6T 1Z2
www.ubcpress.ca

To Alec Brian Deer and Roy Wright

Contents

Illustrations

Foreword

THE OSGOODE SOCIETY FOR CANADIAN LEGAL HISTORY

*T*he *Laws and the Land* is a history of the relationship between Kahnawà:ke and Canada. It is the story of land and law set in the territory of the sovereign Kanien'kehá:ka Nation near Montreal, focused on its interaction with the expanding settler state of Canada over the course of the nineteenth century. That relationship was marked by the asymmetrical encounter between Kahnawà:ke law and Canadian "Indian laws," in the context of Confederation, the *Indian Act,* Indigenous history, and the global history of settler colonialism. Using extensive archival research, Daniel Rück reveals an increasingly powerful and belligerent Canada interfering in the governance of Kahnawà:ke, one of the most populous and influential Indigenous communities in nineteenth-century Canada. Yet the colonial state described in this book was not simply a well-organized, irresistible machine; it was also a polity defined by contradiction, inconsistency, and weakness, which themselves become sources of oppression for colonized people. This is the story of the meeting of two legal traditions in a settler colonial context and of the lawlessness and violence that can emerge from the colonization process.

The purpose of the Osgoode Society for Canadian Legal History is to encourage research and writing in the history of Canadian law. The society, which was incorporated in 1979 and is registered as a charity, was founded at the initiative of the Honourable R. Roy McMurtry and officials of the Law Society of Ontario. The society seeks to stimulate the study of legal history in Canada by supporting researchers, collecting oral histories, and publishing volumes that contribute to legal-historical scholarship in

Canada. This year's books bring the total published since 1981 to 114, in all fields of legal history – the courts, the judiciary, and the legal profession, as well as the history of crime and punishment, women and law, law and the economy, the legal treatment of Indigenous peoples and ethnic minorities, and famous cases and significant trials in all areas of the law.

Current directors of the Osgoode Society for Canadian Legal History are Constance Backhouse, Heidi Bohaker, Bevin Brookbank, Shantona Chaudhury, David Chernos, Paul Davis, Doug Downey, Linda Silver Dranoff, Timothy Hill, Ian Hull, Trisha Jackson, Mahmud Jamal, Waleed Malik, Rachel McMillan, Roy McMurtry, Dana Peebles, Paul Reinhardt, Paul Schabas, Robert Sharpe, Jon Silver, Alex Smith, Lorne Sossin, Mary Stokes, Michael Tulloch, and John Wilkinson.

Robert J. Sharpe
President

Jim Phillips
Editor-in-Chief

Acknowledgments

It gives me great pleasure to acknowledge and thank the many people and organizations who contributed to this project. I want to thank grad school friends, departmental colleagues, administrators, friends, family members, collaborators, examiners, editors, committee members – so many of you supported me in small and big ways. My heart is full when I think of your kindnesses. I am naming only a select few to whom I am particularly grateful as I wrap up this manuscript. My first thank-you goes to Elsbeth Heaman at McGill University, who trusted me and advocated for me in the early years of this project. Colin Coates at York University supported me many generous ways during a particularly difficult time in my career. Legal historian Philip Girard carefully read my work on several occasions and sent me generous and constructive responses to various parts. One of my most important mentors at the University of Ottawa has been my colleague Brenda Macdougall – the support and leadership of scholars like her gave me the space and energy to complete this book. I am especially grateful to the linguist Roy Wright for his friendship, helping me with Kanien'kéha texts and names, and bringing his encyclopedic knowledge of multiple disciplines to bear on my project. He died in 2018, and this book is dedicated, in part, to his memory. I miss him.

This project could not have been accomplished without the help, advice, and encouragement of a number of people and organizations in Kahnawà:ke. I particularly acknowledge the Kanien'kehá:ka Onkwawén:na Raotitióhkwa Language and Cultural Center, which for outside researchers tends to be the first point of connection in the community. For me, it remains an important place of learning and sharing. I am grateful to Oskenontona Philip Deering, Teiowí:sonte Thomas Deer, Katsitsenhawitha Christine Zachary Deom, Kahente Horn-Miller, Orenda Boucher-Curotte, Steve Bonspiel, Ka'nhehsí:io Deer, Martin Akwiranoron Loft, the late Lori Niioieren Jacobs, and others for the small and large ways in which they contributed in this project. The late Tionerahtoken A. Brian Deer played a key role in introducing me to the community, offering advice, and commenting on portions of my work (I say more in the Introduction). Over the years, I frequently consulted with language teacher and community historian Kahrhó:wane Cory McComber on a wide range of issues including orthography, sources, and historical interpretation. This book is much better thanks to his corrections and suggestions – I am deeply grateful.

I also wish to thank the numerous entities that provided institutional support and funding, beginning with the Social Sciences and Humanities Research Council of Canada, the Fonds québécois de la recherche sur la société et la culture, the Bibliothèque et Archives nationales du Québec, the McGill Institute for the Study of Canada, and the Osgoode Society for Canadian Legal History. I am grateful to Jim Phillips and the Osgoode Society for their enthusiastic and patient support for this project. I also wish to thank supportive colleagues at the University of Ottawa Faculty of Arts, Department of History, and Institute for Indigenous Research and Studies. Finally, my gratitude goes out to the editors, designers, board members, and anonymous reviewers at UBC Press.

Abbreviations

BANQ	Bibliothèque et Archives nationales du Québec
CPR	Canadian Pacific Railway
DIA	Department of Indian Affairs
LAC	Library and Archives Canada
OIC	Order-in-Council

The Laws and the Land

Introduction

In geopolitical terms, the impact of settler colonialism is starkly visible in the landscapes it produces: the symmetrically surveyed divisions of land; fences, roads, power lines, dams and mines; the vast mono-cultural expanses of single-cropped fields; carved and preserved national forest, and marine and wilderness parks; the expansive and gridded cities; and the socially coded areas of human habitation and trespass that are bordered, policed and defended. Land and the organised spaces on it, in other words, narrate the stories of colonisation.

— *Tracey Banivanua Mar and Penelope Edmonds*

From the vantage point of the colonized, a position from which I write, and choose to privilege, the term "research" is inextricably linked to European imperialism and colonialism. The word itself, "research," is probably one of the dirtiest words in the indigenous world's vocabulary. When mentioned in many indigenous contexts, it stirs up silence, it conjures up bad memories, it raises a smile that is knowing and distrustful.

— *Linda Tuhiwai Smith*

One of my first experiences in Kahnawà:ke came as a student in 2006, when the elder Tionerahtoken A. Brian Deer informally welcomed me to the community by taking me for coffee and giving me an extensive tour in his minivan. I was concerned about my positionality as a white settler outsider who was interested in doing historical research on Kahnawà:ke, and I asked Brian for his opinion on what

Kahnawa'kehró:non (people of Kahnawà:ke) would think about my plans to look into the history of land surveying and property.[1] He surprised me by saying that my topic would seem obscure to most people, that I shouldn't worry too much about it, and that I should instead focus on being a responsible, accountable researcher. Looking back now, I realize that Brian knew full well my topic was potentially controversial and deeply connected to important and possibly divisive issues such as race, land, inequality, and membership. He also knew that I would make mistakes, but he chose to encourage me anyway. That meeting was the beginning of a mentorship and friendship that lasted until his death in January 2019.

Brian was an unusual and talented person: a kid with a lung condition who was told he wouldn't live past sixteen but proved everyone wrong; a community historian who didn't consider himself a historian; an avid hockey fan with a bachelor's degree in mathematics; a film buff who owned and ran a video store; a professional librarian who in the 1970s developed a new library classification system for Indigenous libraries, now known as the Brian Deer Classification system. Brian taught a regular course at Concordia University on Indigenous religions and wrote articles and reports on topics ranging from Rotinonhsión:ni diplomacy to the history of the Kahnawà:ke sewer system.[2] For our first meetings, I often brought research questions or particular archival tidbits to discuss, and I would get frustrated when he sometimes didn't seem very interested and wanted to talk about something else, whether it was the Kanehsatà:ke Resistance (Oka Crisis) or the Latvian national hockey team. I think this was his way of teaching me to put my agenda aside and listen.

Years later, when I was planning my dissertation defence (a kind of accountability process to my academic community), I asked Brian and his brother Oskenontona Philip Deering how I could be accountable to Kahnawa'kehró:non while completing my work. They told me that decades before, when they still regularly invited outsiders into longhouse meetings, people like me would be given a few minutes during a social event to publicly explain their work. Afterward, anyone could talk with the speaker about it. Since this is no longer done, they suggested I present my work on local radio, in the Kahnawà:ke newspaper, and with a public presentation at the library. That summer, I shared my work on the *Party Line Talk Show* of K103.7 and gave a formal presentation at the Skawenniio Tsi Iewennahnotahkhwa (Kahnawà:ke Public Library). When a reporter for the newspaper the *Eastern Door* asked Brian for a comment, he said, "I've met many researchers over the years and it's refreshing to meet someone who's interested in Kahnawà:ke without an agenda."[3] I was surprised by his remark, since I definitely did have an agenda, but I understood it to mean that he saw me as willing to listen and to change it if necessary – to be accountable.

Brian was one of several people in Kahnawà:ke who took an interest in me and my work, who set aside time to teach me and mentor me (see Acknowledgments). I am deeply grateful to all of them, whether or not they knew they were my teachers. Brian later supported me and my career by writing letters of recommendation for dozens of university departments where I applied for faculty positions. I hope this book honours his memory, and I continue to strive to be worthy of his trust in me, as well as the many others who trusted me with their time, energy, and knowledge.

I have opened *The Laws and the Land* with this story about Brian because his comment about agendas gets to the heart of the colonial problem I want to address. Settlers have been coming to Kahnawà:ke for centuries with agendas, and their actions have often caused incredible harm. Their agendas have not always been explicitly to harm, but even many well-intentioned settlers did great damage because they were not willing to listen or take Kanien'kehá:ka points of view seriously. Sometimes it was white men who married into the community and then refused to live according to Kahnawà:ke laws so that they could enrich themselves (Chapter 2). Sometimes it was missionaries who preached their truth rather than listen for the truth of others. It was storytellers like me – anthropologists, historians, journalists – who came in with their minds already made up, saw what they expected to see, and reported their "findings" back to their audience. It was Indian agents who imposed the agenda of the Department of Indian Affairs (DIA), or their own personal agendas, and meddled in every aspect of Kahnawà:ke lives.[4] In the period covered by *The Laws and the Land,* the DIA was defined by paternalism: officials projected an unshakable certainty in Indigenous people's helplessness and savagery, and in their own ability to identify and solve Indigenous problems for them. In writing this book, I have striven to avoid this colonial hubris but acknowledge that I may have failed in ways that escape my attention. As a white, cis-gender man living in a settler colonial state, I continue to cause harm in ways I do not yet fully understand, but I have tried to remain accountable to Kahnawa'kehró:non in ways that I hope will make this book more valuable, helpful, and true.

The Laws and the Land tells the story of a settler colonial state (Canada) operating on Indigenous lands and its invasion of one Indigenous community (Kahnawà:ke) living on a tiny portion of its vast traditional territory (Figure 0.1). Kahnawà:ke is an Indigenous community and nation, part

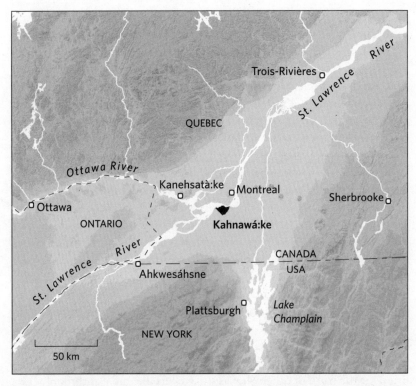

FIGURE O.1 Kahnawà:ke in regional context. Kahnawà:ke and Montreal are near the northern boundary of the historical Kanien'kehá:ka homeland. | Map by Eric Leinberger.

of the Kanien'kehá:ka (Mohawk) Nation and Rotinonhsión:ni (Haudenosaunee) Confederacy. The invasion described here was not conducted with soldiers and guns (although the threat of military violence always lurks); it is an invasion of colonial values and laws, and it was headed up by bureaucrats, Indian agents, politicians, land surveyors, and businessmen.[5] The same battle also raged within the community, as Kahnawa'kehró:non disagreed about how to respond to colonial advances and how best to defend their nation. This book is thus a story of colonial interference in Indigenous lives, rooted in the idea that settlers and settler governments have all the answers and licence to do what they want to Indigenous people. Colonizers believed it was their right and duty to impose their laws on Indigenous peoples and lands, even while Indigenous peoples continued to assert their own laws and values.

The Laws and the Land is an account of colonial harm. Although colonizers often had "good" intentions, meaning they intended to impose their idea of "good" on colonized people and lands, it is the story of the dramatic failure of these intentions to bring about improvement in Indigenous lives. The rhetoric of good intentions has too often distracted historians from seeing the harm for what it was.[6] There was no benefit or improvement. It is also a story of Indigenous resistance to settler colonialism, of an Indigenous nation that collectively refuses Canadian laws and rejects the conditions imposed on it. But the focus here is on the colonial invasion: How are colonial laws imposed? When does this occur? What does the transition look like, and how long does it take? What happens when people do not know which laws apply? What if some people continue to live by Indigenous laws while others adopt colonial laws? How does the state respond to Indigenous resistance and refusal? These are some of the questions explored in this book, which presents an Indigenous community governed by its own leaders and laws that in various circuitous, chaotic ways came to be partially governed by Canada under the rubric of the *Indian Act*.

In her essay "Unmaking Native Space," historian Paige Raibmon calls for a genealogical approach to studying and understanding the history of settler colonies. This approach combines the study of settlement history and that of Indigenous dispossession, two fields that do not generally engage with each other. The tendency rather is for certain historians to examine the history of settlers and settlement, whereas others concentrate on Indigenous history in a colonial context. Raibmon argues that contextualizing the way in which settlers interacted with what was for them a new land within a larger history of violences toward Indigenous peoples can produce a fuller picture of colonial geographies (including Indian reserves and homesteads), colonial processes (including intermarriage and racism), and the "figurative kinships" between countless great and small events and actions.[7] *The Laws and the Land* aims to contribute to just such a discussion. My own ancestors were indigenous to Europe, and I lived as a guest on Rotinonhsión:ni and Algonquin territory while writing most of this book. Thus, I invite readers not to interpret it as a Kanien'kehá:ka history of Kahnawà:ke – it is not. Of course, it is a contribution to the historical writing on this community, but its focus is on the fraught relationship between Kahnawà:ke and Canada, and it probably says as much about Canada as it does about Kahnawà:ke. Although it contains much Indigenous history, it is also a history of Canadian settlers and our relationship with First Peoples on their lands – a genealogical approach to understanding our shared history and differing responsibilities.

A Settler Colonial "Frontier"

Situated only a few kilometres from Canada's largest city, Montreal, nineteenth-century Kahnawà:ke was one of the most populous and influential Indigenous communities in the country. Yet, despite being so close to the heart of Canadian economic and political life, it was one of the few places in the densely populated St. Lawrence Valley of the 1880s that had never been systematically surveyed or mapped for its internal boundaries. The border or "frontier" between Kahnawà:ke and Canada thus represents an important, if ambiguous, dividing line between Indigenous and settler, between colonized and colonizer, and between spheres governed under Indigenous laws and those governed under colonial laws. It is perhaps unexpected to read a book on the "frontier" (a space of settler colonial violence and Indigenous dispossession) that is set in the St. Lawrence Valley of the nineteenth century. In the United States, "the Frontier" is often visualized as a wide line drawn on a roughly north-south axis that, through time, moved west from the Appalachian Mountains to the Mississippi and across the Great Plains along with waves of white settlers. In Canadian history, such a visualization is complicated by the geographical fact of the Canadian Shield, which put a thousand kilometres of rock between the fertile soils of southern Ontario and the Red River Valley, but many Canadians still have a similar concept in their minds as they imagine their own history.

But the frontier was never just a line. There are always many frontiers, and they have never been straight or straightforward; they did not move at a steady pace or in only one direction; and they can look very differently across time and space. Historian Frederick Jackson Turner famously declared in 1893 that the American Frontier was closed, and he publicly worried how the nation would fare without what he considered its democratizing and liberating effect.[8] Turner might have been surprised to learn that today the field of settler colonial studies (which itself is built on decades of research by Indigenous scholars) is premised on the idea that the Frontier never closed, that the work of settler colonialism continued long after settlers took most of the land, and that settler colonialism exists in both the past and the present. In other words, the Frontier as Turner saw it (capitalized, in the singular) is a limiting concept, because all of the land is Indigenous land, settler colonialism is everywhere, and Indigenous people continue to build their nationhoods in ways that defy typical "Frontier" thinking. I think of frontiers (lower case, plural) simply as places where the forces of settler colonialism meet the forces of Indigenous sovereignty. In this definition, a frontier can be a well-known event such as the Kanehsatà:ke Resistance (Oka Crisis), but it can also be a sidewalk conversation between strangers, a tense moment in a classroom, or the physical boundary around Kahnawà:ke.

Historian Patrick Wolfe makes a useful distinction between two kinds of frontiers. He describes the demise of the Frontier (massacres, removals, armed conflict) as a moment when "elimination turned inwards." This was not the end of the invasion but simply the beginning of a different one:

> The western frontier met the one moving back in from the Pacific, and there was simply no space left for removal. The frontier had become coterminal with reservation boundaries. At this point, when the crude technique of removal declined in favour of a range of strategies for assimilating Indian people now that they had been contained within Euroamerican society, we can more clearly see the logic of elimination's positivity as a continuing feature of Euroamerican settler society.[9]

The end of the Frontier was the end of a particular kind of settler territorial expansion but just the beginning of countless new frontiers and forms of invasion into Indigenous lives and land, as well as Indigenous resurgences and assertions of sovereignty. If we wish to understand Kahnawà:ke (and everywhere, really) as part of a frontier where Indigenous people constantly confront all manner of settler colonial forces, we must put aside the heavy burden of the stereotypical Frontier – a lawless "west," where cowboys and cavalry battle "Indians" in a tragic, endless, repeating dance of death. I agree with Wolfe that it is useful to think of settler colonialism as "a structure, not an event," meaning that the settler invasion can occur in any geographical location and never really ends (as we know it thus far).[10] Instead, the invasion turns itself into bureaucracies, systems, and mindsets, hiding its true self behind justification stories, failed memory, and bald-faced lies. As such, settler colonialism is a profoundly modern phenomenon, not a historical land-grabbing prelude to the modern reality, and it should not be conceptionalized only as a struggle between Indigenous peoples and settlers but as a tension within the minds and hearts of settlers and Indigenous people alike. Wolfe argues that settler colonialism is actually integral to modern nation-states and the modern international order because it builds and maintains chains of command and international market forces, and depends on modern racial ideologies that are incongruously synched with the rhetoric of democratic liberal individualism.[11]

Anthropologist Ann Laura Stoler suggests that settler colonialism, like other types of colonialism, can be understood as "the effect of a failed or protracted contest over appropriation and dispossession that is not over when the victories are declared, killings are accomplished, and decimation is resolved as the only 'solution.' Settler colonialism is only ever an imperial process in formation whose security apparatus confirms that it is always at risk of being undone."[12] Settler colonialism, in other words, is the settler invasion and everything that comes after, including the continuing attempts of the settler polity to naturalize, indigenize, and justify itself.[13] Furthermore, the colonization of Indigenous lands and peoples was not as complete as many metanarratives of the Frontier make it out to be. Indigenous peoples have continued to build their nationhoods, and nation-states continue their attempts to co-opt and undermine them. The struggle persists to this day. *The Laws and the Land* is situated within the ongoing settler colonial invasion, which Indigenous peoples and their allies still resist long after most settler narratives have placed the Frontier firmly in the past, rather than in the unfolding present.[14]

I agree with several of my colleagues and students who point out the danger of fatalism in formulating settler colonialism as a structure, not an event, and the hopelessness inherent in the suggestion that we cannot escape our settler colonial predicament. But I also stand with Indigenous peoples and decolonial settlers in rejecting that hopelessness and cynicism. I also share the concerns of many Indigenous, Black, and racialized scholars that the relatively new field of settler colonial studies still foregrounds white scholars and does not adequately recognize the work of Indigenous scholars who have been pursuing similar approaches for decades. I also share the perspective of many scholars in Indigenous studies and Black studies who have pointed out that settler scholars, and particularly white scholars (often historians), tend to naturalize and understate the violence of settler colonial conquest. This can be seen in common features of historical writing, such as the passive voice in which a scholar describes genocidal violence against Indigenous people or in the assumption that colonization and imperialism were somehow inevitable and natural. The tendency of white scholars to portray settler colonial violence and Indigenous death in what they might describe as "neutral" or "unbiased" language is particularly telling, because the violence in question was unprecedented in its scale and horror, so much so that words are often inadequate to describe it. As Tiffany Lethabo King states:

Because conquest ushered in such a world-altering rupture, it is almost impossible for the human imagination to fully conceive of the reach of its violence. Beyond the unfathomability of the scale of conquest's historical violence, the fact that its violence does not cease makes it even more difficult for the critical imaginaries that produce critical social theories to contain it or find the appropriate level of abstraction or texture to make it legible.[15]

King does not advocate for an abandonment of settler colonial studies per se but instead points toward the often unacknowledged work of Indigenous women scholars in laying the groundwork for the field. In particular, she refers to Hawaiian political scientist Haunani-Kay Trask, one of the first to use the term "settler colonialism," who explicitly argues that genocides of all kinds are central to settler colonial processes.[16] Rather than focusing on the damage and destruction suffered by Indigenous communities in settler colonial contexts (as white scholars have often done), King points out that Indigenous scholars "direct our attention to the methods and processes of genocide that settlers/conquistadors use to self-actualize."[17] *The Laws and the Land* follows her lead by eschewing a focus on settler massacres of Indigenous people in favour of describing the actions that directly contribute to genocidal processes, settler benefit, and Indigenous death. In other words, this approach refuses the sensational to concentrate on the systemic elements of settler colonization.

The definition and use of the word "genocide" are hotly contested among some scholars in Canada.[18] In this book, I employ it in accordance with the 1948 Convention on the Prevention and Punishment of the Crime of Genocide, which states that

> genocide means any of the following acts committed with intent to destroy, in whole or in part, a national, ethnical, racial or religious group, as such: a. Killing members of the group; b. Causing serious bodily or mental harm to members of the group; c. Deliberately inflicting on the group conditions of life calculated to bring about its physical destruction in whole or in part; d. Imposing measures intended to prevent births within the group; e. Forcibly transferring children of the group to another group.[19]

When I mention attempts to destroy Indigenous nations (as political entities), I am usually referring to part c. of the United Nations definition, but historians have written about all five variants in Canadian history. Many Indigenous people and scholars recognize that a central goal of settler colonial states has been the elimination of Indigenous peoples – some use "genocide" (or a qualified version of it, such as "cultural genocide"), some use "ethnic cleansing," and others use "elimination."[20] I have opted for "genocide," "attempted genocide," and "genocidal" because these seem to me the best descriptors for what happened and because so many Indigenous survivors feel that they best describe their experience.

In *Mohawk Interruptus,* Kanien'kehá:ka anthropologist Audra Simpson describes the historical and contemporary disposition of Kahnawa'kehró:non toward colonial intrusions as "refusal." They "have survived a great, transformative process of settler occupation, and they continue to live under the conditions of this occupation, its disavowal, and its ongoing life, which has required and still requires that they give up their lands and give up themselves."[21] Yet, despite the overwhelming power imbalance and explicit genocidal intentions of the Canadian state, Kanien'kehá:ka continued to be themselves. "They refuse the 'gifts' of American and Canadian citizenship; they insist upon the integrity of Haudenosaunee governance," which sometimes manifests in a refusal to vote and pay taxes.[22] My research and analysis follow Simpson's work by holding that, in her words,

> [Kanien'kehá:ka] are Indigenous nationals of a strangulated political order who do all they can to live a political life robustly, with dignity as Nationals. In holding on to this, they interrupt and fundamentally challenge stories that have been told about them and about others like them, as well as the structure of settlement that strangles their political form and tries to take their land and their selves from them.[23]

I have frequently seen this "refusal" among many Kahnawa'kehró:non, who steadfastly and creatively refuse colonialism, even when the consequences are unpleasant or terrible. This book includes many such examples and further contextualizes Simpson's analysis of the history of Kahnawà:ke and of Canadian settler colonialism.

The Laws and the Land also builds on the important work of Rotinonhsión:ni historian Susan Hill, whose book *The Clay We Are Made Of* traces the relationships between Canada and Six Nations of the Grand River.[24] Hill uses archival sources to offer detailed accounts of Canadian efforts to dispossess and destroy Six Nations through the nineteenth and twentieth centuries, and focuses on the actions of Rotinonhsión:ni to maintain their governance structures and lands. Both this book and Hill's give a history of Rotinonhsión:ni relationships with colonial governments, and both concentrate thematically on law and land. This book is very different from Hill's, however, in that hers is a history of her own Indigenous nation in relation to the settler state, whereas mine is a history of the settler society in relation to an Indigenous nation. My hope is that the two books can be read alongside each other and that they complement each other.

ENVIRONMENTAL HISTORY AND LEGAL HISTORY

Environmental historians have often emphasized the agency of nature in shaping the decisions of human beings, but *The Laws and the Land* is more about the kind of agency that humans are able (and unable) to express through laws and practices related to the environment. Of course, environments and other-than-human creatures always shape human behaviour, but the focus here is on human beings interacting with each other politically and environmentally as they shape their environments. Kahnawà:ke, like many Indian reserves, is a kind of bio-geographical island in that its ecological communities look quite different from those outside its borders (Figure 0.2). This is due less to geographical factors than to cultural and political ones. For example, there is no environmental reason why the Châteauguay suburbs should stop abruptly at the Kahnawà:ke border or why farmlands become forests when they reach the reserve's eastern boundary. Nevertheless, the boundaries of Kahnawà:ke are today inscribed on the land, testifying to the importance of history and law in shaping landscapes. As historians Tracey Banivanua Mar and Penelope Edmonds put it, the lands themselves "narrate the stories of colonialism."[25] Environmental history is the story of human beings in relationship with other-than-human creatures and forces; this book is an environmental history because it discusses a human story in relationship to particular places, forests, fields, animals, and plants.

The narrative of *The Laws and the Land* unfolds in the context of nature and in relationship to other-than-human creatures, but it does not begin in a "wilderness" – in fact, Indigenous people have been trying to teach settlers for centuries that none of their lands are "wilderness," places that are untouched by humans. Instead, Indigenous people have been, and continue to be, engaged in ancient and ongoing relationships with creatures and places throughout their homelands.[26] Environmental historians have more recently recognized the deeply problematic nature of settler conceptions of wilderness: one common Western understanding is that a pure and good environment is one without humans, that human presence and

FIGURE 0.2   This satellite image of Kahnawà:ke clearly shows the outlines of today's
"reserve," a dark-green, triangle-shaped territory amid suburbs and farmland. | Map
screenshot, accessed on 4 March 2021, copyright 2020, Google.

interaction are inherently negative.[27] Indigenous stories about human relations with other-than-human creatures tell a different story: one of intimate
relatedness. The story here unfolds in a landscape that humans have inhabited and intimately known for thousands of years.

The "frontier" in *The Laws and the Land* is not a geographical boundary
or an ambiguous space of conflict between Indigenous and settler cultures;
rather, the narrative unfolds in the space where Canadian colonial governance and law meet Kanien'kehá:ka governance and law. This book is a
legal history because it shows how these two legal traditions interacted in
a colonial context. Anishinaabe legal scholar John Borrows argues that Indigenous legal traditions have always been practised in the country currently known as Canada, and he summarizes Canada's long tradition of
recognizing and affirming the existence and legitimacy of Indigenous law.
Borrows sees Canada as a legally pluralistic state where "civil, common
and indigenous legal traditions organize dispute resolution in different
ways, though there are similarities between them."[28] In this view, Canada
is a place where different legal traditions are constantly interacting, where
ancient Indigenous legal orders come into contact with newer settler legal
systems in many ways over time and space.

Although settlers repeatedly declared and insinuated that Indigenous peoples had no government or law, their own actions contradicted these assertions. Europeans arriving in North America understood that they had entered a complex and sophisticated Indigenous socio-legal landscape, and even if they disliked doing so, they adopted Indigenous diplomatic and legal practices.[29] Canada's history of negotiating international treaties with Indigenous nations (despite the many problems and illegalities associated with treaty making) is itself an affirmation of Indigenous sovereignty and a continuation of international diplomatic relations that date back to first contact.[30] Add to this the fact that Canadian settler courts have repeatedly acknowledged the existence and importance of Indigenous legal traditions. Thus, settlers' own historical legal engagements with Indigenous peoples give the lie to pronouncements that Indigenous peoples do not constitute real nations with real legal orders.[31]

I follow Indigenous legal scholar Val Napoleon in using the term "legal order" for Indigenous law, which is "embedded in social, political, economic, and spiritual institutions." This is in contrast to "legal system," which describes state-centred (in this case, mostly Canadian) legal systems in which "law is managed by legal professionals in legal institutions that are separate from other social and political institutions."[32] Law itself is something that people do together; it is how they govern themselves.[33] Recently, Napoleon told an allegorical story involving discussions between murdered Indigenous women, highlighting moments and spaces when laws fail to do what they are intended to do, or when there are gaps in laws. Debbie, one of the murdered women in the conversation, says that "today the problem is that while our laws have not gone anywhere, they have been undermined – there are gaps, and there are distortions. Where there are gaps in our laws, and where Canadian law has failed, these are spaces of lawlessness, and violence happens in these spaces."[34] *The Laws and the Land* is situated in one such space. It is about what happened when two legal traditions met in a colonial context over the course of the nineteenth century, the lawlessness and violence that happened in the gaps, and the distortions that emerged.

Kahnawa'kehró:non are a part of the Rotinonhsión:ni Confederacy, a political federation many centuries old. Some consider it to be the oldest continuously functioning democracy in the Americas. A central part of the legal framework that holds the confederacy together is the Kaianerehkó:wa, the Great Law of Peace, often referred to as the Rotinonhsión:ni constitution. With the explicit goal of allowing people to live together in peace, it lays out the legal framework for managing territories and boundaries, interacting with others based on kinship responsibilities, relating to the land both individually and collectively, and choosing and replacing leaders.[35] Rotinonhsión:ni are also part of a complex international political system that pre-dated contact with Europeans and employed wampum as mnemonic devices. The place of Kahnawa'kehró:non in this confederacy through the eighteenth and nineteenth centuries was complicated by internal disagreements over the kinds of relationships with colonial powers that would produce the healthiest outcomes for Rotinonhsión:ni nations and communities. Kahnawà:ke, along with other Indigenous villages of the St. Lawrence Valley, allied itself with France, whereas some southern Rotinonhsión:ni communities favoured Britain. Similar divisions emerged later when Kahnawà:ke was among Rotinonhsión:ni communities allied with the British, whereas some southern Rotinonhsión:ni allied with the United States. These divisions often had damaged Rotinonhsión:ni political and interpersonal relationships. Even as they often managed to avoid fighting each other, they sometimes found themselves on opposite sides in colonial wars.[36] Some of these broken ties between Rotinonhsión:ni nations and communities have been restored or are in the process of being restored today. During the entire period covered by this book, however, Kahnawà:ke continued to govern itself according to the principles of the Kaianerehkó:wa and even established a powerful regional confederacy called the Seven Nations of Canada, including Abenakis, Algonquins, and Wendats of the St. Lawrence Valley.

The Laws and the Land is set at a historical moment when Kahnawà:ke was geographically and politically distant from southern and western Rotinonhsión:ni nations, and it is difficult to know exactly how Kahnawa'kehró:non saw themselves in relation to the rest of the confederacy at the time. We do know that Kahnawà:ke leaders saw their people as a sovereign nation, and colonial authorities largely agreed until the late eighteenth and early nineteenth centuries, often accepting Indigenous laws and the authority of Indigenous leaders. This book begins at the historical moment when this mutual respect and balance of power began to break down, and it follows through to the ways in which Canada imposed its own laws on Kahnawà:ke: it concentrates on the years 1790 to 1900. Audra Simpson summarizes the current situation thus:

> The Mohawks of Kahnawà:ke are nationals of a precontact Indigenous polity that simply refuse to stop being themselves. In other words, they insist on being and acting as peoples who belong to a nation other than the United States and Canada. Their political form predates and survives

"conquest"; it is tangible (albeit strangulated by colonial governmentality) and is tied to sovereign practices.[37]

The Laws and the Land tells the story of Canada's legal and environmental conquest of Kahnawà:ke, a conquest that succeeded in some ways and failed in others. It also tells the story of the many Kahnawà:ke responses to these incursions. The following section considers the ways in which the Department of Indian Affairs (DIA) operated in the nineteenth century and the ways in which I have approached this topic as a historian. I often use the past tense here to describe colonial phenomena, but I invite the reader to remember that most of these continue to this day in some form.

The Department of Indian Affairs and Settler Colonialism

While writing this book, I struggled to find a true and useful way to think about morality in the story I wished to tell. Not every story needs to be about good and evil, but I do see colonialism in those terms. That is not to say that the history of colonialism is a simple story of good and evil or that all people fall starkly on one side or the other, but simply that settler colonialism harms Indigenous peoples – by definition, it attempts to destroy and replace them – and I consider that evil. The colonial evil described here is one that colonized people around the world will probably recognize. At its most extreme, it results in massacres, stolen children, genocide. Yet even when the genocidal elements of settler colonialism are less obvious (in, for example, the imposition of patriarchy, Christianity, capitalism, and representative democracy), the impacts are still destructive and deadly – they still serve the same ultimate goals.[38] The story here is not simply one in which two societies come into conflict, and I do not see my job as a historian as "telling both sides," as if there were a moral equivalent.

Recognizing settler colonialism as evil or wrong, however, should not be confused with applying a simplistic or naive analytic framework to a complicated subject. The point of the book is not simply to condemn what happened but to better understand how it happened. For example, I delve deeply into the contradictions of Canadian colonialism: into the ways it has been both honest and dishonest, non-violent and violent, orderly and disorderly, constructive and destructive. It should also be understood that this account of colonialism is not so much one of individual people who are "bad" and other people who are "good" but of a conflict that occurs in every sphere of life, where everyone takes part in some way and where different sides of the conflict may play out within a single individual. Another complicating aspect is the bureaucratic nature of many of the colonial processes described here, which became more pronounced over time. It is not that bureaucracy is necessarily bad or good but that its growth allowed for new kinds of surveillance, intrusion, and oppression. Readers may also want to remember that settler colonialism can be recognized just as much in its "successes" (assimilation, dispossession, enfranchisement, racialization) as in its "failures" (the survival and thriving of Indigenous peoples, the ability of many to maintain a land base, the refusal of many to be defined in colonial terms). The evil described here is thus not simply a monstrous, well-organized, irresistible machine (although surely it sometimes appears that way to those who suffer under it) – it is also wracked by contradiction and weakness, which themselves can become sources of oppression for colonized people.

Sociologist and lawyer Yael Berda discusses aspects of the Israeli permit regime, which restricts Palestinian people's movements, in terms of "effective inefficiency." For Palestinians who live under Israeli colonial administration, the difficulty of navigating the constantly changing bureaucratic landscape amounts to "bureaucratic cruelty" in which "conflicting decisions created recurring moments of disorientation and alienation."[39] The *Indian Act* and the way in which the DIA implemented it had a similar impact on First Nations people. DIA governance has sometimes been effective and brutal in accomplishing its explicitly racist goals, but it has also been marked by inconsistency, confusion, inefficiency, and contradiction. Berda argues that these seeming weaknesses of the colonizing legal regime can further remove the agency of colonized people, who cannot find ways to navigate a legal system that is often contradictory, constantly changing, and impossible to understand. In the Israeli context, even fighting against the permit regime appeared to give it legitimacy and power: "Taking on any part of the permit regime, including petitioning against it, meant it solidified its ad hoc activities into a legitimate institution; created a jurisprudence around it; normalized the completely impossible, absurd, and unacceptable situations; and rendered it part of the repertoire of the security justifications that made it grow."[40] In Canada, Indigenous resistance can similarly be viewed as futile at certain moments: the power imbalance was so great that even strong resistance could often lead to deeper colonial intrusions. In the words of historian Keith Smith, "while the DIA regularly spoke of promoting self-sufficiency, it took nations of independent peoples and enmeshed them in a web of regulation, restriction, and incompetent, inadequate, and inappropriate 'assistance.'"[41]

A key way in which the DIA accomplished its goals was by identifying Indigenous leaders who would cooperate with it and undermining those who would not. The band council system of governance established in the *Indian Act* was designed to project a semblance of representative democracy while ensuring that the department could eliminate or sideline oppositional leaders.[42] On the other hand, Indigenous leaders were often confused as to what was expected of them and what *Indian Act* law meant for them in practice. DIA officials were often equally confused, working as they did in an understaffed and underfunded environment, tasked with implementing contradictory policy goals. But of course they did not have to live in the chaotic conditions they facilitated. In a colonial context, such confusion tends to benefit the colonizing agenda, as Berda points out for the Palestinian context. It also worked this way in Canada, which is one of the truths I wish to show. *The Laws and the Land* demonstrates the "effective inefficiency" of Canadian colonialism, dogged as it was with contradiction and absurdity but nonetheless effective in undermining Indigenous sovereignties.

In the decades following Confederation, the DIA expanded from a department employing only a handful of officials to a multitiered, hierarchical system that generated voluminous records. The volume of its correspondence doubled in the 1870s and 1880s, and doubled again in the 1890s.[43] The Victorian society that produced the department believed itself to be at the pinnacle of civilization. It was simultaneously enthralled by its own romantic conception of Indigenous people and disgusted or horrified by actual Indigenous people and societies. What was holding Indigenous people back from progress, believed the Victorians, was their aversion to individualism and private property. Furthermore, DIA officials were active proponents of common racist stereotypes about Indigenous people, as for example, that they were lazy, prone to alcoholism, and unable to manage their own affairs. Like many white elites at the time, they saw plow farming as a solution to the "Indian Problem" because they believed it would teach private property, sedentarism, Victorian gender roles, and capitalist work habits. Agriculture and Christianity together would lead Indigenous people toward "civilization," by which Victorians meant assimilation.[44] I use the past tense here, but I want to remind readers that these racist beliefs are still common everywhere, from newspapers to textbooks to dinner tables. They were institutional dogma at the DIA – it did not matter whether reality lined up with belief; officials were

expected to make these assumptions about their "wards."[45] In the case of
Kahnawà:ke, DIA officials did not care that Kanien'kehá:ka already had
their own legal orders and leaders; that they already farmed; that their
literacy rates were similar to those of neighbouring settler populations.[46]
Indian agents still spoke about them as savages who were, at best, partway
down the path toward civilization.

In many historical narratives (in Canada and elsewhere), settlers are
cast as largely innocent parties in their relations with Indigenous peoples.
Authors of these histories find ways to excuse settlers for any harms they
caused, blame Indigenous people for their own defeats, losses, and deaths,
and see tragic outcomes as natural and inevitable.[47] Recently, many settler
historians have tried to do more to reveal the imbalance of power and the
asymmetry of harm and benefit, but some still attempt to excuse settler
colonial harm, sometimes by pointing to supposed misunderstandings,
by suggesting that both sides were equally responsible for particular conflicts,[48] or by doubling down on the "good intentions" of the perpetrators.
In *The Laws and the Land,* I follow a growing number of Indigenous and
settler scholars who discuss Canada in the context of global settler colonialism, racism, white supremacy, and imperialism, and do so in the global
context of anti-colonial struggles and Indigenous resurgences. I am not
trying to show "both sides" of the conflicts between Canada and Kahna-
wà:ke – I show the ways in which settler colonial processes, and resistance
to them, played themselves out in this particular time and place.

Organization of the Book

This book is organized roughly chronologically. Chapter 1 describes some
of the pre-contact and early-contact Rotinonhsión:ni ways of living on
and sharing the land. It gives an overview of the history of Kahnawà:ke,
its origins within the French colonial seigneurial system, the roots of current land claims, and elements of Rotinonhsión:ni environmental law and
governance. Chapter 2 focuses on early-nineteenth-century formulations
of Kahnawà:ke law and the dominant (but always contested) legal system
in place throughout most of the nineteenth century, contrasting it with
the growing power of the colonial state and its interest in constructing a
polity based on the sanctity of private property. Kahnawà:ke laws treated
the community's immediate land base as a Dish with One Spoon, a
Rotinonhsión:ni metaphor (also shared by other Indigenous nations of
the region) for an ecological commons where individual land-use rights

were limited and of a non-commercial nature.[49] This chapter discusses how the chiefs defended their nation, laws, and values when a small number of acquisitive Kahnawà:ke men began to oppose them and the legal framework they represented. Chapter 3 delves into some of these conflicts in the 1820s and 1830s, many of which centred on questions of race and belonging. This period saw massive influxes of settlers who appropriated Indigenous lands; thus, many Indigenous people could not access their lands and found themselves in crisis. During this period, Indigenous peoples lost a great deal of political influence, since colonial governments increasingly saw them as weak and doomed to extinction. Canadian colonial law and Kahnawà:ke law coexisted uneasily, and the power dynamic became increasingly asymmetrical.

Covering the years 1850 to 1875, Chapter 4 begins with the completion of the first railway to bisect Kahnawà:ke and the abolition of the seigneurial system. Kanien'kehá:ka recognized that these developments, coupled with much more intrusive Indian laws and the rapid growth of Montreal, represented serious threats to the integrity and viability of their community. The chapter reveals the continuity of Kahnawà:ke law and land practices in the face of these pressures, as well as the exasperation, concern, and decisions of Kanien'kehá:ka leaders who feared that their nationhood would end. After attempts to move the entire community elsewhere failed, Kahnawa'kehró:non again reoriented their resistance efforts toward defending their existing territory and jurisdiction. Chapter 5 focuses on the chaotic environmental and social consequences that followed the increased DIA interference of the 1870s. With the ascendant DIA constantly undermining the political power of chiefs but unwilling or unable to step into the void it created, Kahnawa'kehró:non were unsure of who would enforce laws and which laws those would be. The resulting confusion, though caused by the department, served to confirm its stereotypes about lawless "Indians," which were used to justify the Walbank Survey, the subject of Chapter 6. The survey was an attempt by the Canadian state to radically transform the community and landscape of Kahnawà:ke. From the perspective of state officials, it was largely a failure, but it did succeed in freezing previously dynamic lot lines and implanting, albeit imperfectly, some of the private property norms contained in the *Indian Act*. Chapter 7 covers the last fifteen years of the nineteenth century with the imposition of the band council system and DIA attempts to gain political control. Although its efforts succeeded to some extent, this chapter shows the ways in which Kahnawa'kehró:non refused its control and continued to live according to their laws.

The transition from Kahnawà:ke law to *Indian Act* law was not seamless or linear. The process took decades and involved many people and situations. Nevertheless, the results year after year tended to benefit Canada's settler colonial project and undermine the sovereignty of Kahnawà:ke. Although this study demonstrates the power of the early Canadian nation-state to transform Indigenous communities and lands, it also reveals the disorganized, inconsistent, and contradictory ways in which that power was brought to bear. It shows how the people of Kahnawà:ke survived, adapted, endured, and sometimes even thrived despite colonial incursions. But in the final analysis, *The Laws and the Land* is a historically based argument for a return to Indigenous self-government and an indictment of the DIA, which claimed to serve the interests of Indigenous communities but in reality sought their destruction.

Although the book follows chronological order, some chapters discuss overlapping years. Some are pegged around major events, such as the construction of the first railroad or the Walbank Survey, but in other cases I did not feel that this was necessary. Part of the historian's job is to distill an infinitely complicated past into a comprehensible narrative, but I hope that this book gives readers a sense of the multiple stories and competing timelines in this and every story.

SOURCES

The Laws and the Land draws on a number of archival sources, including the records of the Department of Indian Affairs, personal papers, period newspapers, travel literature, censuses, legal records, maps, government reports, and a broad array of judicial sources. I conducted the largest part of my research at Library and Archives Canada, particularly with Record Group 10, the records of the DIA. These include correspondence between Indian agents, department officials, and their superiors, as well as petitions, newspaper clippings, letters from third parties, and maps. There are advantages and problems with each of these types of materials. Documents produced by the DIA tend to obscure as much as they reveal. In a number of cases, my own interpretation of a set of texts changed dramatically over time based on further experience and knowledge gained elsewhere. Among the material written by DIA officials are letters and petitions written by Kanien'kehá:ka themselves, sometimes in Kanien'kéha (the Kanien'kehá:ka language). I have used these whenever possible to provide Kahnawà:ke perspectives. However, they were usually crafted to appeal to the sensibilities of officials who knew little about, and had little sympathy for, Indigenous points of view. Thus, I have understood that many such documents produced by Indigenous people in the records of the DIA may not express the true feelings and beliefs of their authors but may have been pitched to achieve a desired result.

DIA officials, including Indian agents, were often motivated by a need to make themselves look good, cover up mistakes, or justify decisions. In the climate of institutionalized racism that characterized the department, it was exceedingly easy to blame lazy, vindictive, and obstructionist "Indians" for any problem. The correspondence of department officials and Indian agents is saturated with negative stereotypes and racist assumptions that are easy for an experienced researcher to recognize, but the silences are more difficult to identify. Topics such as women's work and leadership or small-scale gardening are rarely mentioned, but I have tried to highlight them whenever possible. Finally, it is also important to note that DIA records, by their nature, highlight conflict instead of harmony. Thus, the action in this book turns on a number of conflicts over land, and readers will be left with a picture of Kahnawà:ke as less peaceful than it probably really was.

As I researched and wrote this book, I spent a lot of time in Kahnawà:ke and spoke about my archival findings with a number of Kahnawa'kehró:non. I often gained valuable insights in this way, and I found that these conversations gave me important added insight into my archival sources. I did not conduct formal interviews but have drawn from a few taped and transcribed oral histories conducted by others.[50]

ORTHOGRAPHY

I have had to make some difficult choices regarding terms and orthography and have done so in consultation with a number of Kahnawà:ke readers, especially language teacher and community historian Kahrhó:wane Cory McComber. The archival texts I consulted most frequently refer to the residents of Kahnawà:ke as Caughnawagas, Iroquois, Sauvages (in French), and Indians, but I have used Kahnawa'kehró:non (People of Kahnawà:ke), Kanien'kehá:ka (People of the Flint, Mohawk), and Rotinonhsión:ni (Haudenosaunee, Iroquois). I have generally opted for proper nouns that are in use today and correct according to current Kanien'kéha spelling conventions. I have not changed proper nouns that appear in quotations. Since the use of Indigenous language terms for self-identification is an important part of Indigenous political and cultural resurgence, and some colonial-origin proper nouns seem to be falling out of favour with Indigenous people, I have made language choices along those lines.[51]

In most instances, I refer to nineteenth-century Kanien'kehá:ka by their Kanien'kéha names when these are known, and if I know their English/French names I have included these in parentheses at first appearance. In the case of multiple spellings, I opted for what appears to be the most common one. When a name is given in the Walbank Survey, I adopt that spelling because the names in the survey were recorded by a single person (Owakenhen Peter Stacey) in a consistent way. I did not alter them to reflect the spelling norms of today. I transcribed English-language quotations much as they appear in the original, and I included spelling and grammar irregularities without always flagging them. To make *The Laws and the Land* more accessible to those who do not read French, including many Kahnawa'kehró:non, I have translated French quotations into English, giving the French original in an endnote. Unless otherwise noted, all translations are my own.

1

Kahnawà:ke and Canada

Relationships of Laws and Lands

*Then Dekanahwideh continued and said: "We have still one
matter left to be considered and that is with reference to the
hunting grounds of our people from which they derive their living."*

*They, the lords [Rotiiá:ner, or Confederacy Chiefs], said with
reference to this matter: "We shall now do this: We shall only have
one dish (or bowl) in which will be placed one beaver's tail and
we shall all have coequal right to it, and there shall be no knife
in it, for if there be a knife in it, there would be danger that it
might cut some one and blood would thereby be shed."*

     — The Constitution of the Five Nations (version of the
        Kaianerehkó:wa recorded by Arthur Parker)

*It has been the impression of many people that the Indian
nations of America had no conception of national boundary
lines between nations and that all they did was just wander
around the country and help themselves to any spot that took
their fancy. Even the late Theodore Roosevelt believed this to
be true. Another popular belief has been that all Indians in a
community had no ideas of individual ownership of things and
that everything was shared by any and every member of the tribe.
Both ideas are erroneous. Instead we find the strictest ideas of
both these concepts were believed in and practiced by all Indians
to the fullest extent. Each individual had property rights and
these rights were highly respected by every member of the tribe
or nation. I mean to say by this that while no Indian had much
more than his neighbor at any time he certainly did have sole
title to whatever he did possess.*

     — William B. Newell, 1965

In the seventeenth and eighteenth centuries, Rotinonhsión:ni kept and used feast bowls to symbolize the lands that each nation shared. The clans of each nation dipped their spoons into the common bowl to share a meal, symbolically sharing in the bounty of the lands.[1] The principle of the Bowl or Dish with One Spoon is a powerful political and moral metaphor for sharing land and its bounty, common to Indigenous nations of the larger Great Lakes region. The Kaianerehkó:wa (the Great Law of Peace) quoted in the first epigraph above employs this concept to explain how Rotinonhsión:ni shared their hunting grounds, but other versions refer to cultivated fields as well.[2] This legal formulation of land use and rights established the people's rights to freely live on the land and to live in right relation with each other and the land.[3]

In this chapter, I introduce readers to the early history of Kahnawà:ke and to Rotinonhsión:ni and Kahnawà:ke law in relation to land. I give a brief history of the community itself and its relationship with French and British colonial governments. I explain aspects of Kahnawa'kehró:non involvement with the French colonial seigneurial system, which is necessary to understand if we are to appreciate the land grievances and concerns of the community that are detailed in this the book, which continue to affect the community to this day. I also introduce aspects of the legal pluralism in that Indigenous and colonial legal systems operated side-by-side, and the ways in which settlers and their laws began to intrude in Kahnawà:ke in harmful ways.

Many Indigenous people did not and do not believe that land should be bought and sold, but it is also true that all human societies have ways of assigning legal rights to territory to individuals and groups.[4] Although abstracted, decontextualized "territory" is a colonial imposition in North America, and the English language has been shaped and defined by capitalist and instrumentalist assumptions about nature, it is nevertheless a fact that Indigenous legal orders deal with questions around who should have access to land and its bounty.[5] Another myth about Indigenous people (noted in the epigraph by the Kanien'kehá:ka scholar William B. Newell) is that they held all property in common and had no concept of individual property rights. In reality, every Indigenous society had a concept of collective territorial sovereignty, individual rights to territory, and also individual and collective rights to other items. Some things were/are held in common; other things were/are not. Note that even the words "thing," "held," "sovereignty," and "rights" may not be appropriate in this context, because they assume social hierarchy and ownership. The English language is not well equipped to speak about non-capitalist forms of territoriality or about land practices that do not involve permanent villages and perpetually cultivated lands. Thus, certain English words related to landownership and property do not fully capture, and potentially distort, the meaning of non-capitalist forms of land tenure such as the ones discussed in this chapter. I do use these words, if sparingly, but ask readers to remember this caveat. Although fee-simple ownership is now widely assumed to be the normal way for people to relate to land, it is only one way to assign legal rights to territory; the imposition of fee-simple landownership is also at the heart of the settler colonial project. I see the current human-caused climate and ecological crisis as intimately connected to colonial and capitalist relations with land, nature, and other-than-human creatures. Indigenous conceptions of nature point us toward a relationship of love and relatedness, recognizing other-than-human creatures as kin, water as sacred, and land as powerful life-giver.[6]

Kahnawa'kehró:non share a common legal tradition with other Rotinonhsión:ni, and when they joined with Kanien'kehá:ka, Abenaki, Wendat, and Algonquin Nations of the St. Lawrence Valley in a political alliance called the Seven Nations of Canada, they were guided by these principles. The continuity of these legal principles is revealed by a 1796 petition in which Seven Nations leaders, along with Odawa, Mi'kmaq, and Malecite counterparts, protested a newly imposed British prohibition against hunting northeast of Quebec City that was intended to reserve hunting in that area for the Innu (Montagnais). The leaders addressed General Robert Prescott, saying that

> we are the true Native Inhabitants of this Country and that God had placed us first on these Lands. It is there that our ancestors to preserve peace had resolved to make use only of one Dish and one Platter ... and to eat all together. This parable signifies that there was no Limits for the indian Hunting, that all the country should be free: When the King of France set foot on our Ground He did not conquer us, He came as a Father who wishes to protect his Children. We communicated to Him this parable of the dish and spoon, He approved of it and encouraged us to continue in our way of acting, He did not tell us Children I want to share in your dish and have the Best bit in it. When our Father the king of England drove away the king of France, We were so earnest in nothing as communicating to Him this parable. He did more than the King of France, for he had the goodness to prop up the dish telling us that He did not wish that we should make use

of knives to eat our Meal least they should hurt us, and as a proof of it we
preserve his Word / parolle /. He did not tell us that He wished to eat with
us, being accustomed to a different kind of Food.[7]

In this case, Seven Nations leaders employed the metaphor of the Dish
with One Spoon to explain why Europeans had no right to interfere with
the ways Indigenous peoples managed their hunting territories but also
to emphasize the communitarian nature of their relationships with the
land and other-than-human creatures.

Rotinonhsión:ni lived and hunted in the St. Lawrence Valley for centuries, but the first people to form the village of Kahnawà:ke arrived in the
mid-seventeenth century, well after first contact with Europeans. French
settlers were moving quickly to settle the St. Lawrence Valley at this time,
and the French Crown laid claim to the entire territory. Kahnawa'kehró:non
(as allies of the French) accepted the French presence and French legal
jurisdiction over settlers but have always asserted jurisdiction over their
own lands and people. By 1672, residents hailed from at least twenty-two
Indigenous nations, including about three hundred Wendats, who represented the single-largest nationality. But following the subsequent arrival
of several hundred Kanien'kehá:ka from the Mohawk Valley, many non-
Kanien'kehá:ka moved elsewhere, and the community became increasingly
Kanien'kehá:ka in character.[8] Most of the original Kahnawa'kehró:non
had fled the insecurity of war, the ravages of disease, and the upheavals of
religious factionalism.[9] In addition to these negative factors, according
to the Kanien'kehá:ka leaders Joseph Brant and John Norton in 1801, the
original Kahnawa'kehró:non were attracted by the prospect of having access to better and cheaper trade goods compared to what was available in
Albany.[10] They came from many nations and many places, but they all
believed that Kahnawà:ke offered what they needed: safety, economic
opportunity, and religious and social harmony. They saw it as a place where
they could live as they wished, with the freedoms they expected. Their
intent was not to put themselves under the thumb of the French monarch
or missionaries, as early commentators and historians erroneously believed.[11] Rather, many saw themselves as moving into a different part of
their own national territories, and they formed a political and military
alliance with the French in exchange for political independence, economic
opportunity, and land security. Moving to the Montreal area was not an
admission of defeat or a sign of submission to colonial authorities but a
calculated decision that equated living near a centre of French colonial
power with the best opportunity to recover and thrive on their own

terms.[12] This chapter shows that though they brought with them a legal and agricultural tradition, they also adapted certain European ideas and practices.

LAND AND LAW IN EARLY KAHNAWÀ:KE

Kahnawa'kehró:non come from a tradition where villages were not permanent, moving approximately every generation. This Rotinonhsión:ni practice continued well into the contact period but generally ended in the eighteenth century. Kahnawà:ke itself was moved for the last time in 1716. Before that point, a village site remained in use until a number of factors converged to make a move necessary: soil became compacted and less fertile, and weeds became unmanageable; firewood became too distant for easy collection and transport; and insect and rodent pests invaded fields and homes.[13] More and more effort and time were required to produce crops, collect firewood, and maintain the longhouses, until finally the community decided to relocate.[14] A new village site was chosen carefully on the basis of various factors, including the quality of the soil, access to water, and availability of firewood. Uplands were favoured, not only for military reasons, but also because the lighter soils were relatively easy to turn with wooden tools.[15] Rotinonhsión:ni referred to the area in and around villages as "the clearing" and to the spaces beyond them as "the forest." This binary was so foundational to their everyday reality that the clearing and the forest became powerful metaphors for everything from international politics to gender relations and family life.[16] Rotinonhsión:ni land practices included fishing and hunting (usually associated with the forest), but my focus here is on activities linked with the clearing.

I interpret the origin of Kahnawà:ke in light of this settlement tradition; although it is true that the mid- to late seventeenth century was a time of crisis for the people who chose to move to Kahnawà:ke, it was also normal for them to periodically relocate. It is also true that the cultural/linguistic makeup of particular villages could change dramatically based on such facts as decisions of families to leave or join.

Agriculture and Law

Settler writers over the last two hundred years have propagated the false idea that Indigenous land practices, including agriculture, were primitive at best and that Indigenous people underutilized the land. Rotinonhsión:ni

storytellers, scholars, and historians, by contrast, remember their ancestors as innovative, prosperous, and productive farmers. Recent scientific
research tends to confirm early colonial reports of highly productive,
large-scale Rotinonhsión:ni agriculture.[17] Early colonizers and missionaries
describe substantial villages and large surrounding fields ranging in size
from ten acres to several hundred. For example, French soldiers in 1669
described a Seneca clearing of cultivated land that was nearly 10.0 kilometres in circumference, which equates to about 7.5 square kilometres
(750 hectares or 1,850 acres). In 1687, French soldiers claimed to have destroyed 400,000 minots or 1.2 million bushels of corn during an attack on
four Seneca towns.[18] To put this into perspective, 1.2 million bushels of
corn would fill seventeen Olympic-sized swimming pools. The Dutch
traveller Harmen Meyndertsz van den Bogaert, who visited Kanién:keh
country in 1634–35, described affluent towns whose longhouses were full
of beaver pelts, grains, and dried venison. Everywhere he went, he saw
huge stores of corn, in some cases entire longhouses dedicated to this
purpose. One town consisted of fifty-five longhouses used for habitation
and a few more used only for grain storage, but even the inhabited houses
were full of grain and beans.[19] Although many European observers derided
swidden cultivation (a technique of rotational farming practised by
Rotinonhsión:ni in which land is cleared for cultivation and then left to
regenerate, also known as shifting cultivation or "slash and burn" farming)
as backward and unproductive, it was actually an innovative and sustainable practice that enabled Rotinonhsión:ni to build a secure and stable
society over many centuries.[20]

Agriculture was feminized in Rotinonhsión:ni thinking and practice.
Women had jurisdiction over village and agricultural activities (the clearing), and were responsible for planting, tending, harvesting, and processing
crops, storing and cooking food, and conducting rituals that promoted
successful harvests.[21] Rotinonhsión:ni leaders over the centuries have consistently stated that women are the owners and caretakers of the land, and
the Kaianerehkó:wa includes this gendered legal distinction.[22] Men played
a limited role in the clearing: they built houses and cleared fields, but it
was the women who directed these activities. Dutch colonial observer
Adriaen van der Donck noted in the 1640s that old men and children also
worked the fields under the direction of the women.[23] Agricultural work
was feminized to such an extent, according to historian and museologist
Arthur Parker, that even men who simply helped to clear the fields did
not want to be seen; old men who were caught with a hoe in their hands
often "excused themselves"; and if a man helped his wife in the field, it

was a sign of his extraordinary love for her.[24] This gendering of the clearing, of village governance, and of agricultural labour meant that Rotinonhsión:ni men often deferred to women on questions of land. There are numerous instances of treaty negotiations breaking down or being delayed because the men were unwilling to make agreements involving land without the approval of the women of the nation.[25]

Joseph-François Lafitau (1681–1746), a Jesuit missionary who lived in Kahnawà:ke during the 1710s, was an astute observer of its everyday life.[26] Writing about how women organized their work, he stated they "make numerous different bands according to the different quarters where they have their fields and pass from one field to the other helping each other."[27] One woman was designated the coordinator, or in Lafitau's words "the mistress of the field" *(la Maitresse du Champ)*, whose job it was to distribute seeds and assign each working group to a particular area. Moving from field to field was relatively easy because there were no hedges or ditches between them, unlike the European fields that Lafitau knew. In fact, he noted that they "give the appearance of only a single farm where there are no disputes over boundaries because everyone knows how to recognize them clearly."[28] Although many would have assumed that the open character implied a lack of divisions, Lafitau understood that Kanien'kehá:ka landownership included both communal and individual elements. Indeed, his remarks are unusual in that he made no negative judgments about the openness of the Kanien'kehá:ka agricultural landscape, unlike many of his contemporaries. For example, van der Donck had written sixty years earlier that Rotinonhsión:ni farmers were "not neat and cleanly in their fields," paid very little attention to their crops, and left their fields open, unenclosed, and unprotected. Nevertheless, even he admitted that these methods produced massive surpluses, on which the Dutch depended to stock their ships with food.[29]

"Property" Relations

Closely connected to the false notion that Indigenous people had no real governments or laws is the belief (still widely held) that their lands were a kind of undifferentiated, collective property. Kanien'kehá:ka scholar William B. Newell confronted this damaging truism in 1965 when he wrote the passage that opens this chapter. Whereas all Indigenous peoples organized their territories in ways that excluded some and granted access to others, Newell also gives examples of individual ownership of horses, cows, dogs, cats, and chickens as evidence of individual property among

Rotinonhsión:ni. To further argue for a kind of Rotinonhsión:ni private property, he cited such practices as ritualized gift giving, as well as the borrowing and lending of tools.[30] Sir William Johnson, long-time British superintendent of Indian Affairs in the eighteenth century, also recognized that Rotinonhsión:ni had their own laws and understandings regarding land, ownership, and use rights. In 1764, he wrote that it was easy to find the "true" Indigenous owner of a particular parcel of land. "Each nation," he explained, "is perfectly well acquainted with their exact original bounds, the same is again divided into due proportions for each Tribe, and afterwards subdivided into shares to each family ... Neither do they ever infringe upon one another, or invade their neighbours' hunting grounds."[31] Among Rotinonhsión:ni, land was not bought or sold, but it could be allocated to families for exclusive agricultural use.

Historian Arthur Parker gives a good example of the complexity of property relations among Rotinonhsión:ni:

> The function of the men was to hunt, to bring in the game and stand ever ready to defend their people and their property and to engage in war expeditions. An Iroquois man must be ever generous and give to every one who asked for his arms or his meat. If he brought his bear to the village it became public property, to the material injury of himself and family. He therefore left his game hidden in the outskirts of his town and sent his wife to bring it in. She was not bound to give of her husband's bounty and could properly refuse the appeals of the hungry, lazy or others who loved to prey upon generosity. After the meat was cooked, however, the case was different and she was bound to feed any who came to her door.[32]

This passage reveals a great deal about the relationship of property to gender, as well as the differing moral and legal norms that applied to the bear depending on where it was, who possessed it, and whether it was cooked or uncooked. Parker also discussed Rotinonhsión:ni land-use traditions in terms of "ownership." According to him, individuals could freely cultivate their own fields, but if they wanted to share in the communal harvest they had to work in the communal fields. He even claimed, on the basis of oral histories, that individually owned fields were marked out "by a post on which was painted the clan totem and individual name sign."[33]

Rotinonhsión:ni women were the managers and "owners" of land, houses, and food stores, and individual women had jurisdiction over the plots they cultivated. Scholars have often understood this gendered relationship to land as one of the bases for the political power that women wielded in Rotinonhsión:ni societies.[34] Anthropologist Elizabeth Tooker points out, however, that such an interpretation does not take into account the fact that particular cultivated plots and houses were not viewed as the permanent holdings of individuals to be passed down to children. Because residents abandoned old longhouses and fields when the village moved, roughly once a generation, and built new longhouses and cleared new land, land was not hoarded, bought, sold, or passed along to children. Thus, it could not be easily instrumentalized and translated into political power.[35] Tooker also emphasizes that though tools and other objects were "owned" by those who used them, Rotinonhsión:ni law did not articulate property in terms of a transferrable ownership right to a certain object or a delineated space, but as recognized rights in the context of use.[36]

Likewise, nineteenth-century anthropologist Lewis Morgan was told by his informants that "no individual could obtain the absolute title to land, as that was vested by the laws of the Iroquois in all the people; but he could reduce unoccupied lands to cultivation, to any extent he pleased; and so long as he continued to use them, his right to their enjoyment was protected and secured."[37] The late Ahkwesáhsne leader and scholar Kaientarónkwen Ernie Benedict recounted that in the days before European interference, "when a man wished to build a home and take some land for his family, he simply went to the desired location and indicated that this was to be his property."[38] Shakokwenniónkwas Tom Porter, a leader in Kanatsiohareke, explains that according to traditional principles a person who owns a certain number of horses has a right to use an area of land appropriate for that number of horses but no more.[39] Rotinonhsión:ni property law did not consider land as a commodity to be transferred to heirs, but it did recognize the rights of an individual to exclusively use particular objects and to delineate specific spaces under certain conditions.

Village Architecture

Over the course of the eighteenth century, Kahnawa'kehró:non continued to live in longhouses, farming and working in ways not so different from those of their ancestors. Some acquired domestic animals for agricultural and transportation purposes, but certain things also remained the same. Women were still the primary farmers, growing traditional foods along with newly introduced crops such as potatoes and wheat.[40] Kahnawa'kehró:non still relocated the village every ten to twenty years until 1716, when they moved to the current location.[41] Just as every society changes over time, so did Kahnawà:ke. And just as every society disagrees about changes, so also Kahnawa'kehró:non disagreed among themselves from time to time. Many of the conflicts discussed here were about whether to incorporate European practices and how Indigenous law should be applied in new contexts. Such disagreements first appear in the archival record in the late eighteenth century, when there was a clash between those who wished to adapt settler norms and those who drew a line in the sand and refused any more change (and many perspectives between these two extremes). It should be said, however, that the people who favoured continuity of Kahnawà:ke law and gradual change tended to outnumber those who wanted radical change.[42]

The most fundamental changes in Kanien'kehá:ka land practices during the eighteenth century came when the community decided not to relocate again. After establishing their village on the shores of the St. Lawrence in 1667 at the location of today's La Prairie, they had moved four times.[43] But, due to expanding French Canadian settlement, little land remained available for further moves after 1716. When, in 1750, thirty Kahnawa'kehró:non families moved to a new location, it was one hundred kilometres upriver at Ahkwesáhsne, where they settled with families from other communities.[44] The new reality of a permanent village had important implications for the way in which Kahnawa'kehró:non lived and used their land. One of these was the architectural trend away from longhouses and toward single-family dwellings.

Historian Gretchen Green argues that most Kahnawa'kehró:non were still living in longhouses at the end of the eighteenth century, but she does not indicate when the change to smaller dwellings occurred.[45] The evidence is scant and contradictory, but the transition must have been under way by the middle of the eighteenth century, even if traditional-style longhouses were still common at that time.[46] One early-eighteenth-century drawing shows around fifty longhouses of fairly consistent sizes (Figure 1.1). When the military engineer Louis Franquet visited Kahnawà:ke in 1752–53, he observed that people lived in longhouses but also that some were starting to build smaller houses using squared timber or stone.[47] Franquet's fortification map (Figure 1.2) includes both long and short dwellings, but it is difficult to draw conclusions from such scant evidence. Archaeologist Kurt Jordan shows that Rotinonhsión:ni had already been innovating with dwelling size and design for decades and that their villages had included both long and short buildings for quite some time.[48] French army officers Louis Antoine de Bougainville and Pierre Pouchot visited Kahnawà:ke in the 1750s and also mentioned the presence of longhouses.[49] A decade later, when an English fur trader named John Long visited the village, he said

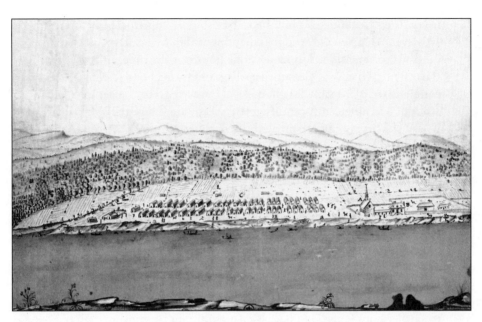

FIGURE 1.1   "Veue de la Mission du Sault Saint Louis," c. 1732. | Service historique de la Défense, Département Bibliothèque, Réserve, Génie, Folio 210e, Bibliothèque nationale de France, http://gallica.bnf. fr/ark:/12148/btv1b7911862h.

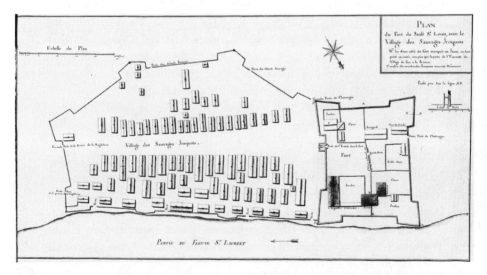

FIGURE 1.2   "Plan du Fort du Sault St Louis avec le Village des Sauvages Iroquois," Louis Franquet, 1752. Most of the fortification depicted was never completed. | Louis Franquet, "Mémoire des remarques faites sur les principaux endroits que j'ai parcourus dans ma tournées de Montréal au lac Champlain et autres lieux depuis le 24 juillet jusqu'au 23 août 1752," Ministère des armées, Service historique de la Défense, Ms. in-fo 210e, ex. ms. 703.

it consisted of about two hundred houses, most constructed of stone.[50]
However, Gretchen Green argues that this cannot be accurate, because no
other visitor mentioned so many stone houses at the time. In 1796, Irish
travel writer Isaac Weld described a village of fifty log houses, which Green
contends were probably longhouses.[51] However, given the complete absence of any nineteenth-century references to longhouses, it seems likely
that Weld simply underestimated the number of houses and that longhouses had already been replaced by stone and wood cottages.

By the early nineteenth century, most Kahnawa'kehró:non were living
in smaller dwellings. This transition left no paper trail, but there is no evidence that it caused conflict or even debate. It is likely that the architectural change was not as disruptive as outsiders might suppose. Longhouses
had always been partitioned into "apartments," each of which, according
to Lewis Morgan, was "in fact, a separate house, having a fire in the centre,
and accommodating two families, one upon each side of the fire. Thus a
house one hundred and twenty feet long would contain ten fires and
twenty families."[52] Since families already lived in separate spaces, the move
to smaller houses need not have been a significant rupture or a sign of acculturation. Nor did it happen quickly. It was instead an adaptation to the
new opportunities and influences but also to the reality of a permanent
village: since the village would no longer move, erecting more permanent
structures made sense. Another likelihood is that the new smaller houses
had many features of longhouses. Historian Carl Benn mentions that
houses at Six Nations of the Grand River in 1812 looked outwardly like
European houses, but the interiors of some resembled longhouses, with
double rows of bunks for seating, sleeping, and storage.[53]

Eighteenth-Century Adaptations

A permanent village also required a reinvention of the community's relationship to the land. Instead of moving when conditions became unfavourable, Kahnawa'kehró:non now needed to find new ways to manage their
lands. This did not mean completely abandoning the old ways and adopt-
ing the methods and laws of their settler neighbours. Instead, many Kahnawa'kehró:non retained certain practices and fundamental principles while
also embracing some new practices, technologies, and regulations. They
continued to practice swidden cultivation on their limited land base and
to maintain legal principles such as tying individual rights to land to
active use. Nevertheless, questions of landownership and inheritance became important, and the legal principle of women's jurisdiction over land

was de-emphasized in an increasingly patriarchal colonial context. No particular event in the archives marks this change, but by the eighteenth century both men and women were acknowledged as the owners of plots of land. I discuss possible reasons for this change in Chapters 4 and 5.

One serious problem related to living in a permanent village while practising shifting agriculture was the distance to fertile fields and fire-wood.[54] Lafitau wrote:

> As the Indians never manure their ground and do not even let it lie fallow, it is soon exhausted (and worn out). Then they are forced to move their villages elsewhere and make new fields in new lands. They are also reduced to this necessity, at least in North America and the cold countries, by another more pressing reason for, as the women have to carry firewood to their lodges every day, the longer a village stays in the same place, the farther distant the wood is so that, after a certain number of years, they can no longer keep up the work of carrying the wood on their shoulders from so far.[55]

The solution to this problem was the horse. By the early eighteenth century, many Kahnawa'kehró:non were using horses to transport firewood and produce. Lafitau was there at the time of the transition:

> The Indians in the neighbourhood of the French cities of New France have wished to avoid this inconvenience and have, some time since, gotten horses of their own to take the wood to their lodges on their toboggans in winter and on the backs of these same horses during the summer. The young people, delighted to have the horses to lead, undertake this task willingly and the wives, freed by this means of a heavy burden, are no less pleased than they.[56]

But the presence of horses brought new problems:

> The horses, which are very numerous, spread in droves over the cornfields wherever there are no hedges or enclosures to stop them. They lay the fields waste entirely. No one can remedy this situation for, since the Indians lack stables in which to feed them, all that they can do is to shut them in by poor fences which the horses cross easily whether, not finding food enough in these enclosures they proceed to go get it elsewhere in the form of corn which tempts them more than hay, or whether the children who are con-stantly stirring them up to make them fight, press them and force them to jump their fences.[57]

Whereas horses resolved certain difficulties, they created new ones related to housing and feeding them, as well as requirements for fencing, so that they would not destroy crops. A century later, in 1810, an English actor named John Bernard toured Kahnawà:ke.[58] He was impressed by its system of communal horse ownership:

> In the course of our walk round the town our guide pointed out to us a field in which all the horses belonging to the settlement were running loose, and told us it was the practice whenever a man wanted one for him to take the first that came to hand, whether it was his own or not, to make use of it, and then return it at his convenience to this general repository. This may be a very good practice, thought I, in Cognawagha, but I doubt how it would be found to work in any other part of the world.[59]

The common pasture that Bernard observed remained in place until the latter decades of the nineteenth century, but I have encountered no other sources that describe Kahnawà:ke communal horse ownership in this way.

Declining returns from hunting and fishing posed another serious problem for Kahnawa'kehró:non, especially as all arable land in the vicinity had been taken up by settlers, who hunted and fished without any legal or personal accountability to their Indigenous neighbours. Overhunting and overfishing caused significant harm to Indigenous communities, especially beginning toward the end of the eighteenth century.[60] Although historians and anthropologists have long emphasized the centrality of horticulture, Rotinonhsión:ni economies also depended on fish and meat obtained by hunting. Van den Bogaert, for example, described seventeenth-century Rotinonhsión:ni diets as rich and meat-heavy, and Rotinonhsión:ni chiefs who visited Paris in 1666 were not much impressed by anything except the meat market.[61] Decisions to incorporate livestock into Kahnawa'kehró:non land practices in the eighteenth century may have been made to retain access to meat at a time of diminishing returns from hunting and fishing.[62] By the second half of the eighteenth century, colonial officials and observers already remarked that Kahnawa'kehró:non depended less on hunting than did other Indigenous peoples, because they raised their own crops and were heavily involved in trading.[63] By 1801, many, if not most, raised livestock and poultry.[64]

Nevertheless, declining returns from hunting, trapping, and fishing led to friction with settlers and other First Nations. For example, Algonquins and Nipissings from Kanehsatà:ke complained that Kahnawà:ke hunters trespassed on territories they claimed along the Upper Kitchissippi

(Ottawa) River and Lake Nipissing.[65] These conflicts were another reason Kahnawa'kehró:non had chosen to hunt less by the late eighteenth century. In 1796, Indian Agent M. Stacey and Indian Affairs storekeeper John Lees wrote that Kahnawà:ke men had "no hunting of any consequence" and were becoming more "laborious" as a result. They also mentioned that the cultivation of corn (maize) was a significant part of the Kahnawà:ke economy, estimating average annual production at one hundred bushels per family. Although Kahnawa'kehró:non incorporated domestic animals and new crops such as potatoes and wheat into their daily lives, they continued to grow their traditional crops.[66] Some became commercial farmers in the nineteenth century, and others leased out their lands to white farmers. Subsequent chapters explore questions and conflicts related to this transition.

Kahnawà:ke Governance

Rotinonhsión:ni societies were organized in ways that discouraged the establishment of political and economic hierarchies and inequalities, restrictions that were closely related to limits on the accumulation of individual wealth. European observers, their own assumptions often shaken by what they saw, remarked excitedly (both positively and negatively) on the egalitarian nature of Iroquoian society and politics. French military officer Louis Armand, Baron de Lahontan, noted that among seventeenth-century Wendats (an Iroquoian society whose cultural and legal traditions resembled those of Rotinonhsión:ni), "every one is as rich and as noble as his neighbor; the women are entitled to the same liberty with the men, and the children enjoy the same privileges with their fathers."[67] Jesuit missionary Paul Le Jeune wrote that they "are born, live, and die, in a liberty without restraint; they do not know what is meant by bridle and bit."[68] He added that "they are very generous among themselves and even make a show of not loving anything, of not being attached to the riches of the earth, so that they may not grieve if they lose them."[69]

Kahnawa'kehró:non maintained fierce independence throughout the eighteenth century, forming political alliances with colonial and Indigenous powers according to their own interests.[70] For example, although allied with the French, they were suspicious of French efforts to "protect" their village with new fortifications and garrisoned soldiers, as depicted in Figure 1.2.[71] Kahnawà:ke diplomats, as representatives of their sovereign nation, negotiated agreements with colonial powers, probably expecting to continue to share the bounty of the land like a dish with one spoon.

Around the turn of the eighteenth century, Kahnawà:ke leaders had the authority to concede land, construct and lease a community-owned mill, and make legal agreements with external institutions.[72] It is not known whether Kahnawa'kehró:non as a whole sanctioned or respected these powers, but both French and British colonial governments benefitted from these relatively new exercises of chiefly power, and they encouraged it.

A number of contemporary observers and historians have commented on aspects of the political system in Kahnawà:ke before the establishment of the elected band council in 1889. The military engineer Louis Franquet noted in 1752–53 that Kahnawà:ke was divided into three "familles" (clans), each of which consisted of two "bandes" (sub-clans) led by individual chiefs who were accountable to a grand chief.[73] This council structure of seven chiefs (six clan chiefs and one grand chief) persisted until the late nineteenth century.[74] There may have been up to thirty-three chiefs if sub-chiefs are included in the count.[75] The seven principal chiefs were elected by their respective clans, named for life, and confirmed by the Grand Council of the Seven Nations, as well as by colonial authorities.[76] In 1830, the influential resident missionary Joseph Marcoux compared the position of Kahnawà:ke chief to that of an elected member of parliament in which the chief represented the members of his clan.[77] Grand Chief Kanasontie declared in 1840 that the confirmation of the chief by the colonial government was a mere formality, but this approval became more important over time, and there are plenty of mid-century examples of the colonial government attempting to interfere in the nomination process.[78]

By the late eighteenth century, male leaders had taken some authority over the clearing, previously held by women. The colonial archive for Kahnawà:ke contains almost no explicit mention of this change, but it is clear that certain patriarchal political values took hold during this period. Even so, women certainly continued to lead in ways that were not perceptible to colonial observers, and these roles became more visible again toward the end of the nineteenth century (Chapter 6). It was a Rotinonhsión:ni norm for the leading women of each clan to choose the male leaders, and women played this role in Kahnawà:ke as well. In 1835, James Hughes, superintendent of Indian Affairs for the district of Montreal, observed that the widows of chiefs seemed to wield political power equal to that of living chiefs.[79] In early-nineteenth-century Kahnawà:ke, clan mothers continued to play a key role in nominating and recalling chiefs, even if this power was shared with clan men, but the practice eroded over the course of the century.[80] By the late nineteenth century, the DIA was refusing to confirm the replacement of any chief, and it became difficult to raise up new chiefs under the traditional system with the approval of the department. Refusing to confirm new chiefs was almost certainly a colonial tactic to pressure Kahnawà:ke into accepting the band council system. When the first band council was elected under the rules of the *Indian Advancement Act* in 1889, only three traditional chiefs remained.

The Seigneury of Sault Saint-Louis

To better understand the history of Kahnawà:ke land and law, we must consider its shared history with French colonial settlement under the seigneurial system. The territory of Kahnawà:ke was long known to settlers as the Seigneury of Sault Saint-Louis, a legal entity created by the French Crown in 1680, long after the village was established in that location. Its more than forty thousand acres were initially composed of two separate concessions: the first ran two leagues upriver from the Lachine Rapids and two leagues inland; the second, of about the same size, is just upriver from the first (Figure 1.3). The deeds specify that the lands were granted to the Society of Jesus (the Jesuits) for the benefit of the "Iroquois" of

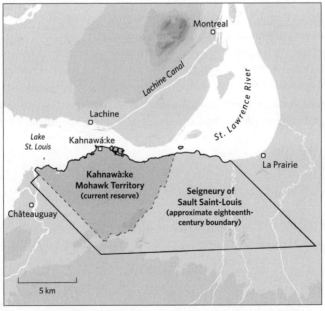

Figure 1.3   Kahnawà:ke and the Seigneury of Sault Saint-Louis. | Map by Eric Leinberger.

Kahnawà:ke until the day they should abandon it. The documents also forbade any French settlers on the tract from keeping cattle or establishing taverns.[81] Nevertheless, the Jesuit missionaries came to believe that they were the owners of the seigneury.[82] In 1718, the two concessions were joined into one territory about four times the size of the current reserve.[83]

Some scholars, such as legal historian Michel Morin, suggest that Sault Saint-Louis should not be considered a true seigneury. Morin notes that the deeds of concession made no provision for how the lands would be settled and developed and did not give the parameters as to the relationship between seigneur and censitaire (i.e., the rights and obligations of each), central features of most other seigneurial concessions.[84] Unlike most seigneurial deeds, these deeds state that the land would revert to the Crown if the Indigenous inhabitants were to abandon it. This suggests that French authorities expected Indigenous occupation to be temporary, an unfulfilled expectation that produced what historian Isabelle Bouchard calls an "ambiguous" legal status.[85] Morin argues that Sault Saint-Louis should simply be seen as "lands belonging to Indigenous people,"[86] not a seigneury. Similarly, historical anthropologist Carmen Lambert maintains that Sault Saint-Louis was never intended for non-Indigenous settlement and that any concessions made to non-Indigenous people should have been considered illegal.[87] Even if the territory was not initially conceptionalized as a typical seigneury, however, the practices of the Jesuits and Kahnawa'kehró:non over many decades resulted in what was, to all intents and purposes, a seigneury under French and then British colonial law. Jesuits acted as seigneurs, and Kahnawa'kehró:non, both before and after the British conquest, referred to themselves as "seigneurs and owners" of these lands.[88] Even Arakwente, discussed in Chapter 2 as a dissident who consistently opposed Kahnawà:ke leaders, identified himself in a court deposition as "one of the Indians of the Seignory of the Sault Saint Louis who are Seignors and Proprietors of the said Seignory."[89]

Sault Saint-Louis under the French and British Regimes

Despite the absence of any legal provisions allowing them to do so, Jesuit missionaries began to concede lands to French settlers on the borders of the seigneury in 1704. Colonial authorities finally responded to pressure from Kahnawà:ke leaders in 1718, when they ordered the Jesuits not to make any further concessions. However, the Jesuits ignored the order and in 1720 began to concede lands at an even faster rate. By 1759, they had conceded some 13,065 arpents (27 percent of the seigneury) to French

Canadian settlers. Continuing Kahnawà:ke protests led the colonial government to revisit the matter at mid-century. In 1754, the président du Conseil de la Marine determined that the lands in question belonged neither to Kahnawa'kehró:non nor the Jesuits but ultimately to the Crown. He ruled that the Jesuits did not have the right to concede lands (a ruling the Jesuits again disregarded), but he made no judgments on more specific questions regarding the legal status of the Sault and allowed previous concessions to stand.[90] Historical consultant Joan Holmes finds that "the Jesuits succeeded in taking over land in Sault St. Louis by canceling concessions and uniting them to the domain of La Prairie, by manipulating boundaries between lots, and by describing conceded areas as being shared between the seigneuries of La Prairie and Sault St. Louis."[91]

When British forces invaded the St. Lawrence Valley in 1760, and it became clear that Montreal would fall, leaders of nations previously allied with France, including Kahnawà:ke leaders, met with British commander Jeffrey Amherst at Oswegatchie in February to negotiate the terms for their neutrality. The British promised Indigenous nations that in exchange for ending their military defence of New France, they would enjoy the same privileges under British rule as they had under the French, including their land rights to seigneuries and hunting territories.[92] Then, in September 1760, the Treaty of Kahnawà:ke, a confirmation and expansion of the Treaty of Oswegatchie, transformed the previously negotiated neutrality into an alliance with the British.[93] The 1763 Royal Proclamation and 1764 Treaty of Niagara subsequently affirmed the territorial rights of Indigenous peoples and set apart large territories as "Indian lands," which were to be off limits to settlers without the permission of the Crown. Legal historian John Borrows shows that the Royal Proclamation, as well as post-1764 treaties in British North America, must be understood in light of the Treaty of Niagara. The latter included promises of the continuation of Indigenous sovereignty, free trade and travel for Indigenous people, prohibition on settlement on Indigenous lands without Indigenous consent, annual presents, and general promises of mutual respect and peacefulness.[94] The Royal Proclamation stipulated that settlers could not purchase lands directly from First Nations; only the Crown was authorized to negotiate for them. The goals of the proclamation were to limit European settlement to the eastern seaboard, to thus prevent hostilities between settlers and Indigenous peoples, and to allow the Crown to control the pace and character of colonial settlement.[95] The promise of a vast western territory free of European settlement was broken almost as soon as it was made, but certain elements of the Royal Proclamation became embedded in subsequent Indian policy. One of these is the idea that settlers should not be allowed to buy Indigenous land, that only the Crown can do so.

Despite the treaties protecting Indigenous lands, Jesuit missionaries took advantage of the administrative chaos following the conquest of New France by conceding Kahnawà:ke lands at an accelerated pace, to the concern and fury of Kahnawa'kehró:non.[96] When they asked the British in 1762 to put an end to Jesuit mismanagement, the governor of Lower Canada, General Thomas Gage, conducted an investigation. He concluded that the Jesuits did not own the land since the sole purpose of the original arrangement was for the benefit of the Indigenous inhabitants. Although he ruled that Kahnawa'kehró:non should be considered possessors of the whole territory (including church buildings) and revenue, he believed that their land rights were intended to be temporary and that underlying ownership was vested in the Crown. Nevertheless, Gage refused to annul Jesuit concessions made under the French regime.[97] A later DIA interpretation (1879) determined that following the Gage Decision Sault Saint-Louis was "entirely and exclusively vested in the Iroquois, under the supervision of the Indian Department."[98]

The Gage investigation also resulted in the creation of the position of "receiver," who was legally authorized by both the colonial governor and Kahnawà:ke chiefs to collect rents and to enter into certain contracts on behalf of the chiefs. After the Gage Decision removed the Jesuits from the process of granting lands, the chiefs and their receivers issued only a small number of concessions (Isabelle Bouchard identifies twenty-two between 1760 and 1820). This arrangement lasted until 1821, when the position of receiver was replaced by an agent commissioned by the governor, and the chiefs discovered that they had only limited influence over who would be appointed.[99] Although the arrangement under the British regime slowed the loss of land through concessions, Kahnawa'kehró:non to this day have not been able to recover illegally conceded lands.

With the danger of illegal and unauthorized concessions largely removed, Kahnawa'kehró:non turned to other threats to their land base. These included boundary incursions, unpaid rents, and settlers who continued to squat on unconceded land.[100] According to historian Maxime Gohier, more than 34 percent of petitions from Indigenous people who lived in the St. Lawrence Valley during the British period concerned land and territory, and many of these came from Kahnawà:ke.[101] Most of *The Laws and the Land* pertains to unconceded seigneurial lands – that were principally occupied by Kahnawa'kehró:non and that form the basis of the reserve today. Bouchard refers to this part of the territory as an "ambiguous space," largely because colonial officials were unsure about its legal status.[102] That apparent ambiguity was partly the result of the legal complexity of the seigneury as a whole, but it was also due to the strident, unambiguous, and asymmetrical assertions of both the Crown and Kahnawà:ke chiefs to exercise authority over it. The Crown solidified its claim by seizing all Jesuit estates in 1800.[103] The perception that the Crown held the underlying title to Kahnawà:ke land was of course very convenient and lucrative for the Crown, but it is based on the legal interpretation of Indigenous seigneuries as ultimately vested in the Crown. This, in turn, became one of the legal bases for the creation of the Indian reserve system under the administration of the federal government after Confederation.[104]

The Boundaries of Sault Saint-Louis

A major concern for Kahnawa'kehró:non throughout the British colonial period was the location and integrity of the boundary around the seigneury. A July 1762 survey ordered by Gage and completed by the surveyor Jean Péladeau marked out the border between Sault Saint-Louis and La Prairie, which Gage inexplicably moved only two months later to add a large strip of land, measuring thirty-seven arpents by two leagues, to the Jesuit-owned seigneury of La Prairie.[105] After Kahnawa'kehró:non bitterly disputed the alteration, Brigadier General Ralph Burton, Gage's successor, had three surveyors re-examine the boundary in 1763. They found that the Péladeau survey had been correct and subsequently reintegrated the tract with Sault Saint-Louis. Three years later, the Jesuits asserted their claim to the tract before the Court of Common Pleas in Montreal but lost. That decision was reversed, however, when the Jesuits appealed to the Superior Court of Quebec, and so the tract was restored to La Prairie in 1768. Surveyor General John Collins retraced the boundary in 1769, officially adding the strip of land to La Prairie.[106]

In 1798, the Crown, on behalf of Kahnawà:ke, successfully sued the Jesuits regarding the same boundary issue, but the Jesuits won again on appeal the following year.[107] Kahnawa'kehró:non pointed out in 1794 and 1797 that the Jesuits had moved a boundary marker so that a grist mill would be fraudulently included in the La Prairie seigneury and that settler farmers routinely moved boundary markers to enlarge their properties.[108] Since the Crown seized the Jesuit estates in 1800, all subsequent Kahnawa'kehró:non litigation was against the Crown.[109] In 1807, Kahnawà:ke sent a delegation to London to protest the location of the boundary, but it failed to convince the secretary of the colonies to take action.[110] In the

1820s, Kahnawà:ke petitioned Governor General, Lord Dalhousie, but he too rejected its claim.[111] The nation also sent a delegation to the governor of British North America, James Kempt, in 1828, saying that the most valuable part of the seigneury, including the grist mill and other buildings, should be restored to it. As evidence that the land belonged to Kahnawa'kehró:non, they reminded him that the Jesuits had needed their permission before building the mill, but Kempt rejected their claim. An 1829 delegation to the king on the same matter also accomplished nothing except to bring in some money for church renovations.[112]

On the western boundary of the seigneury, Kahnawà:ke leaders repeatedly accused the Grey Nuns of encroaching on their lands. Chiefs protested the location of that boundary, which was surveyed in 1769 and ran through fields cultivated by Kahnawa'kehró:non.[113] They objected to the loss of a boundary tract of ten arpents, which they had used and occupied for many years. Governor Guy Carleton and other colonial officials eventually came to agree with them, and thus the western boundary was resurveyed by John Collins in 1773.[114] Nevertheless, it remained contested at least until the mid-nineteenth century, when Kahnawà:ke leaders asserted their claim to all of the land between Kahnawà:ke and the Châteauguay River.[115] They also pointed out that they had been dispossessed of St. Bernard Island, formerly under cultivation by Kahnawà:ke farmers, without ever having sold or ceded rights to it.[116] Successive colonial governments dismissed many Kahnawa'kehró:non claims as unfounded but repeatedly promised to send surveyors to fix the boundaries. However, the entire border around the unconceded portion of the seigneury was not surveyed until the end of the nineteenth century, and much of the land in question remains in the hands of neighbouring settlers.[117]

Collecting Seigneurial Rents and Managing Money

Another major concern of Kahnawà:ke leaders was unpaid seigneurial rents and government agents who failed in their task of collecting and delivering rents. In 1821, Indian Affairs Superintendent John Johnson began to take a more active role in appointing and supervising agents to handle these tasks. Johnson asked Kahnawà:ke chiefs to recommend "some Respectable Person to be their Agent for the collection of their Rents, and the Transaction of all other Business connected with their Lands." They recommended Châteauguay land surveyor Charles Archambault, who had already served in that capacity for two years and had "acquitted himself entirely to their Satisfaction."[118] However, when the influential parish priest

Joseph Marcoux raised objections to Archambault and recommended notary Nicolas-Benjamin Doucet of Montreal instead, Johnson complied with his wishes.[119] This was an important moment in the erosion of chiefly power amid the increasing interference of the Indian Department. Furthermore, the fiscal affairs of the seigneurial lands were generally disorganized and inconsistent, meaning that Kahnawà:ke could not derive significant revenue from the lands it had otherwise lost.[120] Three years later, Kahnawà:ke chiefs complained that Doucet was a man "whom we don't know, distant from us, who does not know the censitaires who pay us rent, does not know how much each is required to pay, does not know the extent and location of their lands, and who does not give us wheat or money to relieve the ills of our poor."[121] They added that Doucet was afraid to leave his home, refused to speak to them, and had hired someone else to collect the rents in his stead. Doucet was eventually replaced, but crooked and unreliable agents continued to be the scourge of Kahnawa'kehró:non. Income from rents fluctuated over the years but could be significant. In 1830, the income from conceded lands was about £200 in currency and £800 in agricultural produce. It was used for church maintenance, public infrastructure, legal services, salaries for the miller and the guardians of the common pasture, upkeep of the mill, and hosting visiting delegations.[122] According to contemporary departmental reports, revenue could have been much greater if it had been properly managed.[123]

Throughout the 1820s, 1830s, and 1840s, one agent after another was investigated for irregularities and quickly replaced, and records on seigneurial income were incomplete at best. The 1858 report by the special commissioners into the affairs of the Indian Department revealed that the annual public revenue of Kahnawà:ke was small, amounting to $1,062, of which about $1,000 was derived from "rents in money and kind from their leased lands." The rest was paid by the Séminaire de Montréal as interest on money loaned to it during the previous decade for the construction of the Notre-Dame church (today Notre-Dame Basilica) in Montreal. The rents were collected by the Indian agent, who received no government salary but had the right to retain a portion of the rents. An indication of the importance and lucrative nature of this position is the fact that a new agent was required to give the Indian Department a $4,000 security.[124] The department felt that the seigneurial arrangements for the 14,257 conceded acres produced rents below market value, but it excused itself from intervening because Kahnawà:ke finances were still largely out of its hands. As the special commissioners emphasized in 1858: "Over most of this money the Indian Department has no control, nor does it pass through their hands. The above named rents are collected by the local agent who is bound to render annual returns to Head Quarters of his receipts and expenditure."[125] Yet colonial law came to treat Indigenous communities such as Kahnawà:ke as not possessing a corporate legal personality, which prevented them from pleading their case before the courts except through their "tutor," the king. They had little recourse when censitaires paid no rent, agents failed to collect it, and the Crown refused to intervene.[126] An additional but related blow to the independence of the chiefs occurred at the end of the 1830s, when the Indian Department imposed the requirement that the chiefs provide it with accounts of the seigneurial revenue.[127]

Abolition of the Seigneurial System

The abolition of the seigneurial system in 1854 directly affected the Kahnawà:ke economy and land base. The law enabled censitaires to transform their feudal ownership (with its rights and responsibilities) into the equivalent of fee-simple ownership, free of all seigneurial rights and duties. Thus, the parts of the seigneury that were occupied by settlers were now to become private property and would no longer produce revenue for the community.[128] Seigneurs were to be indemnified by the government for their losses at an amount arrived at by calculating the value of seigneury land using a *cadastre abrégé* (cadastral summary document). The law made exceptions for seigneuries that were owned by religious orders and First Nations, so changes there occurred a little differently.

The cadastre abrégé for Kahnawà:ke was created between 1858 and 1860 by land commissioner H. Judah, who assessed the value of the conceded portion of the seigneury at $99,209.83. This was the compensation that Kahnawà:ke would be owed for territorial losses brought on by the abolition of the seigneurial system. Judah listed the seigneury as belonging to "la tribu des sauvages Iroquois, etc." (the Indian tribe of the Iroquois, etc.), but this was corrected to remove the "etc." Its inclusion would have indicated some doubt as to the sole ownership of the seigneury, but its removal may have signified that the creators of the cadastre abrégé recognized Kahnawa'kehró:non as the sole owners. At least as late as 1890, representatives of the Quebec government cited the Gage Decision of 1762 to argue that Kahnawa'kehró:non were in possession of this territory and that federal government claims to it were thus invalid.[129]

No indemnity was paid at the time, however. Finally, in 1881, $10,000 (about 10 percent of the amount determined in 1860) were paid to a trust fund managed by the DIA. The department subsequently used this money to fund the Walbank Survey, an intrusive, expensive land subdivision conducted against the wishes of the community (Chapter 6).[130] In an attempt to encourage censitaires to pay their rental arrears, the federal government passed the *Act Respecting the Seigneury of Sault St. Louis* in 1894, which reduced the arrears of most tenants by 25 percent, but most were unmoved by the law and paid nothing. The 1935 *Seigneurial Rent Abolition Act* provided for commutation of rents by payment of "a capital sum the interest on which 6 percent equals the rent and which applied to Sault Saint Louis." It set up a fund from which censitaires could borrow at low interest to make the lump-sum payment, but few opted even for this. In 1967, the Kahnawà:ke band council unanimously rejected a lump-sum payment in exchange for which the community would have given up its seigneurial rights.[131] Negotiations on this matter are still ongoing.

There was never a decisive moment when Sault Saint-Louis concessions were transformed into fee-simple ownership, and government agents continued to collect rents in a haphazard way after Confederation. But by the time of seigneurial abolition, rents were already falling off, largely due to neglect by Indian agents and the unwillingness of the colonial government to intercede. Mentions of seigneurial income in the DIA archives became increasingly rare as the nineteenth century drew to a close. Historical anthropologist Carmen Lambert suggests that some censitaires stopped paying rent in 1871, and others followed suit. By 1891, almost no one was paying.[132] Kahnawa'kehró:non, however, did not forget that this income was their right and inheritance, and they often brought the matter to the attention of the Indian Department. For example, in 1874, the chiefs complained that agents had not been collecting rents and that the books had not been kept since 1848.[133] Ottawa sued one censitaire for thirty years' arrears in 1889, but instead of producing any income for Kahnawà:ke, the case turned into a drawn-out legal dispute between Quebec and Ottawa over who had the right to collect rents.[134] In the early twentieth century, federal and provincial governments again locked horns over the question of whether a small island in the St. Lawrence River was part of Kahnawà:ke, with the courts siding with Quebec's claim that it held title.[135]

Subsequent chapters of this book continue the story of Canadian colonialism during the nineteenth century and Kahnawa'kehró:non efforts to defend their territory and assert their sovereignty over it. Though my focus does not go much beyond 1900, I would note that perhaps the most serious twentieth-century blow to Kahnawà:ke territorial sovereignty came with the massive expropriation of its most valuable land to build the

St. Lawrence Seaway in the 1950s. In that instance, the DIA helped the
St. Lawrence Seaway authority to commute seigneurial rents (eliminate
the debt of accumulated rents owed to Kahnawà:ke with a much smaller
lump-sum payment), and these commutations continued in later years
against the wishes of Kahnawa'kehró:non.[136] The Kahnawà:ke band council
vociferously protested these unilateral attempts to eliminate its interest in
conceded seigneurial land, and since the 1980s the council has pursued its
claim to seigneurial lands and revenues through Canada's Specific Claims
process.[137]

CONCLUSION

An 1864 map made by P.L. Morin (Figure 1.4) shows the Seigneury of
Sault Saint-Louis, including conceded lots (long rectangles in the bottom
half of the image) that still produced rental income for the Kahnawà:ke
community. It is one of the last nineteenth-century maps to depict the
seigneury including both conceded and unconceded lands – the latter
would become Indian Reserve No. 14. The caption on the map (not shown)
reads "Plan of the Seigniory of Sault St. Louis or Caughnawaga," which
indicates that the entire seigneury was equated with Kahnawà:ke and that
conceded lots occupied by French Canadians were still seen as part of the
territory. In the process of transforming seigneurial tenure into private
property, Canadian governments worked to impose the status of Indian
reserve onto Indigenous seigneurial lands.[138] First, seigneuries had to be
dismantled before what remained of Indigenous seigneuries could become reserves. In 1880, when the DIA set out to survey the boundaries of
the reserve, it effectively cut off the rest of the seigneury, both on the
ground and in the colonial imagination (Chapter 6). In this way, the federal government ensured that the reserve would be much smaller than the
seigneury had been and that more land would be available to settlers as
private property. Thus, in a way that Kahnawa'kehró:non could not have
foreseen in the seventeenth century, both the seigneurial system and its
abolition became frontiers where settler society was able to undermine
Indigenous nationhood.

Many readers may be surprised to learn that Indigenous peoples, including Kahnawa'kehró:non, voluntarily inserted themselves into a seigneurial
legal framework during the seventeenth and eighteenth centuries. But one
should remember that power relations at that time were very different
from what they would become; the relatively weak French colony depended

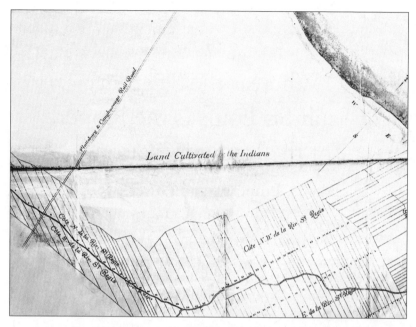

FIGURE 1.4   Detail of "Plan of the Seigniory of Sault St. Louis or Caughnawaga,"
P.L. Morin, 1864. The horizontal and vertical lines running through the map are fold-
marks. | RG88, R214, box 2000211384, LAC.

on the military and political might of its Indigenous allies, and Indigenous
nations did not see French colonial law as a serious challenge or threat to
their own legal orders. That would change over time as colonial power
grew, but given their actions and words in subsequent decades and centuries, it is clear that Kahnawa'kehró:non tended to view their seigneurial
arrangements with French Canadians as highly compatible with their own
conceptions of land sharing and reciprocity. Rotinonhsión:ni leaders in
many places and times (in the Mohawk Valley, in the Grand River Valley),
for example made serious and innovative attempts to share their lands
with settlers in ways that would be mutually beneficial, seeing these relationships through the metaphor of the Dish with One Spoon and the legal
principles of the Kaianerehkó:wa.[139] Most of these efforts were sabotaged
by settlers who refused to be good neighbours and by colonial governments,
who invariably sided with them. But it was not until the late eighteenth
century that Kahnawà:ke leaders would have to face the new threat of
Kahnawa'kehró:non who openly challenged Kahnawà:ke law in colonial
courts.

2

"Whereas the Seigniory of Sault St. Louis Is the Property of the Iroquois Nation"

Dissidents, Property, and Power, 1790–1815

> *Hitherto it has been usual in all disputes among the Indians*
> *of the said village [Kahnawà:ke], that the chiefs in Council*
> *have decided and determined; The same agreeable to those Laws*
> *and Usages which have been handed down to them from their*
> *Ancestors, and this right having been constantly permitted*
> *through the indulgence of the British Government, it became*
> *at last generally understood by their Nation, that the Chiefs*
> *had the power of determining, and that the Nation was*
> *bound to submit to their decision in all such cases.*
>
> – *Kahnawà:ke chiefs, 1799*

D uring the first centuries of contact, there were many moments when the relationships between settlers and Indigenous people were relatively balanced and mutually beneficial.[1] *The Laws and the Land* begins at such a moment, with prosperous Kahnawa'kehró:non, who ruled themselves according to their own laws, spoke their own language, and took part in formal and informal colonial economies as they saw fit. The colonial powers (first France and then Britain) had to adjust their practices to accommodate Indigenous cultural, economic, and political practices. Of course, not everything was fine: Indigenous societies had dealt with their own problems since time immemorial, and the arrival of European microbes, ideas, and products brought new death, turmoil, and destruction. Nevertheless, Indigenous peoples saw benefits in the

European presence and could still impose their narratives and laws in ways that would become unimaginable in the nineteenth century. Until the late eighteenth century, Kahnawà:ke chiefs rarely felt the need to defend their authority. The nation governed itself according to its own laws, and colonial authorities were unable to interfere a great deal in its internal affairs. But the relatively functional, symmetrical relationship was beginning to un-ravel. In 1799, the chiefs petitioned Governor General Robert Prescott in defence of their rights and authority (their petition is quoted in the epigraph), expressing shock and consternation that the colonial leaders did not seem to understand their relationship. This chapter explores how an increasingly asymmetrical power dynamic developed between Kahnawà:ke and British authorities through legal disputes that occurred decades before Confederation and the passage of the *Indian Act*. It looks at how colonial law, specifically land law, made inroads into Kahnawà:ke in the late eighteenth and early nineteenth centuries.

Kahnawa'kehró:non experienced tremendous change during the century between 1716, when they moved to their present location, and the years following the War of 1812. At the beginning of this period, Rotinonhsión:ni nations were important actors throughout the region, but they had lost much of their economic and military power by the 1820s. Britain had become the dominant power, and throughout the nineteenth century many Kahnawa'kehró:non became involved in the fur trade in the Northwest and in other colonial projects far away from their homelands.[2] Montreal, no more than a village in 1716, had grown into a city on the brink of an explosive industrialization, and settlers were transforming its environs into villages and farms.

This chapter details how Kahnawa'kehró:non adapted their laws and practices to these changes, and the conflicts and debates that resulted. It describes the beginnings of various kinds of colonial intrusions that made it increasingly difficult for Kahnawà:ke leaders to enforce their authority. At times, dissident community members challenged Kahnawà:ke leaders and laws, with support from settler outsiders. Successive colonial governments, and their courts, became more willing and able to take advantage of these cleavages to undermine Kahnawà:ke sovereignty. Kahnawà:ke leaders recognized such threats for what they were and responded in innovative ways but were unable to win decisive victories due to growing colonial power imbalances. This chapter looks at the various legal challenges to the authority of the chiefs in council, which contextualizes the creation of the Code of 1801 as the chiefs' response meant to limit the intrusion of colonial legal regimes into Kahnawà:ke.

An important sign of growing conflict in the colonial record involved Kahnawa'kehró:non who wished to circumvent Kahnawà:ke chiefs and Kahnawà:ke laws. Already in 1771, a delegation of twenty-two Kahnawà:ke diplomats had approached the Indian Department to express concern about two Kahnawà:ke families who intended to allow French families to settle on Kahnawà:ke lands. Legal historians Philip Girard, Jim Phillips, and R. Blake Brown refer to them as "a small group of inhabitants of Kahnawake [who] were clearly trying to evade seeking the approval of the Kahnawake council of chiefs, which would be required before any land could be alienated to outsiders, pushing community leaders to seek back-up from British colonial officials."[3] The first court records of such clashes date from the 1790s, when dissident Kahnawa'kehró:non tried to bypass the authority of the chiefs by taking their disputes to court – to have their matters resolved according to colonial law rather than Kahnawà:ke law.

CONFLICT AND LAW IN KAHNAWÀ:KE, 1790–1815

Before 1800, disputes in Kahnawà:ke were handled internally according to Kahnawà:ke law and left no written records. In practice, colonial authorities recognized that Indigenous people were governed by their own laws. Even though French law did not technically differentiate between Indigenous and non-Indigenous people, French authorities almost never put Indigenous people on trial for crimes committed against non-Indigenous people. Instead, the accused were usually transferred to their home communities for proceedings according to Indigenous legal protocols.[4] During the first decades of British rule, a few Indigenous people begin to appear in Montreal legal records, but only in cases where an individual had broken colonial laws outside Indigenous-controlled territory.[5] Conflicts within Indigenous nations continued to be resolved by the nations themselves.

A case from March 1799 signalled a shift, however, when the Court of King's Bench sentenced Kiatharatie, a Kahnawà:ke man, to death for the murder of Kaheghtiaks, a Kahnawà:ke woman. Kahnawà:ke chiefs petitioned to have Kiatharatie pardoned, given that he had never expected to be judged by colonial law (chapter epigraph).[6] Referring to themselves as "your memorialists," they reminded Governor General Robert Prescott that they had always mediated all disputes in the village according to the "Laws and Usages which have been handed down to them from their Ancestors."[7] They did not suggest that Kiatharatie was innocent, but only that their people understood themselves to be governed by their own laws and that everyone, including the British government, had recognized this practice. Indeed, if colonial laws were to be applied to their people, they should be the first to know:

> Had your memorialists been taught to believe that they as chiefs exercised an improper or ill founded jurisdiction over the disputes arising between individuals of their nation, had they been taught to consider the general law of the land as the rule of their conduct, it would have been their duty to declare and make this known to their nation, that they might have no excuses for their delinquency.[8]

Clearly, the chiefs were not referring to themselves as delinquent. They were emphasizing their consternation, not only that the colonial government had expanded its jurisdiction into Kahnawà:ke, but also that they had not been informed. They noted that the case in question "awakens them from their dream of security under their own usages." Their petition expressed great surprise that colonial officials should attempt to impose their laws on Kahnawà:ke and indicated that the chiefs were disturbed about this change. This event in 1799, then, seems to have been a moment of clarity for Kahnawà:ke leaders, when they recognized that an important shift was under way that would place colonial law over their own.[9] This criminal case was a strong indicator that colonial officials did not intend to respect Indigenous jurisdiction, and subsequent land disputes would bear this out.

Arakwente and Sagosinnagete

In all the years of colonial rule before 1796, there is only one known case in which an Indigenous person appealed to the courts to resolve an internal problem. But between 1796 and 1820, there are thirty such cases, almost all of them involving Kahnawà:ke.[10] This explosion in cases is particularly noteworthy because it does not correspond to a general increase in court activity for the period.[11] Nearly half of the cases (fourteen) involved one married Kahnawà:ke couple, Arakwente (Thomas) and Sagosinnagete (Agathe).[12] The colonial archive gives almost no background information on Sagosinnagete – more is known about Arakwente. He was an orphan from another Indigenous nation, adopted by a Kahnawà:ke family. He inherited some wealth from his parents and became an influential merchant who ran a Kahnawà:ke inn that was said to illegally sell liquor. He was also a fur trader, landholder, speculator, and moneylender, and he possessed a lucrative ferry licence for moving goods and people across the St. Lawrence River.

An Irish writer named Isaac Weld met Arakwente in the mid-1790s near Lake Champlain when Arakwente was on his way to trade furs in Albany. According to Weld,

> Thomas appeared to be about forty-five years of age; he was nearly six feet high, and very bulky in proportion: this is a sort of make uncommon among the Indians, who are generally slender. He was dressed like a white man, in boots; his hair untied but cut short; the people who attended him were all in the Indian habit. Not one of his followers could speak a word of English or French; Thomas, however, could himself speak both languages. English he spoke with some little hesitation, and not correctly; but French seemed as familiar to him as his native tongue. His principal attention seemed to be directed towards trade, which he had pursued with great success, so much so, indeed, that, as we afterwards heard, he could get credit in any store in Montreal for five hundred pounds. He had along with him at Chimney Point thirty horses and a quantity of furs in the canoe, which he was taking for sale to Albany. His people, he told us, had but a very few wants: he took care to have these always supplied; in return they brought him furs, taken in hunting; they attended his horses, and voluntarily accompanied him when he went on a trading expedition: his profits therefore must be immense.[13]

Weld added that Arakwente had invited him to Kahnawà:ke, where he promised to make him and his men very happy, and to introduce them to Kahnawà:ke women who might become their wives.[14] Weld promised to visit. He had the impression that Arakwente was very wealthy, and it is also worth emphasizing that Arakwente dressed like a white man, unlike his companions. Though I am skeptical about Weld's claim that none of Arakwente's associates spoke English or French, the more important point is that Arakwente was adept at conducting business in both colonial languages, whereas his associates were probably less comfortable doing so. Finally, in light of the problems that Kahnawà:ke was just beginning to experience with white men who married into the community, Arakwente's claim that he would provide Weld and his men with wives is important and telling (I return to this below).

Weld was quite taken by Arakwente's swagger, but he was later told that Arakwente was "not a man respected among the Indians in general, who think much more of a chief that is a good warrior and hunter, and that retains the habits of his nation, than of one that becomes a trader, and assimilates his manners to those of the whites."[15] Arakwente's aggressive commercial activities and assimilationist tendencies had earned him little respect in the community, it seems. And this was not simply a matter of jealousy among his neighbours: many Kahnawa'kehró:non saw him as putting his own interests above those of the nation. In the 1790s, when he began to take his neighbours to court, he broke with the traditions and laws of his people. In 1791 and 1792, Arakwente successfully sued white people who owed him money in the colonial courts, but it was in 1796 that he became the first of his nation to take a fellow Kahnawa'kehró:non to a British court.[16]

When Kahnawà:ke chief Onashetaken removed a fence that Arakwente had erected around a piece of land, Arakwente sued.[17] The chiefs (supporting Onashetaken) rightly considered such a lawsuit an affront to their authority; eight of them met with the attorney general to protest this action. They argued that a colonial court was no place for a conflict between Indigenous people. According to Indian Department official Joseph Chew, the chiefs stated:

If they [Indians] were indebted to a White man and he sued them they would appear [in court] and do what they could to discharge the Debt, but that one Indian should serve a Writ on another and make him appear in a Court of Law is a New and unprecedented Matter, and they hoped His Lordship would take the same into Consideration and have stop put to such Proceedings.[18]

A few weeks later, two chiefs again met with Chew. After the meeting, he wrote,

I thought I knew the Rules and Customs of Indians pretty well, but one of these [chiefs] had so much to say beginning with the Mohawks going thro' the customs of the Six and many of the Western Nations, all tending to Prove that Indians had no Right to bring Each other into a Court of Law; that I found it in vain for me to dispute with him.[19]

Attorney General John Sewell, however, believed that any person who lived under British protection should have the right to appeal to its courts.[20] Thus, despite the protests of the chiefs, the case went forward in the Court of King's Bench. Both parties agreed that Kahnawà:ke law required a person to occupy a parcel of land for more than one year in order to be put in possession of it. In other words, everyone agreed that a legitimate claim to land required occupancy and, presumably, use. In this case, British judges recognized Kahnawà:ke law and attempted to enforce it, without knowing much about it. The court heard witnesses: Arakwente claimed to have fulfilled the Kahnawà:ke requirement for ownership, but Onashetaken and his three witnesses argued that according to Kahnawà:ke law it was the chiefs who decided such matters. The court found for the defendant, but it is not clear why.[21] Girard, Phillips, and Brown find this case interesting, not only because the court upheld and enforced Kahnawà:ke law, but also because both Arakwente and Onashetaken were represented by prominent Montreal lawyers.[22] This reveals how much was at stake, and how familiar the contemporary Montreal legal community would have been with the case. The colonial legal establishment was clearly taking an interest in Kahnawà:ke law, but this interest can be understood as a prelude to a more aggressive expansion of colonial law.

In 1798, Arakwente again sued a Kahnawa'kehró:non, Jacob Joseph Hill, in a Montreal court. He claimed that Hill had threatened him with death when he demanded repayment of a debt. Hill's affidavit states that Hill came to Arakwente's house carrying a rifle in one hand and a pistol in the other, tried to force him outside, insulted him by calling him a coward and a woman, threatened to kill him, and finally shot at one of his windows.[23] Documents showing the outcome of the case are missing from the archived court files.

Arakwente brought suit again in the Montreal Court of King's Bench in 1799 after he hired labourers to cut trees (for commercial sale of the timber), and the chiefs intervened to stop him. He argued that they were depriving him of his own wood and that "a custom or usage exists and for time immemorial hath existed" that each and every Kahnawà:ke Indian had the right to "cut down and take any quantity of wood which he may choose to take." In other words, his commercial woodcutting on Kahnawà:ke territory, for which he employed two lumberjacks, was in line with Kahnawà:ke law. He believed the chiefs had violated his ancient rights when they prevented him "with force and arms" from cutting and from taking away wood.[24] One witness for the defence, Claude Duranseau, testified that for the previous twenty or twenty-two years only the chiefs had the authority to sell wood from the seigneury, but that during the last four or five years certain Kahnawa'kehró:non had been taking and selling as much as they wanted. Arakwente had approached the chiefs during the previous fall and winter to ask about taking wood, but they told him he was not to sell it, "not even an axe handle."[25] The case ended with Arakwente withdrawing his complaint for unknown reasons, but Arakwente continued to advance his agenda despite community opposition.

Although these initial attempts to use the courts to settle land disputes were not successful, Arakwente and Sagosinnagete sued several other Kahnawa'kehró:non during the following decade. They brought a case against a chief for ejecting Sagosinnagete from the church and threatening to banish her from the community. The court required the chief to enter into a bond to keep the peace. Arakwente received a similar judgment after he complained that in 1799, two Kahnawa'kehró:non had threatened to kill him.[26] In an 1806 case, he accused a man of threatening him, and a bailiff was sent to Kahnawà:ke to arrest the suspect. The bailiff was met by a group of at least fifty Kahnawa'kehró:non armed with clubs and sticks, who said "they had not any business with the law of Montreal."[27] Girard, Phillips, and Brown argue that Arakwente and Sagosinnagete's success was greater in cases that involved their personal safety and mobility than in cases involving land and wood.[28]

The same year, 1806, the chiefs followed through on their threat to expel Arakwente because he would not, in the words of his court declaration, "renounce the laws of this country nor abandon his trade and commerce." Kahnawa'kehró:non were asking him to renounce British law and to stop breaking Kahnawà:ke law. He refused. Aided by a large number of armed Kahnawa'kehró:non, the chiefs stormed Arakwente and Sagosinnagete's house, and according to Arakwente's declaration

> seized upon him with violence carried him from his said house and imprisoned him during the space of six hours, That they then conducted him by force out of the said village, like a criminal, to the distance of about two Leagues from the Said Village to the first settlements of the parish of Laprairie, when they set him at liberty, with an injunction not to return to the Said Village on pain of his life.[29]

He returned to his house that very night, but the following day he was again apprehended on a road east of the village. His captors brought him to the centre of the village, where they gathered a large crowd and "under the pretence that he ... would not renounce the laws of this country [colonial Lower Canada] nor give up his trade and commerce, seized upon [him] anew." Seven men were then tasked with removing him – this time, they escorted him five or six leagues to the upper reaches of the Turtle River (Rivière de la Tortue), probably near today's village of Saint-Mathieu.

There, in an area of woods and swamps, they set him free on condition that he never return. Arakwente, Sagosinnagete, and their children then moved to Montreal for their own safety while they sought the protection of the courts, and two of his sons-in-law attempted to look after his Kahnawà:ke business interests for him.[30] The Court of King's Bench at Montreal, however, decided in Arakwente's favour, and the chiefs were required to allow him to return home and pay him thirty pounds in damages.[31] Girard, Phillips, and Brown see this decision as "depriving the government of Kahnawake of the authority to enforce its decisions regarding expulsions of inhabitants believed to be a fundamental threat to the community's well-being" and thus as a "serious blow to the integrity of customary law and authority, indeed to the community itself."[32]

The courts of Lower Canada were marked by considerable inconsistency at the time, and little is known about the kind of justice that Indigenous people could expect to find there. Legal historian Jean-Philippe Garneau shows that during the latter decades of the eighteenth century, judges and lawyers who had little or no formal legal training struggled to navigate the provisions of the *Quebec Act*. The new justice system, which came into effect with this act in 1775, was a hybrid of the British common law tradition and the civil law tradition of France, and several decades elapsed before it worked smoothly.[33] Between 1780 and 1835, Indigenous people represented only about 0.5 percent of defendants in quarter sessions complaints in the district of Montreal, and even fewer appeared as plaintiffs. Indeed, legal historian Donald Fyson uses the example of Arakwente and Sagosinnagete to illustrate the rarity of Indigenous plaintiffs during this period.[34] Merchants, on the other hand, were always over-represented in the courts compared to their demographic weight in the population at large.[35] All of this suggests that Arakwente's actions and values were in line with those of merchants but not with those of other Indigenous people.

It is worth considering how Arakwente fits into the overall pattern of litigation in Quebec at the time. Historian Evelyn Kolish's quantitative analysis of civil court records for this period shows that the British population was over-represented in litigation compared to the French Canadian population. She suggests that this could arise from the fact that most litigants were urban and that anglophone populations tended to be urban. She hypothesizes "that the British population relished litigation more than the Canadians or that they relied more on the courts and less on the informal networks of family and local communities."[36] Although Kolish does not present direct evidence to corroborate this claim, it seems reasonable that cultural and political factors explain the difference. Censitaires (mostly francophone farmers) almost never entered the court system as plaintiffs. According to Kolish:

> The economic and social realities of life would have made litigation unlikely if not impossible for most censitaires: hence a relatively low level of litigation on seigneurial rights ... No doubt the fact that the majority of landowners were rural small-holders, running owner-occupied farms, also reduced litigation, since the rural agricultural population would appear to have resorted much more systematically to local arbitration, especially in matters such as boundaries, fencing, rights-of-way, and so on. This was a tendency undoubtedly reinforced by the urban bias of the court structures.[37]

Kolish argues that the courts were "distinctly marginal in their impact on the lives of most of Lower Canada's rural agricultural population."[38]

Like French Canadians, Kahnawa'kehró:non avoided the colonial courts (until the time of Arakwente) at least in part for cultural and political reasons. Of course, geographical distance also played a role. Since people who lived at the greatest distances from Montreal and Quebec City were least likely to go to court, and since Kahnawà:ke was closer to a major urban centre than most Indigenous communities, it is not surprising that it was among the first Indigenous communities to become involved in civil litigation.[39] Arakwente's litigiousness was unusual for Kahnawà:ke, but it was also unusual for rural Lower Canada in general. The position of Kahnawà:ke as a ferry-hub across from Lachine, and with easy access to Montreal, facilitated Arakwente's urban connections despite the rural locale of Kahnawà:ke itself.

Since Arakwente had regular contact with anglophone merchants in the Montreal region, he may also have shared their assumptions about the superiority of British civilization and law, and the inferiority of Indigenous ways. He certainly recognized a useful legal mechanism that could advance his interests and behaved much like other merchants he knew. It is also likely that he encountered rhetoric that linked seigneurial forms of land tenure to backwardness and tyranny, and freehold forms of land tenure to British liberties. It would not be hard for him to see himself as the oppressed victim of an outdated and unfair system of land tenure, whether Kanien'kehá:ka or French or both. Later in the century, British merchants, along with their government patrons, would use legislation to systematically attack the seigneurial system. Arakwente challenged Kahnawà:ke land laws in Montreal courts.

Although his contemporaries saw him as a wealthy man, his controversial land and timber grabs could also have been grounded not in a sense of immunity, but in desperation, perhaps because his usual sources of income were drying up. This interpretation would fit with Allan Greer's portrayal of a country merchant in the latter half of the eighteenth century as perennially indebted and searching for new sources of revenue (except in times of war). However, Arakwente's practices challenge Greer's characterization of rural merchants as "parasitic intermediaries between productive systems over which they exercised little control." In Greer's account, rural merchants bought low and sold high but made no attempt to transform the feudal order into a capitalist one.[40] It is not known whether Arakwente's ambitions included the creation of a capitalist society in Kahnawà:ke, but his actions were clearly aimed at upsetting the existing order in favour of one that favoured people like him. Kahnawa'kehró:non long held a reputation as innovative, entrepreneurial traders, but Arakwente stepped out of that tradition by defying the laws of his own community and appealing to colonial law.

In the early nineteenth century, Kahnawà:ke chiefs were facing an increasing number of internal challenges from people like Arakwente, and they would have to find a way to assert their authority and the primacy of their laws on their territory. There is evidence that Arakwente sometimes gained the support of a few chiefs, but mostly he seems to have been at odds with his community. Several years after a British court order allowed him to return to Kahnawà:ke, a traveller named John M. Duncan, who had read Isaac Weld's account, saw Arakwente and wrote: "He was formerly a trader and in good circumstances, but is now in poverty and bloated with dissipation; two of his sons were educated at the Seminary in Montreal."[41] Here is evidence that despite his successes in court, Arakwente had not been able to maintain his wealth and status in Kahnawà:ke. We do not know what led to his poverty, but his downfall might have served as an important cautionary tale for anyone who wished to defy Kahnawà:ke law. Nevertheless, it also reveals new vulnerabilities and dangers for Kahnawà:ke sovereignty.

Claude Delorimier

Another influential and controversial Kahnawà:ke man during this period was Claude Delorimier (Guillaume Chevalier de Lorimier), a French Canadian militia officer and merchant who served for many years as an Indian agent for the Indian Department. Delorimier helped the British recruit Indigenous soldiers, took part in a number of military operations, and later led Kanien'kehá:ka warriors into battle during the War of 1812.[42] He settled in Kahnawà:ke in 1783 when he married a Kahnawà:ke woman whose name is recorded as Marie-Louise Schuyler. After she died in 1790, he married a French Canadian woman who died in 1800. He then married Skawennetsi (Anne Gregory or McGregor), who was probably Kanien'kehá:ka. His three wives bore twelve children in total.[43]

Initially, Delorimier developed a network of allies in Kahnawà:ke and cultivated the trust of its leaders. He was adopted into the nation in 1790 and given the name Teiohatekon. After swearing never to sell lands to non-Kahnawa'kehró:non, he was given land rights under Kahnawà:ke law.[44] It is understandable why Kahnawà:ke leaders would perceive Delorimier as valuable, given his significant military experience and connections in the colonial government. His inclusion in the community is in line with Rotinonhsión:ni legal principles promoting the naturalization of outsiders to strengthen the nation. Not long afterward, however, Delorimier showed himself unworthy of trust, and Kahnawà:ke public opinion turned against him. Already in 1794, a large group of Kahnawa'kehró:non submitted a list of complaints against Delorimier: that he made false promises, was sexually promiscuous, engaged in liquor trafficking, and involved in corrupt political and economic practices. The most serious accusations were that he accumulated land, cattle, and wood to the detriment of the poor and of the nation, and that he enriched himself with funds intended for the community.[45] Kahnawa'kehró:non repeatedly raised similar complaints during the following two decades and later against his children.

By 1801, Delorimier had obtained fifty-three lots in Kahnawà:ke totalling 107 acres, and many in the community agreed, on the basis of Kahnawà:ke law, that he had no right to own so much. There were also complaints that his cattle damaged others' crops, which suggests that he did not maintain his fences or that he simply allowed his animals to roam. In 1809, five chiefs described him as "one of those Whites who sometimes want to be Indians for the advantages, and sometimes White men in order to humiliate and crush us."[46] By the 1810s, Delorimier had few allies left among the chiefs or in the community as a whole, but the chiefs were in a difficult position since they relied on him as official interpreter and Indian agent, positions that were determined by the Indian Department. They finally managed to have him dismissed as agent in 1821, but he was well connected at a number of levels of government, and he used these relationships to keep his rights to live and own land in Kahnawà:ke. In 1821, the chiefs "disavowed and annulled" all land grants to Delorimier and ruled that his land would revert to the nation upon his death. However, after he died in 1825 his children managed to sell and repurchase his land and buildings, and they fought for years to maintain their rights in Kahnawà:ke.[47]

Arakwente and Delorimier were both motivated by the desire to accumulate land and property in ways that were out of step with Kahnawà:ke legal norms, but the two men do not appear to have been allies. In fact, they clashed in one of the major legal disputes of the time. In 1803, Arakwente took Delorimier to court, claiming that the latter had cut wood in his sugarbush.[48] According to Kahnawà:ke law, living trees could be felled by any Kahnawa'kehró:non for their own use, but this did not extend to maples that were actively tapped. Delorimier defended himself by saying that the sugarbush did not belong to Arakwente and in fact was owned by all.[49] The two squared off, not only in a Montreal court, but also in the court of Kahnawà:ke public opinion. Arakwente had the favour of a few people in Kahnawà:ke, among whom were five minor chiefs, but Delorimier managed to sway the majority, including most of the chiefs, to support his position.[50] Each man constructed his arguments to appeal to both British colonial and Kahnawà:ke legal norms. But since Arakwente could not prove that Delorimier actually had logged in the sugarbush, the court ruled in favour of Delorimier.[51] In making this decision, it sidestepped the question of Kahnawà:ke law and focused on the absence of evidence.

Both men represented a threat to the community. Arakwente was a Kahnawa'kehró:non who undermined chiefly authority by taking internal matters to a colonial court, where he attempted to reframe Kahnawà:ke law to his own benefit. He was not always successful, but Kahnawà:ke leaders were very concerned about this challenge to their authority and the potential for others to follow his lead. Delorimier was a white man who gained Kahnawà:ke rights by developing a relationship of trust with Kahnawà:ke leaders and marrying a Kahnawà:ke woman. He then used his new status to enrich himself in a way that Kahnawa'kehró:non saw as illegal and immoral. When the community demanded that Delorimier and his family relocate, he and his children fought for many decades to keep their rights and accumulated wealth. Thus, in the 1790s, Kahnawà:ke leaders began to encounter relatively powerful, insubordinate members of their nation who were willing to enrich themselves at the expense of the community. The power and danger represented by these men came not just from the men themselves, but from the colonial courts that were increasingly willing to claim legal jurisdiction over Indigenous lands and people.

Arakwente and Delorimier cut and sold wood in unneighbourly ways and appropriated large swaths of land for themselves, both of which were illegal actions under Kahnawà:ke law. At a time when people grew most of their own food and burned wood to heat their homes, the threat posed by their behaviour was very real. On a cultural level, Arakwente and Delorimier can be seen as acting normally when compared with white men across colonial North America, but as abnormally in the context of Kahnawà:ke. It was precisely because they were importing colonial norms into Kahnawà:ke that they were such a danger.

The 1801 Code

Kahnawà:ke chiefs responded to the threats posed by these men in several ways. First, they fought back in court when they had to, and sometimes they won. They also appealed directly to colonial authorities, as they did in 1799 when eight chiefs met with the attorney general to explain why their internal conflicts should not be tried in a court of law. When cases did go forward, they found themselves attempting to explain Kahnawà:ke laws in the face of an opposing Kahnawa'kehró:non who interpreted those same laws in another way. Arakwente, for example, argued in court that Kahnawà:ke law allowed him to cut as much wood as he wanted on communal land and to sell it. The chiefs vehemently rejected his interpretation. In addition, Delorimier told the court that because he had a right to own land in Kahnawà:ke, he could acquire as much as he wished. Again, the chiefs asserted an opposing view. In effect, this situation made non-Indigenous colonial judges the arbiters of Kahnawà:ke law, which was unwritten at the time, even though they had no expertise in the subject. Kahnawà:ke law was part of the larger Rotinonhsión:ni legal tradition that was rooted in centuries of thought and practice, and it was absurd to have its finer points mediated by people who were ignorant of it, as they themselves admitted. Kahnawà:ke chiefs certainly believed that engaging in these conflicts in such a way was completely inappropriate, unprecedented, and harmful to their community and nation.

In 1801, the chiefs drafted the 1801 Code,[52] which put Kahnawà:ke laws onto paper for the first time. The translated archival document (probably translated from Kanien'kéha into French and then into English, but the Kanien'kéha document has not been preserved) refers to these laws as "Regulations and Conditions granted and agreed upon by the chiefs of the Iroquois of Sault Saint-Louis assembled and convened for this purpose in the Council Chamber of the village of Sault Saint-Louis."[53] The document marks an early and ambitious attempt to codify Kahnawà:ke law. The chiefs approved it before witnesses and notaries on February 26, 1801, signing and thus ratifying each of its twenty-one articles, except article 8 (more on that below). Historians Denys Delâge and Étienne Gilbert argue that the chiefs wrote down their laws to protect their collectivity from those who wanted to twist and use their traditions for personal gain.[54] Because this document is so important, I have given a translation of the entire original here:

TRANSLATION OF THE 1801 CODE

Rules and conditions granted and agreed upon by the chiefs of the Iroquois of Sault Saint-Louis assembled and called together for that purpose, in the council room at the village of Sault Saint-Louis, this 26th day of February 1801.[55]

Article 1

Whereas the Seigniory of Sault St. Louis is the property of the Iroquois Nation of the said village and that it is in common with any member composing the said Nation, and that they have all equal shares therein, without however it being in the power of any individual to subdivide, sell or alienate any part of it in any manner. It is expressly agreed that the Seigniory, and the mills, which can or may hereafter belong to it, as well as the revenues which may arise therefrom, shall be governed and administered by the Chiefs of the village and their Councillors, or by all other persons who shall be then given power, by Notarial Act, and delivered in full Council called together for that purpose.

Accepted

Article 2

It shall be lawful for the Chiefs of the village in council, to appoint one or more persons to receive, to collect, and even to have the management and administration of this Seigniory and mills and to [illegible] any salary for his pains and care, which is to be amply explained in the procuration [illegible] for that purpose.

Accepted

Article 3

As the lands of the said Seigniory of Sault St. Louis are held in common by all the individuals who make up the Iroquois Indians including children adopted by the Nation, it is agreed upon, that each and anyone of them shall not hold nor distribute more land than they could clear without putting another person in their place to do the work, be it a farmer, agent, procurer, or other.

Accepted

Article 4

It shall not be permitted to any Individual holder of land in the said Seigniory, to sell or carry away any firewood or timber, the whole being reserved for that individual's use, and for the use of each member of the village in general. As it shall not be permitted for anyone to cut maples of sugarbushes of any owner without their expressed consent.

Accepted

Article 5

No owner of land and sugarbushes shall sell or cede their right to the same except in the presence of, and with the consent of the Council assembled for the purpose, because without this formality any discussion that may arise on this subject will not be heard, and without which the transactions will be considered null and void.

Accepted

Article 6

If an owner of cleared land abandons it for three years, it shall be permitted for another to take possession of it and profit from it.

Accepted

Article 7

It shall not be permitted for any owner to cut on their land nor on any part of the domaine of said Seigniory: sugarbushes, oak wood, nor cedar, seeing as these are expressedly conserved for public use of the said Seigniory and for the church of the said village.

Accepted

Article 8

And to protect the cornfields and other cultivated land, each owner of said fields and lands shall be required to build their part of the enclosure, to protect said fields and other cultivated land from animals that could cause damage to them, and if such owners should fail to conform to the present article, it will be possible for the chiefs to have it done at the expense of the owner and to have them legally constrained.

Not Accepted

Article 9

Any person who is convicted of having cut, torn out, or otherwise taken any fences of his neighbours, will be brought before the council and condemned to pay one Spanish piastre (half to the conciliator and half to repair the damaged fence).

Accepted

Article 10

Every spring as soon as the snow melts, each owner who has pigs will be required to mark them and if any one of the said pigs, after the public announcement in the village, be found grubbing in cultivated land or gardens, it will be permitted for the offended landowner to kill it on the spot, and to leave it at that place so the owner can come to pick it up, if he judges it appropriate, so that the pig cannot do any more damage to the one who killed it.

Accepted

Article 11

Any person convicted of riding another person's horse without their agreement will be required to pay one piastre fine, half of which goes to the informer, the other half to the public fund of the village for the general good of all the members of the Nation.

Accepted

Article 12

Any person convicted of having milked another person's cow will be required to pay 40 sols for each time they milked the cow, half of which goes to the informer and the other half to the owner of the cow.

Accepted

Article 13

No owner of a village house or tenant currently living in the village may shelter or receive any stranger in their home, nor give such a person asylum who wants to reside in the village under whatever pretext, unless they have first consulted the village chiefs in council and have received their expressed permission.

Accepted

Article 14
It is expressedly agreed that no owner of uncleared land may sell, cede, convey, lease, or alienate any part of such land without the consent of the chiefs in council and having received their agreement and expressed consent, and in writing.

Accepted

Article 15
If any person is convicted of having taken or seized a boat, canoe made of wood or bark, for crossing or navigating the river without permission of the owner, they will upon conviction be punished and obliged to pay a fine of 40 sols for each offence, half of which goes to the owner of the canoe, and the other half to the informer.

Accepted

Article 16
Any person who upon testimony of one or several trustworthy people before the council will be convicted of having stolen, taken, or taken away vegetables, corn, or other farm or garden products, will be condemned to pay a fine of two piastres of which 3 pounds or schillings of eight coppers to the informer and nine pounds same schillings to the owner of the land who was thus wronged.

Accepted

Article 17
Any person who will graze their horse beyond the fences of the village commons, will, upon conviction, be condemned to pay a fine of one piastre that will be delivered to the mass at the church of the Parish of Sault St. Louis and used to pray to God for rest for the souls of the departed of the Iroquois Nation.

Accepted

Article 18
In the future, there will be no stables nor barns built in the village of Sault Saint Louis, and that as of today. And that such buildings that already exist shall in the next four years be dismantled and taken away by their owners and erected beyond the village, behind it in a place deemed appropriate; and if four years expire and the said stables and barns are not moved, they will be destroyed by order of the council and will be a pure loss for the owners who will have no recourse for damages.

Accepted

Article 19

And since many vagabonds and vagrants in the village have stolen and taken chains and other hardware of carriages, it is decided that upon conviction before the assembled council, such a convicted person convicted in the future of such an infraction will immediately restore the item to its owner or pay them a sum of money that will be determined by the council, but also a fine of two piastres, of which three pounds go to the informant and nine pounds to the church of the parish of the village or used for other pious works to be determined by council.

Accepted

Article 20

It will not be within the power of the council to raise the penalties and fines related to the present regulations, but can modify these according to circumstances, the regulations being in effect until revoked in council.

Article 21

Whoever does not wish to submit to these present regulations may be punished by the council as disobedient and expelled from the village, according to the will of the members of the council.

Little is known about how the 1801 Code was created or how it was perceived in Kahnawà:ke. The archives in which it is held possess very little contextual information. One interesting but unanswerable question is for whom it was created. Was its purpose primarily to make Kahnawà:ke law more legible to outsiders, or was it intended for internal consumption? Many questions remain unanswered, but we can gather quite a lot from the code nonetheless.

As with any laws spelled out by a group of people, the 1801 Code reveals where Kahnawa'kehró:non perceived tensions and dangers to lie. But it is not merely a list of laws; it is also a declaration of legal sovereignty and jurisdiction. The code begins and ends by emphasizing the authority of the chiefs, whose legitimacy resides in the will of all the people. Kahnawa'kehró:non clearly had many concerns around land use, use rights, and property. The code contains several prohibitions against stealing boats, horses, agricultural produce, carriage hardware, and milk (or using them without permission); it forbids strangers from being housed in Kahnawà:ke without leave; it specifies when and where livestock may graze; and it bans stables and barns in the village. The laws reveal the continuity of Rotinonhsión:ni legal traditions, as well as the integration of certain European legal concepts and practices.

Article 1, which lays the foundation for all the rest, states that "the Seigniory of Sault St. Louis is the property of the Iroquois Nation of the said village," thus asserting that the entire territory is owned collectively and that no one person has the power to subdivide, sell, or alienate any part of it without the consent of the chiefs. The 1801 Code recognizes only the chiefs as having authority over the seigneury and only the citizens of the nation as its owners. This seems directed at colonial governments that vested ultimate sovereignty over the land in the Crown, but it also speaks to individual dissidents such as Arakwente, who tried to claim Kahnawà:ke land under colonial norms of ownership. Article 1's insistence on the collective ownership of the nation must have been particularly salient at a time when acquisitive men, backed by powerful colonial interests, were asserting rights over land in ways that threatened to undermine the sovereignty of the nation. This danger, clearly addressed by the chiefs, still disrupts and undermines Indigenous sovereignties today, so much so that international legal conventions now recognize the property rights of Indigenous peoples as collective rights.[56] Article 1 probably drew on the Kaianerehkó:wa, in which "rights" exist insofar as "one has a right to enjoy life and the gifts of creation so long as one fulfills the responsibilities to the other beings of this world and the Sky World." Historian Susan Hill points out that in the Kaianerehkó:wa, "rights" are always collective rather than individual.[57]

Nevertheless, certain articles of the code explicitly recognize individual rights to use land. The relevant clauses here are article 3 (limit on the extent of land one person can claim), article 4 (collective ownership of trees), article 5 (council jurisdiction over land sales), article 6 (unworked land reverts to the collective), article 7 (cedar and oak reserved for the collective), article 9 (fences), article 10 (pigs), and article 14 (council jurisdiction over leasing). Kahnawà:ke law allowed for individuals to claim and cultivate relatively small lots and sugarbushes, and it protected their fences. Just as individuals were prohibited from hoarding land (more than a person could work), so also were they forbidden to cut more wood than they could use. These limits to acquisitiveness were explicitly for the good of the nation, so that the land wealth could be shared relatively equally.

The 1801 Code was rescinded in 1808, though we do not know why. It had been submitted for ratification to Sir John Johnson, superintendent of Indian Affairs, and perhaps he never approved it. Nor do we know whether it was enforced or even enforceable, but important for this discussion are the context of its creation and the principles embodied in it. Of key importance here are the following: The entire territory is communally owned.

The chiefs arbitrate on disputes about land (there is no mention of colonial courts). Land may be individually owned only as long as it is worked. If it is left uncultivated, it becomes available to others. Individuals may own only as much land as they themselves can work. Standing trees may not be owned by individuals, except for maples that are being tapped for sugar. Most other trees, including those on lots owned by individuals, are available to any Kahnawa'kehró:non who wishes to fell them. Wood cut on Kahnawà:ke territory may not be removed from Kahnawà:ke and may not be sold; it is for the personal use of the person who cuts it. Although the 1801 Code was not kept on the books as such – we do not know the circumstances under which it was rescinded – Kahnawà:ke chiefs consistently maintained its principles throughout the nineteenth century.

The code gives evidence of a number of characteristic land practices in Kahnawà:ke around 1800. For example, livestock such as cows and pigs were widespread, as were horses. Cattle and horses grazed in a fenced common area, whereas much cultivated land was not fenced. Pigs were allowed to run free in winter but had to be confined during the rest of the year so they would not destroy crops. Kahnawa'kehró:non had by this time adopted animal husbandry, which provided them with many benefits but also required some regulation for the good of all. The 1801 Code was not written simply to preserve old laws, but to provide legal guidance in its contemporary context. It shows that chiefs were incorporating some colonial norms and practices, such as recording laws in writing, while also maintaining Rotinonhsión:ni values and traditions. One long-standing political value that is not mentioned in the code is the central leadership role played by clan mothers in raising up and deposing chiefs, but this absence could be explained by the fact that the code is not concerned with the mechanics of Kahnawà:ke government.

The code also confirms that Kahnawa'kehró:non found individual landownership to be acceptable under certain conditions. Rotinonhsión:ni always had a kind of individual land tenure practised by women farmers (Chapter 1), but in a non-capitalist world and non-permanent villages, and thus without intergenerational transfers of accumulated land. Individual tenure was also tempered by the communitarian emphasis of Rotinonhsión:ni law.[58] The framers of the code were clearly trying to square traditional practices with the new reality of land scarcity and individual acquisitiveness. Just as Rotinonhsión:ni legal orders reject the idea that land and its bounty are commodities, the code also opposed the commodification of nature, and it forbade, in no uncertain terms, the accumulation of land for the purpose of hoarding wealth. Finally, article 4 prohibited private woodlots and declared the entire territory a communal woodlot. With the exception of sugarbush, no one could prevent others from logging on wooded land, as long as it was not for commercial reasons.

A number of other factors are worth noting regarding the 1801 Code. For example, the chiefs were very concerned about strangers who stayed in the village and thus made it illegal to house an outsider without permission (article 13). This may have been a response to Arakwente's hotel business, or it may have demonstrated apprehension about white people in general – perhaps the sort who would have accepted Arakwente's invitation to come to Kahnawà:ke in search of a wife and the associated land rights. The chiefs' recent experience with Delorimier would have made them particularly sensitive to the dangers of giving an outsider citizenship through marriage.

Interestingly, article 8 was not ratified. It would have required everyone who cultivated land anywhere in Kahnawà:ke to help build and maintain the fence around the communal pasture. Given that the article was rejected, it must have generated considerable controversy. The problem was surely not the need for a fence but rather who should be required do the work to maintain it. For farmers and gardeners who did not use the common pasture, the expectation that they contribute to maintaining its fence may have seemed unfair. Alternatively, Isabelle Bouchard suggests the issue may have simply been the difficulty of legally compelling individuals to do this work.[59]

In 1804, the chiefs prepared another version of the code and a strategy aimed at getting the recognition of the House of Assembly of Lower Canada. The 1804 version was very similar to the 1801 Code, especially in articles related to land use, but it also diverged on certain points. It was more explicit about the consequences (fines) for breaking laws, changed the numbering of some articles, and consolidated others. It omitted two articles from the 1801 Code: article 9 (prohibition against removing the fences of others) and article 19 (fine for stealing hardware from carriages). It also added regulations that imposed fines for disturbing the peace, racing horses, participating in dances on Sundays and holidays, organizing an assembly at the church doors before or after Mass, and refusing to bury animal cadavers. It also authorized the chiefs or missionary to stop an individual from entering the church for Mass, or to have an individual removed. These differences notwithstanding, the 1804 version maintained the legal principles of the 1801 Code, especially those related to land and property.[60] Bouchard argues that the chiefs were attempting to establish "a coercive authority" and that having their code recognized in colonial legislation "would give the chiefs access to the coercive authority of the colonial courts for the resolution of internal conflicts."[61] Whatever the motives of the chiefs, their attempts to achieve this kind of recognition from colonial authorities suggest to me that they still saw settler governments as possible allies for building their nationhood and that their new political opponents – men like Arakwente and Delorimier – represented such an existential threat to their nationhood that they were willing to take this risk. Nevertheless, there is no evidence that the 1804 document was ever submitted to the Lower Canada House of Assembly for ratification or that it was ever endorsed by any colonial authority.[62]

The 1801 Code (along with the 1804 version of the same) reveals that Kahnawà:ke leaders believed that the rights of individuals to lands emerged from the collective sovereign rights of the nation over its territory. They did not oppose commerce and trade per se, but they believed that buying and selling Kahnawà:ke land and wood was wrong because these belonged to everyone. Under Kahnawà:ke law, an individual's land and wood rights were circumscribed so that all Kahnawa'kehró:non would have equitable access. In this way, the 1801 Code is a marker of continuity with the Rotinonhsión:ni past, but it was also a highly innovative attempt to establish jurisdiction and sovereignty through written rules. In the context of growing asymmetrical relations between settler governments and Indigenous peoples, and resulting internal political turmoil, Kahnawà:ke's leaders drew on settler practices and ideas in an effort to strengthen their sovereignty and nationhood.

CONCLUSION

Due to his military experience, Delorimier was chosen to lead Kahnawà:ke warriors in battle against United States forces in the War of 1812, which probably paid off handsomely for him in the years following the war.[63] Nevertheless, the Indian Department dismissed him from his post as agent in 1821 after it could no longer deny or ignore the many ways in which he abused his position. Complaints against him included that he failed to properly collect rents from censitaires, accumulated land, livestock, and houses, showed sexually inappropriate behaviour toward Kahnawà:ke women, sold liquor, and skimmed off the top of supplies and presents destined for Kahnawa'kehró:non.[64] Also in 1821, Kahnawà:ke chiefs decided that all land grants to him would be annulled when he died and that his lands would revert to the community. On his death in 1825, however, they could not enforce the wishes of the community, and his children retained much of his accumulated land.[65] Many Kahnawa'kehró:non continued to work for the expulsion of the Delorimier family throughout the nineteenth century. Some Delorimiers were forced out, but a number of them became fully integrated into Kahnawà:ke society.

Little is known about Thomas Arakwente's biological children, but his agenda lived on through his adopted son, Jarvis McComber. Arakwente adopted McComber, originally from Massachusetts, after he arrived in 1796 as a teenager under unknown circumstances. He married one of Arakwente's daughters and, after serving as land agent for the chiefs, obtained lots totalling ninety-seven acres. In 1817, the chiefs brought their grievance to the Court of King's Bench, which ordered him to return these lands. It is notable that by this time the chiefs were resorting to the courts to enforce their laws, something they had been loath to do a decade earlier. McComber returned the lands but repurchased them the same year. Over the course of his life, he married three different Kahnawà:ke women and fathered twenty-eight children. He served as resident interpreter during the 1820s and 1830s, and died in 1866.[66] In contrast to Arakwente, who played a mostly antagonistic role in relation to the majority of Kahnawa'kehró:non and their leaders, McComber may have modelled his strategy on the more ambiguous and arguably successful path taken by Delorimier. Although the acquisitiveness of both McComber and Delorimier ran counter to Kahnawà:ke laws and values, neither tried to challenge them as directly as Arakwente had. Instead, they offered their cross-cultural, linguistic, and military skills to the community, while also accumulating land and maintaining allies. Many Kahnawa'kehró:non remained skeptical about their true loyalties, as they did not seem to share the community's core values and received much of their income from the colonial government.

Court records of the disputes involving Arakwente and Delorimier reveal ruptures, conflicts, and power struggles in Kahnawà:ke around the turn of the nineteenth century. Conflict in any community is normal, but these particular disagreements acquired added significance because of increasingly asymmetrical colonial power dynamics. The chiefs responded to the challenge by crafting the 1801 Code, a legal innovation in defence of the nation that was rooted in Rotinonhsión:ni political tradition and the values of the Kaianerehkó:wa. It was explicitly based on the claim of Kahnawa'kehró:non and their leaders to exclusive political and legal jurisdiction over their lands. The code spelled out the rules by which Kahnawa'kehró:non presumably already abided, or new laws they felt were necessary. Putting these previously unwritten laws on paper can be interpreted as an innovative attempt to give them added legitimacy – perhaps for outsiders who knew very little about Kahnawà:ke law but also perhaps for Kahnawa'kehró:non who wished to have the kind of clarity and rigidity that written laws provide. Although the code was not ratified by colonial authorities, Kahnawa'kehró:non continued to assert its principles throughout the nineteenth century. The following chapters show how they continued to act on their rights, just as the code spelled out.

3

"Out of the Beaten Track"

Before the Railroad, 1815–50

*The village of Caughnawaga ... consists of a church, a house
for the missionary, who resides with them, and about 140
others, principally built of stone formed into two or three rows,
something resembling streets, but not at all to be remarked either
for interior or exterior cleanliness or regularity; their occupants
may be altogether about 900, who chiefly derive a subsistence
from the produce of their corn-fields and rearing some poultry
and hogs, sometimes assisted by fishing, and the acquisitions
of their hunting parties, which however they do not, as in an
uncivilised state, consider their principal employment ...*

*Notwithstanding the remote period when their ancestors
were induced to abandon their forests, and the barbarous customs
of savage life, and the present inoffensive demeanour of their
offspring, they have not yet acquired the regularity of habit and
patient industry that are necessary to the complete formation of
civilized society, nor indeed will the hopes of those who have had
opportunities to observe the peculiarities of their character, and
try them by the opinions of philosophers and humanists, ever
be very sanguine that longer time or greater exertion will effect
a more radical conversion; to prevent a falling off from the
improvement already made is perhaps as much as may reasonably
be looked for. That the fierce and restless spirit of the wandering
savage has been tamed into something like docility cannot be
denied; as a proof, it may be adduced, that some of the men
of this village, and also some of those of the village of two
mountains, have lately been employed as auxiliaries of the British
army, and during the periods of their service no difficulty has
been found in bringing them under strict subjection, or confining
their operations within the laws of modern warfare.*

– Joseph Bouchette, 1815

S hortly after the War of 1812, the prominent cartographer and surveyor
    Joseph Bouchette (also surveyor general of British North America)
    described Kahnawà:ke as a quiet village inhabited by docile but only
partially civilized "savages." In the passage quoted above, he seems conflicted about Kahnawà:ke; on the one hand, its residents met some of his
criteria for civilization (agriculture, inoffensive demeanour, obedience),
but on the other hand, they had "not yet acquired the regularity of habit
and patient industry" that he believed necessary for civilized life. In other
words, they did not resemble the fearsome "Indians" of his imagination,
who instilled so much terror in his ancestors, yet they still were not white
people – and their difference repulsed him. Finally, he showed his deeply
anti-Indigenous ideology (even compared to many of his contemporaries)
when he expressed pessimism about the possibility of further "civilizing"
them. The best he felt one could hope for was to prevent "a falling off from
the improvement already made."

At first glance, Bouchette's description appears to be a factual account
of the village: its tone is self-confident, scientific, and objective. However,
a closer look reveals that it is far from objective. Bouchette waffles between
assumptions about the inevitability of progress ("they have not *yet* acquired
the regularity of habit") and his certainty that Indigenous people can never
really be civilized – that docility and obedience are the best that can be
hoped for. His tone is distant but judgmental; morally certain but practically unsure; paternalist but uncaring. Although Bouchette did not work
professionally in Indian Affairs, his tone was typical of imperial elites
around the world of the time. It was not reserved only for Indigenous
people, but it certainly defined the communications of the Indian De-
parment in the nineteenth century and found its way into every part of
the Indigenous-colonial relationship. This chapter reveals some aspects
of how this colonial relationship came to be.

This chapter covers the period after the War of 1812 and before the
passage of the first Indian laws in Canada, which saw a massive influx of
white settlers into Indigenous lands and a relative steep decline in the
power, influence, and wealth of those nations vis-à-vis settler states. For
many Indigenous people living in proximity to white settlers, this was a
time of unprecedented poverty and crisis. Most colonial officials came to
see Indigenous people as an inevitably dying race and a financial drain
on government coffers.[1] Of course, there was little inevitable or natural
about the settler invasion, although it no doubt seemed that way to those
who participated in it. The European global land grab and unprecedented
settler population booms on newly seized lands led directly to Indigenous

poverty and death.[2] The situation was less dire in Kahnawà:ke due to its proximity to Montreal, its relatively stable agricultural economy, and its well-established involvement in colonial economic enterprises such as the fur and lumber trades, but Kahnawa'kehró:non during this period saw some ominous signs pointing to the growing power imbalance.[3]

This chapter begins with a selective history of the early colonial Indian Department and its impact on Indigenous communities, then describes Kahnawà:ke land law and practices during this period. It includes a short discussion of the emerging problem of citizenship – who had the right to live in Kahnawà:ke and belong to the nation, and who had the right to make that determination. I end the chapter by considering other land-related conflicts of the early century, which leads into Chapter 4 and the period of railroads, industrialization, and new colonial Indian legislation.

The Department of Indian Affairs and Indian Policy to 1850

The Indian Department began the nineteenth century as a branch of the military, assigned the responsibility of maintaining diplomatic relations with Indigenous military allies. By mid-century, it would be transformed into a civilian department tasked with protecting First Nations from harmful influences while also facilitating their assimilation (destruction of their peoplehood). The department thus began the century as an agency designed to serve the needs and demands of First Nations (to maintain their loyalty), but fifty years later its mandate was explicitly both to protect them and eradicate them as a people.[4]

Following the upheaval of the War of 1812 and the rapid influx and growth of settler populations, First Nations in Upper and Lower Canada experienced a decided decline in political influence, one that was directly related to their diminishing demographic and military weight. They still played a significant role during the rebellions of 1837 and 1838, and their involvement on behalf of the Crown briefly improved some treaty relationships, as historian Nathan Ince shows.[5] However, the general trend over the first half of the nineteenth century was that colonial governments perceived First Nations increasingly less as important military allies (or threats) and simultaneously more as financial burdens. It was for this reason that the Indian Department would become part of the civilian administration.

The new civilian department was funded almost entirely by the sale of Indian land, which was clearly at odds with its stated goal of protecting First Nations. But selling off Indigenous lands, and thus eliminating Indigenous access to the same, was certainly in line with the department's assimilative ("civilization") agenda. Responding to calls that the department be abolished, Deputy Superintendent Henry C. Darling argued in 1828 that maintaining it would save the government money in the long run. Since Indigenous people would lose their lands in any case, Darling suggested that the department could at least help them assimilate while they went through the dispossession process. Without the department, Darling warned, they would either become more dependent on the government or would turn to violence, both expensive outcomes. He thus argued that maintaining the Indian Department was money well spent because its presence would head off the possibility of even larger expenditures.[6] At the same time, the department began to de-emphasize its former mission of maintaining good relations through the distribution of presents, focusing instead on its civilizing agenda. This meant sponsoring missionaries and schools, and encouraging Indigenous men to become farmers.[7] As early as 1829, boys from Kahnawà:ke were admitted to a school in Châteauguay as boarders, where they learned certain farming skills. This was made possible through government grants.[8]

As Rotinonhsión:ni in the British sphere of influence lost territory, wealth, and standing after the War of 1812, many in American-occupied territory had it even worse. The 1815 peace and the 1825 completion of the Erie Canal facilitated a massive influx of settlers into upstate New York, and American authorities did little to stop them from squatting on Rotinonhsión:ni land and illegally exploiting their small remaining territories. Due to genocidal settler violence and immense pressure from land companies, speculators, collaborating officials, and all levels of government, a number of Rotinonhsión:ni communities had no option but to sell their lands and move elsewhere.[9] In British-occupied territory, colonial officials also tried to move Indigenous people away from valuable agricultural land, from southern Ontario to Manitoulin Island in Lake Huron, but with relatively little enthusiasm compared to their US counterparts.[10] Large Rotinonhsión:ni communities such as Ahkwesáhsne, Six Nations of the Grand River, and Tyendinaga were able to remain in place, but they lost much of their land during this period. Between 1820 and 1835, Tyendinaga was reduced from 175,000 to 94,000 acres.[11] In the decades leading to 1841, settlers appropriated 95 percent of the territory of Six Nations of the Grand River, leaving that community with only 55,000 acres.[12]

The pre-1850 dispossession in Kahnawà:ke occurred in stages, as we saw in Chapter 1: first, Jesuit missionaries conceded most of the seigneury to French farmers; second, British authorities accepted these illegal concessions as legitimate; third, colonial agents tasked with collecting rent on behalf of Kahnawa'kehró:non did so inconsistently, and authorities did not effectively respond to the concerns of Kahnawà:ke chiefs about the situation. Meanwhile, throughout all periods in question, farmers and administrators were busy moving boundary markers on all sides of the seigneury to increase their holdings at the expense of Kahnawà:ke. Finally, the abolition of the seigneurial system in the 1850s separated conceded lands from the rest of the seigneury and deprived Kahnawà:ke of seigneurial rents.

Kahnawa'kehró:non were well aware of the dispossession experienced by other Rotinonhsión:ni communities, as well as policy changes at the Indian Department. They travelled far and wide in North America and beyond, participated in the fur and lumbering trades, and regularly shared information with Indigenous people from around the continent. They knew their nationhood and land base were in jeopardy, but their range of alternative options was shrinking as the century progressed.

Land Law and Practice

As part of its "civilizing" mission, the Indian Department intended to inculcate colonial notions of private property into Indigenous people. As early as 1839, it offered to have the unconceded portion of Kahnawà:ke territory subdivided. It wished to survey the reserve so that each head of household would be apportioned a lot of thirty to fifty arpents (an arpent is about 0.845 acres or 3,419 square metres). The chiefs politely declined the offer, pointing out that most of the desirable land was already individually owned. Chief Sawenoenne explained that Kahnawà:ke would have been more open to such a survey at an earlier date, when much of the land was still forested, but "now that most of the good land was cleared and become private or individual property, it would be impossible to lay out a farm of one hundred arpents without taking in several possessions." Sawenoenne also objected to the survey because he believed that "many of the young men to whom uncleared land might be apportioned would sell the timber growing thereon and then abandon the lands."[13] Even had the department's plan been feasible, Sawenoenne could see that such a subdivision would undermine community cohesion and stability. A few years later, in the context of an 1846 boundary dispute, the chiefs and warriors of Kahnawà:ke again declared that the entire territory was already divided between families and that it was well used.[14] Another forty-two years would pass before the Indian Department finally succeeded in its bid to impose a subdivision, against the wishes of the nation (Chapter 6).

Most good land was indeed individually owned but not according to colonial legal logics, and the meaning of landownership was continually contested in Kahnawà:ke. Certain Kahnawa'kehró:non were dissatisfied with Kahnawà:ke law in regard to owning and managing land, so they hired notaries to draw up deeds for their lands similar to what their settler neighbours had. They then proceeded to buy and sell these plots among themselves to the chagrin of many of their neighbours. In 1827, a Kahnawa'kehró:non named Gaihonate (Michel Perthuis) petitioned Lord Dalhousie, governor of British North America, for a piece of land. He specified that he wanted to own it like a white settler and to leave it to his children on his death: "That in imitation of the Canadian habitants, your supplicant wants to establish himself in a stable and permanent manner, by procuring a lot of land appropriate to his work and industry, and for the needs and sustenance of his family, not just during his lifetime but after his death."[15] There's no evidence that Dalhousie ever read his petition, but Gaihonate's approach to acquiring land was in contrast to those of Arakwente and Delorimier, discussed in Chapter 2. They had pushed the boundaries of Kahnawà:ke law to enrich themselves and had then fought in colonial courts to keep the lands they acquired. The arguments in court on both sides concerned different interpretations of Kahnawà:ke law. By contrast, Gaihonate made no mention of Kahnawà:ke legal orders. In fact, he wanted a lot (which measured three arpents by twenty-five to thirty arpents) to be conceded to him in the seigneurial tradition so that he became a censitaire like his French Canadian neighbours.[16]

One can imagine a number of good reasons why Gaihonate wanted to own and farm a large lot under the same conditions as French Canadians. It is also understandable that the chiefs unanimously opposed him. Jesuit missionaries had conceded most of Kahnawà:ke territory in just the way that Gaihonate asked, and Kahnawà:ke leaders had been trying for decades to ensure that no more was lost in that way (Chapter 1). A key concern of the chiefs, according to Indian Agent Duncan Campbell Napier, was that granting Gaihonate his wish would "establish a precedent for similar claims from many other individuals of their tribe, which if permitted, might lead to the dissolution of their common property."[17] Although such a land grant would clearly have interested some Kahnawà:ke individuals, the chiefs were unwilling to carve up their common lands, because doing so would weaken their nation. This is not to imply that Gaihonate cared nothing for his nation – he obviously did. Indeed, he turned down a seigneurial concession near Sorel (a hundred kilometres from Kahnawà:ke) because, according to Napier, "he cannot think of separating from his tribe under any circumstances."[18] It is to be expected that the views of an individual farmer on such a subject might differ markedly from those of a nation's leaders, even if they all care deeply about their people.

In asking for a land grant, Gaihonate argued that much of the territory was uncultivated and going to waste. He claimed that

> within the borders of the fief of Sault St. Louis, there is a large expanse of vacant and uncultivated land which in its current state is of no use and brings the tribe or anyone else no profit, so it appears to your supplicant that it would be in the communal profit of the tribe and to the individual advantage of its members, to concede a part of it so it can be cultivated instead of leaving it in its natural uncultivated state.[19]

The chiefs addressed this matter directly when they explained "that the petitioner is aware that the only unconceded part of their seigniory is the Domain or Champ which has been reserved by their fathers for the free use and advantage of the tribe generally, and, that they are in consequence, most anxious to preserve this land for their children, free from any encroachment."[20] For the chiefs, the land Gaihonate wanted for himself and his children was not underutilized but the inheritance of generations of Kahnawà:ke children yet unborn. Both Gaihonate and the chiefs saw the land as the inheritance of their children, but the chiefs meant the intergenerational inheritance at a community or nation level, whereas Gaihonate meant individual or familial inheritance.

Gaihonate was not alone in referring to Kahnawà:ke land as underused. An 1843 report by Joseph Marcoux, the priest in Kahnawà:ke, stated that of the 12,400 acres left of the original seigneury, around 10,000 were still in a "primitive state."[21] The chiefs did not talk about their land in this way since they were doing everything possible to keep it from the hands of settlers. In settler colonial discourse, declaring land uncultivated and underused is a powerful argument for dispossession and the imposition of capitalist land markets. Both Marcoux and Gaihonate knew this and used the language of "unimproved land" for their own ends. Gaihonate also asserted in his petition that Kanien'kehá:ka had sustained themselves since time immemorial primarily through the hunt, thus obscuring the agricultural history of his people. Presumably, he employed these powerful tropes about Indigenous people that he knew would resonate with colonial officials.[22]

In contrast, other archival data suggest that most arable land in Kahnawà:ke was already under cultivation at the time and that much of the rest was unsuitable for agriculture. Napier's 1845 report quantifies and classifies the 42,336 acres of the seigneury thus:

Conceded to Canadians	15,000 acres
Under Indian Cultivation	2,296 acres
Sugar Bush	1,953 acres
Common near village	1,500 acres
Irreclaimed swamps	4,004 acres
Total	24,753 acres
Residual	17,583 acres[23]

We do not know how Napier arrived at these numbers. Nor is there an explanation of what is meant by 17,583 acres of "residual" lands. Considering the many uncertainties inherent in these figures, we cannot place too much stock in them, but by looking at various other sources we can get a general picture of Kahnawà:ke land use at this time. Archival sources differ greatly on how much land was under cultivation and how many people farmed the land. Marcoux asserted in 1836 that Kahnawà:ke men had practically ceased to hunt but still avoided farming. Instead, many of them piloted river boats and rafts in the summer and sold moccasins, snowshoes, and beadwork in the winter. Marcoux saw these men as having a particular aversion to agriculture and to sedentary life in general.[24] His successor, Father T. Eugene Antoine, added that Kahnawà:ke men also showed little inclination toward learning trades that would keep them in the village.[25]

Although many Kahnawà:ke men did gravitate toward work that involved travel, early commentators and later scholars stressed this fact to such an extent that few scholars have taken an interest in how Kahnawà'kehró:non interacted with their land. For example, a statement by historian Gerald Reid that farming in the late nineteenth century "was an economic option, but few pursued it in an important way" is based on a number of such commentators.[26] Since most commentators were men who tended to be interested only in the economic activities of men and plow agriculture, the available sources for the period probably underestimate the extent of land that was farmed on a small scale and by women. A good example of the overemphasis on mobile male labour appears in the report generated by a major 1856–58 inquiry into the operations of the Indian Department, which concluded that Kahnawa'kehró:non were

> of such mixed descent, as scarcely to reckon a single full blooded individual among their number, retain the aboriginal apathy and disinclination to settled labour of any sort. They still cling to their roving habits, and many of them are Voyageurs and Canoemen in the employment of the Hudson's Bay Company. A considerable number too are occupied during the summer in rafting timber and as pilots through the rapids of the St. Lawrence.[27]

The report goes on to claim that "they cultivate a limited quantity of land, but most of the Reserve which is in their own hands, is lying idle, unprofitable alike to themselves and the country at large."[28] Women performed much of the agricultural labour, and it was typical for officials to dismiss this work as unimportant and insubstantial. Similarly, repeated assertions that the land was uncultivated tell us more about the author than about the land and the people who worked on it. It is no accident that discussions of "idle" lands were often paired with a description of Kahnawa'kehró:non as characterized by an "indolence which is natural to them, and an apathy which, is the greatest obstacle to their advancement and improvement."[29]

Contradicting these truisms, as well as his own firm assertions that Kahnawa'kehró:non did not farm, Marcoux estimated in 1843 that the average Kahnawà:ke family cultivated about ten acres and that a few farmed more than forty.[30] Surprisingly, his account of the typical day of a Kahnawa'kehró:non man included farming. He wrote in 1843:

> Generally speaking, the Indian begins the day by eating between eight and nine o'clock. When the sun begins to throw out its rays he goes to his field, where he works in the greatest heat until the afternoon. He then returns home to take another meal. In winter between the morning and the afternoon meals, he goes to cut wood, but when he remains at home he eats several times a day. No word is found in his tongue for *dinner, breakfast* or *supper;* he always used the expression *to eat.* The Indian has no stated number of meals, nor any fixed time for taking them; it all depends on circumstances.[31]

Although Marcoux saw farming as a good and civilized profession, his Kahnawà:ke farmer is undisciplined and irrational – he eats his meals at irregular times and works during the heat of the day instead of in the early morning. Like many educated white men of his time, Marcoux interpreted any Indigenous difference in behaviour as a problem and a defect. Although Kahnawà:ke men generally preferred livelihoods other than farming, many were involved in growing food, at least seasonally. An example of this is found in an 1817 Hudson's Bay Company contract for the employment of nine Kahnawà:ke men on a return trip to Fort William (Thunder Bay): "If they are away from their homes for a period lasting more than two months and eight days the honourable company is obligated to put a man on their land to help with the work up till the moment of his return."[32] The seasonal agricultural labour of these men was so valued by their families that the company promised to hire replacement workers if they had not returned by the time of the harvest.[33]

The average mid-century Quebec farmer cultivated between thirty and forty-five acres, compared to the average Kahnawà:ke farmer's ten acres.[34] Kahnawà:ke averages were thus decidedly smaller, but nearly every family cultivated plots of land. Of an estimated population of 1,100 in 1843, Marcoux stated that 50 families farmed.[35] It is possible that he was referring to 50 *men* who farmed on a relatively large scale, incorporating Euro-American techniques and technologies such as field rotation, draught animals, manuring, and harrows.[36] But aside from the 50 families, it is likely that several hundred women and their families also cultivated lands on a smaller scale and using different techniques. After all, Marcoux noted in 1847 that traditional gender roles (although changed) were still in place: young men plowed and harrowed the fields, but women and old men handled the rest of the agricultural work. He also noted the continued existence of the Kahnawà:ke legal principle that unused land was available to any Kahnawa'kehró:non who wanted to work it.[37]

Small-scale farming and gardening were largely the domain of women, children, and older men, and larger-scale farming was done by a minority of men who had the necessary land and capital (and by a few white farmers who leased land unofficially). But most Kahnawà:ke men, like their ancestors, pursued livelihoods that took them away from the village for long periods. The Rotinonhsión:ni community of Ahkwesáhsne followed land-use and livelihood patterns that resembled those of Kahnawà:ke. The Indian agent there, Solomon Chesley, stated in 1834 that the majority of Ahkwesáhsne farmers were women. In his account, many of the men worked as boaters in the summer while the women cultivated the fields.[38]

In her work on Six Nations of the Grand River, another large Rot-inonhsión:ni community, historian Susan Hill discusses changes and continuities in gender roles that seem similar to those in Kahnawà:ke. Six Nations experienced the devastating trauma of the American War of Independence followed by the turmoil of relocating from its homelands to what would later become known as southern Ontario. Hill contextualizes changes in gender roles in light of the adjustments required in the new community. The trauma of war and dispossession, along with harsh new colonial realities, led these Rotinonhsión:ni to develop and embrace the Karihwí:io (Good Message of Handsome Lake) spiritual tradition. Based on the visions of the Seneca leader Handsome Lake, the Karihwí:io gave Rotinonhsión:ni men divine sanction to become more involved in agriculture but continued to emphasize the matrilineal and clan-oriented government structure of the Great Law of Peace.[39] By the 1840s, Hill shows, "heads of household" in Six Nations of the Grand River were usually men.[40] The Karihwí:io did not have a particularly obvious impact in Kahn-awà:ke until much later, but the community's trajectory of normalizing patriarchy and private property while also maintaining certain traditional views and practices resembled that of Six Nations.

Similarly, Kahnawà:ke land practices after 1815 can be seen as a continuation of the Rotinonhsión:ni tradition, along with the incorporation of certain Euro-Canadian elements. By then, Kahnawa'kehró:non had fully embraced livestock raising alongside traditional horticulture.[41] Marcoux wrote in 1830 that gardens and fields were not fenced but that the community maintained a fenced common pasture. This suggests that Kahnawa'kehró:non used fences to keep livestock away from fields and gardens, at least at certain times of the year.[42] Men of the village gathered every summer to spend a few days building and repairing public roads and fences, and chiefs paid for their food and drink from the community purse. The public road bisected the common pasture, so the community employed gatekeepers to ensure that traffic could go through it without allowing animals to escape.[43]

The 1858 special commissioners' report into the affairs of the Indian Department stated that Kahnawa'kehró:non possessed "a very considerable quantity of live stock."[44] It listed 251 cows, 15 oxen, 226 horses, and 517 swine, as well as 119 carts and wagons among the 1,342 counted inhabitants. The village was "the largest, and one of the best built Indian Settlements in Canada," and its farms produced oats, barley, peas, hay, and wheat. Kahnawa'kehró:non produced maple sugar "to a very considerable extent." In the same report, the new resident priest in Kahnawà:ke, Father

Antoine, revealed his ignorance of Rotinonhsión:ni history and culture when he claimed that the "Indians have been taking an interest, before not known, in agricultural pursuits."[45] The idea that First Nations were beginning to take an interest in agriculture was frequently repeated in Indian Department reports over the decades to indicate progress toward assimilative goals. One finds virtually the same sentence in reports written three decades later, and no one in the department seemed to know or care that Rotinonhsión:ni had had a keen interest in farming for centuries before Europeans even knew they existed. Instead, we can conclude that Kahnawa'kehró:non always practised agriculture, adapted new methods from time to time, and continued to do so after contact with Europeans.

The 1815 and 1831 maps of Kahnawà:ke by Surveyor General Joseph Bouchette (Figures 3.1 and 3.2) juxtapose a largely forested and undifferentiated Kahnawà:ke with neatly parcelled settler farmland all around. He depicts the only cultivated lands in areas known to be occupied by Kahnawa'kehró:non as next to main roads. Both maps portray the land in this way, but the 1831 version adds the label "Indian Woodlands." The two maps show the areas conceded to French Canadian farmers within the Seigneury of Sault Saint-Louis. Both maps are composites, constructed by Bouchette from earlier maps. Considering the lack of accurate maps of Kahnawà:ke, and that Bouchette probably never penetrated beyond the main roads shown on his maps, there is no reason to give these depictions a great deal of credibility as faithful representations of the geography. However, they do show that settlers thought of Indigenous lands as under-utilized and uncultivated. Settlers seemed unable to perceive Indigenous land use, agency, and labour, an inability that, not coincidentally, proved very useful to both them and their governments. Bouchette, and others like him, showed little interest in actual Kahnawà:ke land uses – for example, Kahnawa'kehró:non valued their ready access to firewood for heating during the long winters and surely did not see their forests as "waste." Also, outside observers may have constructed such incomplete pictures of Kahnawà:ke because their patriarchal mindset led them to ignore the economic contributions of women and their engagement with the land. Nevertheless, Kahnawa'kehró:non were clear and consistent in their repeated claims that all of it was theirs to distribute and use according to their own laws and needs. It was becoming more and more difficult, however, to ignore the growing power and influence of colonial ideologies and institutions. One important space in which colonial Canada began to undermine Indigenous sovereignty during this period was the question of belonging and citizenship.

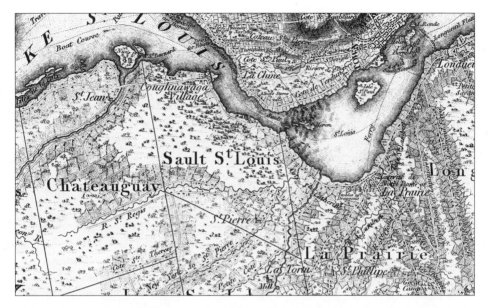

FIGURE 3.1   Detail of "Topographical Map of the Province of Lower Canada," Joseph Bouchette, 1815. | G/3450/1815/B68 CAR, BANQ.

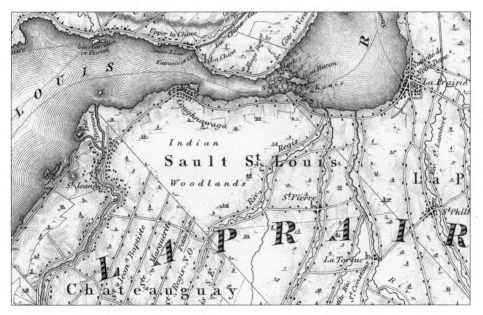

FIGURE 3.2   Detail of "Topographical Map of the Province of Lower Canada," Joseph Bouchette, 1831. | G/3450/1831/B68 CAR, BANQ.

BELONGING AND LAND

Like all Rotinonhsión:ni communities, Kahnawà:ke has a long and proud history of successful adoption and naturalization of outsiders.[46] This success was key to the long-term survival of Rotinonhsión:ni against great odds in the seventeenth and eighteenth centuries. But issues around belonging, citizenship, and membership became thornier during the nineteenth century, as it became clear that the landlust and colonial mindset of adopted white men could threaten the sovereignty of the nation. The previous chapter touched on questions of inclusion and exclusion in connection with Arakwente and Claude Delorimier. Arakwente was banished after he repeatedly broke Kahnawà:ke laws, challenged the authority of the chiefs, and sued fellow Kahnawa'kehró:non in court. No one disputed his rights as long as he adhered to Kahnawà:ke laws, but he refused to do so. In the case of Delorimier, a naturalized citizen who started to abuse his rights almost the moment he received them, the chiefs revoked his rights, but by then his children were so well established in the community that they managed to retain much of his land. For Kahnawa'kehró:non, the problem may not have been their rights to reside and own land, but their possession of their father's illegally held properties.[47] The conflict with the Delorimier family alerted Kahnawa'kehró:non to the fact that outsiders were not being integrated as well as they once had been.

Instead of becoming Kahnawa'kehró:non in their thoughts and behaviours, white men like Delorimier, who had been adopted into the nation, maintained many of their old ways and made no effort to hide it. Within a few years of their arrival, they could become wealthy at the expense of the community, and their considerable influence presented a challenge to the nation. Not all challengers came from the outside, but Kahnawa'kehró:non understood that colonial ideas about land and property were incompatible with their own. Many individuals who pushed for drastic reform were adoptees, children of adoptees, or white men who had established themselves with the approval of the Indian Department and sometimes of the chiefs. It is therefore not surprising that their opponents labelled them "white men" even if they had once seen them as "Indians" or Onkwehón:we (true person).[48] Many who wished to maintain the sovereignty of Kahnawà:ke believed that white men like Delorimier were responsible for causing conflicts over land and wood, so an obvious solution was to remove them and to severely restrict the practice of naturalizing white men.

Until 1850, the colonial government had no legal definition of "Indian," and the Indian Department did not concern itself greatly with questions of who belonged to particular Indigenous nations. It expected the nations themselves to determine their citizens according to their own laws. Over time, the department increasingly prioritized this question because keeping the numbers of "Indians" as low as possible would reduce its expenses. This also aligned well with another goal that emerged with the enfranchisement legislation of the 1860s and the *Indian Act* of 1876: the elimination of Indigenous nations.[49] During an 1836 discussion about how people in Kahnawà:ke defined "Indian," Indian Agent James Hughes said that in Kahnawà:ke "all children begotten by Indian parents or an Indian father and a white mother are looked upon as Indians; all children by white men and Indian women are looked upon as whites."[50] On the basis of his experience in Kahnawà:ke, Hughes believed that women who married white men lost their Indian status, but we cannot know if this view represented the community at all.[51] If it did, it represents a major shift from only a few decades earlier, when the nation regularly adopted white men. By the 1830s, Kahnawa'kehró:non had adjusted their legal norms so that white men could no longer gain land rights and Indian status through marriage.

With the removal of Jesuit missionaries as land managers and the 1762 Gage Decision to end seigneurial land concessions, it became difficult for white men to acquire land in Kahnawà:ke. One of the few avenues was via marriage with a Kahnawà:ke woman, and many Kahnawa'kehró:non were concerned about this practice. As early as the 1780s, they were protesting against non-Indigenous men gaining land through marriage and were doing everything possible to prevent it. In 1812 alone, they physically intervened to prevent at least two white men from entering the Kahnawà:ke church where they intended to marry Kahnawà:ke women, precisely because of the threat these men posed to Kahnawà:ke sovereignty if they were granted land rights through marriage. Ten years later, the newly hired Indian agent Nicolas-Benjamin Doucet mentioned growing frustration and unrest regarding this problem. In his view, preventing white men from gaining land rights through marriage was legally justified, given that the Royal Proclamation of 1763 prohibited the establishment of non-Indigenous people among Indians.[52] The 1828 Darling Report noted repeated complaints about white people living in Kahnawà:ke who sold liquor.[53] Kahnawà:ke chiefs had difficulty ejecting white people without the cooperation of the colonial government, which rarely intervened to expel anyone, so these problems continued to fester.

Whereas many Kahnawa'kehró:non wanted to find expedient ways of evicting white people, the colonial government took an ambiguous stance on the question. Through its agent, the Indian Department exerted significant control over who could live on the territory, but it had no defined or consistent rules regarding who was an "Indian" and who was not. In reality, it often issued residency permits on the basis of personal favours, and it rarely forced people to leave once they had settled. In 1835, white people reportedly held 188 acres in the unconceded part of the seigneury, but of course there was disagreement as to whom the label "white" could be applied. That year, the chiefs petitioned the newly appointed governor general, Lord Gosford, to have these people removed and their lands returned to the nation. They described the white landholders as "bad birds with black hearts who use honeyed and bewitching words to turn the heads" of the people. In response, they were told that since the suppression of the Jesuit Order, the Crown was now the true owner of the seigneury, and thus any conflicts should be brought before the courts.[54] Later, the Indian Department would do everything possible to keep land conflicts from going to court; and the courts, in any case, often referred cases involving Kahnawa'kehró:non back to the department because of the "irregularities" in landownership in Kahnawà:ke.

Thus began the problem of regulating "membership" in Kahnawà:ke, a problem deeply rooted in colonial interference and one that remains acute today. Kahnawà:ke leaders, who under ideal circumstances embodied the will of the community, wanted to maintain the power to include and exclude people based on their laws. As the nineteenth century wore on, the Indian Department became increasingly involved in this issue by intervening to prevent white people from living in Kahnawà:ke but also by protecting certain people from expulsion once they had established themselves there. Without any particular legislation to support its actions, or explicit agreement from Kahnawà:ke leaders, the department became an arbiter of membership questions. It sometimes used this power to support the decisions of chiefs but could also use it to block their path or to prevent any action.[55]

Conflicts in the 1830s

Not all conflicts during this period were concerned with questions of citizenship and belonging, but many were. One particular conflict boiled over in 1833 and 1834, when Bernard St-Germain, the department interpreter, tried to have the ferry licence held by George Delorimier (son of Claude Delorimier) revoked and given to a man named Kaneratahere (Ignace Delisle).[56] St-Germain argued that Delorimier should be expelled from Kahnawà:ke because he was not a member of the nation and should not have Kahnawà:ke rights. Father Marcoux defended Delorimier, and the recently hired Indian agent, James Hughes, backed St-Germain and Kaneratahere. In an unprecedented move, Hughes used his influence to have all chiefs deposed who would not oppose Delorimier. According to Marcoux, this was the first time that the colonial government had interfered in the nomination of Kahnawà:ke chiefs.[57] The remaining chiefs, now unanimously allied with Hughes, petitioned against Marcoux, complaining that he was not acting in the best interests of the people because he sided with white men such as Delorimier. They also petitioned against the presence of white people in general. According to them, peace would be restored in the village only when all its white residents were removed, their property was returned to the nation, and Kahnawà:ke laws enforced.[58]

In December 1834, the Supreme Court of Montreal ruled that Delorimier was an Indian, and thus he was able to keep his ferry licence.[59] Despite the ruling, however, and probably due to the influence of Hughes, the Indian Department cancelled his annual presents. It would soon abandon the practice of annual gift giving altogether, but at the time, every citizen of the nation was eligible. The following year, Hughes found a way to get the ferry licence transferred to Kaneratahere and to open an official inquiry into the conduct of Marcoux (who was later acquitted). Agent Robert McNab, who investigated the question of white people in Kahnawà:ke, concluded that the McComber and Delorimier families (among others) had no right to Kahnawà:ke land and no legal status as Kahnawà:ke Indians.[60]

The battle between Hughes and Marcoux continued into 1836, with Hughes compiling a list of sixty-one white people in the village and Marcoux claiming that there were fewer than ten, none of whom had taken any land.[61] Marcoux went on to say that everyone in Kahnawà:ke was of mixed ancestry and that white people and half-breeds had been "sauvagifiés" (made savage, made Indian) in any case.[62] In 1836, the majority of the chiefs sent another petition, asking for the removal of white people and for the formalization of a law forbidding the sale or lease of land to non-Indians.[63] The white people in question, including the McComber and Delorimier families, counter-petitioned. After the upheavals of the 1837–38 Rebellions, the tide turned in favour of the Marcoux-Delorimier faction but only briefly. First, the chiefs removed Kaneratahere, the Hughes-backed ferry operator, from the council. Then they reconciled with Marcoux and Delorimier and petitioned against Hughes and his allies in the village. The colonial government held another inquiry, this time into the behaviour of Hughes. It found in his favour and recommended the removal of Marcoux and Delorimier.[64]

In 1840, forty-four Kahnawa'kehró:non, apparently fed up with the entire situation, sent a petition that criticized both factions. They opposed Kaneratahere *and* blamed Delorimier and Marcoux for stirring up trouble.[65] Around the same time, at least two other petitions were launched, calling for the removal of white people, one stating the primary concern as wood, the other as land.[66] The summer of 1840 saw a final inquiry, which acquitted Marcoux, and in December 1840 the factions signed a peace agreement. Hughes and St-Germain were transferred to positions in which they would have no further contact with Kahnawà:ke, and a membership agreement was reached that all children of "Indian" women would be considered "Indian," regardless of the identity of their father.[67] This solution would have appealed to those who valued and supported Rotinonhsión:ni matrilinealism, and it was also agreeable to the descendants of white men like McComber and Delorimier who had married Kahnawà:ke women. However, many Kahnawa'kehró:non continued to worry about white men and their children gaining Kahnawà:ke rights via marriage.

The Indian Department recognized that the clashes concerning citizenship or membership in Kahnawà:ke were really often disputes over land. Thus, in 1839, near the end of the Hughes-Marcoux struggle, it offered to solve the entire problem by having the territory subdivided among families (see page 81). The department argued that regular lots of thirty to fifty arpents, properly surveyed, would prevent conflicts because land would be more equally and securely held.[68] The chiefs rejected this proposal, not because they had a distaste for private property or because they opposed it in principle. They simply did not see it as feasible, and they did not believe that it would ultimately benefit either the community or the young men who would gain possession.[69] Nevertheless, the idea of subdividing the territory simmered for decades in the files and minds of Ottawa officials, surfacing again in the 1870s and 1880s (Chapter 6).

Conclusion

In 1848, James Duncan, a Montreal painter, spent some time in Kahnawà:ke, where he produced two watercolours (Figures 3.3 and 3.4). In contrast to the tumultuous picture of Kahnawà:ke presented in much of this book, they portray the village as quiet and calm. One shows the church in the background, while in the foreground are several houses, fences, and

FIGURE 3.3   *View of Caughnawaga/Caughnawaga au Canada-Est,* James D. Duncan, 1848. | Item no. 02206, Accession no. 1970-188-2206, Collection reference no. R3908-0-0-E, W.H. Coverdale collection of Canadiana, LAC.

FIGURE 3.4   *View of Caughnawaga/Caughnawaga au Canada-Est,* James D. Duncan, 1848. | Item no. 02148, Accession no. 1970-188 PIC, Collection reference no. R3908-0-0-E, W.H. Coverdale collection of Canadiana, LAC.

two Kahnawa'kehró:non in traditional clothing having a conversation. The other presents a vista of the village, with a defunct mill in the foreground along with two figures. Both watercolours depict a peaceful place that seems a world away from the hustle and bustle of Montreal.

Many visitors described the village in similar terms, and there is reason to believe that its daily life was generally peaceful and calm. "Caughnawaga was out of the beaten track," wrote the Jesuit historian E.J. Devine, "strangers were rarely seen, and the native population were far enough away from the contaminating crowd to enable them to live their lives in peace and quiet."[70] A comparable sentiment comes through in the writings of mid-century visitor John H. Hanson, whose book *The Lost Prince* contended that the Dauphin had escaped the French Revolution and had taken refuge in an Indigenous village, perhaps even Kahnawà:ke. Hanson described Kahnawà:ke thus:

> Caughnawaga is a straggling Indian village on the St. Lawrence, opposite Lachine, and within sight of Montreal. It consists, besides a number of scattered huts, of two long narrow streets varying considerably in width. The houses are low and shabby, most of them of wood, but some of dark stone. The masonry is of the rudest kind. A Roman Catholic church, a solid stone building, of some slight pretensions to architecture, stands in the middle of one of the streets. In looking at the dingy houses, the narrow streets, the crowd of little Indian children; and considering the loneliness of the spot in former years before railroads and steamboats had brought it into connection with the busy world, one cannot help feeling how secure a hiding-place for a poor scion of royalty this village presented.[71]

Even as Hanson described the "loneliness of the spot" as a perfect hiding place for a fugitive royal, he noted that it was a thing of the past – the quiet and isolation would end with the arrival of railways and steamboats.

Kahnawa'kehró:non may have had a sense that things were about to change. In 1848, the year that James Duncan painted the village, Kahnawà:ke residents believed that it had been invaded by evil spirits, and local medicine men could not eject them. What the spirits were said to be doing is not entirely clear, but Kahnawa'kehró:non felt that the problem was serious enough to expend public funds on bringing in a Mississauga medicine man. After spending some time in the community, he claimed to have killed the spirits and left, but they returned soon after. Kahnawà:ke then sent a delegation to Onondaga, a Rotinonhsión:ni nation that had resisted Christianity for a long time. There, the delegation found a medicine man who was willing to come to Kahnawà:ke. He visited in 1851 and was apparently able to solve the problem by suggesting that a certain "possessed" young woman be married.[72]

More qualified people than I can unpack the spiritual meanings of this incident, but it certainly suggests that Kahnawà:ke was not as Christian as many settler narratives assumed, and it also points to the continuing relationships with other Rotinonhsión:ni communities. But in the context of this chapter, I see the event as an indication that Kahnawa'kehró:non felt something was deeply amiss or that big changes were afoot. First Nations across the region were facing major land losses and other setbacks. Kahnawa'kehró:non would have heard how settler governments broke treaty agreements and undermined the sovereignty of Six Nations of the Grand River, Tyendinaga, and many other communities. Thousands of land-hungry settlers were arriving every year, often squatting on lands the Crown had allocated for Indigenous people, and colonial governments did little to protect Indigenous lands from this onslaught.[73] The reorientation of the Indian Department from nation-to-nation relationships to a "civilizing" agenda was, in practice, a severe blow to Indigenous communities. The department severely cut spending on annuities, choosing instead to pay the salaries of missionaries and teachers, most of whom were white, all while working to frame and categorize indigeneity within colonial conceptions of race.[74] At the same time, the city of Montreal was on the cusp of its own industrial revolution, with the requisite demographic explosion, all of which would deeply affect nearby Kahnawà:ke. An especially important early impact was the construction of one of Canada's first railways, which ran through Kahnawà:ke, with a terminus and ferry dock in the village itself.

I opened this chapter with a quotation from Joseph Bouchette that articulates his unshakable faith in human progress while also expressing his certainty that Indigenous people would not take part in it. Not all colonial elites shared his pessimism, but by the mid-nineteenth century most agreed that Indigenous people were doomed in some way. "Civilization," by way of education, agriculture, and Christianity, became the new organizing principle for a genocidal program that would persist into the next century.[75] The following chapters show some of the ways in which Kahnawà:ke experienced this new orientation and the growing power and intrusiveness of settler governments.

4

"In What Legal Anarchy Will Questions of Property Soon Find Themselves"

The Era of Confederation, 1850–75

The railway that now runs the full depth of the seigneury will inevitably cause many difficulties. Already the whites, attracted by the commerce the railway is stimulating, have spread throughout the village and on the road. We will soon see, due to the Indian political fact, in what legal anarchy will questions of property soon find themselves, in a place where everyone is owner and nobody is.

– Joseph Doutre, 1852

These words by Joseph Doutre, a lawyer and the president of the Institut Canadien, are from "Les sauvages du Canada en 1852," a speech he delivered to a gathering of Montreal's francophone liberal professionals. Its subject was Kahnawà:ke, and Doutre was convinced that the opening of the Lake St. Louis and Province Line railway that year would cause serious problems. Considering the racial tensions already at play (regarding who had land and residency rights, discussed in Chapter 3) and the competition between two seemingly incompatible legal systems, the only outcome he could foresee was legal anarchy. Although he admitted to his audience that his "frivolous" observations were collected over a mere two or three years and "stitched together" by a twenty-four-hour study, he showed considerable insight.[1] Unlike most of his contemporaries, Doutre traced the cause of the chaos he foresaw, not to any defect in Kahnawà:ke governance or law, but to racial tensions, industrial development, and outside political interference. He also recognized that all these issues were ultimately rooted in concerns over land.

As he explained, the problems he foresaw "will not be caused in any way by [Kahnawà:ke's] form of government, but solely due to the mixing of heterogeneous races, who are all subject to different laws."[2] This was an important insight. Other outside commentators in the following decades, including officials with the Department of Indian Affairs (DIA), operated under the assumption that the fundamental problem in Kahnawà:ke lay in the people who lived there. They saw Kahnawa'kehró:non as savage and uncooperative, and their laws as retrograde, the product of conservative and irrational minds. This was in line with the contemporary settler belief that "Indians" were uncivilized, lazy, ignorant, and devious, and that their primitive collective instincts impeded their "improvement" as individuals. Nineteenth-century government records, travel reports, historical writing, and newspaper articles are infused with these racist tropes, and uncritical historians have tended to repeat them. How convenient it was for the global imperialist colonist to disparage Indigenous peoples around the world in this way, while taking their land and wealth. Similar rhetoric and logic are still employed against Indigenous peoples to this day, from Palestine to Australia to Canada. Colonial governments have long assumed that Indigenous people have defective land practices and have used this as a pretense for taking the land and imposing new land-management regimes.[3] Like Doutre, I argue in this chapter that problems around land management and governance did not arise from internal deficiencies, but from industrial development, population growth, the racial tension inherent in the settler colonial project, and external political interference in many forms. More broadly speaking, the argument of this chapter points toward the way that settler colonies around the world use(d) racist logics to undermine Indigenous claims, blame Indigenous people for problems directly inflicted by colonial regimes, and to make the taking of Indigenous lands appear commonsensical and inevitable.

Although Doutre's analysis was far from perfect, this chapter builds on his insights and further discusses the impacts of new legislation and the expanded powers of the Indian Department, and industrial development and railway construction in Kahnawà:ke from 1850 to 1875. Unlike DIA officials who traded unceasingly and uncompromisingly in victim-blaming racist tropes (and unlike innumerable tourists and visitors who repeated tired stereotypes), Doutre visited Kahnawà:ke with a fairly open mind. Thus, he was able to listen and to say something insightful and useful to his audience. People like Doutre suggest to me that no one is simply "of his or her time," that people can choose to do the right thing even in dark times, and that gives me hope.[4]

DOUTRE ON KAHNAWÀ:KE:
GOVERNANCE, GENDER, AND PROPERTY

The Institut Canadien was a literary and scientific society whose membership comprised several hundred of Montreal's most prominent francophone liberal professionals. Doutre's 1852 presentation to this society was based on an extensive tour of Kahnawà:ke that he took with George Delorimier, one of its residents already mentioned in the previous chapter. The only Kahnawa'kehró:non whom Doutre had previously encountered were the women who sold moose and deer hide footwear in the city. His speech conveys his impressions of Kahnawà:ke behaviour, dress, and architecture, but thanks to his interaction with Delorimier, he could also discuss Kahnawà:ke politics and culture. Delorimier, considered by many in Kahnawà:ke to be a white man, gave Doutre a rather simplified explanation of his battles with the community concerning his own dubious citizenship, saying that he was disliked because he was unwilling to wear a "couverte," the traditional dress for certain occasions.[5] In fact, the problem was rooted in the Delorimier family's accumulation of land and wealth at the expense of the nation. On many other points, however, Delorimier helped Doutre to see beyond what an outsider could otherwise have observed.

As a lawyer himself, Doutre showed interest in Kahnawà:ke governance and law. His observations reveal that Kahnawà:ke governance, as discussed in Chapter 1, showed remarkable continuity. The chiefs still held political sway, but their power was frequently challenged both inside and outside of the community. He reported that there were five clans (but the Bear and Turtle Clans were each split into two, making a total of seven), each of which elected a grand chief for life, and that the colonial government recognized them, confirmed their election, and gave them medals as symbols of their authority. Grand chiefs were responsible for governing land issues within the territory, including the management of the common pasture, seigneurial rights, and the seigneurial mill. What Doutre did not know was that governance in Kahnawà:ke, as in many other Indigenous communities, was not characterized by rigid hierarchies or high levels of coercion. Yet, despite the fact that leaders had little power to enforce laws, people generally behaved themselves and followed community norms.[6] Historically, Rotinonhsión:ni placed great value on individual freedom and strongly resisted those who sought to limit that independence (including their own leaders), but they accepted certain kinds of authority and law.[7] They did not create written legal codes until the nineteenth century, but in the words of Kanien'kehá:ka scholar William B. Newell, "a knowledge of the principles of good morals and ethics" was reflected in their everyday lives. Anyone who did something wrong "would not be told that he was wrong, but rather he was ignored, ridiculed, or subjected to social ostracism, and in major offenses he might even be killed."[8]

Doutre was particularly impressed by the matrilineality of Rotinonhsión:ni society and governance. At the death of a chief, his medal remained in the hands of his mother, if she were alive, or his sister, brother, or closest maternal relative.[9] Incredulously, he reported that Kahnawa'kehró:non (including men) actually believed that children belonged to the mother and that women were morally superior to men. All of this sounded so unusual that Doutre had to have it confirmed by several people.[10] He finally recognized it was true:

> They take it as a maxim that the child belongs to the mother, and that the father is only, as Balzac said, *l'editeur responsable*. Then, in order to effect a legitimate transmission of the insignia of authority [the medal], from the dead chief to his successor, they wanted the mother and her line to keep it safe until the election of the successor. The father of the chief is considered an outsider for this purpose.[11]

There is no hint in his speech that matrilineality was weak or declining, which is probably a good indication that the end of longhouse living had had little bearing on the continuity of matrilineal values and practices. If Doutre had thought otherwise, he probably would have seized the chance to mention it.

In discussing Kanien'kehá:ka jurisdiction over Sault Saint-Louis, Doutre emphasized the collectivity of their ownership. According to him: "At Sault Saint-Louis, the Iroquois possess collectively, not individually, in an uncontested way, a seigneury measuring three leagues wide and two leagues deep between Châteauguay and Laprairie. The whites cultivate a part of it as censitaires, and the rest is standing trees and tall forest, a part cultivated by the Indians, a common pasture, and the village of Caughnawaga."[12] Kahnawà:ke leaders always underscored the collective nature of their territorial sovereignty, and Doutre picked up on this. He also learned that Kahnawa'kehró:non could gain a kind of individual ownership over pieces of land but that the rights of individuals were always subject to the right of the collective. Doutre understood the territory in seigneurial terms, with French Canadian censitaires who paid rent to Kahnawa'kehró:non, who acted as seigneurs. He seemed not to know of the highly contested nature of the ownership and boundaries of the seigneury or of the frequent delegations Kahnawà:ke sent to England on this matter (Chapter 1). He discussed Kahnawà:ke laws on landownership in some detail, comparing Rotinonhsión:ni legal norms to the ideals of the communists and socialists of his day:

> Those who have considered the phalanstery, communism, and socialism, as unrealistic dreams, would be astonished if they saw an almost analogous system functioning with perfect regularity, and if they knew that this kind of communism has existed here for centuries and is still fully operational. Because the current government of the Iroquois is the traditional government of the American Indians, and European civilization has not changed it.[13]

Obviously, Doutre was not aware of the great diversity of political systems in Indigenous America or of the European influences on Indigenous governance to that time. However, he was impressed by the fact that here was a very old political institution operating according to principles that European theorists had only recently formulated.

Doutre had also learned that Kahnawà:ke had a kind of individual landownership. Rather idyllically, he stated that every Kahnawa'kehró:non possessed a piece of cultivated land, sugarbush, and timber:

> Since long ago, each of them has had a piece of land to cultivate, a sugar-bush, and a woodlot, and all of this is an inheritance that is transmitted, without the intervention of the commune. But since the commune is obliged to concede uncultivated lands to Indians who ask for them, one can see that the mixture of communism and individual property would give rise to great difficulties if the population were to exhaust all of its unconceded lands.[14]

Doutre's story on this front was better than the reality, but even so, he was right in pointing out that any eligible Kahnawa'kehró:non could obtain a modest lot for a house and garden. His reference to the transmission of land from one generation to the next suggests that the practice had become normal by this time or that he was simply repeating Delorimier's point of view. In another part of his speech, Doutre even seemed to be aware that Kahnawa'kehró:non could cut trees on unconceded parts of the seigneury, including on lots claimed by other Kahnawa'kehró:non. But though he admired the way in which the land system seemed to run itself, he was concerned about how the "commune" would function when there was no longer any unclaimed land to be had. As Kahnawà:ke grew, more people would be competing for land, a problem that would lie at the heart of future conflicts.[15]

Although he was a white man and an outsider who did not know much about Kahnawà:ke, Doutre visited it with an open mind and thus gained important insights that DIA officials were never able to, or allowed to, have. He could see that worsening tensions and problems over land and race would not be the fault of Kahnawa'kehró:non themselves but would spring from the growing asymmetry of the colonial relationship between Canada and Kahnawà:ke. He understood that Kahnawà:ke operated according to its own laws and that the colonial state and capital were increasingly at odds with Kahnawà:ke leaders and law. His ominous premonition was that the situation would end in legal and political chaos. He identified various other threats as well, two of which were industrialization and the railway.

Montreal Industrialization and Its Effects

During the nineteenth century, Montreal was transformed from a fur-trading town of about 9,000 people on the colonial margins to an economic powerhouse with a population of 300,000. In the 1850s, as the city was becoming the most important transfer point, depot, and manufacturing centre in British North America, it experienced spectacular population growth, with rates averaging 5 percent each year. This rapid urban development was made possible by significant increases in public spending on transportation infrastructure such as canals and railroads, as well as political and judicial reforms that favoured industrial growth.[16] Economic expansion went hand-in-hand with the geographical expansion of the city and the steady rise in land prices throughout the region. Although Kahnawà:ke lay several miles from the city core and was separated from it by a large river, it was significantly affected by all this change. Like most developments associated with industrial and urban expansion, the impacts were not all negative: for a time, there were opportunities for entrepreneurship, new jobs, and easier river crossings. But the higher regional population densities and industrial infrastructure also brought new anxieties, problems, and hazards.

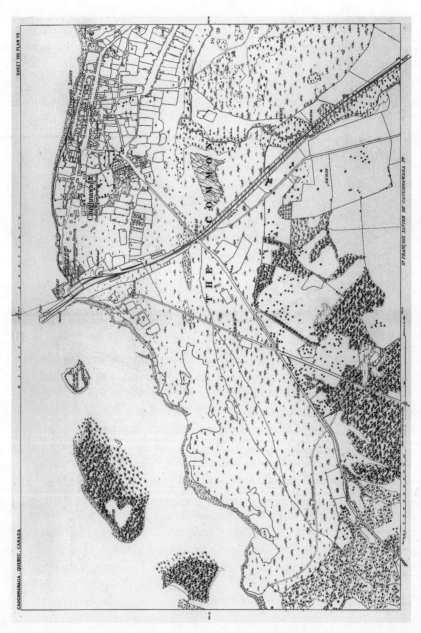

FIGURE 4.1 "Lachine and Caughnawaga, Province of Quebec," 1868. The railway line runs from the southeast (bottom right) to the wharf on the west side of the village. | William Francis Drummond Jervois and H.S. Sitwell, *Fortification Surveys Canada: Lachine and Caughnawaga, Province of Quebec* (Southampton, UK: Ordnance Survey Office, 1868), sheet VIII, plan VII.

Probably the greatest mid-century impact of Montreal industrialization on Kahnawà:ke was the construction of the Lake St. Louis and Province Line (LSL&PL) railroad in 1852. Running thirty-five miles from Mooer's Junction, New York, to Kahnawà:ke, it facilitated the transport of goods and passengers from Lake Champlain to the St. Lawrence River. At the Kahnawà:ke terminus, the aptly named ferry *Iroquois* carried railway cars across the river to Lachine, which were then pulled to Montreal along an eight-mile rail line that paralleled the Lachine Canal. Figure 4.1 shows an 1868 military map with part of the village of Kahnawà:ke, the rail line, and the infrastructure for the rail terminus and wharf. The LSL&PL was financed by Montreal businessmen who believed the economic well-being of their city was threatened by recently completed lines in New York State, such as the Northern Railroad that ran from Ogdensburg to Rouses Point (connecting the Upper St. Lawrence River to Lake Champlain) and thus cut Montreal out of the trade between New England and the Great Lakes.[17]

By the time the first LSL&PL train ran from Montreal to Plattsburgh, however, several companies were already competing for essentially the same route, each hoping to capture the traffic between Montreal and the eastern seaboard. The advantage of the LSL&PL over its downstream (and down-rapids) competitors was that goods arriving at Lachine could be shipped south of the border without paying Lachine Canal tolls, but its disadvantage was that Plattsburgh did not yet have rail connections to the south.[18] This meant that railway cars had to be transported by steamer across Lake Champlain to the nearest railway terminus. After several unprofitable years, a merger, and a bankruptcy, the Grand Trunk Railway absorbed the LSL&PL in 1863 and thus gained control of the line serving Kahnawà:ke (Figure 4.2).[19] In 1859, the completion of the Victoria Bridge linked the island of Montreal to the south shore, which diminished the competitiveness of the bridgeless LSL&PL. It was abandoned in the early 1880s and turned into a public road. The wharf was still used as a ferry terminus and for loading quarried stone onto barges, and the abandoned Grand Trunk warehouses and workshops were taken over and used by Kahnawa'kehró:non for a variety of purposes, including residences. Figure 4.3 is a painting of the busy Kahnawà:ke riverfront in spring 1860 from the point of view of the wharf.[20]

This first railway was short-lived, but since Kahnawà:ke was a terminus and transfer point, it experienced significant impacts, including the construction of piers, docks, and other structures to accommodate freight and passengers. Aside from changing the character of the village, the railroad also caused damage to land and landowners all along its path. Kahnawà:ke

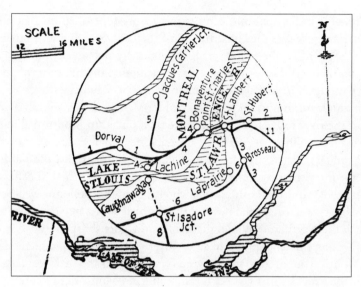

FIGURE 4.2   Detail of map of the rail network around 1880. The stretch from St. Isadore Junction to Kahnawà:ke is given as a dotted line, signifying that it was inactive. | Stevens, *Canadian National Railways*, 300.

FIGURE 4.3   *Indian Village of Caughnawaga,* 1860, by George Henry Andrews. | Delia Millar, *The Victorian Watercolours and Drawings in the Collection of Her Majesty the Queen,* 2 vols. (London: Philip Wilson, 1995).

farmers were so infuriated by the way in which the company treated them that they refused to have further dealings with it after construction was completed. The last straw was the company's demand for thirteen acres to house its terminal at the village waterfront, which some interpreted as a plot to gain possession of the village itself. Tension and threats of violence ensued. Kahnawà:ke chiefs quite reasonably believed that compensation for the expropriated lands should stay in the community, but the government kept the money, brandishing the convenient racist argument that "Indians" were not capable of managing money.[21] This may have been the first time that the DIA held Kahnawà:ke money in trust for the chiefs, but I was unable to find more archival information on this event. By the time the band council system was imposed in 1889, all public Kahnawà:ke money was held in trust by the department.[22] The physical, cultural, and economic changes wrought by the railway, along with the sense that Kahnawà:ke leaders could no longer effectively lead, prompted much concern about the future of the community.

The advent of quarrying also had a major impact on Kahnawà:ke. The Trenton limestone found closer to Montreal was not hard enough for cutting large construction stones, whereas the grey, medium- to coarse-grained Chazy limestone in Kahnawà:ke was ideal for this purpose.[23] As early as 1822, an area behind the village was being quarried for the construction of the Lachine Canal. The quarry workers were mostly settler labourers who were housed in and near the village.[24] Kahnawà:ke stone was used in many transportation structures, including the Cornwall Canal and the piers of the Victoria Bridge. For the latter project, Kahnawà:ke boatmen were hired to transport stone to the building site.[25] The quarries were in operation until the mid-twentieth century, and most are now filled with water. Although they did provide jobs and some benefits for Kahnawa'kehró:non, they were also sites of dispute over air and noise pollution. In the late nineteenth century, they became another battleground when the DIA attempted to extract royalties on quarried stone and favoured settler-owned companies over Kahnawà:ke operators.[26]

A development that could have further disrupted the lives of Kahnawa'kehró:non was the construction of a shipping canal to connect the St. Lawrence with the Richelieu River. This project was seriously discussed from the 1840s until the 1870s but never came to fruition. Its most ardent proponent was John Young, a steamship entrepreneur, long-time president of the Montreal Harbour Commission, and lifelong proponent of harbour and waterway modernization. Several studies were commissioned mid-century, most recommending that the canal be constructed from

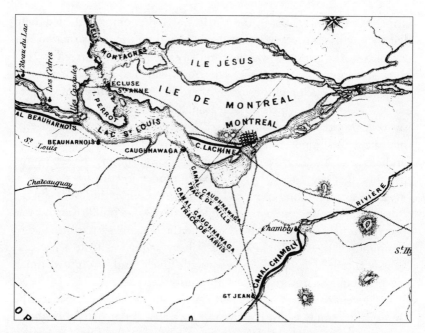

FIGURE 4.4   Detail of "Canaux Construits et Projetés, District de Montréal,"
1867. | Canada, "Annual Report of the Commissioner of Public Works," June 30, 1867,
Sessional Papers 5 (1867–68), 62.

Kahnawà:ke to the Chambly Canal, which led south to Lake Champlain
(Figure 4.4). Because Kahnawà:ke is located above the Lachine Rapids, it
is only 29.0 feet below Lake Champlain, whereas Montreal is 73.5 feet
below. Situating the canal terminus in Kahnawà:ke would have meant
fewer locks, and thus lower construction and operational costs. The canal
was to have been about 32.5 miles long, and the cost of construction was
estimated at $1,814,408 in 1848 and at $4,267,890 in 1855.[27] Promoters
claimed in 1870 that the canal would reduce the cost of shipping Ottawa
wood to the United States by one dollar per thousand board-feet.[28] In
1855, construction seemed set to begin, and Kahnawà:ke chiefs asked for
protection against surveyors of the canal who were causing damage to
their crops, as well as compensation for removed trees and fences.[29]
Although engineers declared the plan to be perfectly feasible, and although
Young kept bringing it to the attention of the prime minister as late as
1871, it was never carried out.[30] A century would pass before life in
Kahnawà:ke was turned upside down by the construction of a canal whose
size was much greater than anyone in the nineteenth century could have
imagined – the St. Lawrence Seaway.[31]

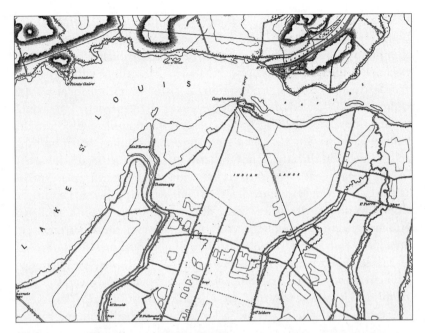

FIGURE 4.5   Detail of "Frontier of Canada East, Plan 3," 1865. | E21, S555, SS1, SSS8, P37/4, BANQ.

The growth of Montreal also affected Kahnawà:ke in other ways. Land prices skyrocketed; wood became more expensive and had to be brought in from farther away. Wood shortages began to be felt in Kahnawà:ke as outsiders cut and took wood to which they had no right. Some Kahnawa'kehró:non also began to sell it for profit, thereby breaking Kahnawà:ke law and depriving other Kahnawa'kehró:non of wood. A detail from an 1865 map of the area (Figure 4.5) shows the proximity of Kahnawà:ke to nearby towns and extensive "Indian lands," which were more heavily wooded than neighbouring areas. The regional shortage meant that Kahnawà:ke wood, which had been relatively abundant, became increasingly vulnerable to unauthorized depredations (I return to this problem in Chapter 5).

THE DEPARTMENT OF INDIAN AFFAIRS AND INDIAN POLICY TO 1875

Kahnawà:ke's difficulties were worsened by an increasingly strident and ambitious Indian Department with an intensified "civilizing" agenda.

During the 1830s and 1840s, the newly constituted department concentrated on First Nations in Upper Canada because many Lower Canada communities already lived in permanent villages, which officials saw as essential in the civilizing process. Permanent Indigenous villages experienced particular kinds of dispossession associated with white squatters and white men who gained access to Indigenous lands by marrying Indigenous women. More mobile Indigenous peoples at this time were subject to the kind of dispossession associated with large-scale logging, settler hunting and fishing, and direct violence inflicted by frontier settlers.[32] Thus, the Indian Department established its first Indian reserves in Upper Canada as places that would supposedly keep Indigenous people safe from the vices of white colonial society while also preparing them to be assimilated into that society. Due to budget constraints, however, the department did little more than administer the distribution of annual presents and relied on missionaries to run missions and schools.[33] The Lower Canadian government already considered Indigenous nations in the St. Lawrence Valley as "mission villages" and would soon begin to refer to them as "reserves."

Although Indigenous people in Lower Canada had protested against white settlement and hunting competition in their hunting grounds since the late eighteenth century, the issue came to a head during the 1840s. An 1844 report commissioned by Governor Charles Bagot suggested that Indigenous peoples throughout the St. Lawrence watershed were in crisis: wild animals were scarce, farmers and loggers were invading hunting territories, and the closer proximity of settlers had produced widespread poverty and desperation. The colonial government was bombarded by petitions and demands from many Indigenous nations, asking for protection and compensation.[34] In response to this crisis, both Upper and Lower Canada made the protection of "Indian lands" a priority. However, the lands were not the vast area guaranteed by the Royal Proclamation of 1763 (or claimed by Indigenous peoples themselves), but only a few small spaces that would interfere as little as possible with white settlement. The colonial government set them aside, not because it particularly cared about Indigenous nations, but because it was eager to avoid the expense of feeding starving people or dealing with an Indigenous military insurgency. The Indian Department had worked with missionaries since the 1830s in Upper Canada to establish and operate "Indian reserves," but such language was not normally used in Lower Canada until 1850.[35]

The 1850 *Act for the Better Protection of the Lands and Property of the Indians in Lower Canada* aimed to stop encroachment on Indigenous land, but it also empowered the Crown to manage that land, thus undermining the authority of Indigenous leaders. The commissioner of Indian lands named in the act was accountable to the colonial government, not to the chiefs.[36] Indigenous seigneuries such as Kahnawà:ke were also vested in the commissioner, who began to call them "reserves," whereas hitherto they had usually been referred to as Indian villages or seigneuries. The 1851 *Act to Authorise the Setting Apart of Lands for the Use of Certain Indian Tribes in Lower Canada* established 230,000 acres as reserves, including Indigenous seigneuries, reserves for hitherto mobile communities, and hunting reserves for non-mobile communities, among them Kahnawà:ke.[37] The 1850 act was the first piece of Canadian legislation to legally define an "Indian." Not only did it help to establish the idea of an "Indian" as a legal category, it also granted the Crown legal jurisdiction over who would be considered as such. In addition, it specified that if an Indian person married a non-Indian person, the latter would become an Indian.[38]

Indigenous leaders immediately perceived that this law would enable white men to gain control of Indian land through marriage, as they already had a history of doing. After a sustained outcry from Kahnawà:ke and other communities, Lower Canada changed the law so that non-Indigenous men could not gain access to Indigenous resources and land through marriage. Henceforth, a non-Indian man who married an Indian woman would not gain rights in her community; instead, she would lose her rights. A non-Indian woman who married an Indian man would assume his status.[39] Considering the relatively powerful political position of women in Kahnawà:ke and other Rotinonhsión:ni communities, it may seem puzzling that leaders would countenance a situation in which many women would be deprived of their Indian status, land, and ties to their community. Why would a matrilineal nation demand a provision that removed women who married non-Indian men? And why would it want to grant full status to non-Indian women who married Indian men? The answers to these difficult questions can surely be found in the fact that Indigenous communities had very few options in the context of settler colonial assaults. More specifically, their approval of these patriarchal provisions must be seen in light of the real threats posed by white men who gained access to lands and rights by marrying Indigenous women, and the decades-long struggles of Indigenous communities to prevent this. It is also likely that at least some Indigenous leaders had internalized colonial patriarchal values.

Kanien'kehá:ka anthropologist Audra Simpson suggests that in this situation, white men ... as status Indians were far more threatening [than white women] because they could be landowners, band councillors, and voters. Although the presence of white women (as de jure Indians) may have been profoundly aggravating to Indian women, who had to leave upon out-marriage, it probably was not *threatening* to the stability of the broader community in terms of property or land ownership.[40]

Thus, the extinguishment of Kanien'kehá:ka women's rights, according to Simpson, "may have been less of an attempt at discriminating against their own people than at protecting the community from a possible take-over by non-Indian men."[41] Patrilineal landownership and inheritance norms were also adopted by other Indigenous communities during the nineteenth century. An important corollary is Six Nations of the Grand River, which incorporated patrilineal legal norms as a way to protect what little remained of its land base in the 1840s.[42]

Five years after the 1850 and 1851 acts came into effect, the chiefs of the Seven Nations (the confederacy of First Nations along the St. Lawrence River) met to discuss their experiences with the acts and to draft recommendations for the colonial government. They understood that the laws had ostensibly been drafted to protect their lands from acquisitive settlers, but they detailed the unanticipated effects:

Those who were not entitled to Indian right before became entitled to Indian rights by the passage of the act of A.D. 1850 which has done us a great deal of harm, such whites residing amongst us paid rent even for Cattles pasturage before the Act of A.D. 1850 but after the passage of said Act, no rent is paid either for cattles pasturage. We then became as it were slaves although we are principal men of our Tribes. It (the Act) does us a great deal of harm and trouble.[43]

Although the aim of the legislation had been to stop Indigenous land loss, it had undermined the authority of the chiefs and emboldened settlers to stop paying rent for pasturing cattle on their territories. Chiefs also reported that some settlers had gained Indian status because of the laws, against the wishes of the community.

The chiefs of the Seven Nations went on to suggest that all Indian legislation related to land be based on the laws in effect in Kahnawà:ke. They outlined six key points that should be part of Canada-wide Indian legislation:

1 An Indian should not have the right to sell land house or wood to a white man and that a punishment should be made for both the seller and buyer.

2 That an Indian should not have the right to let land, house or give farm to a white man to sow in half.[44]

3 An Indian if lawfully married to a white woman his wife becometh an Indian and her Children reputed to belong to the particular Tribe or Body of Indian. But if male of the Children as above mentioned should marry to a white woman the Children issue of such marriages lose all rights of Indians.

4 An Indian woman who is lawfully married to a white man loses all her Indian rights.

5 That the Chiefs of each Tribe should be incorporated with full powers to superintend the affairs of their respective villages and to make a Law for the same subject to the approval of the Governor General.

6 That at the expiration of five years there should be a general election of grand Chiefs for each Tribe, and that the names of the Chiefs so elected should be submitted for the approval of his Excellency the Governor General.[45]

Some aspects of this list would remain a feature of Indian law for many decades. For example, selling or leasing reserve land to non-Indians is still forbidden, and a woman's Indian status depended on that of her husband until the passage of Bill C-31 in 1985. In their fifth point, the leaders requested that the chiefs of each village be given the legal authority to govern and to make laws for their communities, which also suggests the elimination of Indian agents. In the final point, they asked for a standardized practice of chiefly elections, which would be certified by the governor general. This request should not be seen as proof that they intended to submit to the authority of colonial governments. Instead, they seemed to be asking for the right to govern themselves in much the same way as the governments of British colonies aspired to govern themselves.

That same year, the governor general, Edmund Walker Head, received a petition from fifteen Kahnawa'kehró:non who represented another point of view. They portrayed themselves as the enlightened minority in the community, with an interest in agriculture, and said that they had followed the "recommendations, opinions and advice" of the government to build houses and cultivate land outside the village.[46] They claimed that during the previous winter, Kahnawà:ke chiefs and a large number of other

Kahnawa'kehró:non had "destroyed, looted, and burned down their homes."[47] Furthermore, they themselves had cut and sold wood, for which the chiefs were now pressing charges in court. They admitted to doing this but claimed that the buyers had purchased only standing trees and had cut them down themselves. This is the only instance I have found in the archival record when anyone tried to interpret Kahnawà:ke law in this way – that cut wood may not be sold but that standing trees may be sold as long as the purchaser fells them. This interpretation clearly violates the spirit of the 1801 Code, since its point had been to prohibit the commodification of wood and to preserve the forests for Kahnawa'kehró:non to use. It is also worth noting that by mid-century, the chiefs believed they needed the courts to enforce their laws on their own territory.

The petitioners could have asked simply for protection and compensation for their losses, but they went much further. They pointed to the high population numbers in Kahnawà:ke and proposed a solution: "That since their tribe now numbers thirteen hundred, and in order to avoid any future difficulties between its members regarding the occupation of the common lands, and to come to the assistance of those members who want to cultivate land, your petitioners believe it would be greatly advantageous to have the lands divided."[48] Their idea was that a subdivision survey would define the boundaries of lots within the reserve. They believed that individual private property with defined borders would produce a more harmonious agricultural community.[49]

When asked about this petition, Indian Agent Édouard-Narcisse Delorimier claimed that several names had been forged and that the chiefs had never stopped any of the signatories from settling on particular lands. As he explained, the chiefs were merely trying to prevent the petitioners from selling wood to settlers because it belonged to the entire community. If the petitioners had simply been cutting wood and cultivating land, no one would have bothered them. Instead, they had logged several thousand cords of timber and had been selling pines and oaks valued at fifteen to twenty dollars for thirty to forty cents.[50] He stated that the chiefs had been doing everything in their power to prevent these men from selling wood, including sending messengers to ask them to stop. Kenthokwen, one of the petitioners, apparently attacked and nearly killed a messenger with a hatchet. When the chiefs realized that they had no other options, "the people rose up en masse against the wood sellers, fifteen or twenty who take the wood belonging to thirteen or fourteen hundred."[51] According to Delorimier, it had always been understood that selling wood to settlers was illegal under any pretext. In defence of those who had attacked the dwellings of the petitioners, he said the buildings were merely log shacks without chimneys or floors. Finally, he utterly rejected the idea of a sub-division survey, saying that the petitioners simply wanted the reserve to be sold at a very low price, an outcome that would be "a great misfortune for this tribe."[52] This was one of several times in the nineteenth century when Kahnawà:ke leaders rejected the idea of subdividing their territory (Chapter 6). Clearly, supported by many of their people (and the Indian agent, in this case), the leaders were enforcing their laws against a few dissidents, but they required the aid of the courts to do so.

New Indian legislation would further facilitate the advance of colonial law. The 1857 *Act to Encourage the Gradual Civilization of the Indian Tribes* (known as the *Gradual Civilization Act*) was supposed to create legal conditions that would break down the barriers between Indian and non-Indian.[53] It established the conditions under which an Indian man could become "enfranchised" – a non-Indian. An Indian could apply to become enfranchised if he were male, at least twenty-one years old, literate in French or English, of good moral character, and free of debt. In exchange for enfranchisement, he gave up all his Indian rights and was entitled to a new name, as well as a fifty-acre parcel taken from the territory of his former community. In this last provision, one can see the intention to break up Indian reserves into individually owned lots and thus extinguish nations.[54] The requirements for enfranchisement were so high – literacy, freedom from debt, and good moral character – that few white people at the time could have satisfied them. "The 'civilized' Indian," concludes historian John Tobias, "would have to be more 'civilized' than the Euro-Canadian." Even in the eyes of colonial governments, the law proved a dismal failure since few Indigenous people could meet the requirements even if they wanted to be enfranchised.[55] Subsequent legislation would give colonial governments more power to enfranchise Indians involuntarily, with the long-term goal of eliminating Indigenous nations. Practically speaking, enfranchisement legislation undermined Indigenous sovereignty because the colonial government empowered itself to define "Indianness," and it did so on the basis of racial and financial logics.

The 1867 *British North America Act* gave the newly formed Canadian federal government exclusive jurisdiction over Indians and Indian lands, without the consent of Indigenous people. The next year, parliament passed an act that summarized and standardized Indian legislation from all four of the founding colonies, *An Act Providing for the Organisation of the Department of the Secretary of the State of Canada, and for the Management of Indian and Ordnance Lands.*[56] In the words of Duncan Campbell Scott, who would later head the DIA, this act brought together all the "best features" of previous legislation.[57] With the passage of the *Gradual Enfranchisement Act* of 1869, it was clear that the central goal of Indian policy was now assimilation and that the short-term objective was the transformation of Indigenous political institutions. Aimed squarely at Rotinonhsión:ni and other eastern First Nations with a long history of European contact, it enabled the governor-in-council to impose elected band councils on Indigenous communities to replace existing Indigenous governments. The band councils could pass bylaws on relatively minor municipal matters but only with the approval of the superintendent general of Indian Affairs.[58]

The DIA was in regular contact with Indigenous communities of the St. Lawrence Valley and the southern Great Lakes region regarding the provisions of these early Indian laws. There was considerable debate within Indigenous communities about each of them, and the DIA did make some attempt to respond to their concerns. The problem was that Canada imposed a rigid, global legal framework that did not recognize the multiplicity of Indigenous legal frameworks and jurisdictions. Although historian Theodore Binnema argues that the Indian Department acted in good faith when it consulted with Indigenous peoples regarding the definition of "Indian," his research also reveals the absurdity of a colonial government attempting to define a rather new term (Indian) according to "ancient customs."[59] In addition, any departmental responsiveness and accountability had evaporated by the end of the nineteenth century. Already in the 1860s and 1870s, the DIA regularly exploited political fissures within Indigenous communities to impose the band council system of the 1869 act, as it did in Tyendinaga in 1870. Although a general council of the Rotinonhsión:ni (including two Kahnawà:ke chiefs) unanimously rejected the *Gradual Enfranchisement Act* in 1870, the DIA was no longer consulting with Indigenous communities in good faith.[60]

It is evident that the trend in Indigenous-Canada relations was intensifying political, cultural, and economic interference in Indigenous affairs. Indigenous people understood that the Canadian government was increasingly indifferent to their demands and hostile to their existence. The fact that the Indian Department in the 1850s consulted extensively with Indigenous communities before and after drafting Indian laws did not mean that colonial governments were kind and generous toward Indigenous people. But it did mean that the DIA was still following precedents that were set when settler-Indigenous relations were more in equilibrium. By the 1870s, the DIA cared little about the opinions of

Indigenous people except insofar as they might impede its ability to impose its will. Kahnawa'kehró:non felt this change, along with other changes mentioned earlier in this chapter, and contemplated their options. One option was to move the community elsewhere.

Attempts to Relocate

Through the centuries, many Kahnawa'kehró:non decided to leave Kahnawà:ke and not return. But during the latter half of the nineteenth century, Kahnawa'kehró:non made some extraordinary attempts to move the community in its entirety to a place where its way of life would be less threatened. In some ways, this was a traditional response to collective hardship, since their ancestors had regularly relocated their villages to more favourable sites for any number of reasons. By the mid-nineteenth century, there were few good options for this kind of collective mobility, yet many in Kahnawà:ke could no longer see a future for themselves and their children in their current location.

A number of Kahnawa'kehró:non were so disturbed by the expropriations and permanent changes wrought by the Lake St. Louis and Province Line in 1852 that they decided to leave. They asked the Saugeen First Nation on Georgian Bay for permission to settle in its territory. The colonial government had been toying with the possibility of moving Indigenous communities westward, as the United States had been doing, so it was open to the idea.[61] The Saugeen Ojibway and the Indian Department agreed to the plan, and some twenty Kahnawà:ke families moved to the Bruce Peninsula. But the scheme was short-lived. All but three of the families returned to Kahnawà:ke in 1857.[62] Of those who remained, some intermarried with local families and were adopted by their communities.[63] Thus, the effort to transfer the nation to the Bruce Peninsula failed, but the idea to move Kahnawà:ke continued to gain traction.

In the 1850s, Kahnawà:ke leaders made the first of several attempts to sell their lands and move the entire village. The reasons for this were economic (such as the impact of the railway, land loss, and illegal wood cutting), but they were also political and cultural.[64] Kahnawa'kehró:non could see that maintaining their way of life would be difficult in the face of economic and environmental upheaval, as well as increasing political and cultural interference by the DIA. The first Kahnawà:ke petitions to sell the seigneury in its entirety date from the early 1860s, and efforts persisted until the mid-1870s. Chiefs asked the Indian Department to enforce

Kahnawà:ke laws against commercial logging as early as 1859, and when the response was inadequate, they asked for their lands to be sold on terms that would be acceptable to them. George-Étienne Cartier, co-premier of the United Canadas, was a major proponent of the sale.[65] A Kahnawà:ke referendum in 1863 approved the sale of the reserve by majority vote, but for unknown reasons the Indian Department did not approve the sale.[66]

In March 1870, three Kahnawà:ke chiefs wrote to the DIA, protesting its refusal to facilitate the sale of the territory and removal of the community. According to their letter, Indian Affairs Superintendent Hector-Louis Langevin had refused to sanction the purchase of their land and to allow the community to move. The chiefs planned to travel to present-day Oklahoma later that year to negotiate with Cherokee leaders for a land purchase there.[67] Apparently, the majority in Kahnawà:ke supported the sale, but some key wealthy and influential individuals opposed it and were able to stop it from going through.[68]

In June 1875, four Kahnawà:ke chiefs again asked the DIA for approval to sell the reserve:

> In March 1862 the Honorable George E. Cartier, as his predecessor in 1859, was of the opinion that the best means of putting an end to these complaints of the said Tribe, would be a Public Sale of the Reserve of Sault St. Louis. The said Mr. Cartier suggested at the same time a new division of the Reserve between the members of the Tribe, or the Cession, by the said Tribe of the Reserve to the Government in order to emigrate into another place of Canada or to the United States. But as the members of the Tribe were not unanimous on the best mode to adopt, it was understood that those of the Indians who would be willing to remain at Sault St. Louis, might buy there some lots or farms, the Government being bound to give them credit for their share out of the Product of the Sale of the Reserve, and as to those who would prefer to emigrate to a foreign country they were to receive in cash a proportionate amount out of the price of said Sale.[69]

The subdivision proposed by Cartier and his predecessor (possibly Sir Antoine-Aimé Dorion, who preceded Cartier as joint premier of the United Canadas) would have continued the cadastre abrégé of 1860 onto unconceded Kahnawà:ke lands, so that the entire seigneury would have been divided into lots and sold. The nation would be compensated for the value of the land, and this money would enable it to move elsewhere. Since the entire community would not agree to such a move, however, the four chiefs suggested that those who wished to stay should be permitted to buy one of the new lots with their part of the collective indemnity. Those who wished to leave both the community and the territory would receive a cash payment. The chiefs stated that they had been complaining for twenty years about illegal wood sales, which were causing great damage to the community. They claimed that "the great majority of the members of the said Tribe, viz: over eight hundred, are ready and desirous to surrender their lands to the Government of the Dominion of Canada, for the price of twenty five dollars, currency, an acre."[70] A letter from four chiefs the month before stated that they did not have the unanimous support of the tribe but did have majority agreement. They also noted that if the sale were to go through, "we shall pass the boundary line in the Dominion of Canada as we are going to be settled of Indian Territory or Charekee Nation if you would be answer to us in satisfactory then we shall commence of preparation" (more on this letter in Chapter 5).[71]

In response to the June 1875 petition, Lawrence Vankoughnet, DIA deputy superintendent general, wrote a memo explaining that the petition came from only four of the seven chiefs and claimed to represent the opinion of only 800 of Kahnawà:ke's 1,557 residents, not the strong majority he was looking for. This was completely disingenuous, since all seven chiefs had signed letters with similar opinions during the previous two months.[72] Demanding the explicit approval of all women and children (presumably most of the missing votes) was also inconsistent with department practice. Vankoughnet calculated that at $25 per acre, the government would pay $393,575 to purchase the 15,743 acres of unconceded land. He noted, however, that the land along the riverfront was worth $100 per acre and the rest $40 per acre, and that the reserve possessed some very valuable quarries. These were estimated to yield about 2,420,000 toise (9,912,854 square metres) of cut stone, which he valued at $32 per toise or $77,440,000. This estimate did not include stone of lesser quality, which would sell for $8 per toise. Vankoughnet also stated that

> the reserve is very favorably situated being opposite Lachine with which there is constant communication by Steamer during the regular season of navigation, and twice a day during the winter as the ice never takes at this point. Caughnawaga is the terminus of the Caughnawaga and Plattsburg R.R. and all the traffic by that line for Montreal passes through this place for transportation by Steamer to Lachine.[73]

Clearly, the offer to sell the reserve for $25 an acre was attractive to the DIA, and the outcome of the sale would have been in line with its goal of eliminating Indigenous communities. Most Kahnawa'kehró:non would leave Canada and those who stayed would be enfranchised. Furthermore, this prime land near Canada's largest city would be parcelled out and sold and would produce long-term revenue. Vankoughnet's memo did not give the reasons for not proceeding with the sale, but perhaps the United States government had declined to take in another Indigenous nation when it was in the midst of an aggressive campaign of dispossession against those already within its borders. Perhaps the $393,575 price tag was also prohibitive, even if it were a bargain. Although this money would have been recovered from land sales, the Indian Department might have been unable or unwilling to access large sums for such purposes.[74] In September 1875, Agent Joseph Pinsonneault followed up with his superior on the chiefs' petition, reiterating the wishes of those who "desire to go to the United States, to get land they propose to buy, if it suit them."[75] No response is included in the file, and the sale did not go through.

CONCLUSION

The year 1875 was the last time Kahnawà:ke leaders tried to move the community to another location. From that time forward, Kahnawa'kehró:non sought to find ways to continue to live on their lands while negotiating the efforts of the DIA to impose increasingly invasive Indian laws and dismantle the reserve. DIA actions to half-heartedly impose colonial notions of private property would create a short period of lawlessness in the 1870s that led to the cutting of much of the Kahnawà:ke forest (Chapter 5). Using this chaos as justification, the DIA decided to survey and subdivide against the wishes of the community (Chapter 6). The goal of the department was to transform the territory into a private property grid and Kahnawa'kehró:non into enfranchised farmer-proprietors. In this light, the attempts of Kahnawa'kehró:non to collectively move elsewhere can be seen as forward-thinking and astute, since they foresaw trouble and tried to move to a place where they could live according to their own laws. After 1875, they put this strategy on the backburner and focused on other ways to defend and build their nationhood.

During the middle decades of the nineteenth century, the Montreal region was dramatically transformed through rapid population growth and the rise of an industrial economy. Over the same period, Indigenous nations saw their political influence decline and their territories subjected to increasing depredation and incursion. Kahnawa'kehró:non continued to use their lands much as their ancestors had done, but also in new ways, showing adaptation to changing demographic, economic, and political realities. Whereas outsiders claimed that Kahnawà:ke was an anarchic, underutilized space, and scholars have emphasized the economic activities of Kahnawà:ke men away from the village, this chapter shows that these outsiders tended to underestimate or overlook farming, gardening, foraging, and woodcutting activities. Although a few men took up farming using Euro-Canadian approaches, women still produced much of the food for their families, and although some Kahnawa'kehró:non owned and enclosed land according to the legal customs of their settler neighbours, most continued to live according to Kahnawà:ke law. The two legal regimes coexisted uneasily in the first half of the century, but a more aggressive DIA in the second half worked to undermine Indigenous law and to impose colonial law.

Kahnawà:ke lost an important source of revenue with the demise of the seigneurial system (Chapter 1), and the Indian Department took control of community finances, making it nearly impossible for leaders to lead. Colonial patriarchal norms undermined the position of women as leaders, and Kahnawà:ke chiefs in the 1850s promoted the legal marginalization of women. Archival sources do not indicate the level of support among men and women in Kahnawà:ke for this measure, but many believed it was the best way to protect the nation's land base against white men who could otherwise gain access to land through marriage. They believed this would help the nation to survive in the context of a colonial legal system that restricted women's property rights to such an extent that women-owned properties in Kahnawà:ke were considered extremely vulnerable. By the 1870s, the largely self-governing Seigneury of Sault Saint-Louis had been transformed, through circuitous routes of dubious legality, into a reserve. Federal legislation had stripped local leaders of some of their powers, and more such laws were on the horizon. All of these changes were related to the emergence of the view of Indigenous people as wards of the state, a paternalist legal relationship that went hand-in-hand with the judicial declaration that traditional councils of chiefs did not possess legal personality. When Indigenous people were declared wards of the Crown, they became subject to a "legal disability" like that of minors or married women, and their leaders faced numerous legal barriers as they attempted to govern and lead.[76] The DIA continually tried to insert itself into the power vacuum of its own making but never managed to claim the entire balance of power. But the land conflicts described in this chapter were only the beginning. Chapter 5 relates the hesitant and reactive way the DIA attempted to step into this power vacuum and details the human and environmental costs of this awkward transition. As Joseph Doutre pointed out, the problems that would plague Kahnawà:ke were not grounded in its "form of government but will be solely due to the mixing of hetero-geneous races who are all subject to different laws."[77] Doutre knew that the conflict was legal and political in nature, and that trouble lay ahead as one legal system stepped up its assault on the other. Kahnawa'kehró:non had also seen it coming and had attempted to move the community. After 1875, they made no further efforts to relocate, focusing instead on other ways of defending and building their nationhood while negotiating DIA efforts to impose increasingly invasive Indian laws and to dismantle their reserve.

5

"The Consequences of
This Promiscuous Ownership"
Wood and the *Indian Act,* 1867–83

*The cutting of wood on our Forest land has not abated nor has
any Steps been taken to arrest the unwarranted trespasses that are
daily committed by white persons at the instigation of unruly and
unmanageable Indians besides which hundreds of Cords of wood
have been taken away through the roads opened by these Indians
and white trespassers, during the past Summer, of which we
cannot find out the offenders.*

– Kahnawà:ke Chiefs to Edmund Walker Head, 1855

In the years following Confederation, the federal government concentrated on territorial expansion and asserting its control over territory it believed it owned. Canada was able to expand west of the
Great Lakes after the Hudson's Bay Company transferred its dubious
land title in 1869. After significant conflicts with Indigenous peoples on
the Prairies in 1869–70, the Canadian government employed surveyors
to create an agricultural settlement grid that would allow for the dispossession of First Nations and the emplacement of mostly white farmers.[1]
On the heels of surveyors came police officers whose job was to protect
the new settlers and to supervise the continued dispossession and disenfranchisement of the original inhabitants. Federal officials and First
Nations negotiated treaties requiring the latter to relinquish lands in
exchange for small reserve territories as well as certain rights and privileges.
All of this occurred while Indigenous nations on the Prairies faced ecological and economic disaster, particularly the decimation of the bison
herds on which they depended.[2]

All eyes, especially in the Department of Indian Affairs (DIA), were on the Northwest, as the newly constituted dominion strove to expand its reach across the continent. Many historians have looked at Canadian policy and action in the Northwest during this period, which was focused on the dispossession and acculturation of Indigenous peoples.[3] But fewer have studied the DIA's dealing with eastern communities such as Kahnawà:ke, which the department considered to be more advanced along the path to civilization and thus more prepared for enfranchisement. This chapter examines the human and environmental consequences of DIA legal and political intrusions into Kahnawà:ke, at a time when Canada was invading Indigenous territory farther west. In these years immediately following Confederation, legislators enacted a number of policy changes that enabled DIA interference in the daily life and governance of First Nations. To become the primary authority in the lives of Indigenous people, the department focused on strengthening its own hand while diminishing the ability of Indigenous leaders to govern. It had no interest in supporting the legal orders of Indigenous nations, but it was also often unwilling to impose itself and its laws in a decisive way. Whether it was actively interfering with Indigenous governance or maintaining a stance of strategic indifference, it did all it could to weaken Indigenous nations. This chapter unfolds in the midst of the power vacuum created in Kahnawà:ke by the actions and non-actions of the DIA, and its focus is wood: Who has the right to fell and use trees, whose laws apply, and how does colonial interference affect ordinary Kahnawa'kehró:non?

The Department of Indian Affairs and Indian Policy, 1876–84

The 1876 *Indian Act* summarized, replaced, and updated all previous Indian legislation and was the foundation on which all subsequent Canadian Indian policy was built. It advanced the assimilationist, genocidal thrust of Indian policy while also maintaining aspects of previous legislation that were supposed, in the thinking of colonial elites, to protect Indians from Euro-Canadian vices. The most significant change from the 1869 *Gradual Enfranchisement Act* was the provision of an elected band council system that could be applied only to a community that officially requested it.[4] The *Indian Act* also maintained the rule, dating from the 1851 act for Lower Canada (Chapter 4), that an Indian woman who married a non-Indian man lost her status, which also meant that such men could not gain status through marriage. Most amendments to the *Indian Act* in later years strengthened the hand of the DIA in its relationships with Indigenous communities. For example, an 1879 amendment enabled the DIA to allot reserve land, whereas this power had previously rested with the band.[5] The 1880 *Indian Act* allowed the superintendent general to recognize only Indigenous leaders who were elected according to the provisions of the act.[6] Indian agents were given the powers of justice of the peace in an 1881 amendment and the same power as stipendiary magistrate or police magistrate the following year.[7] Each of these amendments reduced the power of Indian bands (racialized political institutions created by the *Indian Act*) and made it more difficult for Indigenous peoples to determine their own path. The *Indian Advancement Act* of 1884 was an even more aggressive attempt to transform Indigenous political institutions. Under this policy, which followed the model of Canadian municipal government, traditional councils were replaced by band councils elected on an annual rather than a triennial basis.[8]

In terms of land, the 1876 *Indian Act* laid out extensive rules for the alienation and leasing of Indian lands. A key feature was the "location ticket," which lawmakers saw as an important step in putting Indians on the path away from communitarianism toward enfranchisement and private property. The legislation envisioned that reserves would be surveyed and divided into individual lots. Each lot would be assigned to individual members (heads of households – mostly men, but also some widows) by the band councils, and each owner would be given a location ticket as proof of his title to that lot. To acquire a location ticket, a man needed to prove his suitability; essentially, he had to be literate, morally upright, and debt-free. After the ticket had been issued, the owner had a probationary period of three years to prove that he was capable of behaving in a "civilized" way, which included improving his land according to colonial standards. If he met all the requirements, he would become officially enfranchised and would own the lot in the same manner as a white settler. Those who held a professional degree (such as minister, lawyer, teacher, or doctor) could receive a location ticket and be enfranchised without going through a probationary period.[9] The assumption, initially, was that Indigenous people would desire to become enfranchised – which turned out to be mostly false, since few voluntarily applied for the change in status.[10] Subsequent amendments to the *Indian Act* envisioned unilateral imposition of location tickets and enfranchisement.[11]

The *Indian Act* was genocidal in the sense that its purpose was to eradicate Indigenous nations, first, by legally transforming Indians into non-Indians.[12] Enfranchisement policies were designed to remove the most educated and talented people from the community, but the point was also to shrink its remaining land base by giving each enfranchised person a portion of the reserve. Historian John Tobias sums up the importance of the 1876 *Indian Act* by saying that it was the "first piece of comprehensive legislation by which the government exercised its exclusive jurisdiction over Indians and Indian lands" and that it had "as its purpose the eventual extirpation of this jurisdiction by doing away with those persons and lands that fell with the category of Indians and Indian lands."[13] In other words, the DIA claimed to protect Indigenous people and their lands, but it actually worked to do the opposite.

In the guise of promoting civilization, the *Indian Act* also attacked Indigenous laws related to marriage, divorce, sexuality, race relations, freedom of movement, the actions of Indigenous women, and the legal status of children born out of wedlock.[14] It aimed at the eradication of Indigenous law, practices, leadership, and identity, and sought to create new persons in the image of idealized Euro-Canadian Christians. First Nations east of Lake Superior, toward whom this legislation was largely directed, generally rejected the *Indian Act*.[15] Most opposed the band council system because they understood that it would make their leaders primarily accountable to the DIA. The department chose to interpret this rejection as a sign that even these communities were not yet ready to make choices that were in their own best interest and thus needed more heavy-handed guidance.

But as historian Sarah Carter notes, Indian policy in Canada was not driven by long-term planning or unified purpose. Instead, it was tentative and ad hoc, driven by official ideologies and common beliefs, and not subject to public discussion.[16] The department was often unresponsive to warnings and appeared to do very little advance planning, but legislation relating to First Nations had a clear direction: granting the DIA more and more authority over Indigenous people and lands. In thinking about this situation, I borrow the phrase "effective inefficiency," which sociologist and lawyer Yael Berda coined to describe the colonial effectiveness of the Kafkaesque Israeli bureaucracy to subjugate Palestinians.[17] As the department expanded rapidly during the 1870s, its power over First Nations quickly grew, with very little oversight or interest from the general public and virtually no accountability to First Nations themselves. In such circumstances, the effective inefficiency of the DIA – its failure to plan for the long term and to take a firm policy direction, its tentative and often contradictory decision making – made it very difficult for Indigenous people to resist.

For their part, DIA officials felt that Kahnawà:ke was one of the most advanced Indigenous communities in Canada and so they intended to showcase their assimilative tactics there. At the same time, they were concerned about its strong tradition of political independence and resistance to outside interference. They often characterized those who upheld Kahnawà:ke law as primitive and irrationally conservative, seeing self-interested Kahnawa'kehró:non who broke that law as acting rationally. In their view, a core problem that required a solution, not only in Kahnawà:ke but in all First Nations, lay with the deficiencies in, or absence of, private property. To get control and establish private property, the DIA repeatedly destabilized the authority of Kahnawà:ke leaders and law through the 1870s. But, as we shall see in this chapter, its acts generated a chaotic period of environmental destruction and economic damage, which it blamed on Kahnawà:ke troublemakers.

WOOD, LAW, AND RACE

Although wood and land shortages in Kahnawà:ke had provoked some problems during previous decades, they came to a head in the 1870s. Kahnawà:ke had experienced significant upheaval and uncertainty due to Montreal industrialization and railway development, DIA interference, shortages of land and resources, and racial tensions. It was these concerns that led so many Kahnawa'kehró:non to favour moving the community elsewhere – something the Canadian government would not allow (Chapter 4). At the same time, Kahnawa'kehró:non experienced growing internal political problems. Within this fraught context, a touchstone debate emerged about the legal framework for cutting down trees.[18]

All interested parties (including DIA officials, Kahnawà:ke leaders, and landowners) realized that trees were being cut faster than they could grow and that everyone would suffer as a result. Since most Kahnawa'kehró:non relied to some extent on the land for food, raw materials, timber, and firewood, these shortages affected everyone. There was great disagreement about both the reason for the lack of wood and its potential solution. Already in 1855, the chiefs believed that the problem was white people who stole wood, sometimes with the help of a few Kahnawa'kehró:non (chapter epigraph). To solve the problem, the chiefs needed help in enforcing their laws, but the DIA had no wish to support either the chiefs or their laws. Instead, it attempted to strengthen its position by exhorting its Indian agent to do more. In 1873, the department instructed the incoming agent, Joseph Pinsonneault, to focus on regulating woodcutting and preventing white people from squatting on Kahnawà:ke territory.[19] The DIA solution to Kahnawà:ke's problems rested in asserting its own authority and legal framework, but its own authority remained weak, whereas most Kahnawa'kehró:non still considered their traditional chiefs as legitimate leaders.

In the winter of 1873–74, the situation deteriorated to such an extent that the chiefs hired men to guard the trees.[20] Chiefs Thaioronhiote and Otonharishon informed the DIA (now part of the Department of Interior) in the spring of 1874 that a number of people had taken hundreds of saw-logs to the sawmill with the intention of selling the wood. The chiefs planned to seize the logs whenever they found proof that someone had been selling them. Without the help of a first-language English speaker, they wrote to David Laird, minister of interior, that

> few of them had been cleared the wood or trees of their farms and had sold to the white people and this time chopping their fuel to other's farms and selling to the said White to whom have no Ideas to sell keep for the tribe only. As we intend to punish with them by ceased of their annuities money although is not equal, to encourage of the obedience.[21]

In other words, the chiefs wished to withhold annuity payments from those who were selling wood. Instead of supporting them, Deputy Minister of the Interior Edmund Allen Meredith rebuked them, saying it was not their responsibility to end the sale of timber, but that of the Indian agent. He agreed, however, that Kahnawa'kehró:non who sold it would have the amount of the sale deducted from their share of the annuity.[22] He subsequently berated Agent Pinsonneault for not keeping watch over the wood of the reserve, but the agent could do very little to stop the cutting.[23] Thus, although colonial officials recognized the importance of the chiefs' concerns, they refused to support proven and respected Indigenous leaders in their efforts to protect their forests and people, choosing instead to rely on the Indian agent, an ineffective outsider.

Kahnawà:ke law regarding woodcutting is most clearly spelled out in the 1801 Code (Chapter 2), but it was restated and upheld by Kahnawà:ke leaders throughout the century. Aside from active sugarbushes and a few tree species that were reserved for public uses, Kahnawà:ke citizens could legally take down a tree anywhere on the territory. The wood was only for personal use, however, and Kahnawa'kehró:non were forbidden to sell it. Thus, one can envision nineteenth-century Kahnawà:ke as a commonly owned woodlot or a Dish with One Spoon, a forest commons that was to be shared by everyone under strict conditions. Like all successful historical examples of a commons, this was not a free-for-all, but a regulated space.[24]

Opponents of Kahnawà:ke wood law tended to be landowning, wealthier Kahnawa'kehró:non who sided with the DIA on this issue. I refer to them as "dissidents," which is my own term; it was not used at the time. "Dissidents" is a slippery category and may indeed encompass people who did not see themselves as siding with the DIA on most issues, but it does tend to include those with questionable Indian status and/or questionable residency or citizenship in Kahnawà:ke. Dissidents on the wood issue understood landownership as conferring exclusive rights to the trees on one's land. Like the DIA, they saw the Kahnawà:ke laws as the source of the problem, but they felt powerless to change things because they themselves were in the minority. They did, however, have a powerful ally in the DIA, and the two parties often worked together to undermine Kahnawà:ke chiefs and laws, and to promote the idea that colonial laws should be in force.

On December 20, 1873, five dissident landowners petitioned the DIA for an Order-in-Council (OIC), a highly specific law that would make it illegal to cut wood on someone else's lot without permission.[25] One of the petitioners was Marie-Louise McComber, the widow of George Delorimier, whose family possessed much land despite the widespread view in Kahnawà:ke that they were white people without the right to own land there (Chapter 3). The petitioners complained that under the current circumstances, "they and others are subjected to much annoyance and loss by a custom which prevails in the said Seignory from any member of the tribe to cut down and remove the timber from the said farms contrary to the wishes and without the consent of the owners thereof." Aside from any actual damage this practice might cause to forests, the petitioners saw it as "a serious impediment to the cultivation and improvement" of Kahnawà:ke lands and as "the discouragement of agriculture generally among the Indians of the Sault St. Louis."[26] The dissidents thus argued that Kahnawà:ke law was an impediment to agriculture and productive land use, which they knew would please the DIA, itself deeply invested in promoting "civilization" through farming.

Through their lawyer, M. MacIver, the five dissident landowners described Kahnawà:ke law: "It has hitherto been the custom for any member of the tribe to appropriate to his own uses the timber throughout the

Reserve, regardless of the rights of those who, in virtue of the usual Indian title, are acknowledged owners of lots of land."[27] MacIver summarized "the consequences of this promiscuous ownership and destruction of timber":

> Valuable trees are cut down for the most ordinary purposes, and not unfrequently to gratify a spirit of revenge; the farms are denuded of wood for building, fencing and firewood; and as a natural result few persons are inclined to spend money or labor in improving properties always liable to such ruinous depredations. To add to the evil, threats are now held out of cutting down several valuable "Maple Sugaries" which have hitherto been exempt from spoliation, and considered to be the exclusive property of those persons on whose land they were; and it is feared that perseverance in that design will be attended with serious breaches of the peace.[28]

The dissidents and their lawyer knew that this framing would get the attention and sympathy of the DIA. They cast themselves as rational and even-keeled, surrounded by vengeful, unreasonable, destructive neighbours. In the current situation, they argued, responsible and industrious landowners such as themselves had no incentive to "improve" their property, which is why so much of it remained uncultivated.[29] They stated that their primary concern was the preservation of both the trees and peaceful relations. They feared that all the trees would be felled due to defective laws and poorly behaved Kahnawa'kehró:non, with violence the probable result. Their portrayal of Kahnawà:ke law is consistent with other nineteenth-century accounts, but their interpretation of the actions and motivations of their neighbours was clearly a minority view and deeply offensive to those being described.

The dissidents contended that Kahnawà:ke laws led to conflict and discouraged agriculture. It is impossible to know whether conflict in Kahnawà:ke was greater than in settler villages, but it is unlikely. The trope that Indigenous peoples are marked by unusual levels of violence and internal clashes has long been used to weaken their political interests.[30] The dissidents also made a direct connection between the level of discord and a lack of farming. They said that Kahnawà:ke laws accounted "for the backward state of agriculture among the Indians of Sault St. Louis, for though many of them are anxious to cultivate their lands, they are deterred from so doing by the condition attached to the possession of them." If these laws were allowed to stay in force, they warned, the land would remain underused and friction would escalate. They asked the DIA to imagine what would happen if the entire province were subjected to such a law:

The irritation and mischief caused by the circumstances described may be realized by supposing that all the inhabitants of the Province held their lands burdened with a similar incident of tenure. Were it so, it is scarcely too much to say that the country would either be a wilderness (as the greater part of Sault St. Louis is) or the scene of lawlessness, strife and violence.[31]

It is worth noting that dissidents made a direct association between "wilderness" and lawlessness, one that has been employed in colonial contexts around the world to justify Indigenous dispossession.[32]

Those who wanted to engage in practices that contravened Kahnawà:ke law, such as these dissidents, often stated that Kahnawa'kehró:non did not farm, which was not the case. Government officials made numerous references to their agriculture throughout the 1870s; and outside observers tended not to recognize smaller-scale, women-directed farming as agriculture. Even families that relied on income from wage labour and itinerant professions depended on locally cultivated and gathered food.

In light of the harms caused by the legal status quo, the dissidents asked the DIA to have a law passed that would protect landowners.[33] Their lawyer quoted from section 37 of the 1868 *Act on the Management of Indian Lands*, reminding the DIA that the law authorized the governor-in-council to "make such Regulations as he deems expedient for the protection and management of the Indian lands in Canada or any part thereof, and of the timber thereon or cut from off the said lands, whether surrendered for sale or reserve or set apart for the Indians."[34] The five landowners, in other words, were asking the Canadian government to expand its jurisdiction into Kahnawà:ke.

The DIA turned down their request, saying that no new OIC was needed, because the rights of landowners were already protected by the *Crown Timber Act,* which had been made applicable to Indian lands so that "no Timber can be cut except under license or by white men or by Indians on Indian lands (save when cut by an occupant of land for his own use upon the lot occupied by him), and any cut without license may be dealt with as cut in trespass."[35] But to enforce that law, the DIA believed that Kahnawà:ke needed a cadastral survey to establish the boundary lines between its lots in a way that it could understand. Until then, it could do nothing to stop the conflict. In effect, it insisted on a legal framework that could not be enforced until a cadastral survey had been completed. In the meantime, it would not enforce existing Kahnawà:ke laws, because it did not acknowledge their validity. The DIA suggested that "should it be the general wish of the Iroquois owning that Reserve to have it subdivided by

Survey into farm lots, the Department would be prepared to carry it into effect."[36] This suggestion was apparently a hint about what was needed from the dissidents before the DIA could proceed.

Two months later, the department received exactly what it had requested. It was a petition from nineteen Kahnawà:ke "possessors of farms and other real property therein ... to have a survey made" and to "establish division lines between the different properties."[37] The nineteen signatories included the five individuals who had launched the original petition of December 20, 1873, and the new petition was forwarded by the same lawyer, M. MacIver.[38] The DIA then asked Indian Agent Joseph Pinsonneault to determine whether the opinion of the petitioners represented the majority view. He reported that the petitioners were in the minority; the majority was opposed to a survey that would give landowners exclusive possession of standing trees. Most had no woodlots of their own and thus would never support a position that would deprive them of fuel to heat their homes.[39] It is important to note that the DIA was interested in Kahnawà:ke public opinion, not because it intended to respect the wishes of inhabitants, but only because it needed to know how difficult the execution of its plans would be. Thus, in 1875, even after learning that the majority was opposed, the DIA asked Pinsonneault to collect information about landowners and lots in preparation for a subdivision survey. Many families refused to cooperate, with the result that Pinsonneault could not complete his task at that time.[40]

A few weeks later, four Kahnawà:ke chiefs – Jarvis A. Dione, Joseph K. Delisle, Joseph T. Skye, and Thomas Asennase – responded to the unilateral approach of the DIA with a poignant letter. Their petition lays out the objections of the majority in detail. Although it is written in non-standard English (presumably without the help of a first-language English speaker), I quote it at length because I believe it gives the perspective of most Kahnawa'kehró:non in a relatively unmediated way. The phrasing is sometimes difficult to decipher, so I follow each section with my understanding of what it means in square brackets, along with some explanatory comments afterward. The chiefs began the letter by emphasizing that the request for a survey had come from a minority group:

> In a various opinions of the whole tribe and some of them nothing but wasting the Interests of the tribe, we are much complaining on it for there is quite evident in further will fall to a destitution part of our tribe, though they were been elected us as a Chiefs for maintenance and ruling to them as far as will stand the obedience as we acknowledge we had done in our

duty as much as in our power even to these very days, desires to obtain of release and to protecting to them that they were not possessed a farm or sugar-bush and for using of our interests.[41] [My interpretation: The majority of the tribe believes that this small group is undermining the interests of the entire tribe and has been very vocal about this. The tribe elected us to govern our people – we have done so to the best of our abilities under the circumstances – and our priority has been to protect those who do not possess a farm or sugarbush and to protect the interests of the tribe as a whole.]

The chiefs thus explained that the request for a survey had come from a small group of people who were trying to undermine the nation for their own reasons. The chiefs presented themselves as the only legitimate leaders of Kahnawà:ke, who were acting in the interests of the entire nation, especially the many people who did not own farms or sugarbushes.

They then explained Kahnawà:ke law regarding woodcutting:

As they were a certain party, they have an Idea (the owners of the sugar-bushes) of their own use of the Maple wood and even when will consumed the rest of the woods and one of the tribe had been tried and convicted by the judge of Laprairie, the act 1869. As in our general rule if a man has sugar-bush as long as he kept the maple for making a sugar. He have no privilege, for if he shall convert to a farm or choping himself or servants and selling, there shall we have rights to chop or cut down the maples of our own use the way we understand by the treaty May 29th 1680, of Louis XVI Six Mile Square for the Iroquois tribe.[42] [My interpretation: The small group of dissidents (owners of sugarbushes) have the idea that they can keep their maple wood for their own exclusive use even when all other wood has been cut, and one Kahnawa'kehró:non has already been convicted by the La Prairie judge under the act of 1869. Our general rule is that a man can have a sugarbush as long as he is actively producing sugar. If he cuts down the trees to sell the wood or converts the forest to farmland, he loses his privilege; and all community members have the right to cut the wood. We understand this rule to be supported by the treaty of May 29, 1680, of Louis XVI regarding the six square miles of land for the Iroquois tribe.]

According to the chiefs, the petitioners were a few landowners who claimed an exclusive right to maple wood, even when they were not tapping the trees. The chiefs reiterated the long-standing Kahnawà:ke legal principle that land and trees could be owned in the sense of excluding others from them only when they were *used*. Thus, maples could be claimed as a person's individual property only as long as they were being tapped for sugar (Chapter 2). It is also important to note that the chiefs saw the May 1680 seigneurial concession as a treaty with the French Crown, now inherited by the British Crown, and that this treaty had recognized their laws as applying to the lands in question.

Next, the chiefs discussed their loss of fiscal independence and how it impeded their ability to govern:

> Since disestablished the Act 1867 and the Officers resigned themselves by misunderstood of their duty and our funds are escheat to the Crown, ever since to them that they were misdemeanors have more chance to waste of fuel &c, because we have no power to chastise them and neither of any Agent willing to prosecute them.[43] [My interpretation: Since the act of 1867, Indian agents have misunderstood their duties, and our funds have been managed by the Crown. Since then, lawbreakers in the community have been emboldened to waste wood, because we have no power to chastise them, and the agent is not willing to prosecute them.]

Incidents of illegal woodcutting had been on the rise since 1867, when the chiefs said that Canada had taken over management of their finances. Once the people knew that they no longer had either complete financial control or the full backing of the department, incidents of illegal wood-cutting increased. But the chiefs also recognized that the trend had started before Confederation:

> Some of them they were begun about 25 years ago and multiplying every year and in this year the greatest number ever employed of selling fuel &c, and the parties accusing the Chiefs and were the sellers of wood but we held the peace as our own concern if they were only obedient enough we should live in peaceably.[44] [My interpretation: Some of these people started illegally cutting and selling wood about twenty-five years ago, and more people are doing it every year. This year, the greatest number ever are selling wood illegally, and those who are breaking the law are accusing the chiefs of causing the problem, but we were simply trying to keep the peace, which could be achieved if everyone obeyed the law.]

The writers believed that the problem of wood pilfering had begun about twenty-five years earlier (around 1850) but had never been more severe than now. Colonial interference in Kahnawà:ke did not begin with

Confederation – it dated from much earlier – but the chiefs here explain one concrete way in which things had worsened for them in recent years.

Kahnawa'kehró:non were acutely aware of how little land they had left and were concerned about the real-life impacts of any land survey, legal change, or land redistribution. According to the chiefs:

> For they were conscience most of the tribe it will parpied the interests of the tribe,[45] and if to subdivide the land or reserve, for we have only a small piece of land according to the number of the tribe and beside we have to pay to be surveyed of the land and after received the shares some will oblige to sell and emigrant and nothing to take with the annuity or Indian's pound. For the shares it will containing swamps, rocky or stoney grounds and creared without fuel. As we are considered the present time some more illegal possessed of our land and to them that same license for [using] in the reserve the way one understand if we shall take these actions, all those illegal possessed it shall be theirs in future of the Seignory &c but part of the tribe shall be gone one place to another.[46] [My interpretation: We knew that if the reserve were to be subdivided, each person would have only a small piece of land, and we would have to collectively pay for the surveying of the land, and after it is completed, some would have to sell their lot and leave the community, and lose their access to their annuity. This is because many lots will contain swamps, rocky or stony grounds, and cleared land without fuel. If the minority who are currently in illegal possession of our lands are given licence to continue in this way, and if the reserve is subdivided, those who are currently acting illegally will be given legal rights to lands, and many others will have to leave.]

Since the land was of uneven quality, a redistribution would aggravate inequities, and a new private property regime would spell the end of accessible firewood. Even if everyone were given a piece of land, many would find themselves in dire straits, with poor land and no access to wood. Add to this the high cost of the survey that would be borne by the community, and the chiefs believed these interventions were unsustainable. They wanted only for the colonial government to support them as they enforced their own laws. But if the DIA would not do this, they asked it to approve the sale of the reserve and the removal of the community to Indian Territory (Oklahoma), where they had apparently made arrangements with the Cherokee (for more on this, see Chapter 4).[47]

The DIA knew very well that the majority in Kahnawà:ke opposed a cadastral survey and the imposition of colonial land law. Only a small minority ever asked for these, and information submitted by the Indian agent regularly confirmed that most people supported the position of the chiefs on this issue. But of course the chiefs did not enjoy unqualified support, and the DIA fully intended to exploit these rifts. A number of Kahnawa'kehró:non even favoured having the council of chiefs replaced by an elected band council under the *Advancement Act*. An 1875 petition, signed by more than a third (190) of Kahnawà:ke men who were obviously unhappy with their current leadership, asked for an elected council in line with the *Enfranchisement Act of 1869*. Historian Gerald Reid's demographic analysis of the signatories for this petition (and others) shows that opponents of the traditional chiefs were typically younger men and also tended to be landholders. Supporters of the chiefs tended to be small landholders or people without land.[48] An important point here is that the colonial archives tell us nothing about the views of women in this case. This silence is particularly striking in light of the role that Rotinonhsión:ni women traditionally played in raising up and deposing chiefs. Of course, they still took an active political role at this time, but it is difficult for historians to access specifics about it.

Reid argues that the dissatisfaction with Kahnawà:ke leadership was related to land inequalities and resource scarcity,[49] which is no doubt true, but it was more specifically a response to the chiefs' inability to effectively govern due to colonial interference or strategic indifference. An example of the latter is the DIA's repeated refusal to support the chiefs in enforcing Kahnawà:ke law.[50] This had the effect of damaging their credibility and creating a situation in which people would be willing to accept the band council system as the price for obtaining a functional government. The DIA also now controlled the finances and would allow chiefs to spend money only on things that it saw as priorities. For instance, they were not permitted to spend community funds to help poor families.[51] For leaders who wished to promote economic equality among their people and to show care for the poor, this would have been both infuriating and a serious blow to their credibility.

Conflicts surrounding resource and land management were closely related to questions of race and belonging. Although the *Indian Act* did not specify legal pathways for a non-Indian man to become a status Indian (non-Indian women legally became Indians when they married an Indian man), the DIA regularly granted permanent residence permits to non-status men who had some reason for living on the reserve, acceptable to the DIA. The department was inconsistent in granting such permits, and thus white people lived in Kahnawà:ke under many pretexts. If permits had been renewed a number of times, the DIA sometimes saw this as adequate grounds for granting the permit holder full status rights. In other cases, the courts made decisions about Kahnawà:ke membership rights. The DIA's preferred approach was to take no action, another example of strategic indifference. The department saw evicting people as expensive and risky, whereas allowing white people to stay in place advanced the cause of "civilization." In practical terms, DIA inaction promoted a porous community boundary, weakened community cohesion, undermined the authority of Kahnawà:ke leaders, and increased the number of DIA supporters.

Chiefs repeatedly petitioned the DIA to help them to expel white men residing there illegally, and who often illegally cut and sold wood. According to the chiefs, some of these men held DIA residency permits that should never have been granted, and even those whose permits were legitimate did not pay their annual rents.[52] Of course, white people were not the only wood poachers, but the chiefs believed that they had set a precedent, which Kahnawa'kehró:non had followed when it became clear that they themselves could not enforce the laws.[53] Throughout the 1870s, the DIA made several half-hearted attempts at compiling a membership list for Kahnawà:ke, as well as lists of white people who lived there illegally. The department did not even have a complete list of permit holders; nor did it keep accounting books that would inform it as to whether a permit holder had paid rent.[54] DIA officials often instructed the Indian agent to evict white men or to collect rent from them, knowing that he would not be able to do it.[55]

The inability of Kahnawà:ke leaders to enforce their own citizenship or residency laws led some Kahnawa'kehró:non to great frustration and vigilante justice. Indian Agent Georges Cherrier reported that the first barn fires occurred in 1865, when two barns belonging to people who were seen as white went up in flames.[56] The most high-profile of such attacks came in 1878, when someone torched a barn belonging to Osias Meloche, a Kahnawà:ke resident considered by many to be white. He died trying to save his animals. The *Montreal Daily Witness* reported that

> no doubt is entertained but this is the work of an incendiary, as this is the fourth attempt to fire the village within a short time. It is believed that these attempts are the outcome of animosities which exist between the Indians and the French-Canadians. The deceased was 48 years of age, and leaves a wife and family. He was an industrious man and owned considerable property in the village.[57]

The following year saw five more barn fires, and the arson continued into the next decade. It is clear that in the context of mounting colonial interference, a number of concerns and frustrations were building over the 1870s, all of which resulted in instability and violence.

THE ORDER-IN-COUNCIL OF 1876

In November 1875, Tekanonnowehon (Alexander Delorimier) wrote to the DIA on behalf of a number of "respectable" owners of sugarbushes.[58] They feared that people would cut maple trees on their lands that winter. The parents of Tekanonnowehon, George Delorimier and Marie-Louise McComber, had been part of a number of controversies over the previous decade, and most Kahnawa'kehró:non saw them as white. The DIA was inconsistent in its stance (Chapters 3 and 4). Tekanonnowehon and other members of his family continued to hold considerable land in Kahnawà:ke, including large and valuable sugarbushes. These were the focus of concern for Tekanonnowehon and his fellow dissidents:

> Up to this day only a few young men have dared to chop several trees in these bushes. This winter I have reasons to fear that some serious trouble will take place among them with regard to the maple trees. Such trees according to the usages here are not allowed to be cut down only by those who are actually in possession of them for their own private use but now the ill disposed parties or I may say those who have sold illegally their own portion to the white people have come to the conclusion of chopping these maple trees to the great detriment of the actual owners who wisely have had the good sense to preserve them.[59]

It is not clear whether Tekanonnowehon intended to tap the maples or fell them, but in either case, he believed that no one else had the right to log in his sugarbush. According to his interpretation of Kahnawà:ke law, maples could be cut only by the owners of the land on which they grew, and then solely for their own private use. He asked the government for an Order-in-Council (OIC) to protect landowners' wood and to preserve peace in the community.[60]

Tekanonnowehon's interpretation, however, was not in line with Kahnawà:ke law as it had been expressed to that point. Maples that were used for sugar production were not to be cut by people who did not own the lot, but what might ensue if the owners themselves did so was not at all clear. Did it mean that others could help themselves as well? Perhaps Kahnawà:ke had never faced this particular situation before. Indian Agent Pinsonneault repeated Tekanonnowehon's narrative, adding that the trouble-makers were those who had already felled their own trees to sell the wood illegally, whereas the petitioning landowners wished to preserve theirs. This framing took advantage of the colonial tropes of Indigenous people as savage, whereas these wealthier, whiter individuals could be shown as responsible and civilized. But, Pinsonneault claimed, even they would cut down their maples if the privy council did not issue a new OIC to protect the sugarbushes. His letter ended with a plea: "For the good of the Indian, please intervene to protect the maples."[61]

The chiefs also wished to safeguard the maple trees, but their reasoning was very different from that of Pinsonneault and the petitioners. Their concern was that the owners of the sugarbushes were cutting the maples themselves and planned to take more. In 1874, they had asked the department to stop the practice: "in our opinion the owners of certain sugar bushes should in future be forbidden to chop wood or fuel off the said bushes unless the old Deed shall be altered."[62] What the chiefs meant by "old Deed" is unclear, but perhaps they believed that this rule was contained in the original 1680 seigneurial grants.[63] The DIA also opposed the cutting of maples, but it did so because the sugarbushes were valuable and productive, and because one of its goals was to further the economic development of Indigenous communities. Thus, all parties agreed that sugarbushes should be preserved, but they differed on how to achieve it.

Wasting little time, the DIA acted in accordance with the wishes of the dissidents, ignoring the requests of the chiefs and the majority. On December 9, 1875, it had prominent Lachine industrialist Thomas A. Dawes deputed to enforce section 22 of the 1868 *Act Providing for the Organisation of the Department of the Secretary of State of Canada, and for the Management of Indian and Ordnance Lands,* prosecuting anyone cutting or removing wood, timber, stone, or soil from the reserve.[64] But three weeks later, after apparently finding that the 1868 act was not adequate, the government issued an OIC "for the protection from pillage of Timber on lands occupied by Indians on the Indian Reserve at Caughnawaga." The order stipulated:

1 No timber shall be cut from off any portion of the Indian Lands known as the Caughnawaga Reserve, occupied by individual members of the Band, excepting such as may be required by the occupants of such lands for their own use on the premises.

2 Any infraction of the foregoing Regulation shall subject the parties convicted thereof to a forfeiture of the timber cut and to a fine of not less than twenty or more than two hundred dollars for each such offence.

3 Any timber forfeited under the preceding regulations shall be handed over to the occupant of the land from which it was taken, and the amount of the fine paid shall be carried to the credit of the funds of the Band.[65]

Section 22 of the 1868 act prohibited the removal of wood, stone, and soil from reserves, but it did not specify who owned the wood when it remained on the reserve. This OIC, by contrast, was intended for Kahnawà:ke only. Under its terms, trees belonged to the owner of the land on which they grew, and only the owner was permitted to cut them down or to authorize another person to do so. Interestingly, the OIC made no mention of maples, which were supposedly the reason for its existence. Copies were sent to Agent Pinsonneault, one for each of the chiefs and one to hang on the church door.[66] Alarmed by this development, the chiefs asked to speak to the DIA superintendent general in person, but he refused to see them.

The OIC was drafted without consulting Kahnawà:ke chiefs and was, as a result, poorly considered. The chiefs contacted the department with worries of its dire consequences – that many Kahnawa'kehró:non would no longer have access to firewood. So DIA Deputy Superintendent General Lawrence Vankoughnet asked Agent Pinsonneault if the common areas of the reserve had enough wood to provide for everyone who did not own a woodlot.[67] Pinsonneault assured him that they did and that the supply would last for some years.[68] Only the day before, Thomas Dawes had apprised the DIA of wood shortages in Kahnawà:ke and had asked for clarification of the law concerning wood ownership. "It seems," he wrote, "there is a growing scarcity of timber on the reserve and a consequent quarrelling about it. I would like to know if they possess the timber in common or if any number of them having selected certain portions of land are to have the sole use of the timber on those particular portions to the exclusion of the rest."[69] Dawes had a case before him involving a Kahnawa'kehró:non who had cut wood to build a roof on his outbuilding, whereupon the Kahnawa'kehró:non who owned the property on which the trees were felled took possession of the logs. Dawes had no idea of how to handle the matter, which is why he asked the DIA for guidance.[70] Vankoughnet sent Dawes a copy of the OIC and, echoing the words of Agent Pinsonneault, assured him that "as regards such Indians as have not enough wood on the land they occupy for their domestic use, there is sufficient wood for them on the portion of the Reserve held in Common by the Band."[71]

In February 1876, after having learned about the OIC, Kahnawà:ke chiefs asked the DIA to repeal it. They argued that Kahnawà:ke law had always stipulated that all wood, except maples, could be cut anywhere on the territory. They had

> heard with astonishment and grief that a certain party would have petitioned to the Government of Ottawa and by their instigation a measure would have been adopted in Council that an Indian would no more have right to cut any timber upon the property of another, that the occupant would henceforth have the sole benefit and whoever would infringe the law would incur an enormeous penalty.
>
> Honorable Gentlemen. If it is by pure movement of the Government, we do not blame him in issuing a such an order [the OIC], we like to give him credit that he done is for the greatest benefit of the Tribe; but unfortunately he was not aware of the fatal consequences that would have resulted the the adoption of such measure and the real standing of the Domain, because our usages and habits of cutting wood wherever we find it excepting nevertheless the maple date of time immemorial.[72]

This carefully worded protest gave the DIA the benefit of the doubt, even as it explained in no uncertain terms that the OIC contradicted Kahnawà:ke law. Furthermore, the chiefs argued that the OIC had found favour with only about one-fifth of the population and that many of these people gained access to Kahnawà:ke land under dubious circumstances. Their main point, however, was that regardless of who owned the land the trees belonged to everyone.[73] A few weeks later, after Chiefs Thaioronhiote (Joseph Skye) and Shatekaienton (Louis Beauvais) travelled to Ottawa to make their case in person, Vankoughnet made an exception to the OIC.[74] For the rest of that winter only, Kahnawa'kehró:non would be allowed to cut wood as before (though not maples), but only with the written permission of the landowner. Vankoughnet also suggested that they abandon their long-established habit of cutting wood in the winter and do it during the summer instead. This, according to Vankoughnet, would give the wood time to dry before use – a textbook example of a DIA official believing he had useful advice to offer Indigenous people about how to live on the land.[75]

Meanwhile, Dawes was working with Chief Thaioronhiote to apprehend those who were illegally cutting down trees.[76] As with previous cases, he

had difficulty in getting convictions unless the perpetrators declared themselves guilty. Most of his cases were dismissed, but the court expenses were
paid from Kahnawà:ke funds. Kahnawà:ke, in other words, was required
to pay for the ineffective enforcement of the OIC.[77] In early February,
Dawes asked the DIA to clarify its position on wood and property, on
which he was again sent a copy of the OIC along with a copy of the letter
to Pinsonneault, stating that exceptions would be made this year only.
Evidently, everyone involved was now greatly confused as to whether the
old or the new rules were in effect, and it was not at all clear that breaking
any of them would result in serious negative consequences.

THE ENCLOSURE RUSH OF 1876–77

Since it was unclear which laws now applied to Kahnawà:ke land and
resources, and since no one seemed capable of enforcing them, people
rushed to cut down trees and enclose land with fences. I have employed
my own term, the "enclosure rush," to describe this period. Although
Kahnawa'kehró:non were no longer sure whether woodcutting was governed by their own law or that of Canada, they sensed that the latter would
prevail and acted accordingly. They perceived that the DIA, by way of its
OIC, would recognize the land rights only of those who had individual
claims on particular parcels and that little time remained to lay claim to
whatever parcels were not yet "owned." The traditional way to legally
claim a lot was to clear and cultivate it. Now a number of Kahnawa'kehró:non
realized that the DIA would look favourably on their claim if they also
built a fence around it.

The chiefs were disturbed about the trend of building fences for the
express purpose of claiming land and exclusive rights to trees. Those attempting to bolster their claim to a lot that they already held were building
fences, but so were those who wished to claim a new lot. Kahnawa'kehró:non
recognized that the DIA and its local officials placed great stock in fences
as signifiers of ownership. Dawes reported the following in February 1877:

It seems some of the Indians have been more carefull of their property than
others and have fenced in portions of the reserve for their own use part of
which is under cultivation and part in wood the latter they wish to keep to
use as fuel. Those who have not been so careful are now encroaching on the
others and cutting down this wood for their own use. They say the whole
reserve is owned in common and they have a right to cut down where and

when they please provided they only use for domestic purposes such as fuel &c &c. Will you kindly let me know if those who have fenced in those portions of the land have a right to prevent other Indians from entering upon it and taking away the timber?[78]

In previous years, DIA officials had described wood conflicts in similar terms but had not mentioned fences. Now their presence appeared to bolster, in the eyes of Dawes, an individual's exclusive claim to a lot and its trees. As for his questions regarding fences, the department did not answer directly. A letter from Vankoughnet emphasized that the rules from the year before were still in force, that only those who possessed written permission from landowners might cut wood on their land.[79] Kahnawà:ke had no precedent for claiming land and wood by fencing it, but DIA action and inaction encouraged its residents to adopt the practice. In 1881, the chiefs confirmed that since 1876, all fences built to enclose lots were "for the sole purpose of depriving the community of the wood therefrom."[80]

The most prominent fencing case of the enclosure rush involved part of the lucrative quarry lands in Kahnawà:ke. Commercial quarrying had been under way since at least 1822, but the enlargement of the Lachine Canal prompted a boom during the mid-1870s, and in 1876 between forty and fifty Kahnawà:ke men earned their living in the quarries.[81] That spring, the chiefs leased a portion of the quarry lands to a firm named McNamee, Gaherty and Fréchette, with the approval of the DIA. A Kahnawà:ke man named Ohionkoton (Angus Jacob) claimed that the lot in question was his – that the chiefs had leased it without his permission – and announced that he intended to sue them for damages.[82] The chiefs believed that he had enclosed the land with a makeshift fence only after he knew that it would be leased. According to Agent Pinsonneault, Ohionkoton "has made some improvements on it to the value of $20 to $25. Last year he planted on different places of the quarry on an extent of ¼ of an acre, and he claims the sum of $50 for the extent of 4 acres of uncultivated land."[83] Pinsonneault recounted that Ohionkoton had fenced about five acres next to the quarry and cultivated a portion of it for the first time, harvesting only half a bushel of corn.[84] According to Pinsonneault and the chiefs, Ohionkoton probably knew that the lot was about to be leased and did what he could to claim it and raise its value.

Having cultivated and fenced the lot, Ohionkoton met both the Kahnawà:ke standard for claiming land (clearing and planting) and one of the most important colonial standards (enclosing with a fence). His efforts at farming also bolstered his claim in the eyes of the department because the lot would be classified as "improved." The chiefs rejected his claim and refused to meet his demands, but Pinsonneault suggested that "it might be well to pay him for his improvements in order to prevent any trouble with him."[85] Vankoughnet agreed, asking Pinsonneault to convince the chiefs of the "propriety" of compensating Ohionkoton for his improvements.[86] However, the chiefs refused to do so, probably because they understood that paying compensation would simply generate more such cases. Thus, Ohionkoton made good on his threat, suing the chiefs for five hundred dollars in damages.[87] Neither Pinsonneault nor Chief Taiorakaron thought the lot was worth more than twenty-five dollars.[88] In Pinsonneault's opinion, Ohionkoton was a lazy troublemaker who wanted "money for nothing."[89]

The chiefs offered to pay Ohionkoton fifty dollars to drop the suit, but he refused, holding out for a victory in court. When it seemed that he would prevail, a few others took their cue from him and appropriated portions of quarry land that spring. Pinsonneault felt that they were simply opportunists who had no right whatsoever to the land. He advised that they be dispossessed immediately, especially considering the economic importance of quarry wages and royalties to the community.[90] While Pinsonneault made judgments on the character of the men and the economic impact of their actions, Vankoughnet wanted to know whether Ohionkoton had appropriated the land before or after McNamee, Gaherty and Fréchette signed the lease.[91] In his view, enclosing a piece of common land was illegal only if it had already been leased.

The chiefs claimed to have "strong proof" that Ohionkoton had illegally appropriated the land. According to them, as soon as he heard of their intent to lease it, he encircled the lot with a crude fence of branches. They insisted that the area was not cultivable and that the sole purpose of his quarter acre of planting was to stake his claim. In the days before the trial, they asked the DIA to take the case more seriously, as they were very concerned about the precedent it would set.[92] On September 19, 1877, the court dismissed the action for unknown reasons. However, Kahnawà:ke was still on the hook for more than two hundred dollars in legal fees.[93] Similar enclosures continued after the case was concluded, but Ohionkoton's failure to win meant that the chiefs' worst fears were not realized in this instance.

In the fall of 1876, while the Ohionkoton case was yet before the court, the chiefs petitioned the DIA to have Agent Pinsonneault replaced. They

stated that "he is the author" of the action taken by Ohionkoton in ap-
propriating the quarry lot, which they yet feared "may prove fatal to us."
Unable to "discover a single good act" in Pinsonneault's tenure, they informed the department that "we have dropped him, and no longer consider
him our Agent." Nor had he done enough to ensure that Kahnawa'keh-
ró:non men were hired at the quarry. They warned the DIA that if nothing
were done, it was likely that someone "will make him pass a 'hard time.'"
The chiefs also complained of his "defective education," inability to speak
either English or Kanien'kéha, use of extortion in the quarries, plying
women with liquor to take advantage of them, and letting laden barges
leave without having measured the stone. On the final point, the chiefs
suggested that Pinsonneault was not sufficiently "interested," whereas a
Kahnawa'kehró:non stone measurer "being interested would take more
care."[94] The agent had already been warned by the DIA that his performance was unsatisfactory, and this was the final straw.[95]

Dismissed in February 1877, Pinsonneault was replaced by Georges
Cherrier.[96] Cherrier received a ten-point list on how to do his job, the first
of which read:

> 1. All trespasses should be prevented upon the lands of the Caughnawaga
> Indians whether the same consist in the appropriation by others than mem-
> bers of the Band of locations thereon or by the removal therefrom of wood,
> stone or other materials without the written authority of the Supt. Genl.
> of Indian Affairs, being first had and obtained. You will therefore act with
> promptitude and energy in stopping any attempt at the same and in punish-
> ing the trespassers in the manner provided by law.
>
> With reference to the wood, timber, stone, sand or other material on the
> Reserve, members of the Band have only the right to appropriate such of
> the same as is held in Common, to their own use for domestic purposes,
> but they have no right to sell it; nor can they take any valuables of the above
> or other kinds for domestic use from lands (other than their own locations)
> occupied by individual members of the Band without the written consent
> of the occupant countersigned by you as Agent; and no sugar maples may
> be cut for any purpose whatever by occupants or others.[97]

These paragraphs are a good summary of the department's position on
resource use in Kahnawà:ke at this time and are restatements of the *Indian
Act* and the 1876 OIC in regard to wood, stone, and soil.[98] As Cherrier
began his tenure in February, the height of woodcutting season, he was

immediately faced with complaints of illegal woodcutting. His first letters indicate a steep learning curve, and we observe his further role below.[99]

DIA INTERVENTIONS, 1878–83

The enclosure rush had largely ended by 1878, but conflicts over land continued since it was still unclear what law was in force. The DIA approach was sometimes overbearing and sometimes hesitant but generally inconsistent. Once the weather turned cold in 1878, eighty-seven Kahnawa'kehró:non petitioned the department, complaining about the consequences of the OIC and its approach to solving the land and wood problem. As they explained,

> the proprietors of wood lands have decided to no longer allow us to cut wood on their lots, contrary to our laws existing till about two years ago when the government passed an Order in Council that henceforth the proprietors of wooded lands should alone have the benefit of cutting wood, and this in spite of the protestation of the whole nation.
>
> At present the majority find themselves deprived of this article so useful to a family, as there is no reservation belonging in Common, all being appropriated by enclosing parts with sorts of fences or even branches in places where there is small wood.[100]

The last sentence suggests that most common land (outside the village and common pasture) was now claimed by individuals and enclosed by fences, often only with flimsy structures made from small branches. It is also significant that the petitioners were no longer asking for the OIC to be overturned, but were requesting simply "that every Indian shall have wood for his own use, otherwise great troubles may be anticipated."[101] By this time, they knew that the DIA would not respect Kahnawà:ke law, but since the OIC had deprived them of access to free wood, they asked the DIA to find an alternative solution. No response to the petition is included in the archival file.

The five years following the enclosure rush can be seen as a period of chaotic adjustment, in the sense that Kahnawa'kehró:non were testing the boundaries of the DIA's newly imposed vision of land management. The department also found itself in unfamiliar waters. It was operating rather tentatively under the recently passed *Indian Act* of 1876 and was attempting to impose its will on Kahnawà:ke while maintaining a kind of status quo within the community. In a great many cases related to land, however, the DIA found that the path of least resistance was the path of inaction: if it could avoid making a difficult decision, it usually would, a course that often simply exacerbated the problem. At other times, it made strong and unpopular decisions. It is virtually impossible to discern patterns or logics in the DIA response during this period, but the following cases illustrate the many ways that it chose to intervene – or not – in Kahnawà:ke land conflicts.

Cases of Land Appropriation and Woodcutting, 1878

Although most land outside the village was now enclosed, some people continued to appropriate land in the old way. During the spring of 1878, a man named Taretane (Tom Jacob) "took" and plowed a piece of land claimed by a man named Tewanitasen (Tom 20Months).[102] Tewanitasen claimed that he had owned the land for ten years, and this statement, along with Agent Cherrier's intervention, ensured that the department found in his favour.[103] The key factor for the department was that Tewanitasen was there first, whereas according to Kahnawà:ke law his claim would have been legitimate only if he had recently worked the land. If it lay fallow for longer than three years, Taretane would have been well within his rights to take and use it. Although we do not know whether the land had lain fallow for three years, such cases showed Kahnawa'kehró:non that their law and the authority of the chiefs now counted for very little.

Nevertheless, many Kahnawa'kehró:non also continued to cut wood according to Kahnawà:ke law. Cherrier had been instructed to protect sugar maples under all circumstances, but most Kahnawa'kehró:non saw nothing wrong with cutting maples that were not being tapped. Cherrier was even directed to stop people from felling maples on their own land, although there was no law to that effect anywhere. In January 1878, he confronted some Kahnawa'kehró:non after he noticed loads of green maple logs piled near their dwellings, but they simply laughed at him.[104] For unknown reasons, he did not lay charges. The following winter, he informed the department that many Kahnawa'kehró:non now burned maple wood to heat their homes and that he was ready to lay charges against Karhaienton (Matthew Jocks) for having cut down twelve maples on his own land.[105] When Cherrier asked the DIA where he could find the law under which he could charge Karhaienton, Vankoughnet sent him a copy of the 1876 OIC and a copy of a letter to the previous agent in which he forbade the cutting of maples. Vankoughnet insisted that after reading these, Cherrier would "perceive that it is strictly forbidden that maples shall be cut down or removed from the reserve,"[106] but this was hardly accurate. As noted above, the OIC did not refer to maples, and a DIA letter to an agent did not have the force of law. As in many cases at this time, the DIA hoped that by strongly insisting on a certain course of action, it would convince Kahnawa'kehró:non that there were laws to that effect.

The Case of Sakoraiatakwa

Other Kahnawa'kehró:non tested the new rules by taking actions that were illegal under Kahnawà:ke law but would seem to be legal under the *Indian Act*. Sakoraiatakwa,[107] a former chief, claimed and fenced a piece of land along the Primeau Road in October 1878 but then did nothing with it. Agent Cherrier, perhaps influenced by Kahnawa'kehró:non's sense of injustice concerning someone who claimed land without using it, wrote the department that Sakoraiatakwa's actions were unfair because they deprived poor people of firewood.[108] Surprisingly, the DIA agreed and asked Cherrier to remove him from the lot.[109] This case is another example in which the DIA did not follow its own legislation. There was no clear Canadian legal reason, for example, why Sakoraiatakwa could not appropriate a piece of common land by enclosing it. Several cases from previous years indicated that, as long as his rights were not contested by someone else, the DIA would have recognized his claim. In his case, however, the agent's recommendation regarding wood took precedence. There seems to have been no way that anyone could have predicted this outcome for Sakoraiatakwa.[110]

The Case of Thiretha and Tekaonwake

The DIA was remarkably unpredictable in its responses to cases, sometimes making snap pronouncements and sometimes leaving difficult decisions for the chiefs to handle. One example of the latter came before James P. Dawes in 1879. Dawes, a Lachine industrialist and nephew of the Thomas A. Dawes who appeared earlier in this chapter, had only recently been deputed by the DIA to arbitrate land and wood disputes in Kahnawà:ke. In this case, two men, Thiretha (Peter Diome) and Tekaonwake (Louis Canot), claimed the same piece of land.[111] Thiretha, the occupant at the time, had Tekaonwake arrested for cutting wood on it. In light of their actions in other cases, neither appears to have been a regular DIA supporter;

both opposed DIA interventions in different ways at different times. Agent Cherrier felt that Thiretha was the rightful owner because he had a notarized deed that proved ownership since 1864. Tekaonwake, however, used witness accounts to establish that the lot belonged to him; in fact, people had often asked him for permission to fell trees there. Dawes appealed to the DIA for guidance, but it simply referred the problematic decision to the Kahnawà:ke council of chiefs.[112] In such cases, the department perceived that whatever decision it might make would inevitably turn a large segment of the community against it, so it handed over responsibility to the chiefs. In doing so, it put them in the impossible position of exercising authority only in cases that were destined to damage their standing in Kahnawà:ke. Of course, the DIA could simply have removed the chiefs, but it often chose to exert its power in indirect ways, probably because it feared the consequences if Kahnawa'kehró:non rose up in opposition.

The chiefs decided in favour of Tekaonwake, the man with many witnesses, and against Thiretha, the man with the deed.[113] Cherrier, incensed because they had rejected the party who possessed a contract of sale, thought their decision was due to Thiretha's reputation as a wood-plunderer.[114] The chiefs did describe him as a "well-known plunderer" (*fameux devastateur*) of the forests and referred to the aged Indian agent, "the poor G.E. Cherrier," as easily "dazzled" by old documents.[115] In the end, the department approved the council's decision. As justification, it pointed out that according to Thiretha's deed of sale, the land had been sold by a Kanehsata'kehró:non (Kanien'kehá:ka from Kanehsatà:ke), which made the deed invalid.[116] Had the circumstances been different, the DIA would probably have ignored such a technicality.

The Case of Shorihowane

In the fall of 1881, a Kahnawa'kehró:non named Shorihowane (Louis Leclerc) wrote to Vankoughnet, asking for protection.[117] He had recently cleared and cultivated a portion of the Grand Park (a wetland area on the western side of the reserve today known as the Big Fence), which the chiefs were now demanding that he relinquish. As he explained, he and his large family were so poor that they would starve if the land were taken from them. He could produce four witnesses who would attest that it had been forested and that he had himself cleared and cultivated it.[118] As the case unfolded, it became clear that the chiefs opposed Shorihowane's claim only because he already owned a much larger lot.[119] They offered him fifty dollars to compensate him for his family's move to the other lot and allowed him to sow the land the following summer since he had already plowed it. Shorihowane accepted this arrangement and also agreed to plant the lot in hay before leaving.[120] Vankoughnet accepted the judgment of the chiefs in part because they compensated Shorihowane for his improvements.[121]

In making his claim, Shorihowane seemed particularly adept at navigating both Kahnawà:ke and DIA legal norms. When he wrote to Vankoughnet about clearing the land, he was appealing to the colonial legal right to be compensated for "improvements" made. His claim in terms of Kahnawà:ke law, however, was based on the legal principle that unused land could be claimed by anyone who was willing to work it (Chapter 2).[122] The chiefs did not dispute this right, but they overruled his claim because he already possessed another lot. This was based on the legal principle that individuals could not claim more land than they could work.[123] The case of Shorihowane reveals that both Kahnawà:ke and Canadian legal norms were at play and that Kahnawa'kehró:non had to find a way to navigate both.

The Case of Atianota

Another incident involving land title in the Grand Park area occurred in the spring of 1883, when the DIA was asked for its opinion on a Lachine court case involving Kahnawà:ke. A twenty-seven-year-old Kahnawa'kehró:non named Atianota (Michel Thomas),[124] who had occupied a piece of land for four years, apparently without any previous incidents, brought a legal action against three Kahnawa'kehró:non who cut wood there. Judge J.P. Davies wanted the department's opinion before delivering his verdict on the matter, a request that Agent Cherrier relayed to Vankoughnet.[125] A DIA official then asked Cherrier if Kahnawà:ke chiefs had ever officially located Atianota (assigned him the lot), and the chiefs subsequently passed a resolution stating that they had never permitted Atianota to establish himself on the land in question and that it remained part of the nation's public lands.[126] In light of Kahnawà:ke law until that time, this resolution suggests either that the chiefs had now adapted a more static view of public lands or that Atianota had not adequately proven his claim by clearing and cultivating the land.

In line with the wishes of the chiefs, the DIA advised that Atianota had no valid claim to the land.[127] As in the case of Shorihowane, the department agreed with the chiefs, but not for the same reasons. For the chiefs, the land was part of the Common (probably not the village common but the Grand Park forested area on the western side of the territory), and perhaps Atianota had not claimed it in the customary way by clearing and cultivating it. For its part, the DIA wanted to know whether he possessed legal title according to its own standards, and since he had no documentation to prove his ownership, it agreed that he had no right to stop others from cutting wood there. Two years later, the 1885 Walbank Survey listed him as owning no land.[128]

The Case of Tehowenkarakwen and Edouard DeBlois

In several instances, DIA officials consulted with the Department of Justice regarding the application of the *Indian Act*. One such case in 1877, a year after the *Indian Act* came into force, involved a Kahnawa'kehró:non named Tehowenkarakwen (Michael Delisle), who leased out his farm for two years to a French Canadian named Edouard DeBlois in exchange for a loan of two hundred dollars.[129] According to their contract, DeBlois could sell the farm if Tehowenkarakwen failed to repay his loan by the end of the two years. A merchant who specialized in glass beads, DeBlois had lived in Kahnawà:ke for most of his forty-four years. He held deeds for about fifteen acres of cleared land and thirty-six acres of wooded land, including a sugarbush.[130] His residency permit had been issued in 1874 because he was married to a Kahnawa'kehró:non named Tsawennoseriio (Catherine Desparois).[131] When the two years were up and Tehowenkarakwen defaulted on the loan, DeBlois sold the farm to a Kahnawa'kehró:non named Akwirotonkwas (Tom Phillips).[132] Tehowenkarakwen believed that this was illegal, so he hired a lawyer to bring his case to the attention of the DIA. DeBlois did not have the right to own land on the reserve, but the contract was in the name of his wife, Tsawennoseriio.[133] When the DIA asked the Department of Justice for advice, one of its law clerks stated that, according to section 3 of the 1876 *Indian Act,* Tsawennoseriio had ceased to be an Indian when she married DeBlois. Since section 66 of the *Indian Act* also forbade any person (non-Indian) from taking security from an Indian or offering anything resembling a mortgage to an Indian, the original agreement between DeBlois and Tehowenkarakwen was illegal. In other words, neither DeBlois nor Tsawennoseriio were classified as Indians, and thus neither had the right to own Kahnawà:ke land or to take property from an Indian who had defaulted on a loan. The clerk suggested that the farm should revert to Tehowenkarakwen and that he should pay DeBlois what he owed.[134] But the DIA took no action, the land remained in the hands of Akwirotonkwas, and the problem did not go away.

Tehowenkarakwen complained again in 1879. This time, aside from arguing that DeBlois had no right to sell the farm, he added that it was worth nearly three times more than DeBlois's selling price. DeBlois defended himself, saying that according to his contract with Tehowenkarakwen, the land would become his if the loan were not repaid in two years and that his occupation permit gave him the right to own land in Kahnawà:ke. He suggested that Tehowenkarakwen was pursuing the malicious strategy of deliberately defaulting on the loan and that he was an alcoholic who drank away all of his money.[135] Vankoughnet informed Cherrier that DeBlois's permit did not allow for landownership and instructed the agent to dispossess him on that basis.[136] However, after Cherrier reminded Vankoughnet that DeBlois had played an important role in the community (without specifying what was meant), the matter was dropped.[137] The DIA did not acknowledge Akwirotonkwas, the current occupant, as the legitimate owner of the lot, but it recognized that he had paid DeBlois and was in possession of the bill of sale. Thus, when Tehowenkarakwen offered Akwirotonkwas $280 to get his land back, the department advised him to accept it.[138] This is a fine example of the DIA attempting to resolve conflicts through compromises that had little to do with the law. According to the *Indian Act,* all the transactions in question were illegal, and the farm should simply have reverted to Tehowenkarakwen. But instead of insisting on that course, the department attempted to find a compromise that would resolve a specific difficulty without stirring up any larger problems.

The Case of Léon Giasson versus Tekaonwake

In many cases that involved white settlers illegally occupying land in Kahnawà:ke, the DIA chose to do nothing. One such case was reported by Agent Cherrier in the winter of 1880–81, when land-poor Kahnawa'kehró:non spent several days felling about three hundred maples and other trees on land claimed by a French Canadian named Léon Giasson.[139] Giasson had a residency permit from the DIA, which did not include the right to own land, but like many others in his position, he had claimed or purchased it anyway and had come to see himself as a Kahnawa'kehró:non with land rights. When he tried to stop the woodcutters, they threatened him with their axes.[140] Cherrier, who supported Giasson's cause, did not mention in his correspondence with the DIA that Giasson and his wife, Lumina Mallette, were not Kahnawa'kehró:non (he later claimed they were); he said only that they were among those who wanted to preserve their wood and had always set a good example to "the Indians."[141]

Cherrier identified the leader of the woodcutters as Shatekaienton, one of the chiefs who had travelled to Ottawa in 1876 to protest the OIC.[142] Confusingly, the department instructed Cherrier to warn all Kahnawa'kehró:non that lawbreakers would be prosecuted while also informing him that the Giassons were French Canadians who had no right to wood on the reserve.[143]

In response to Cherrier's reports of widespread maple cutting the previous winter, and specifically to the pleas of the Giasson family, the DIA had an Order-in-Council on maple cutting passed in the summer of 1881. The department had long claimed that the provisions of the *Indian Act* (along with the 1876 OIC forbidding the cutting of wood on another's land) were adequate protection for landowners, but this was obviously not the case. The new OIC specifically targeted maple cutting, stating that "no Indian or other person may ... cut, carry away, or remove ... any hard or sugar maple tree or sapling," without the consent of the Indian agent. The OIC did not differentiate between maples growing on private land and those on common land.[144] It may seem surprising that a government dedicated to the implementation of private property rights would so severely restrict the rights of landowners, but it makes sense in light of the department's inability to use existing legislation to press charges against woodcutters.[145]

In the fall of 1881, Léon Giasson had Tekaonwake arrested and charged with trespassing and taking wood without permission.[146] He may have chosen this course because the DIA had not ruled in his favour earlier that year. The Lachine magistrates found Tekaonwake guilty and sentenced him to prison, but he appealed to the Court of Queen's Bench, where the ruling was overturned. The magistrates ruled that he could not be condemned, because Léon Giasson did not have a location ticket and "therefore [had] no legal title or right to occupy the lands upon which the pretended offence recited in said conviction was committed."[147] Following this unfavourable decision, Giasson asked the DIA for a location ticket, to have the trees on his land protected in the short term, and to have his considerable legal expenses covered by band funds. Quoting the Superior Court's verdict that he had no legal title to the land, he asserted that this was unjust – his title was beyond dispute, "if not legally at least by implication like that of all the other occupants in good faith." Giasson also cited section 28 of the 1880 *Indian Act*, which prohibited trespassing on the land of anyone who possessed "a title of occupation or is otherwise recognized by the Department as occupant of such land." Clearly, this clause could include landholders who did not possess a location ticket. If the judgment of the Superior Court were to be accepted, Giasson warned, "no Indian at Caughnawaga would have the right to protect land occupied by him against the trespassing of another whilst it is a fact that no ticket of occupation 'Location Ticket' has been issued at any time for the Caughnawaga Reserve."[148] Giasson's letter did not mention that he was a non-Indian with a residency permit, a status that should have precluded him from owning land in Kahnawà:ke. When the DIA asked the Department of Justice if the court decision could be appealed in a higher court, it was informed that judgments rendered by the Court of Queen's Bench could not be appealed.[149] Léon Giasson had a number of enemies in Kahnawà:ke, a fact that was probably not unrelated to his irregular landownership and frequent legal actions against neighbours. In the five years preceding this case, he had prosecuted four different Kahnawà:ke men more than twenty times, and he won every time. In each case, the men were fined but were unable to pay, so the costs were covered by the funds of the band. This meant that whenever someone was arrested for taking wood, the community was collectively punished.[150] Giasson employed the trope of the lawless savage when he warned that the precedent set by his lost case would further embolden Kahnawa'kehró:non to help themselves to wood wherever they pleased and that the primary victims would be innocent landowners like himself.[151] The DIA seems to have been unaware that Giasson was a non-Indian with a residency permit, and he spoke about himself as if he had the same rights as Kahnawa'kehró:non.[152]

Giasson was not alone in warning the DIA about what might happen if Kahnawa'kehró:non were not stopped from cutting wood on others' land. Cherrier forwarded letters to the DIA from two other "principal members of the band" in November 1881.[153] The two men, Karonhiaktatie (Jean-Baptiste Jacques) and Kanatsohare (Thomas Patton), submitted a statement to the effect that they owned land "by uncontestable titles" on which they had been growing some small trees "since the existence of our new laws." This statement implies that they would not have tried to grow trees had it not been for the 1876 and 1881 Orders-in-Council. They complained that certain individuals were cutting their trees, the same people who "sold and devastated whole forests." They asked for the application of the *Indian Act,* section 17, which specified the punishment for Indians who trespassed.[154] Both of these men were dismayed about the precedent set by the Court of Queen's Bench ruling on Léon Giasson, since it had been based on his lack of a location ticket. Because the idea of a location ticket was new, and none had been issued in Kahnawà:ke so far, they feared that they would be unable to protect trees on land they claimed.[155] By this time, the DIA had realized that the OICs would not be effective without a comprehensive land survey. Thus, it did not address the immediate fears of these landowners, focusing its energy instead on having the land surveyed (Chapter 6).

The Case of Otseroniaton and Thohenton versus Harhontonkwas

DIA attempts to remake landownership and impose its own law caused unforeseen problems that were difficult to solve and very confusing for the people involved. One 1878 case that illustrates this point is when two men named Otseroniaton (Peter Jacob) and Thohenton blocked the road leading to the farm of Harhontonkwas (Angus Deer).[156] As a result, Harhontonkwas could not work his land. He claimed he had been using the road for twenty-five years.[157] Both the chiefs and the DIA agreed that the blockade should come down,[158] but the DIA believed that it could not legally enforce this view. In its opinion, as the chiefs of Kahnawà:ke had not passed a bylaw on the matter, there was no way to make the men dismantle their barricade. This was an early DIA reference to the need for bylaws, which is the language of the 1876 *Indian Act.* However, the act refers to the bylaws passed by a band council, and Kahnawà:ke would not have this form of government until a decade later. Thus, since the DIA was not particularly interested in addressing individual problems such as this roadblock, Kahnawa'kehró:non had few legal options in resolving such problems as long as they did not have the form of government specified by the *Indian Act.* Nevertheless, despite the absence of any law to that effect, Cherrier was instructed to order removal of the barricade. Archival documents do not provide the end of the story.

Cases Showing the Influence of the Indian Agent

Several of the cases discussed above show how influential the Indian agent could be in determining DIA decisions. The outcome of many cases could be greatly shaped by the way the agent presented them to the department. A case to demonstrate this point arose in November 1881 when Otsitsatakon (Michel Martin) and his father burned underbrush on a lot they intended to cultivate.[159] They also seemed to have offered the trees to anyone who was willing to cut them. Agent Cherrier ordered them to stop, giving as his reason that Otsitsatakon was not interested in the wood and wanted only to cultivate the land, which Otsitsatakon readily admitted.[160] Although he had no need for the wood and told the DIA that he would gladly let others take it, Cherrier interpreted this as laziness. He also complained that Otsitsatakon had fenced the property, thus depriving poor residents of firewood, which made little sense in light of his desire for others to take the wood.[161] Evidently, no one else had claimed the lot, which made it available for cultivation according to Kahnawà:ke law. Nor did the *Indian Act* prevent Otsitsatakon from fencing a parcel of common land. On the basis of Cherrier's intervention, however, the DIA agreed that Otsitsatakon must be made to desist. Although Cherrier claimed that he was concerned for the poor, it is likely that Otsitsatakon's fencing was interfering with his own illegal pasturing on the reserve, which would come to the attention of the DIA in 1883.[162] There is no indication that Otsitsatakon's actions transgressed either the provisions of the *Indian Act* or Kahnawà:ke law; nor did he construct his fence for the purpose of keeping others from gaining access to firewood. Nevertheless, the DIA accepted Cherrier's counsel (without consulting the chiefs) and refused to allow Otsitsatakon to take possession of the lot in a lawful way.[163]

The Indian agent also played a key role in directing the effort to regulate land transactions. In October 1878, Cherrier reported that "some abuses exist among the Indians in their transactions, which have disastrous consequences."[164] According to him, certain unscrupulous notaries visited Kahnawà:ke to draw up notarial conveyances in exchange for high fees. To him, this was evidence that "many Indians are victims either by their ignorance or through the want of good advice," as the documents were of little or no legal value.[165] This is quite rich coming from Cherrier, who had a reputation among the chiefs for placing great stock in such documents,[166] and he would have known that they often gave the claimant a definitive advantage.

To further his point, Cherrier relayed the story of a man named Sonowonhesse, who borrowed fifteen dollars from a man named Kanonwatase (Louis Beauvais).[167] Sonowonhesse gave Kanonwatase the deed to his land as collateral for the loan. When he defaulted, Kanonwatase demanded that he pay five dollars in interest every month until he was able to pay the entire amount. Cherrier said that such cases were very common. This example certainly illustrates the possible problems associated with an unregulated system of deeds in the context of legal and political uncertainty, but Cherrier believed that the solution lay in creating a land registry to be managed by the Indian agent. This would give him the information and power to prevent fraudulent transactions.[168] The DIA approved his suggestion and asked him to present it to the chiefs, as they were authorized under the *Indian Act* of 1876 to establish such a registry.[169] The chiefs, however, had no interest in handing over this kind of power to the agent, and no registry was established until years later.

Conclusions regarding DIA Interventions, 1878–83

As a whole, these cases reveal that by about 1880, the government and laws of Kahnawà:ke had been destabilized to the point that there was no effective government. And the new source of authority, the rather chaotic Department of Indian Affairs, was unprepared and under-resourced. The *Indian Act* was on the books, but the DIA did not know how to implement it and was continually discovering new ways in which the act did not meet its needs. Nevertheless, the department showed no interest in Kahnawà:ke law or in supporting the chiefs as they attempted to lead their community and resolve problems. It consulted with the chiefs in some cases, though not in others, and even when it did accept the chiefs' decision it justified this in terms of its own bureaucratic, colonial logic. The department saw Kahnawà:ke as legally under the *Indian Act,* even though the community had not agreed to it, and the act was clearly unenforceable and inappropriate. The two Orders-in-Council (1876 and 1881) proved ineffective as well. Even the DIA realized that few colonial laws would be effective until lots had been surveyed and location tickets issued, yet Kahnawa'kehró:non were provided with no legal certainty in the meantime.

In the absence of Canadian laws that made sense for the Kahnawà:ke context, the department often resorted to extra-legal measures, such as insisting that the agent act outside of the law. Its response to land conflicts was so inconsistent that most Kahnawa'kehró:non had no way of knowing what to expect from it. Sometimes it followed the precedents established in similar situations of the past. Sometimes it did not. Sometimes it consulted the chiefs, but often it did not. Sometimes it asked the agent to act outside of the law, but at other times the agent himself made this request of the department. Overall, the DIA presented itself as the source of law and order, and Kahnawa'kehró:non as lawless, unreasonable people – but the evidence suggests quite the opposite. The department actively undermined Kahnawà:ke leaders and laws but could not provide a viable alternative. In the meantime, Kahnawa'kehró:non had no way of predicting how the department would react if they plowed a field or cut down a tree, and the high cost of the many court cases was largely borne by the Kahnawà:ke public, which no longer controlled its own money.

A TEMPORARY WOODLOT

By the spring of 1881, the chiefs understood that the DIA could not be relied on to ensure that Kahnawa'kehró:non had access to firewood and that it would not support any such request from themselves. They decided to take matters into their own hands. Calling a general assembly, they asked the community for the authority to pass laws on wood. A majority voted that the chiefs "be empowered to pass whatever measures, concerning the wood, they seem proper." The chiefs immediately gave every community member the right to cut any trees (except maples) anywhere on the territory, including on fenced lots.[170] This was simply a restatement and reassertion of Kahnawà:ke law as it had been articulated throughout the century. In taking this step, Kahnawa'kehró:non chose to acknowledge the authority of their chiefs and the legitimacy of their own legal order. The resolution of the chiefs, delivered to Ottawa in person by Chief Shatekaienton, reads thus:

> Considering the scarcity of fuel to a great number of our Indians, who are not holders of wooded lots, in consequence of the provisions of the law prohibiting them to cut any wood either on the ground pertaining to individuals who deny them the use of said wood taking benefit of the law favouring them; resulting grave inconveniences in many cases by the incarceration of our warriors, and entailing thereby considerable expenses of our funds.
>
> That in future until further orders be it permitted to our Indians to cut any wood standing or on the ground in whatever place be found, either on lots fenced within ten years, as these fences being constructed since eighteen hundred and seventy six for the sole purpose of depriving the community of the wood therefrom, excepting always the cutting down of sugar maple trees.[171]

Fences built before 1876, according to the chiefs, served legitimate purposes, but most fences constructed after that could be legally disregarded.

Alarmed by this turn of events, which threatened DIA power, Agent Cherrier argued that if the department allowed the decision to stand, more disputes would inevitably follow. Reaching for familiar settler colonial and capitalist tropes, he claimed that Kahnawa'kehró:non who lacked access to firewood were irresponsible and wasteful. In his view, the only solution was to establish a woodlot to provide for those who needed firewood.[172] The DIA approved the idea and asked him to set up the woodlot with the help of at least one chief.[173] The next winter (1881–82), Cherrier and Chiefs Taiorakaron and Asennase (Thomas Deer) decided that the woodlot would be a piece of land owned by Thiretha.[174] Why Thiretha would agree to this is uncertain, but perhaps the lot in question was the one that the chiefs had awarded to Tekaonwake in 1879, from which he had never been evicted (see page 148). Perhaps the woodlot scheme was a compromise agreement in which he was allowed to keep the lot if he permitted others to cut trees there.[175] Setting up a community woodlot was not customary practice, but it was a temporary way to give people access to firewood. The woodlot solution was used for some time, and chiefs continued to designate a disputed lot as a place for community woodcutting each winter. For example, in the winter of 1883–84, they decided that a lot claimed by both Shatekaronhies and Thiretha would be a public woodlot.[176] They did the same for a lot claimed by both Satekaronies (also known as Arene Daillebout or Antoine Shatehoronhies) and the heirs of Ononkwatkowa.[177] This practice reveals that Kahnawa'kehró:non could not count on the DIA to prioritize their needs but that they were sometimes able to force its hand. Although the public woodland, as implemented, was probably not the preferred solution of most Kahnawa'kehró:non, it was a solution that was actually useful and at least consonant with Kahnawà:ke traditions.

CONCLUSION

The actions of Kahnawà:ke leaders show that they were determined to protect the best interests of their community even if they had to find ways of working around the unpredictability, inaction, and active harm of the DIA. In the wake of their failure to relocate the community, the chiefs tried multiple creative responses to the DIA challenge to their authority. At times they were careful and accommodating – at other times they were strident and combative. But they always insisted on their sovereignty over their lands and opposed uninvited Canadian intervention in their affairs. The 1870s represent a sea change for the chiefs and the DIA in the everyday lives of Kahnawa'kehró:non, as well as in the relationship between Kahnawa'kehró:non and their land. Every revision of Indian law gave the department more power and new ways to undermine Indigenous leaders. Kahnawà:ke law and the council of chiefs were still in place but on ever shakier ground. Chiefs had greater difficulty asserting their authority in matters of citizenship and land management, and they could no longer spend money according to their own priorities. Population growth throughout the region produced land and wood shortages, which were then significantly exacerbated by a destructive, asymmetrical contest between two legal orders. The final DIA pressure tactic was a refusal to confirm new chiefs to replace most chiefs who died throughout the 1880s.[178] By 1887, the three remaining elderly chiefs had been deemed incapable of fulfilling their duties, and soon afterward the DIA imposed an elected band council to replace them (Chapter 7).

The initial spark of the conflicts described in this chapter was often provided by a few large landowners who wanted to have property rights like white people. In particular, they wanted the right to keep others from cutting wood on their lands. The DIA responded by insisting on existing legislation and passing Orders-in-Council to impose its own view of landownership. It was so inconsistent and so unpredictable that Kahnawa'kehró:non had little legal certainty or recourse. By the 1880s, DIA actions and strategic indifference had led to the elimination of most common-property resources and had made it virtually impossible for Kahnawà:ke chiefs to govern. However, in the absence of surveyed boundaries between lots, the department still had no way of effectively imposing its law. Nor had location tickets been issued, which meant that land was held on the basis of witness testimony or an assortment of deeds and conveyances. More radical and intrusive DIA moves were yet to come: land surveys are the subject of the next chapter. The 1880 *Indian Act* allowed the department to authorize land surveys, including subdivision surveys, without the approval of the community, and Kahnawà:ke was one of its first targets.[179]

6

"Equal to an Ordnance Map of the Old Country"

The Walbank Survey, 1880–93

onen se8ensionson watkeri8aserako kenon8es nii tsi niio tsi
8akien iate katenninons nakonwentsia [Now you gentlemen:
I answer. I like the way that I have. I do not sell my land].

— *Ohionkoton (Angus Jacob), 1885*

In the late nineteenth century, the Canadian state implemented one of the largest land enclosure projects in world history on the Great Plains. The lands and resources of the northern Prairies had been a commons, largely governed by Indigenous law and shared between nations through international agreements.[1] The enclosure of the Prairies, and indeed the entire continent, transformed common lands and resources into private property and transferred Indigenous land to (mostly) white men.[2] The 1885 uprising against the Canadian state in what is today Saskatchewan can be seen, in the words of economic historian Irene Spry, as "a last despairing attempt to protect the commons" on which Indigenous people depended.[3] Although some scholars falsely characterize common-property regimes as particularly prone to environmental over-exploitation, users of commons have historically tend to carefully regulate their actions to ensure sustainable use.[4] While First Nations lost nearly everything to this enclosure and were intentionally excluded from newly imposed property rights, settlers claimed the spoils and benefitted from the newly imposed colonial legal order. The ecological and cultural catastrophes of this period (the collapse of bison herds being the most spectacular and tragic) were not primarily due to the introduction of horses and guns but to the large influx of settlers who did not care about Indigenous law and to colonizing powers that facilitated their progress with surveyors, police, and railways.[5]

How were commons transformed into private property, and how were Indigenous lands transferred to white people? Most such transformations involved a period of disordered, dysfunctional legal pluralism. Chaotic social, political, and environmental conditions marked the transition from common to private property in many colonial contexts, including the one described in the previous chapter. *The Laws and the Land* is not primarily about the ways in which white people took Indigenous lands, though the subject is addressed; it is instead the story of a fraught transition from common to private land and resource tenure under the *Indian Act.* This chapter focuses on the most concerted effort by the DIA to complete the transition it had tentatively begun during the 1870s in Kahnawà:ke.

The words "commons" and "enclosure" are European in origin, but Indigenous peoples throughout northeastern North America employ a term to describe similar phenomena: the Dish with One Spoon. The Rotinonhsión:ni Confederacy itself was based on the principle that the founding nations would peacefully share the "dish" of their fields and hunting territories. Peace agreements between the confederacy and other nations also used this metaphor to express the way in which they would harmoniously share a territory and its bounty, and the Kaianerehkó:wa, the Great Law of Peace, also focuses on it.[6] Given that Indigenous nations invest themselves so deeply in the diplomatic and political language of peaceful sharing, it should come as no surprise that around the world their critiques of colonialism zero in on the unwillingness of Europeans to accommodate, tolerate, and share.[7]

This chapter discusses the Walbank Survey of the 1880s, a DIA attempt to radically transform Kahnawà:ke land and people, and to make them more visible to the state. Unique in Canadian history, the survey was a government project whose purpose was to completely redistribute reserve lands that were already fully claimed and occupied. New reserves on the Prairies were subdivided around the same time, but these subdivisions were conducted after Prairie lands had already been symbolically and legally enclosed, and thus did not involve the elimination of well-established Indigenous property regimes on the reserves themselves. The settler invasion had already all but eliminated the possibility of traditional ways of life before the reserves were subdivided. As we have seen, however, Kahnawà:ke at this time was a community of between one and two thousand people whose ancestors had occupied and worked a territory of some twelve thousand acres for more than two hundred years (for time immemorial, if one considers hunting territories and villages in the region). It had its own well-established laws concerning land management. With the Walbank Survey, the DIA's goal was to coercively "simplify" legal and environmental relationships, meaning that the state would be able to make sense of Kahnawà:ke through its own bureaucratic, capitalist logic.[8] This approach damaged Kahnawà:ke, its people, and land in ways that were both intentional and unintentional, but this chapter also shows how Kahnawa'kehró:non responded to these incursions.

As used in this chapter, "enclosure" does not necessarily refer to the literal installation of fences but to the construction of a market in discrete, bounded parcels of land to the detriment of a non-commercial regime that favoured the well-being of the entire community. In using this word, I make implicit comparisons with the enclosures of the British countryside that began during the eighteenth century and with similar processes later carried out around the world. In Britain, wealthy landowners used enclosure to dispossess peasants who owned land by customary tenure and to overturn ancient rights to common lands. Evicted from their farms, peasants became wage labourers. Their customary rights were based on unwritten laws, the result of centuries of local traditions, practices, beliefs, and norms.[9] Historian E.P. Thompson notes that the first attacks on the English commons did not come from legal enclosures but were related to the growth of towns and cities, which increased the demand for fuel and building materials, and rapidly raised the value of quarries, peat bogs, and gravel pits.[10] Through the efforts of landowners who wished to remove peasants from their lands, parliament extinguished most common rights between 1750 and 1850.[11] During this period, English elites denigrated the peasants with the same language that was used to disparage and dispossess North American Indigenous peoples: lazy, wild, uncontrollable, poverty-stricken, and inexplicably content with their situation.[12] The history of the British Empire can be understood as a global enclosure movement in which land that had been governed under Indigenous law was transformed into lots owned in fee simple, to the detriment of Indigenous nations.[13]

THE WALBANK BOUNDARY SURVEY

Compared to many Indigenous communities in Canada, which faced military invasion and other crises, Kahnawà:ke was a relatively stable and prosperous place in the early 1880s. But the decade was also marked by intensifying and interrelated incursions into Kahnawà:ke lives and lands. Kahnawa'kehró:non experienced territorial invasion in the form of the Canadian Pacific Railway (CPR) bridge and line, political invasion in the imposed band council system, and cadastral invasion in the form of the Walbank Survey, the focus of this chapter. Whereas Kahnawa'kehró:non who experienced these kinds of threats in the 1860s and 1870s had made plans to move the community to a distant location (Chapter 4), most Kahnawa'kehró:non of the 1880s no longer considered this option. In fact, all of these invasions hardened the resolve among Kahnawa'kehró:non to defend their nation and lands, maintain their distinct identity, and resist outside attempts to eliminate their way of life.

An important concern of Kahnawa'kehró:non throughout the 1860s and 1870s was the shortage of firewood, as well as the legal changes that would deprive poor people of this vital energy source (Chapter 5). By the 1880s, firewood was scarce and expensive in Kahnawà:ke, and the situation was becoming increasingly severe. Due to this lack of fuel, Agent Cherrier said that many of Kahnawà:ke's poorest were wintering in the United States. He also identified the shortage as the root cause of the barn burnings, since the arsonists targeted people whom most Kahnawa'kehró:non saw as non-Indians with no right to live there. To Cherrier and other DIA officials, the blame lay squarely with defective Kahnawà:ke governance, primitive customs, and obstructionist individuals. Since the problem was located squarely within the community, the solution had to come from the outside – a typical colonial approach. According to Cherrier:

> These periodical disasters show the necessity for introducing changes in the tenure of the Seigniory. The system of [the] community which was well enough formerly is out of date. A great number of the Indians being jealous and lazy, always look with an evil eye on those who are prospering, even amongst those of their nation, and will be led to regard the goods and earnings of others as their own.[14]

Cherrier here packs his sentences with racist stereotypes: Indigenous people are lazy, jealous, opposed to progress, savage, hopeless on their own, and sinfully small-minded and selfish in the context of their primitive communitarianism. The DIA had long planned to carry out a subdivision survey to accomplish "changes in the tenure of the Seigniory." It knew it had little support among Kahnawa'kehró:non, but it never intended to respect their views. Racist stereotypes repeated ad nauseam in departmental correspondence ensured that only the dominant settler colonial viewpoint would be taken seriously.

The chiefs consistently opposed a cadastral survey (survey of lot boundaries) of Kahnawà:ke territory because they knew that it would be used to diminish their sovereignty. However, they frequently asked for a boundary survey, as this would help to define the border around unconceded parts of their territory, which had been left undefined for so long that nobody knew exactly how much land had been taken by unscrupulous settler neighbours.[15] In the past, the chiefs had directly asked the DIA for a boundary survey; in other cases the Indian agent had requested the survey on their behalf. In 1874, Agent Joseph Pinsonneault wrote:

> Permit me to draw your attention to the boundary line between the Caughnawaga Indian Reserve and the Whites. Many Indians who have land in the vicinity of the Whites, complain that they encroach on their lands; and as no boundary line can be found it is desirable that such a line should be established, so that the Whites should not encroach on their lands.[16]

The DIA at the time agreed to initiate a boundary survey, but only in the context of a subdivision survey, an idea the chiefs soundly rejected. In April 1880, the Kahnawà:ke council of chiefs once again asked for a boundary survey, "that the lines of our property and of the Canadians which adjoins ours should be revised because it has been reported for many years that these neighbors have encroached on our land."[17]

By the nineteenth century, two-thirds of the seigneury created in 1680 (Chapter 1) had been conceded to white farmers, and its border had been modified a number of times, rarely in favour of Kahnawa'kehró:non.[18] Kahnawà:ke leaders often raised their concerns with colonial officials about illegal concessions and other settler incursions, and they sent several delegations to London to seek support on the issue. With the abolition of the seigneurial system in 1854 and the 1860 cadastre abrégé of the Seigneury of Sault Saint-Louis, conceded land was eventually turned into freehold tenure and legally detached from Kahnawà:ke, an action that Kahnawa'kehró:non have contested ever since. Aside from the conceded seigneurial land lost after 1854, the integrity of this subsequent boundary was also a serious issue because of gradual encroachment by neighbouring farmers. The DIA finally agreed to conduct the boundary survey in 1880 but not before asking one more time if the chiefs also wanted the reserve itself to be surveyed and subdivided. The chiefs again declined.[19] Announcing tenders for the boundary survey in June 1880, the department accepted the bid of William McLea Walbank, provincial land surveyor. On August 12, he and his staff were in the field.[20] Walbank's initial contract was to run the boundary survey, but it became clear later that the department intended to have Walbank also do the cadastral and subdivision surveys, against the wishes of the chiefs and most in the community.

Walbank (1856–1909) was born in St. John's, Newfoundland, the son of Matthew William Walbank, a lawyer and Conservative member of the Newfoundland House of Assembly. The younger Walbank studied architecture and civil engineering at Queen's University in Ireland and graduated from McGill University in Montreal in 1877 with a degree in civil and mechanical engineering. He spent his adult life in Montreal, where he worked as an architect, engineer, and land surveyor. Walbank would later be involved in efforts to develop hydro-electric power generation at the Lachine Rapids.[21] At the start of the boundary survey, he was twenty-four years old.

In December 1880, Walbank declared all field operations for the boundary survey complete and submitted his final report.[22] He complained that the survey had been difficult for a number of reasons, first of which was the lack of relevant maps. He had searched high and low for a reliable map or field notes on the boundary but could find none. He concluded that none had ever been made. His second complaint concerned the hostility of white farmers who had gradually taken land from Kahnawa'kehró:non over many decades. Since "the ground had been in possession of the families of the settlers for over one hundred years ... they were loath to give us any information respecting its limits," wrote Walbank. He lamented that the farmers were "willing to swear anything advantageous to them."[23] He had no complaints about Kahnawa'kehró:non resistance to his work. They desired a defined boundary line, and their white neighbours did not. It would seem, then, that they scored a small victory in finally achieving a survey of their external borders, but it was later revealed that Walbank had run only parts of the boundary line. In 1895, DIA land surveyor W.A. Austin wrote that Walbank had failed to submit adequate documentation related to the boundary survey and that he had admitted to leaving the work unfinished due to conflicts with interested parties.[24] Thus, Walbank did not do the job he had been contracted to do, and departmental officials allowed that to happen. The boundary survey was not of much interest to the DIA, and it would quickly become evident that it was just a warm-up for the cadastral and subdivision surveys it intended to impose on Kahnawà:ke. Meanwhile, the undefined boundary would continue to cause problems for Kahnawa'kehró:non.

After claiming to have completed the boundary survey, Walbank suggested that the next logical step was subdividing the entire reserve and that he was well placed to carry out this task. It is very likely that Walbank had taken the job knowing that it would ultimately also include the subdivision. He believed that such a project would be in the interest of "civilizing" Kahnawa'kehró:non, but he warned that since they had not yet reached that level of development, they could not be trusted with full property rights.[25] In this way, Walbank repeated the racist dogma of the DIA as justification for whatever he would do next.

LEADUP TO THE DIA SUBDIVISION SURVEY

The fact that Kahnawa'kehró:non were generally opposed to surveying and subdividing their territory should not be construed as indicating that they were unfamiliar with the concepts. Seigneurial land concessions were a kind of territorial subdivision, and Kahnawa'kehró:non were aware that these concessions were responsible for the loss of most of their land. Already in 1839, Superintendent of Indian Affairs Duncan C. Napier had raised the idea of subdivision. He made an offer to Kahnawà:ke leaders to have the territory divided into thirty- to fifty-arpent lots, one for each "head of family." The chiefs and members of the council refused, saying that this would have been feasible only when the land was still largely forested and not yet claimed by individuals. Even if the subdivision had been technically possible, the chiefs objected to it on the basis that it would lead to territorial loss and land degradation.[26] The response of the chiefs also shows their concern for maintaining the integrity of the territory and nation.

A similar idea for subdivision was raised in an 1856 petition by a handful of Kahnawa'kehró:non who wanted the right to cut and sell Kahnawà:ke wood to white people. Indian Agent Édouard-Narcisse Delorimier made it clear that theirs was a minority opinion and that such a project would be a great misfortune for Kahnawa'kehró:non. Nothing came of the request.[27] In the 1870s, a number of the largest landowners again petitioned for a cadastral survey in Kahnawà:ke, but their requests were only for surveys to define existing property boundaries, not to establish new ones (subdivision). There is no evidence that anyone in Kahnawà:ke ever asked for a subdivision survey. Nevertheless, the DIA informed the chiefs in 1874 that a subdivision was in the works.[28] The chiefs sent two representatives to Ottawa to ask for details and "to ascertain if that provision will be better for the management of our affairs, than what we shall decide upon."[29] The department answered: "Provided the Indians desire it, the Reserve will be surveyed into farm lots so that each family may have a homestead farm with regular boundary lines. If the Indians have any propositions relative to this matter, they should submit them to the Superintendent General by letter."[30] The principal chiefs sent the DIA a powerfully worded response, stating that they had a duty to protect and represent those who would suffer most from a subdivision, the poor majority. The lots created by a subdivision, they argued, would be small and of uneven quality, and with the loss of the common wood and pasture resources the community would no longer be viable.[31]

In February 1878, in the middle of a cold winter and a wood shortage exacerbated by both DIA action and inaction, Agent Cherrier informed the department that he now had the names of sixty Kahnawa'kehró:non who supported a subdivision. He noted that the only people who favoured it did not possess land and now could no longer cut wood on the lots of others.[32] The subdivision scheme was floated again in 1880, this time by James P. Dawes, the Lachine industrialist whom the DIA had hired to arbitrate Kahnawà:ke wood disputes (Chapter 5). He was frustrated by his inability to settle the disputes and attributed his failure to the lack of defined lots.[33] Walbank made the same suggestion while working on the boundary survey, saying that a subdivision survey "could now be done very cheaply in connection with our survey."[34] Indeed, the DIA fully intended to go forward with a subdivision survey after the boundary survey was complete but worried about the reaction of Kahnawa'kehró:non. DIA solicitor Zebulon A. Lash wrote to Dawes that subdividing the reserve would be "rather a difficult matter to arrange as the Reserve has been allowed to remain unsurveyed so long that it will no doubt cause considerable dissatisfaction when some of the land held by the present occupants is taken from them and given to others desirous of cultivating land but not having any to cultivate."[35] Not mentioned here are the very real difficulties encountered by Kahnawa'kehró:non who had to deal with the fallout of DIA actions. The department showed no concern about this. But even from its colonial viewpoint, Lash's observation that the subdivision survey would be "rather a difficult matter" was an understatement, as Walbank would soon learn.

Why was the DIA so intent on subdivision? It publicly offered various reasons, and I have also identified a number of others on which it was less forthcoming. The DIA made five motivations known: poor Kahnawa'kehró:non land use, lack of protection for property owners, inability to resolve land conflicts, inegalitarian land distribution, and the need for enfranchisement. The first point suggested that Indigenous people let the land go to waste – that they did not exploit its full potential. This convenient argument was used against Indigenous peoples around the world to supposedly justify their dispossession and is still employed today. Non-Indigenous farmers and urbanites have long dismissed Indigenous agriculture as disorganized, irrational, and wasteful.[36] The idea that Indigenous people were inefficient farmers also related to their portrayal as lazy, drunken, and uncivilized.[37] These were powerful rhetorical tools for those who benefitted from such caricatures, including land-rich Kahnawa'kehró:non and white residents of Kahnawà:ke, who depicted themselves as simply wanting to farm and make a living, and their neighbours as wasteful, spiteful, violent, and irrational. Dawes suggested in 1880 that more and more land on the reserve was being cultivated, that "most of the respectable" Indians wanted to go into agriculture more extensively, and that a subdivision survey was needed to encourage this trend.[38] Respectable Kahnawa'kehró:non, according to him, were men who wanted to own and cultivate land for large-scale commercial purposes, but he believed it was impossible for them to farm successfully under the present conditions of landownership.[39]

The department's second justification for subdivision proclaimed the necessity of protecting property owners. Some historians contend that Canada's nation-building project is best understood as the construction of a liberal edifice founded on property rights.[40] Within such a context, Indigenous land law and practices came to represent the exact opposite of what the nation builders were working to establish. Forging a nation-state on the security of property holders depended on the creation of rhetorical and legal distinctions between regimes based on law and lawless savagery that supposedly reigned outside of the boundaries of the state.[41] The very existence of a settler colonial regime based on property depended on narratives in which law and individualist property holding was absent. Critical legal geographer Nicholas Blomley describes the construction of this opposition: "Inside the frontier lie secure tenure, fee-simple ownership, and state-guaranteed rights to property. Outside lie uncertain and undeveloped entitlements, communal claims, and the absence of state guarantees to property. Inside lies stability and order, outside disorder, violence, and 'bare life.'"[42] DIA documents from the late nineteenth century presented Kahnawà:ke as a place of chaos and violence, where good people simply could not succeed. Department officials frequently cited "wood stealing" as an example of Kahnawa'kehró:non lawlessness and the natural consequence of the absence of property rights. Survey and subdivision constituted a bold attempt to make manifest what previous Orders-in-Council and laws had failed to bring about.[43]

The third justification for subdivision was that it would enable the DIA to resolve land conflicts between Kahnawa'kehró:non, something it had failed to do in a number of cases. Of course, it bears repeating that the situation was generated by the department's own decision to take on this role at the expense of Kahnawà:ke leaders and law. According to Deputy Superintendent General Lawrence Vankoughnet, the problem was that lands had "been taken up, without reference to the rights of other Indians, by individual Indians on the Reserve from time to time, and the metes and bounds of the locations so taken up" had not been defined. Given this, "innumerable disputes were constantly occurring between the occupants of adjoining locations as to their respective rights to certain portions of the locations; and it was impossible to decide as to the rights of the respective parties, unless a regular survey was made of the locations thus occupied."[44] By insisting on colonial law, the DIA had created the problems that it described, problems that it also exaggerated to justify a cadastral survey and subdivision.

DIA officials also frequently emphasized the unfair nature of current land distribution in Kahnawà:ke as a reason for the subdivision. In 1886, the *Montreal Daily Witness* ran a story on Kahnawà:ke that underscored the supposed problem of land inequality and the goal of fixing it. According to Walbank, quoted in the article: "The land had been common to all, and a man occupied just what be considered suited him. Thus one holding might consist of but three or four acres while another might run up to one hundred and forty acres. This seems to have caused dissatisfaction, and the Government ordered the survey."[45] Whereas of course there was some dissatisfaction about land inequalities, Walbank did not mention that most Kahnawa'kehró:non did not accept the DIA solution. Years after the survey, Vankoughnet wrote that "complaints were made by those Indians who had no lands that the land on the Reserve had been monopolized by those who were able to purchase them or who had taken them up years ago without reference to the rights of [those] who were as much entitled to share in the land on the Reserve as those parties were."[46] Like Walbank, Vankoughnet failed to mention that the Kahnawa'kehró:non who complained requested, not land redistribution but enforcement of Kahnawà:ke laws that would result in more egalitarian sharing of land. Minister of the Interior and Superintendent General of Indian Affairs Edgar Dewdney similarly made much of these egalitarian goals when defending the Walbank Survey in the House of Commons in 1890. The reason for the survey, Dewdney declared, was "that some of the more advanced Indians took up larger portions of the reserve than others thought they were entitled to, and they believed that the survey would give them more equal portions."[47] The idea of giving everyone an equal share of the land greatly appealed to Canadian government officials, who were also deeply engaged in colonizing the Prairies, using a model patterned after the US homesteading ideal, which made 160-acre lots available to white men. Although this project had certain egalitarian aims, it was grounded in the disenfranchisement and displacement of Indigenous peoples, and it excluded most women and people of colour.[48] Similarly, in Kahnawà:ke, equality may have been a stated goal, but even if one ignores the explicit exclusion of most women, egalitarian landownership was not a realistic outcome. It is also telling that the DIA felt that it could solve a land disparity problem by eliminating common property.

The final stated reason for the Walbank Survey was enfranchisement. The supposed mandate of DIA officials was to work themselves out of their jobs by assimilating Indigenous people and eliminating their nation-hoods. They saw themselves as protecting, educating, and guiding First Nations on the path from barbarism to civilization. Once this was complete, First Nations would no longer exist, and the department could be dismantled. The *Gradual Civilization Act* of 1857 had translated this desire into law by setting the standards that a male Indian must meet to discard his Indian status and gain the rights of a non-Indigenous British subject. The act stipulated that if he satisfied the requirements – literacy, moral uprightness, and freedom from debt – he would also receive up to fifty acres from his former reserve. First Nations immediately recognized this law as an attack on their land base, since each enfranchised person would be awarded a piece of their common land. Initially, almost no one opted to become enfranchised, so the DIA had the law revised to permit involuntary enfranchisement. In February 1882, when it announced the upcoming subdivision survey to Kahnawa'kehró:non, enfranchisement was front and centre. DIA clerk J.V. de Boucherville verbally informed Kahnawa'kehró:non, "it is hoped that, at no distant date, the Band, or such members thereof as may be deemed fit for the change, will be enfranchised, the step proposed, namely the Survey of their individual locations on the Reserve, is an essential preliminary to their enfranchisement."[49] In contrast to other Indigenous communities, the DIA saw Kahnawà:ke as "one of the further advanced in civilization in Canada" and therefore intended to use it as an advertisement for the possibilities, benefits, and ultimate inevitability of enfranchisement.[50] And since enfranchisement required private property, a subdivision would enable everyone on the reserve to be enfranchised at the same time.

Aside from the DIA's stated reasons for subdivision, a number of un-stated and contextual factors should be considered. One such factor is the concurrent territorial expansion of the Dominion of Canada that was under way in the 1870s and 1880s, during which the federal government facilitated crisis after crisis for Indigenous people on the Prairies. Faced with rapid dispossession, competition from settlers, confinement on re-serves, and a new legal regime that severely restricted their access to their lands and waters, Indigenous peoples could no longer feed and clothe themselves.[51] Due in part to genocidal policies in the United States, the southern bison herds had been extirpated by 1875, and the northern bison were mostly destroyed by 1883.[52] The Canadian government was obligated by treaty to provide for suddenly impoverished First Nations, but rather than ensure that settlers did not infringe on Indigenous treaty rights, the DIA hurriedly drew up plans to subdivide reserves. Officials hoped that cutting reserves into small, individually owned lots would induce In-digenous people to grow their own food, thus saving the government money. Historian Sarah Carter describes this process in some detail, show-ing how racist policies and actions led to even more Indigenous suffering and disempowerment.[53] The Walbank Survey was done under the same policy rubric and possibly as a trial run for western allotments. When Edgar Dewdney defended the survey in the House of Commons in 1890, he linked it with the concurrent reserve subdivisions in the Northwest. Just as in Kahnawà:ke, the "more advanced Indians" on the Prairies "took up larger portions of the reserve than others thought they were entitled to," and thus the department felt it had to intervene. Speaking of newly created reserves on the Prairies, Dewdney told the House:

> We have already commenced to subdivide our reserves there into forty-acre sections, and, as far as we possibly can, we are inducing the Indians to settle on their own sections of land, not compelling them to remain there if they do not like it, but when they get there, we find that they make their improve-ments, and begin to look upon it as a home.[54]

Although, as we shall see, the Kahnawà:ke subdivision did not go as planned, it might be considered a kind of test run for later subdivisions.

Another unpublicized motive of the DIA was the expected construction of a CPR bridge spanning the St. Lawrence River between Lachine and Kahnawà:ke. The only other crossing, the Victoria Bridge, was controlled by the Grand Trunk Railway. The CPR chose the narrows between Lachine and Kahnawà:ke as the site for a bridge to be constructed from 1885 to

FIGURE 6.1 *Indian Village, Caughnawaga,* c. 1885, by William Notman. | VIEW-2471, McCord Museum.

1887.[55] Figure 6.1, a photograph, probably taken from the ferry, shows the village with the church in the foreground and the CPR bridge under construction in the background. The CPR and government officials worried about how the company would expropriate Kahnawà:ke land if it did not have information about lots and landowners. They hoped that the subdivision would "regularize" landholding in time to facilitate expropriation for the CPR bridge and line. Walbank knew in 1882 that the bridge and line through Kahnawà:ke would be built and wanted to incorporate its trajectories into his subdivision plan so that his new lots would not be awkwardly bisected by the CPR project. The DIA, however, told him not to worry about it.[56] James P. Dawes, initially hired to act as arbiter in conflicts over wood, was now tasked with arbitrating compensation for land expropriated for the bridge and line. An active booster of Lachine industrial development, with interests in banking, insurance, and hotels, Dawes was vice-president of the Dominion Bridge Company, which was building the CPR bridge (see Figure 6.2).[57] His overt interest in the matter explains his involvement in Kahnawà:ke land issues long before the bridge

FIGURE 6.2   *Steel Bridge on the Canadian Pacific Railway,* c. 1885. The CPR bridge under construction. | MG29-B1, R7666-0-8-E, MIKAN no. 3264735, Sandford Fleming fonds, LAC.

itself was constructed. It also shows the important interconnected interests of Montreal industrialists and DIA officials in imposing colonial political and environmental values. Surveying for the bridge approach in Kahnawà:ke began in 1884.[58]

Another factor that made a subdivision attractive to the DIA was its potential usefulness in dominating Kahnawà:ke politics. The department wanted to replace the council of chiefs with an elected band council, but without a membership list – of everyone the DIA considered to be a member of the Kahnawà:ke "band" – there could be no list of electors. However, the subdivision survey would employ a tribunal to determine eligibility in land redistribution, and it would lay the groundwork for the installation of the band council system in 1889 (Chapter 7). The DIA thus wished to use the subdivision survey to further its knowledge and control over Kahnawà:ke land. Although the department did control the collective funds of Kahnawa'kehró:non, it had no way to manage, or even know about, the status of individual lots except through its agent and whatever information the chiefs were willing to divulge. DIA officials never saw Kahnawà:ke law as coherent and legitimate, which merely heightened their confusion about Kahnawa'kehró:non actions and words. Lacking both maps and a membership list for Kahnawà:ke, the DIA was unable to see the land and its people in the way that it wished. A subdivision survey would help to eliminate Kahnawà:ke land law and make its land and people visible (and thus governable) to the DIA.[59]

One final possible motive for initiating a subdivision may have been the substantial amount of money in the band account. The Sulpician Order had borrowed $3,333 from Kahnawà:ke to finance the construction of the towers of Notre Dame church (today Notre-Dame Basilica) in 1844, the largest church in North America at the time of its completion.[60] After a protracted court battle between the federal government and the Sulpicians over the principal of this loan, it was finally paid to Ottawa on behalf of Kahnawà:ke in 1883 along with interest.[61] The Kahnawà:ke band fund also received a payment of $10,039 in 1881, supposedly the seigneurial indemnity for losses incurred by the *Seigneurial Act* of 1854.[62] More research is required to follow the money trail, but the fact that the Kahnawà:ke account was flush with cash at that moment is highly relevant, since the subdivision was expensive. Kahnawa'kehró:non may not have been told about the money until it was spent. The DIA controlled Kahnawà:ke's finances and, without community approval, decided to earmark the money for the subdivision. Had the cash not existed, it is unlikely that the DIA would have initiated the project.[63]

THE WALBANK SUBDIVISION SURVEY

In February 1882, Deputy Superintendent General Lawrence Vankoughnet sent J.V. de Boucherville, a clerk normally in charge of Indian land sales, to Kahnawà:ke to inform the chiefs that the department intended to subdivide the territory. De Boucherville told the chiefs that the DIA was doing so "with a view to tickets covering each location being issued to those who would be entitled to the same." "Under the present system," he explained, "it was very difficult to protect their individual holdings from trespass," and it was hoped "that at no distant date the band or such members thereof as might be deemed fit for the change contemplated would be enfranchised and that the survey of their individual locations on the Reserve was an essential preliminary to their enfranchisement."[64] De Boucherville's announcement was translated into Kanien'kéha and he reported that the chiefs had manifested their contentment with the plan and their hope that the survey would be carried out quickly.[65]

Of course, there is no reason to believe that the chiefs were pleased by de Boucherville's announcement since they had always opposed any sub-division plan. The DIA regularly misrepresented the views of Indigenous leaders to give its own projects an air of legitimacy. In its annual report for 1882, it misrepresented Kahnawà:ke public opinion by declaring that "the survey is greatly appreciated by the band generally."[66] Even if some chiefs did cooperate once they realized that the project could not be stopped, they were certainly not as content as de Boucherville claimed.[67]

The sole leader who appears to have felt genuine enthusiasm for the survey was Chief Skatsentie (Joseph Williams, 1846–85), a young, wealthy trader whose father had done considerable business in Germany, selling "Indian curiosities" and crafts.[68] He had been chosen as a chief in 1878 but stepped down in October 1880, when he lost popular support.[69] The DIA, which saw him as an ally, refused to accept his resignation and helped him to keep his position until September 1883.[70] In exchange for DIA backing, Skatsentie helped to facilitate Walbank's work and wrote a letter to de Boucherville in which he downplayed Kahnawa'kehró:non opposition to the survey.[71] He lived in one of the fanciest houses in the village and owned 103.65 acres outside the village, which were valued at $1,127.[72] As someone who possessed significant wealth and land, he was willing to work with the DIA, which recognized him as an ally in the community. At first, he seemed to enjoy popular support, but when he lost it the department propped him up to ensure that it could continue with the survey.

Vankoughnet informed Prime Minister John A. Macdonald in April 1882 "that the Iroquois Indians of Caughnawaga have recently signified their consent to the lands comprised in the Reserve owned by them being sub-divided by survey into locations for each family and inasmuch as this sub-division is a necessary preliminary to the enfranchisement of an Indian Band."[73] According to Vankoughnet, everything was in place to begin the survey, including the consent of the Indians (which was never given or legally required under the *Indian Act*). He recommended Walbank for the job.[74] At least one other surveyor inquired about the contract, but the DIA never requested tenders. A few days later, Vankoughnet gave Walbank the go-ahead and asked how he intended to proceed.[75]

Walbank duly submitted a hastily prepared subdivision plan, which the DIA accepted without serious scrutiny, and he immediately got to work. He opened an office in Kahnawà:ke and put three teams in the field, each consisting of a surveyor and two Kahnawa'kehró:non assistants.[76] He expected to complete the job during 1883, but it dragged on well beyond that year due to complications he probably should have foreseen.[77]

Kahnawa'kehró:non were often openly hostile to the project, and Walbank found that without their assistance it was very difficult to determine boundaries between lots.[78] Nor did Kahnawà:ke law see land in terms of bounded territories that belonged to only one person, so Kahnawa'kehró:non saw some people as having rights to the same piece of land in one season and others in another season, for one land use and not another, and also perceived boundaries as shifting over time. Thus, Walbank was probably asking questions about lots and boundaries in a way that took no account of Kahnawà:ke law and history, another possible reason why so many Kahnawa'kehró:non chose not to help him.

Despite the delays and cost overruns, Walbank found time to involve himself in organizing an agricultural and industrial exhibition in Kahnawà:ke, beginning in 1882. For him, the survey was simply one part of a larger civilizing project, and he was interested in all aspects of it. He used the opportunity of the 1883 Kahnawà:ke agricultural exhibition to display "plans of former tribal occupation," as well as his own recently drawn maps of the reserve.[79] He was also an organizer of a farming competition in the spring of 1883, where "prizes [were] given to the steady workers." Outsiders had their prejudices shaken when a number of Kahnawa'kehró:non "compare[d] favourably with the best amongst themselves" and "the competition led to no act of excess."[80] Walbank also involved himself with local issues by imposing Christian conceptions of right and wrong. For example, he attempted to teach Kahnawà:ke merchants "that it is not the correct thing to sell on Sundays," "explaining to them what they were laying themselves open to in not closing their shops on Sunday" (he did not specify what these consequences might be).[81] Cherrier was appreciative of Walbank's help on all these fronts and declared that "his presence among the tribe is productive of much good."[82] When Vankoughnet visited Kahnawà:ke in the summer of 1883 to inspect Walbank's work, he "found matters generally in a very satisfactory condition there."[83] A columnist for the *Catholic World,* who visited Kahnawà:ke while the survey was under way, was informed that the project was the brainchild of Prime Minister John A. Macdonald himself. Walbank knew that his project had support at the highest levels of the Canadian government, and he was genuinely enthusiastic about its potential to demonstrate how to transform "Indians" into enfranchised landowners and farmers.[84]

Walbank hoped that he could subdivide the reserve into fifty-acre lots, which would then be allocated to eligible people. The larger the lots, the more attractive the project would be to potential owners, but large lots also meant that fewer people would benefit from the survey. Since the

FIGURE 6.3 "Plan of Kanawake Reserve," William McLea Walbank, 1889. | H1/340/Caughnawaga/ 1889, V1/340/ Caughnawaga/1889, R/340/Caughnawaga/ 1889, LAC.

civilizing project of the DIA involved turning Indigenous people into farmers, the lots needed to be large enough for commercial agriculture. But Walbank was not a farmer and did not know how big the lots would need to be, so he began his survey by measuring out and mapping the existing lots as best he could. Although he was conducting the survey on the fly and according to a vague general plan, its overall purpose was abundantly clear. As Agent Cherrier put it, the survey would be accomplished "with a view to a fair distribution of the land being made, and the location tickets being issued to the Indian occupants. This step, it is hoped, will be eventually followed by the enfranchisement of the majority, if not of the whole, of the band."[85] The goal, in other words, was the end of Kahnawà:ke as an Indigenous community and nation. Everyone would be enfranchised, and Kahnawà:ke would become a town much like any settler town. And then, the DIA would follow the model established there to destroy other First Nations.

After having surveyed and mapped many of the existing lots by June 1884, Walbank began the process of valuing the lots and their "improvements" (such as buildings and fences). The DIA instructed him not to proceed as he would if the lots were off-reserve; instead, he was to value them based on a land market in which only "Indians" could buy from each other. This racist decision had the effect of making Kahnawà:ke valuations much lower than those for similar lots on non-reserve land, and it had important negative economic repercussions for Kahnawa'kehró:non in both the short and long term.[86] By December 1884, Walbank had completed the survey of existing lots and plotted them on a map.[87] Both his map (Figure 6.3) and his record books are preserved by Library and Archives Canada.

The map and the data contained in the record books formed the basis of my Geographic Information System (GIS) analysis, which were used to draw some of the maps for this chapter. A very complex composite, Walbank's map shows existing lot boundaries, projected lot boundaries, and land-use categories. In fact, it is so loaded with overlapping detail that it is difficult to decipher, so I have separated its information into the two maps that appear in Figure 6.4. The upper map (Figure 6.4a) shows the irregular lots that Walbank identified. The lower map in Figure 6.4b shows Walbank's projected lots, regular thirty-acre polygons that were to be given to each household head. Walbank had by this time realized that fifty-acre lots would produce too few in total for the number of eventual claimants, so he had settled on thirty-acre lots (more on this below). The two maps

(a) Existing lots as determined by Walbank, 1885

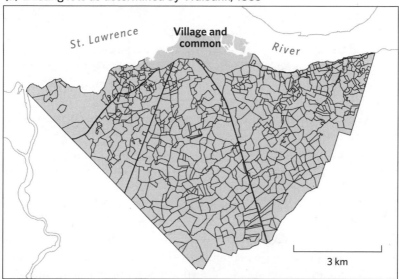

(b) Projected lots as determined by Walbank, 1885

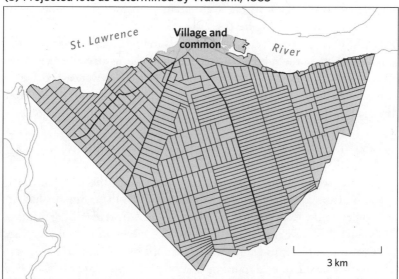

Figure 6.4   Maps of Kahnawà:ke, showing existing and projected lots, c. 1885. |
Maps by Eric Leinberger.

in Figure 6.4 give an easily digested picture of the radical transformation he planned.

The third layer on Walbank's map depicts seven land-use categories: bush and hay, bush, bush and swamp, cultivated, pasture, beaver hay, and sugarbush. For unknown reasons, Walbank did not use these seven categories in his reference books, which contain all the numerical data on each claimant and lot. In the reference books, he employed only five categories (cultivated, pasture, hay, bush, and sugarbush), so direct comparisons between the map and the reference books are hard to make. His map used various colours and patterns to delineate land use, but these are extremely difficult to discern because the colours have faded, and the map is ripped and water-damaged.

In the winter of 1884–85, after having completed his survey of existing lots, Walbank decided on a methodology to determine eligible "heads of household" who would receive a new lot. Knowing who was eligible would allow him to calculate the exact number of lots needed for the new property grid. To this end, Walbank established a process by which anyone who claimed to be a head of household could present himself (and sometimes herself) to a tribunal consisting of the council of chiefs, the Indian agent, and Walbank himself. Figure 6.5 shows the public notice that was read out at the entrance to the church after Mass to invite "all persons claiming a right to share in the subdivision" to file their claims at Walbank's survey office within sixty days of January 15, 1885.[88] Claimants were asked a series of questions in person, and their answers were recorded on standardized forms. The questions were designed to gather information about each claimant, which could be used to disqualify people, as well as details about lots and improvements. Aside from the standard names, birth dates, and birth places, claimants were asked questions that reflected DIA concerns about race, sexuality, and absences from Canada.[89] The tribunal was in operation from February until June 1885. Once all the claimants had appeared before the tribunal, special meetings were held regarding disputed lands and other more complicated claims. The survey and tribunal aroused considerable interest in Montreal, as evinced by a *Montreal Daily Witness* article that included a transcription of all the questions on Walbank's claim forms.[90]

The voluminous data produced by Walbank's tribunal are valuable for learning about Kahnawà:ke land and Kahnawa'kehró:non in the late nineteenth century, but the information is also problematic. The entire process, including the questions on the forms, was designed with colonizing intent and interest. There is no reason to believe that Kahnawa'kehró:non

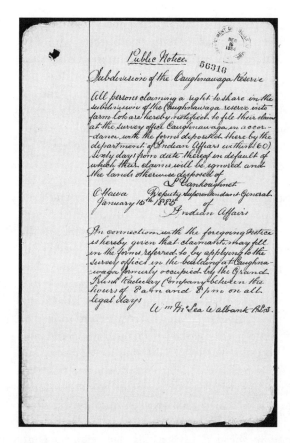

FIGURE 6.5   "Public Notice: Subdivision of the Caughnawaga Reserve," January 15, 1885. | RG10, vol. 2693, file 139,964, pt. 1, LAC.

had any input in framing the questions – thus, it is likely that claimants often disagreed with the questions themselves. But there is no way to know this, because what they actually did say was not recorded. Instead, the tribunal used pre-selected English phrases to document their information, even if the claimant spoke in French or Kanien'kéha, all compiled in the handwriting of one person. For example, for question ten ("Do you hold any land on the Reserve; and how did you acquire such land?"), the recorded answer is often "No" or "Yes, 2 pieces," and Walbank admitted that often he did not attend closely to what claimants said. Although he himself was young and an outsider with limited knowledge of Kahnawà:ke, he believed that "any information I might get from the individual Indians would be very unreliable and inaccurate."[91] For question seven ("How long have you resided on the reserve?"), some of the standardized answers were "All my life" or "All my life except when at college," whereas individuals surely gave a much wider range of responses. Considering Walbank's youth, inexperience, and lack of empathy for those whom he saw as uncivilized, it is likely that many Kahnawa'kehró:non claims are not fairly represented in his records. In addition, the questions did not take into account Kahnawà:ke legal conceptions of ownership, and no doubt they frustrated and angered the people who were forced to reply to them. Nevertheless, there is no reason to think that Walbank intended to falsify information – he just thought he was smarter and more reliable than everyone else.

The tribunal process also allowed some Kahnawa'kehró:non to file claims in absentia. Walbank mentioned people in New Orleans and Lake Superior who could not appear before the tribunal. To have their claims considered, they had to complete claimant forms in the presence of the British consul, mayor, or notary of the town in which they lived.[92] But some absentees did not know that this was possible. At the time, sixty skilled Kahnawa'kehró:non boatsmen were in Egypt, participating in a British military mission to rescue a besieged colonial force in Khartoum. They had left Montreal in September 1884, only to receive word soon after that they should return home if they wished to participate in the land redistribution. Most did so immediately. On arriving in Montreal, one Kahnawa'kehró:non speaking for all the men told the *Montreal Star* that they would have stayed on longer had it not been for the subdivision.[93] Obviously, Walbank had not informed Kahnawa'kehró:non of his timetable in advance and had not provided them with a way to file their claims in absentia. If he had thought ahead and shared his plans with the community, these men might not have agreed to go to Egypt in the first place, or they could have made their claims before leaving.

After all the claims were filed, the DIA (in consultation with the Department of Justice) reviewed the contested claims. These were claims for which at least one chief disputed a person's right to membership. This was the part of the tribunal in which Kahnawà:ke chiefs were most involved. Their council had consisted of seven clan chiefs until that time, but the DIA had refused to allow several new chiefs to replace those who died in the years before the survey. The four remaining chiefs in 1885 were Shatekaienton (Louis Beauvais), Karatoton (Thomas Jocks), Sakoientineta (Michael Montour), and Asennase (Thomas Deer). Historian Gerald Reid determined that of 610 total claims (513 men and 97 women), 175 (27 percent) were contested. Each of the four chiefs on the tribunal could either approve or contest every claim. Chief Skatsentie, an enthusiastic promoter of the survey, died in May 1885 and thus did not play a role in the tribunal decisions.[94] After years of DIA interference, the chiefs had lost some popular support, and many Kahnawa'kehró:non opposed their involvement in the tribunal at all, but their involvement still gave the process a veneer of legitimacy. The chiefs participated in fifteen special meetings of five to six hours each, and the DIA paid each of them one dollar per meeting. The purpose of these meetings was to determine whether applicants had a legitimate claim to a new lot, and their decisions had long-term implications on whether these people and their families would be considered members of the band under the *Indian Act*.[95]

The chiefs unanimously agreed to reject 122 of the 175 contested claims, and the DIA generally concurred with their decisions. But in the other 53 contested claims, the chiefs could not reach consensus. It is nowhere stated how they arrived at their decisions, but it is evident that they and the department were not operating according to the same logic. Reid found that the main reasons the chiefs rejected claims were that claimants were underage men, non-widowed women, born elsewhere or out of wedlock, absent from Kahnawà:ke for a long time, "white" or "half-breed," or because they had parents who were born elsewhere. Final decisions on the 53 most difficult cases resulted from the back-and-forth between the chiefs and the DIA, but the chiefs had little real power. The DIA attempted to apply *Indian Act* membership and status rules, but officials found it impossible to adjudicate the racial provisions of the act since they lacked local knowledge. Thus, they relied heavily on the knowledge and opinions of the chiefs to determine who would be excluded, purportedly on the basis of racial criteria, but on many other factors as well. The *Indian Act* assumed that there was such a thing as "Indian blood," a racist construct that the DIA had no consistent way of adjudicating.[96] Thus, it usually took the chiefs' word on who was sufficiently "Indian" and who was not. It contradicted the chiefs only in the case of the Delorimier family, whom most Kahnawa'kehró:non saw as white but whose Indian status had been confirmed in 1834 by the Supreme Court of Montreal.[97] The chiefs also wanted to exclude certain Kahnawà:ke women who had married white men. However, pointing out that their marriages predated the 1869 *Gradual Enfranchisement Act,* which would have deprived them of their status, the DIA forced their inclusion. Aside from disputed claimants, approximately 130 cases of disputed ownership of lots came before the tribunal.[98] Reid suggests that the chiefs' primary motivation was to limit the number of band members so that each would receive an adequate share of the small territory, but their decisions also reflected their own priorities and beliefs to which the archival documents do not give us access.[99]

RESISTANCE TO THE WALBANK SURVEY

Kahnawa'kehró:non closely watched Walbank's surveying activities and claims process, and the longer they dragged on the more their opposition grew. The survey, however, coincided with events that circumscribed the ability of Kahnawa'kehró:non to resist it. Aside from the tightening noose of federal Indian legislation that repeatedly undermined Indigenous sovereignty and empowered the DIA, these events strengthened the DIA's hand in Kahnawà:ke. When the Métis and their Assiniboine and Cree allies on the Prairies rose up against the Canadian invasion and occupation of their lands in the spring of 1885, settler public opinion turned sharply against Indigenous peoples.[100] Kahnawa'kehró:non surely took this antipathy into account as they registered their complaints about the survey that summer. In July 1885, only three months after the Indigenous provisional government on the Prairies had been crushed, some fifty Kahnawa'kehró:non sent the DIA a carefully worded petition in which they expressed concern over the long duration and high cost of the subdivision survey and asked for an investigation into the matter. They wrote, "it is with anxiety that we look for the completion of said survey: we are inexpert in the nature of the work, but assuredly one acting faithfully should have finished it by this time, comparing to the small size of the Seigniory."[101] Although many opposed the survey regardless of how it was conducted, the petitioners strategically framed their argument in terms of Walbank's technical competence and the expense of his operations. But when the department asked Walbank for a response, he dismissed the petitioners as nothing but a few troublemakers. "The complaint," he wrote, "does not come from the respectable part of the tribe; but from some whom I have prosecuted for bringing intoxicants on the Reserve, and is composed of some fifty or sixty of the most troublesome men of the tribe, and who take no interest in any matters except opposing all progress."[102] Walbank here was describing people who simply wished to live their lives as they thought best and who did not welcome his interference. He knew that the opposition to his work was deeply rooted and widespread, but in light of his serious technical and budget problems, he preferred to attack the credibility of the petitioners with familiar racist tropes about alcohol and irrationality.

The work of the tribunal was mostly complete by the fall of 1885, but the DIA did not release its final decisions on disputed claims until the summer of 1886.[103] As long as the claims remained in limbo, Walbank could not start subdividing the reserve because he did not know how many lots would be needed. He urged the DIA to process the matter quickly, but to no avail.[104] As he waited, he started marking out road allowances that would serve as the basis for the new grid, drew a provisional map of the new lots of approximately thirty acres each, and invited successful claimants to choose among them. He also invited owners of existing lots to review his valuations of their lands and improvements. These notices sparked another round of protests, this time mostly from large landowners.

After two secret meetings in early June 1886, a group of Kahnawa'kehró:non sent the DIA a petition protesting the low valuations of their lands and the high cost of the survey.[105] The petitioners were among the privileged few who owned extensive lands and who thus stood to lose the most from Walbank's low valuations. These were people who had often supported DIA initiatives, and perhaps realizing that it was on the verge of losing even its few local allies, the department cracked down. On June 25, Walbank and Indian Agent Alexander Brosseau called a general meeting to denounce the petitioners and to announce a ban on unauthorized public meetings.

Some landowners hired arbitrators to revalue their properties, but the DIA rejected this move.[106] Vankoughnet stated that "the valuation would be on the basis of values of such property in Caughnawaga, as between Indian and Indian and not as between White people," and he would make no exception to this rule.[107]

A project that would redistribute land from the wealthy to the landless poor should ostensibly have found some approval among the poor themselves, yet most of them opposed it. Whereas overt opposition came from large landowners, some small landowners did not want change either. A good example here is Ohionkoton (Angus Jacob), who added a defiant message in Kanien'kéha to his returned notice: "onen se8ensionson watkeri8aserako kenon8es nii tsi niio tsi 8akien iate katenninons nakonwentsia" [Now you gentlemen: I answer. I like the way that I have. I do not sell my land] (Figures 6.6 and 6.7).[108] Ohionkoton had failed to appear for the tribunal interviews the previous year. Walbank listed him as the owner of a 1.03-acre lot of cultivated land valued at thirteen dollars.[109] It is not known what motivated Ohionkoton, but he and other land-poor Kahnawa'kehró:non realized that the new property arrangement would criminalize woodcutting beyond one's lot and that this would deprive them of free fuel. It is also likely that many saw DIA interference as an attack on their independence and sovereignty, and rejected it even if they could have benefitted individually.

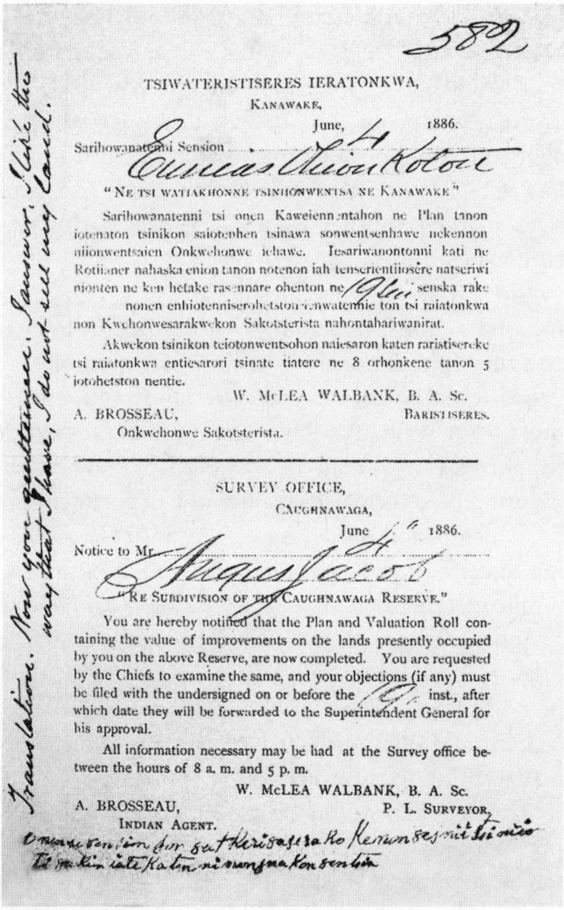

582

TSIWATERISTISERES IERATONKWA,
KANAWAKE,
June, 4 1886.

Sarihowanatenni Sension .... Eneas Ohionkoton

“NE TSI WATIAKHONNE TSINHONWENTSA NE KANAWAKE”

Sarihowanatenni tsi onen Kaweiennentahon ne Plan tanon iotenaton tsinikon saiotenhen tsinawa sonwentsenhawe nekennon niionwentsaien Onkwehonwe ichawe. Iesariwanontonni kati ne Rotiiøner nahaska enion tanon notenon iah tenserientiiosère natseriwi nionten ne ken hetake rasennare ohenton ne 19 senska rake nonen enhiotenniserohetston ienwatennie ton tsi raiatonkwa non Kwehonwesarakwekon Sakotsterista nahontahariwanirat.

Akwekon tsinikon teiotonwentsohon naiesaron katen raristisereke tsi raiatonkwa entiesarori tsinate tiatere ne 8 orhonkene tanon 5 iotohetston nentie.

W. McLEA WALBANK, B. A. Sc.
A. BROSSEAU, BARISTISERES.
Onkwehonwe Sakotsterista.

SURVEY OFFICE,
CAUGHNAWAGA,
June 4 1886.

Notice to Mr. Angus Jacob

“RE SUBDIVISION OF THE CAUGHNAWAGA RESERVE.”

You are hereby notified that the Plan and Valuation Roll containing the value of improvements on the lands presently occupied by you on the above Reserve, are now completed. You are requested by the Chiefs to examine the same, and your objections (if any) must be filed with the undersigned on or before the 19 inst., after which date they will be forwarded to the Superintendent General for his approval.

All information necessary may be had at the Survey office between the hours of 8 a. m. and 5 p. m.

W. McLEA WALBANK, B. A. Sc.
A. BROSSEAU, P. L. SURVEYOR.
INDIAN AGENT.

Translation. Now your questionnaire. I answer, I like the way that I have, I do not sell my land.

FIGURE 6.6 Notice returned to Walbank by Ohionkoton, 1885. | Caughnawaga Reference Books, RG10-B-8-aj, vols. 8968–72, LAC.

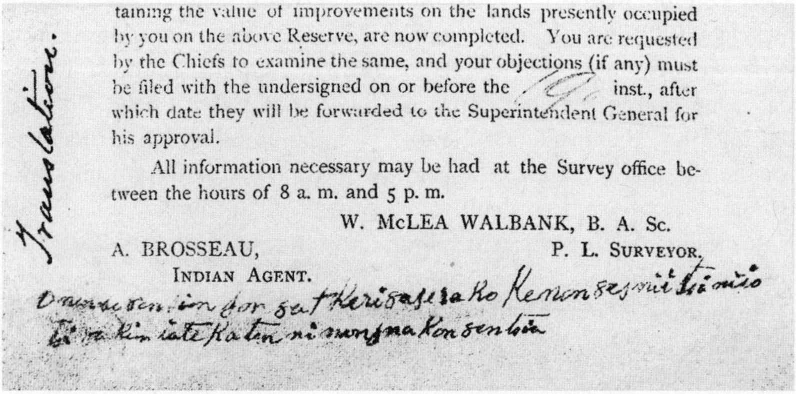

taining the value of improvements on the lands presently occupied by you on the above Reserve, are now completed. You are requested by the Chiefs to examine the same, and your objections (if any) must be filed with the undersigned on or before the 19 inst., after which date they will be forwarded to the Superintendent General for his approval.

All information necessary may be had at the Survey office between the hours of 8 a. m. and 5 p. m.

W. McLEA WALBANK, B. A. Sc.
A. BROSSEAU, P. L. SURVEYOR.
INDIAN AGENT.

Translation.

FIGURE 6.7 Detail of Ohionkoton’s returned notice, showing his response, 1885. | Caughnawaga Reference Books, RG10-B-8-aj, vols. 8968–72, LAC.

THE WALBANK SURVEY STALLED

In the fall of 1886, Walbank began the actual subdivision of the land, which aimed to make his property grid a reality on the ground. By then, he had already assigned each of the projected 387 rectangular lots to an owner (Figure 6.4b).[110] The most difficult part of the process would be to transfer an irregularly shaped lot that was occupied to several new owners on different rectangular lots. He thus started by subdividing the Grand Park, a 506-acre swampy area on the west side of the territory known today as the Big Fence.[111] But how would the more valuable, individually owned lots be transferred to new owners? Since the department was legally obligated to compensate owners for improvements, they had to be paid for buildings, cleared land, fences, and orchards before the new lots could be taken up by their various owners. This process promised to be extremely difficult, time consuming, and expensive – and this on the heels of a subdivision survey that had already gone far over-time and over-budget.

The department was worried about delays and spiralling costs. DIA surveyor W.A. Austin wrote in September 1886 that all the time spent by Walbank's surveyors, who worked mostly during the warm seasons, would have stretched into five full years of employment for a single surveyor. He quoted an 1882 letter from Walbank, which noted that the subdivision survey would be finished in just one year at a cost of $10,000. In 1886, Walbank had already charged the DIA $15,000.[112] After Walbank staunchly defended his expenditures and timeline, citing numerous unforeseen complications and stating that the project could not be compared to any other, Austin went to Kahnawà:ke to inspect his work. His subsequent report expressed a great deal more sympathy toward Walbank and his justifications for time and money spent. Austin reported that Walbank had laid out forty lots and several roads, which left about 273 miles of lines left to run. He estimated that the remaining fieldwork would be finished by the end of August 1887.[113] Early in 1887, Austin again came to Walbank's defence, saying that although the survey had been expensive, the money was well spent. Like Walbank, he claimed that the "peculiar features" of the survey meant that no other project could be compared with it.[114]

Not only had this process involved a lot of money that Walbank did not have at his disposal, he had also not planned ahead as to how the land redistribution would transpire. Once the new grid was in place, existing roads would become useless, barns could be separated from fields, and sugarbushes separated from sugar shacks. The geographical and cultural logics of the original lots would be replaced by the bureaucratic logic of the rectangle and the grid. But how and when would the owners of the old lots be replaced by the owners of the new ones? Figure 6.8 shows that almost every new lot incorporated land from more than one old lot. One can only imagine the chaos at the moment of redistribution. Some people would lose land, buildings, and improvements, whereas others would gain those same things – some lots would be valuable and others not. The idea was to give everyone an equal portion of land, but the lots were not equal in quality. Aside from geographical differences, there were also great differences in how various lots had been used during the long occupation of the site. Landowners would be paid the value of their old lots, and owners of the new ones would be indebted for any improvements found there. They would be required to pay down this debt in instalments, and if they failed in this respect the DIA would lease the lot to a third party until the debt was paid. It was thus foreseeable that some would lose land (albeit in exchange for money), whereas others would gain thirty acres of questionable quality for which they would be heavily indebted. Those who received the most compensation were those who owned land that Walbank recognized as improved (with buildings, fences, and cultivated areas) and those who possessed notarized titles. Walbank's scheme would transform the land-rich into the money-rich (although landowners felt that their improvements had been seriously undervalued) and would indebt the poor for lots they did not request. One likely outcome was that former large landowners would use their compensation money to buy the land of those who could not pay their debt for it, and the inequalities would thus be perpetuated or worsened. On the surface it appeared that the subdivision would redistribute land, but in reality it simply caused disruption and damage to everyone while deepening existing disparities.

In a context where legal forms of protest had been taken from them, Kahnawa'kehró:non increasingly turned to other means of opposition. Walbank informed the DIA in September 1887 that one of his surveyors had been impeded by a number of Kahnawa'kehró:non, who had "offered obstruction to the running of the new lines of Lots; and also threatened personal violence." They had removed pickets and destroyed surveying marks.[115] Walbank accused three men. One was Thiretha, on whose form Walbank noted: "This man resides here upon his land which is very extensive, he refuses to attend here to make his statement." Thiretha was listed as owning four lots totalling 194 acres in all land-use categories, which were valued at $1,473. The second man was Kataratiron (Joseph Jacob), born in 1842, who owned an 80-acre lot, of which a significant

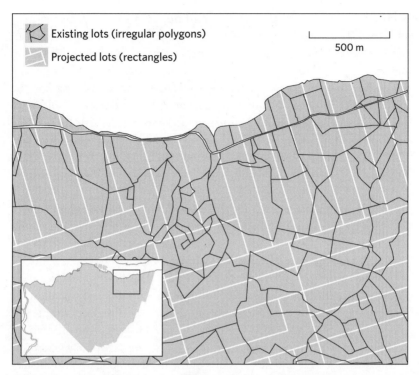

FIGURE 6.8   Detail of part of Kahnawà:ke, c. 1885. Dark lines show the boundaries of existing lots, as drawn by Walbank. Light lines represent the boundaries of projected lots. | Map by Eric Leinberger.

portion was cultivated, valued at $1,804.[116] The third man, a certain Doctor Jacobs, cannot be positively identified in the Walbank record books. Given that two of these men were land-rich and the third was a medical doctor, losing access to firewood would probably not have been the most pressing issue for them. It is to be expected that these large landowners were opposed to losing their lands without adequate compensation, but the colonial archives do not inform of their motives for disrupting the survey.[117] Such wealthier men were typically among the few people whom the DIA had been able to count on as allies, and now the department had succeeded in alienating even them.

Walbank's final requirement for completing the long-overdue land redistribution was a fund of at least $50,000 from which to compensate owners of existing lots when their lands were transferred to new owners. His plan was that the new owners would then make payments back into the fund, so that all the money would balance out in the end. Without such a fund, Walbank felt that he could not move forward, but in May 1887 the DIA refused to gratify his request.[118] Reluctant to concede defeat, Walbank decided to arrange for piecemeal transfers. He staked out sixteen new rectangular lots, lined up owners for each one, and asked the DIA for money to compensate them for the lots they would be giving up. The department, however, declined to make even that money available.[119] In July, Walbank tried again, this time proposing to transfer title for just one new lot to the relatively wealthy Ohonwakerha (Louis Jocko), who was willing to pay for it if the department granted him a location ticket (perhaps as a tactical omission, Walbank did not mention the valuable properties that Ohonwakerha would be giving up).[120] In this way, Walbank intended to set a precedent, but the department refused to grant Ohonwakerha a title before he had been compensated for the lots he would surrender in exchange.[121] Thus, the department was not prepared to pay to compensate owners; nor would it allow new owners to take up lots. In refusing to set aside Walbank's $50,000 fund, DIA officials had effectively doomed the redistribution project and now had no intention of allowing it to proceed, but they did not inform Walbank of this. They simply left him hanging, with no way to complete the job. He ended the subdivision fieldwork in December 1887, remarking that he was "extremely glad to be finished with it." He added: "It is one of the most difficult and unsatisfactory surveys one could possibly have."[122] He finished his paperwork in the spring of 1888,[123] filing a lengthy report with Prime Minister John A. Macdonald, who was also minister responsible for the DIA. After summarizing the project to date, Walbank explained why he needed a large fund and tried to calm financial concerns by emphasizing that if a new owner failed to pay interest on his debt, the department could lease his land to someone else until the debt was paid off.[124] Nothing came of this proposal either, and Walbank soon distanced himself from the project, saying he had done all he could. From then on, his correspondence with the DIA consisted of debates over the quality of his work and the amount of money he was owed.

By the late 1880s, after years of enduring the uncertainty of the Walbank Survey, Kahnawa'kehró:non had rightly concluded that the redistribution would never take place. On the other hand, considering that Walbank and the DIA had often acted without consultation or warning, perhaps some were still bracing for what came next. In November 1887, a number of Kahnawa'kehró:non called on the department to allow them to elect chiefs, but they were told to wait until the subdivision was complete so that the *Advancement Act* could properly be applied to them.[125] White farmers who had DIA permission to live and work in Kahnawà:ke were also left in limbo, because they did not know from year to year whether their land would still be available in the following year. They asked the DIA in 1889 whether the subdivision would be completed that year, so that they could look for farms elsewhere if need be, but the DIA replied that nothing had been decided.[126] The following year, Agent Brosseau asked the department if people who were too old and weak to farm would be permitted to lease their land to white farmers and was told that they would have to wait until the land redistribution was complete.[127] DIA officials appeared to have been strategically indifferent to the fact that so many Kahnawa'kehró:non had to put their lives on hold for a few years while the department sorted things out. Even as the survey itself attempted to overwrite existing cultural, economic, and environmental logics, the "bureaucratic cruelty" and "effective inefficiency" of the department interfered with and disrupted Indigenous lives and livelihoods.[128]

THE END OF THE SURVEY

When it became clear that the subdivision would never take place, finger pointing and blame shifting began in earnest. The department, seeking to deflect attention from itself, discovered numerous flaws and shortcomings in Walbank's work, and Walbank himself blamed the difficulties of an unusual project.[129] Both the DIA and Walbank also blamed the "Indians." Walbank's mistakes and omissions could be chalked up to inexperience – he had never tackled such a large, complicated project before, and it showed – but the DIA also displayed very little interest in the details of the plan until it was too late.[130] The blame game also played out at higher levels of government. From 1887 to 1890, opposition members of parliament frequently peppered Conservative prime minister John A. Macdonald and his ministers with critical questions about the project. The Opposition regarded the botched survey as a liability for the government.[131] Cyrille Doyon, an independent Liberal MP who represented La Prairie, was the most vociferous critic. He had been raising questions about the Walbank Survey, but by 1890 his public demands for information on its costs, quality, and purpose could no longer be ignored. In a particularly poignant comparison, Doyon asked the government why this incomplete survey had cost $1.80 per acre when the Dominion Lands Survey on the Prairies cost only 4 cents per acre.[132] In the face of such attacks, the government distanced itself, and the DIA let the project die.

However, Minister of the Interior Edgar Dewdney, a trained engineer and land surveyor,[133] did attempt to address Doyon's unfriendly cost comparison with the Dominion Lands Survey. As he told the House of Commons in March 1890, the Walbank Survey

> was made on a petition of the Indians themselves ... Of course a survey of this character must cost a great deal more than the survey of the Dominion lands. The cost per acre of the Dominion lands survey, was calculated on millions of acres which had been surveyed. This survey, as the hon. gentleman knows, was cut up into small fields, resembling much the appearance of this chamber, the desks representing the little holdings of the Indians. The location of every house, and fence had to be surveyed, and a most complete and detailed map, *equal to an ordnance map of the old country,* I find has been made. Whether there was a necessity for such a detailed survey as that, I am not prepared to say. I know something about that class of work, and I can say that the map has been very well made, showing the topography of the whole reserve, as well as the various holdings.[134]

Dewdney's comparison of Walbank's map to one produced by the British ordnance survey is particularly striking, given that the latter, a systematic, highly detailed, large-scale rendering, was developed to facilitate the subjugation of the Scottish Highlanders in the 1740s.[135] The point of his comparison was to underscore the quality and level of detail in the Walbank Survey, but it was also apt because the purpose of both surveys was the same – to subjugate and rule over another nation.

As of February 1890, the total price tag for the Walbank Survey stood at over $22,000, which had been taken from the Kahnawà:ke fund managed by the DIA.[136] As the department attempted to wrap up the project, Walbank was still demanding pay for work done years before. In January 1891, the DIA paid him the final $3,000 he was owed, even though Kahnawà:ke's account was empty. The money was loaned to the Kahnawà:ke band fund by the Timiskaming and Sarnia Chippewa band accounts, probably without permission from those communities themselves.[137] After carefully examining Walbank's work in September 1890, W.A. Austin concluded that it had been shoddy and suggested that the department not hire him again.[138] When Austin resurveyed the southwestern boundary of the reserve in 1894, he encountered stiff resistance from white landowners who had enjoyed the status quo, which had allowed them to encroach on the reserve. He came to believe that Walbank had abandoned the boundary survey because of this same resistance.[139]

In 1893, the land redistribution had still not occurred, and most people realized that it never would, but Vankoughnet still believed. Clearly irate about the department's failure, he placed the blame squarely on "the Indians." "The occupants of the old locations," he claimed, "cling to the possession of the same, and are unwilling to part with any portion thereof." He also seemed baffled that landless Kahnawa'kehró:non showed "no special anxiety ... to acquire the thirty acre allotments." He drew on the trope of the complaining, ungrateful, fickle Indian to distract from the culpability of his own department.[140] Although the department had, according to Vankoughnet, done its part in agreeing to grant location tickets to anyone who paid for the improvements on the new lots, individual Kahnawa'kehró:non had not pulled their weight. There is no hint in Vankoughnet's report that the department might bear any blame for forcing an ill-conceived project on an unwilling community, that the band fund had been depleted, and that DIA action and inaction had caused untold damage. In 1893, Vankoughnet was forced into early retirement, and he seemed determined to make the redistribution a reality before he left.[141] Since it now appeared "hopeless to expect ... voluntary action" on the part of Kahnawa'kehró:non, he asked the Kahnawà:ke Indian agent to inform "those who have more land than they are entitled to" that they should be prepared to give up "surplus land." Those who had little or no land should be prepared to pay the agent for improvements on their new lots. Large landowners would be given first choice of lots.[142] That Vankoughnet was promoting such an unworkable idea years after Walbank had left the field suggests that he was truly disconnected from the real world, perhaps in much the same way that his department was often disconnected from, and uninterested in, Indigenous realities.

Vankoughnet's replacement, Hayter Reed, made Kahnawà:ke one of his first priorities after taking up the position. In December 1893, he met with Kahnawà:ke chiefs, who demanded to be compensated for the band funds spent on the Walbank Survey. He said he could not give them money outright, but he promised to enlarge and renovate the school, improve roads and bridges, and pay for the cost of evicting trespassers. All of this, of course, was subject to parliamentary approval of his budget, and there is no evidence that the money was ever forthcoming.[143] Thus, Kahnawà:ke paid for a subdivision survey that it did not want, one that was never truly completed and did not accomplish what it intended. It had certainly failed to impose formalized colonial landownership norms in time for the construction of the CPR bridge (see Chapter 7). Nevertheless, the survey had allowed the DIA to define, number, map, categorize,

and value existing lots, and the tribunal claims process enabled the DIA
to name, number, categorize, and value (in the sense of defining who
owned property) Kahnawa'kehró:non. Kahnawà:ke itself had succeeded
in preventing its own destruction by way of subdivision and enfranchisement, but the survey data still permitted the DIA bureaucracy to better
view, understand, and control the community. Eventually, these data would
enable the department to impose the band council system, as we shall see
in Chapter 7. Thus, even with its failures and shortcomings, the Walbank
Survey is still a classic example of, in the words of historian Raymond
Craib, a "state's fixation with proprietorial transparency."[144] Nation-states
always want to know, and control, property transactions. In the case of
Indigenous communities, the settler state had first to *create* the private
property that it wished to know and control. Even as it contributed to
uncertainty, tension, and inequality in Kahnawà:ke, the Walbank Survey
was instrumental in the formation, surveillance, and control of private
property.

Conclusion

Identifying the Walbank Survey as a land-redistribution scheme does not
capture the full extent of its ambitions. It was no less than an attempt to
destroy an Indigenous nation and erase its people's ways of relating to each
other and the earth. Even though it did not fully succeed, it had significant
damaging consequences for Kahnawà:ke sovereignty. Settler observers
rarely acknowledged that Kahnawà:ke land law and practices had their
own logic and organization – namely, that individuals should be limited
in their ability to profit from lands and wood, and that the community
as a whole should benefit. One thing Canada's colonial elite were sure
about was that communal Indigenous ways of relating to land were backward and harmful. Liberal MP and former superintendent general of
Indian Affairs David Mills expressed it this way: "There was one thing
that impressed itself very strongly upon my mind, and that was the mis-
chievous effects that flow from allowing the Indians, on the various reservations in the old Provinces, to hold their lands in common."[145] The
Walbank Survey was one important step in imposing the legal and ethical
notion that land and resources should be treated as commodities for the
benefit of certain individuals.

The survey was designed to reshape property and land relations to the
detriment of Kahnawà:ke law and the Dish with One Spoon commons

that it upheld. In this, it bears many similarities to the earlier enclosure of common land in England. Most English commoners had depended heavily on common lands to supply food and raw materials because they lacked enough cultivated acreage to meet their needs. When common land was enclosed, many could no longer sustain themselves and were forced off of their lands.[146] Likewise, land-poor Kahnawa'kehró:non relied on common access to firewood, which was cut off once the DIA replaced the Kahnawà:ke commons with a form of private property. The Walbank Survey helped to make these changes more concrete and enforceable. Although it did not attain some of its most ambitious goals, it did succeed in transforming land into commoditized lots, and it further enabled the punishment of people who wished to follow Kahnawà:ke land law.[147]

The ideological rhetoric used to justify the subdivision of Kahnawà:ke was not unlike that used to justify enclosure in England. Late-eighteenth-century English proponents of enclosure sometimes even compared English commoners to North American Indigenous people.[148] In their view, allowing commoners to "wastefully" manage lands and resources was irresponsible, given that wealthier landowners could administer them more efficiently. Promoters of enclosure assumed that Indigenous land use (like that of English commoners) was primitive, bestial, and profligate, and they believed it wrong to leave the land and its inhabitants in such conditions. Common lands provided food and material that did not need to be cultivated, and improvers saw this production in negative terms, tantamount to thievery and pillage. Enclosing common lands was said to increase their productivity by placing larger portions under the control of one enterprising farmer; it also supposedly enhanced the productivity of the dispossessed, who were now required to exchange their labour for wages.[149] Kahnawà:ke chiefs in the 1870s recognized that a subdivision survey would likewise cut off their most vulnerable people from the land and its bounty, and they repeatedly refused the survey because they did not believe that such an enclosure was in the interest of their nation.[150]

Likewise, the Walbank Survey is best understood in light of Canada's rapid westward and northward territorial expansion. In the 1880s, the DIA was preoccupied with the thousands of Indigenous people who lived beyond the Great Lakes, onto whose territory Canada was imposing itself. In contravention of long-standing nation-to-nation agreements, protocols, and treaties, the Canadian state sought to speed the destruction of Indigenous political structures, cultural cohesion, and territories, allowing white settlers to appropriate the land and impose their law. Canada confined First Nations on reserves, tore families apart with residential schools, and ensured that they could not participate in the emerging settler economy. But the next step was to dismantle the reserves by parcelling them into individual lots that would be owned as private property by enfranchised former "Indians." The Walbank Survey was a trial run for this larger plan, an attempt to set a precedent for how to enfranchise an entire community and transform its territory into private property. It should also be viewed in light of the United States allotment policies of the late nineteenth century, and specifically the 1887 *Dawes Act,* which broke up Indian reservations and transferred the land to white settlers, undermined Indigenous sovereignty, and deprived Indigenous people of their land and wealth.[151] Although the purpose of the Walbank Survey was not explicitly to transfer land to white settlers, the outcome would have been similar if the land redistribution and mass enfranchisement had succeeded since the land would have then become available to anyone with money. The survey had indeed undermined Kahnawà:ke law and ways of life, but Kahnawa'kehró:non were able to stop its most destructive elements from being implemented.

Whereas landownership and land use were rooted in Kahnawà:ke law and in ever-evolving relationships between community members, Walbank's cadastral map froze a particular moment in time, imposed a settler colonial understanding of land, and served to preserve and privilege the boundaries it demarcated. Walbank's projected property grid never became reality, but the existing lots were defined, numbered, mapped, categorized, and valued. The people of Kahnawà:ke were likewise defined, named, numbered, categorized, and valued, and the DIA then used this information to impose the band council system in 1889 and to attempt to rigidly define, according to the *Indian Act,* who had the right to belong and who did not. According to its own estimate, the DIA considered Walbank's work incomplete, sloppy, and unreliable, yet his survey became the basis of both the existing cadastre and band membership list. In 1894, Hayter Reed declared, "this Department has accepted as correct the survey performed by Mr. Walbank on that Reserve as well as his plan of the same."[152] What mattered to the DIA was not the "accuracy" of its data as much as projecting authority and control, something it has struggled to do ever since. For detail and precision, the Walbank Survey could not match the ordnance survey, but it was very much like it in the way it aimed to colonize and subjugate a sovereign nation.

7

"It Is Necessary to Follow the Custom of the Reserve Which Is Contrary to Law"

Rupture and Continuity, 1885–1900

He did not tell me that he had a document; but he told me that it was he who had worked on the land.

— Atiataronne (Thomas Jacob), 1895

It has been the custom here that whoever worked a piece of land became the owner of it and was recognized as such by the tribe.

— Louis Norton, 1895

The Indian Advancement act, has created nothing but divisions, enmity and separation among us, it has degraded us rather than promoted.

— Shatekaienton, 1895

lthough the DIA interventions of the 1880s, most notably the Walbank Survey, did not immediately revolutionize the way in which Kahnawa'kehró:non related to their lands, they did have significant long-term impacts. From about 1885 to 1900, there was a distinct move away from Kahnawà:ke law and toward *Indian Act* law, even if neither set were evenly applied. In some instances, the DIA took account of Kahnawà:ke law (or custom, as officials sometimes termed it), but sometimes it did not (Chapter 5). This chapter covers the period during which the *Indian Advancement Act* and the band council system were imposed on Kahnawà:ke. As previous chapters have shown, *Indian Act* law was imposed on Indigenous communities in an uneven and haphazard way, resulting in uncertainty and hardship. Not only were these laws aimed at eradicating Indigenous sovereignty and culture, they were also imposed in ways that made it impossible for people to predict how the DIA would respond to their actions and decisions, and this book has shown some of the harms that arose as a result. Nevertheless, this ambiguity and uncertainty also allowed space for some people to continue to follow their own laws, even as such norms lost ground to state-sanctioned practices and ideologies.[1] This chapter shows some of the strategies the DIA used to try to take political control in the wake of the Walbank Survey and the ways in which Kahnawa'kehró:non ignored or resisted them.

This chapter covers roughly the fifteen years from the time of the Walbank Survey and the construction of the CPR bridge to the turn of the twentieth century and consists of two parts. The first is a history of the DIA's imposition of the band council system on Kahnawà:ke, a move that was designed to strengthen the department and weaken opposition in the community. The DIA and its officers were willing to bend and break laws, disenfranchise voters, slander leaders – anything to get control. Although this chapter shows that the DIA was indeed able to gain some of the control it desired using these tactics, it also shows that even as Kahnawa'kehró:non suffered under colonial rule, they continued to refuse it. The second part of the chapter provides an analysis of a key event that reveals the changing and contested nature of landownership and resource management in Kahnawà:ke in the 1890s, just as the band council system was being established. The lot 205 case arose because of railroad land expropriations, and it produced a remarkable documentary snapshot of Kahnawà:ke legal thought and land practices of the time. The case also reveals a great deal about how the Canadian state attempted to surveil and control Kahnawà:ke land and people, and the ways in which land and resource management continued to be sites of great contestation even after the *Indian Act* and the band council system of government had been imposed. Sometimes the DIA was able to assert itself with no apparent opposition; at other times it seemed impotent in the face of concerted political action by Kahnawa'kehró:non. The chapter title quotes Indian Agent Alexander Brosseau, who admitted even in the year 1900 that it was sometimes "necessary to follow the custom of the reserve," even if it were "contrary to law."[2] Although the chapter does not conclude at a convenient end point, it looks forward to twentieth-century trends, inviting readers to consider

the incomplete and ongoing nature of settler colonialism and the importance of Indigenous responses in defence of their nationhoods.

DIA Imposition of the Band Council System
and Kahnawà:ke Responses

When the Walbank Survey failed to deliver the expected outcomes –
the enfranchisement of all Kahnawa'kehró:non and the elimination of the
reserve – the DIA began to press for the *Indian Advancement Act* to be
applied to Kahnawà:ke, which would establish the band council system.
After decades of departmental action or inaction that had the effect of
discrediting the chiefs and stripping them of their authority, the stage was
set. Through much of the 1880s, the DIA stopped its long-standing practice
of confirming new chiefs who were chosen by the various clans.[3] In 1887,
only three elderly chiefs remained, who were widely seen as unable to effectively lead on their own.[4] Kahnawa'kehró:non needed new leaders, so
they tried to find ways to work with the DIA that did not involve accepting
the intrusive provisions of the *Advancement Act*. In November 1887, fifty-
four Kahnawa'kehró:non petitioned to have section 72 of the 1880 *Indian
Act* imposed. Under its terms, the ineffective council of chiefs would be
replaced by chiefs chosen in a general election.[5] The petitioners referred
specifically to the 1880 *Indian Act,* not the 1884 *Indian Advancement
Act,* because the former provided for a stronger band council and less
potential for DIA interference. They saw this step as a temporary measure
that would provide a functioning government until they could resolve
the problem posed by the DIA refusal to confirm chiefs. These petitioners
represented the anti-DIA side of Kahnawà:ke politics, which opposed the
Advancement Act.[6]

In January 1888, Agent Brosseau called a general meeting in Kahnawà:ke
to discuss the application of the *Indian Advancement Act,* which was not
what the petitioners had requested. Grossly misrepresenting Kahnawà:ke
public opinion, he reported unanimous support for the DIA to apply the
Indian Advancement Act to Kahnawà:ke.[7] That Brosseau lied about the unqualified approval for the act would be obvious to anyone with some
knowledge of Kahnawà:ke politics and history, and it is also revealed by
a letter that Brosseau wrote a few months later. Describing a subsequent
general assembly, he recorded that Tawehiakenra (Louis Jackson) and other
opponents of the act protested the meeting as illegal and demanded an
immediate election to replace deceased chiefs. Brosseau also knew that at

least one of the three remaining chiefs opposed the *Advancement Act*, but he nevertheless recommended that "in the interest of the tribe," it be applied as soon as possible.[8] The DIA planned to impose the band council system and cared little what most Kahnawa'kehró:non believed, but it used evidence of support from small numbers of community members to demonstrate that there was enthusiasm for the plan. When it came to imposing its own legal framework, the standard approach of the department was to take a letter from one person or group as representative, but it rejected outright the demands for the continuation of Indigenous legal frameworks regardless of the number of petitioners.

In the months following the January 1888 general meeting, large numbers of Kahnawa'kehró:non signed petitions demanding the right to elect new chiefs under the old system. Immediately after the meeting, 160 Kahnawa'kehró:non petitioned the DIA, demanding permission to elect leaders without delay.[9] According to historian Gerald Reid's calculations, thirty-two (57 percent) of those who signed the November 1887 petition also signed the January 1888 petition in a last-ditched attempt to restore the council of chiefs under the old system. Each of the seven Kahnawà:ke clans also sent petitions, asking to elect chiefs outside the parameters of the *Indian Advancement Act*.[10] The DIA asked Agent Brosseau for his opinion, and he attempted to discredit the petitioners by calling them troublemakers, ignorant, young, or absent from the reserve.[11] To paint the 160 January petitioners with such a broad brush shows just how negatively the DIA and its agents responded to those who disagreed with its plans. Brosseau also felt that "it would be preferable to have [band] councillors than to reelect chiefs, who in my opinion might place the sound portion of the population at the mercy of the agitators and supporters of intemperance, who are trying their best to create trouble and disorder within the village."[12] By portraying large numbers of Kahnawa'kehró:non in such disparaging terms, Brosseau gave DIA officials the justification to dismiss their opponents and to impose the *Advancement Act*.

Brosseau hoped that new elections under the *Advancement Act* would be held immediately, but DIA officials worried about various legal matters and thus dragged their heels.[13] It even seems likely that they forgot the subject until the following year, when Brosseau reported that he was receiving two or three delegations each week "seeking immediate and precise information in regard to this matter." "It is impossible," he wrote, "to go on with the affairs of the tribe any longer without something being done."[14] In January 1889, nearly 210 Kahnawa'kehró:non, representing all seven clans and making up 43 percent of the adult population, signed petitions asking for "the Election of Chiefs while waiting for the *Indian Advancement Act* applied to us."[15] The wording of these petitions suggests either a strategic attempt at appeasement or resigned acceptance that the act would be installed whether they wanted it or not – that they simply wished to have a working government in the meantime. Like earlier petitions, these were denied (Figure 7.1).

In fact, only a very small number of DIA allies in Kahnawà:ke approved of the *Advancement Act,* five of whom petitioned for its immediate application. Identifying themselves as farmers, they were Taiawensere (Thomas Leclerc), Ohahakete (George Wood), Anatahes (Moise Mailloux),

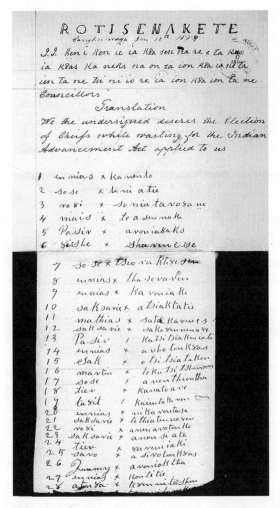

FIGURE 7.1   A page from the petition of January 13, 1889, from over two hundred Kahnawa'kehró:non. | RG10, vol. 7921, file 32-5, LAC.

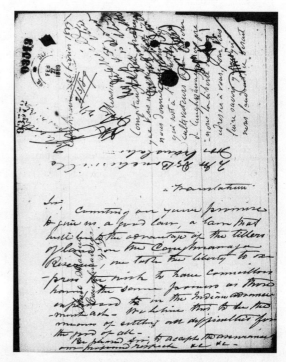

FIGURES 7.2 AND 7.3
Petition from Taiawensere,
Ohahakete, Anatahes,
Teatenhawita, and
Katsitsiio, February 26,
1889. | RG10, vol. 7921, file
32-5, LAC.

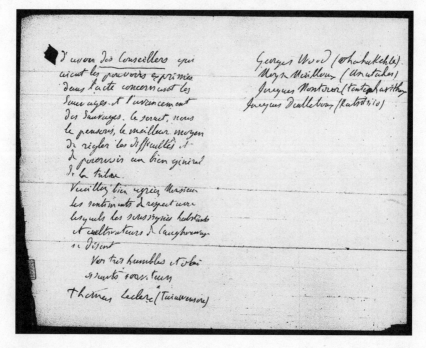

Teatenhawita (Jacques Montour), and Katsitsiio (Jacques Daillibout).[16] In their February 1889 petition (Figures 7.2 and 7.3), they wrote:

> Counting on your promise to give us a good law, a law that will be to the advantage of the tillers of land on the Caughnawaga Reserve, we take the liberty to express the wish to have councillors having the same powers as those expressed in the Indian Advancement Act. We believe this to be the means of settling all difficulties for the good of all.[17]

Given the way in which the department operated, it probably solicited this petition to give the appearance of community buy-in. Less than a week after receiving it, Vankoughnet told its authors that "the matter was now engaging the attention of the Government."[18] On the same day, March 5, 1889, the Privy Council issued an Order-in-Council that applied the *Indian Advancement Act* to Kahnawà:ke.[19] The DIA then abolished the council of chiefs, imposed the band council system, designated the territory "the Caughnawaga Indian Reserve," and divided it into six electoral districts.

The configuration of the districts reveals either that DIA officials hoped to subvert the will of the electorate. According to the *Advancement Act,* each district was to have "a number of male Indians of full age, equal or nearly as may be found convenient to such proportion of the male Indians of full age resident on the reserve, as one section of the reserve will bear to all the sections."[20] But in Kahnawà:ke, almost the entire male population lived in just one district (section 6, the village), whereas each of the other five contained only a handful of men. Thus, even though the village district housed hundreds of electors, and the other five had an average of just fifteen to twenty, every district would choose a representative to sit on the band council.[21] In addition to having already disenfranchised Kahnawà:ke women through the *Advancement Act,* DIA officials knew that the layout of the electoral districts also devalued the votes of most of the men, since most lived in the village. To justify their approach, they pointed out that each district contained an approximately equal number of Walbank's newly surveyed thirty-acre lots, and they expressed the hope that the land redistribution would still go through.[22] Once the demographic shuffle was complete and everyone was ensconced on the new lots, the six districts would have approximately equal numbers of electors.[23] However, virtually none of the thirty-acre lots had houses, so the idea that Kahnawa'kehró:non would abandon their homes in the village was patently unrealistic. Additionally, it was abundantly clear to all involved that the land redistribution would not take place due to the DIA refusal to finance it. Thus, either DIA officials were living in a fantasy world or they had chosen the profoundly anti-democratic layout of the districts because they knew it would produce band councils that were sympathetic to them. Tellingly, some of the largest landowners and strongest DIA supporters lived outside of the village district. The DIA certainly benefitted from the situation in the years to come, and its subsequent attempts to control election results further point in this direction.

Early Band Council Elections

The DIA ensured that the first election under the *Indian Advancement Act* was held almost immediately after the application of the act. Under the act, women could not vote. The adult men who lived in section 6, the village district which contained most of the population, elected Tawehiakenra (Louis Jackson), a respected man who owned no land outside the village.[24] He was a leading opponent of the *Indian Act* system and captain of the Canadian voyageur contingent that went to Egypt in 1884–85.[25] Over two hundred men voted in section 6, whereas no more than twelve did so in each of the other five.[26] Agent Brosseau, however, claimed that Tawehiakenra was ineligible because he was not a resident of section 6 and refused to allow him to attend council meetings. Tawehiakenra produced evidence to the contrary and was eventually vindicated by a Department of Justice investigation, but in the meantime his enforced absence from council ensured the election of a chief councillor, Kanenharoton (Thomas Jocks), preferred by the DIA.[27] The DIA believed that he would advance its agenda.[28] A number of Kahnawa'kehró:non petitioned the DIA to investigate Brosseau's meddling in the March 26 general election and the election of Chief Councillor Kanenharoton on April 1.[29] Three of the newly elected councillors petitioned the department to annul the results of the April 1 election, due to irregularities.[30] The DIA, happy with the election results, sided with its agent and allowed them to stand.[31] Thus, as the first band council election demonstrated, the DIA realized that its own agenda was deeply unpopular and knew that under a lawful band council election, Kahnawa'kehró:non electors would choose leaders who opposed the DIA's agenda. As it was, the department ensured that most of the unfriendly votes went to just one candidate – Tawehiakenra – and then blocked him from running for, or even voting for, the position of chief councillor. As a result, the first band council was relatively friendly to the DIA and vastly over-represented the sparsely populated electoral districts outside the village.

Having ensured a relatively compliant band council, the DIA soon undermined whatever legitimacy the council had in Kahnawà:ke by failing to respond to its resolutions. Since the council could not enact its own laws without departmental approval, and since the DIA simply did not respond to many of its resolutions, even councillors who had supported the band council system became frustrated. Nevertheless, the chief councillor and his allies maintained a deferential disposition toward the DIA, whereas the three opposition councillors boycotted meetings in protest of departmental unresponsiveness.[32] As a result, the council lacked quorum and could not transact business. The three oppositional councillors disrupted its activities to such an extent that the superintendent general of the DIA asked the Privy Council to have them deposed and declared ineligible for re-election. As justification, he cited section 75 of the *Indian Act,* which stated that the Privy Council could depose a councillor for "dishonesty, intemperance, immorality or incompetency."[33] A Department of Justice investigation concluded that the government did not have the power to unseat the three men. Although the correspondence does not indicate how the Department of Justice arrived at this conclusion, it mentions that it intended to insert a clause into the next amendment of the *Indian Act* that would give the government the "necessary power so that we shall have that to hold over their heads in the future."[34]

Under the *Advancement Act,* elections were held every year, and the 1890 race returned Tawehiakenra to office by a wide margin, this time as chief councillor, along with a council dominated by opponents of the DIA. In its first sitting, the council asked to have the *Indian Act* amended so that band councils could enact their own bylaws without the approval of the department. Fifty-two Kahnawa'kehró:non petitioned against this expansion of band council powers, arguing that it was unjust for landowners to be ruled by those who owned no land (as was then the case).[35] In apparent coordination with the band council, however, Liberal MP Cyrille Doyon introduced a bill that would allow the Kahnawà:ke band council to pass rules and regulations without DIA approval.[36] This bill was debated in the House of Commons in March 1890, with the Opposition Liberals supporting it and the governing Conservatives firmly opposed. Doyon argued that Kahnawa'kehró:non were more advanced than other First Nations and should thus be given more responsibility in governing themselves. Liberal Party leader Wilfrid Laurier favoured the Kahnawà:ke council's request, and went further, stating that all band councils under the *Indian Advancement Act* should be given these expanded powers. DIA Superintendent General and Minister of the Interior Edgar Dewdney rejected these suggestions out of hand, asserting that Kahnawà:ke was the one community that did not deserve expanded band council powers and citing the behaviour of Tawehiakenra's "obstructive party." Prime Minister John A. Macdonald added that band councils could not be allowed to act independently as long as all "Indians," including the "wild and dissolute," were allowed to vote for them. The proposed amendment to the *Advancement Act* was defeated.[37] Plainly, Macdonald's government believed that Indigenous people were not human enough to govern themselves and that they should not be given the chance to do so. Nevertheless, these events reveal that Kahnawa'kehró:non who opposed the *Indian Advancement Act* were able to take control of the new band council and even to have their propositions debated in the House of Commons. Their apparent political agency did not translate into the successful political and legal changes they sought, but they continued to use all means at their disposal to agitate for them. They soon realized, however, that even control of the council did not enable them to govern themselves.

Many Kahnawa'kehró:non soon understood that the band council system was itself designed to ensure ineffective governance (and DIA control), regardless of who was elected. At the end of 1890, the DIA received two petitions from Kahnawa'kehró:non, asking for a return to traditional government: one was from seven women of the Bear Clan who blamed the band council form of government for "ill feelings between us Indians." The other was from 121 men who demanded an end to "the republic form of government of electing persons" and a return to the system in which clans chose hereditary chiefs.[38] The department disregarded both petitions. A contentious band council election in 1891 confirmed the split between those who were willing to work with the DIA and those who were not, with the result that the councillors refused to work together. Once again, the council was unable to reach quorum, and there was apparently nothing the DIA could do about it.[39]

In the leadup to the 1892 spring election, Agent Brosseau reported that a number of people were moving from the village to outlying areas in order to be able to vote in those districts. He believed that those who opposed the DIA agenda were in this way attempting to take control of the council.[40] Since so few Kahnawa'kehró:non lived outside the village, even a small change could greatly affect outcomes there.[41] Although the DIA had hoped for a village-to-farm migration when it created the electoral districts, it now found these moves alarming since they threatened to weaken its influence even further. To put an end to them, Brosseau suggested various changes to the *Indian Act* that would allow him to disqualify his political opponents ("men who want to live at the expense of the government") from voting.[42] Although his DIA superiors always agreed with this characterization of those who opposed their agenda, they had to remind him that even if his proposed changes were desirable, the *Indian Act* could not be revised in time for the upcoming election.[43]

Undaunted, Brosseau attempted to manipulate the outcome of the 1892 election by declaring that a number of electors in the rural districts were ineligible to vote because they had moved there only recently or because they did not own property there.[44] When results were tied in three districts, Brosseau cast the deciding vote in each.[45] Thus, the 1892 council was dominated by men who were favourable to the DIA, including the chief councillor, Dr. Thomas Patton.[46] Because of uncertainty around *Indian Act* election provisions and questions about the actions of the agent, the DIA deliberated for two months before ratifying the results.[47]

Further Resistance to the Band Council System

After a number of similarly contested elections, Brosseau recommended in 1896 that the six-district system be eliminated. The system was based on a vision of a future population distribution that never came to be, and in fact the populations of some outlying districts were actually decreasing by 1896.[48] The department initially agreed to the change, but by now the system had been in place long enough for its allies to shift Kahnawà:ke politics, and over one hundred Kahnawa'kehró:non signed a petition asking for the system to be retained. The department agreed. Brosseau said that he attempted to hold community meetings in 1897, aimed at reforming the electoral districts, but these generated only acrimony, since naturally all the councillors who represented rural districts preferred the status quo.[49] The DIA also benefitted from the districts as they were and thus maintained the six-district system until 1906, even though it knew it to be outside of its own law. A single-district system was finally introduced in that year.[50]

Despite colonial meddling and injustice (or perhaps because of it), Kahnawà:ke opposition to the *Indian Advancement Act* did not dissipate as the DIA had hoped. As soon as the act was imposed in 1889, many Kahnawa'kehró:non expressed their dissatisfaction and their desire to return to the traditional council of chiefs. This resistance was often expressed in the form of petitions.[51] One such petition in 1894 was signed by 245 people, who demanded a return to traditional governance.[52] This was only one in a long line of petitions asking for much the same thing. In response, T.M. Daly, the minister of the interior and DIA superintendent general, and his deputy, Hayter Reed, visited Kahnawà:ke to speak to community members in person.

In February 1895, Daly and Reed met with about four hundred Kahnawa'kehró:non to discuss the widespread desire to reinstate traditional governance. Also present at the meeting were representatives from Ahkwesáhsne, Kanehsatà:ke, and other Indigenous nations in the area. One newspaper reported that "the day was regarded as a gala occasion, the houses were decked with flags, and the assemblage singularly bright and animated."[53] The meeting can be interpreted as a continuation of the Seven Nations tradition of large council meetings in Kahnawà:ke that sometimes included representatives of the colonial government.[54] Chiefs gave speeches in their respective languages. Several argued that the current law was unacceptable, that the old system of governance should be revived, and that Indian agents should be removed from their communities. One white reporter noted, however, that "others were found" who had only small grievances with the band council system.[55] This kind of "bothsidesing," which is still common in journalism, served the colonial status quo then just as it does today.[56] Minister Daly, in what must have been an extraordinarily disappointing speech for many of his listeners, promised to seriously consider their request only if there were unanimous support for a return to the old system. Like everyone else, Daly knew that unanimity would be impossible to achieve. He ended his speech by encouraging Kahnawa'kehró:non to give more attention to farming, an insult to an Indigenous people famous for its agricultural tradition and a way of declaring that the department intended to take no responsibility for problems caused by its own interference.[57]

The dismissive response from Daly further infuriated the many who opposed the band council system and were now told there was no way out. Shatekaienton, who had been named a chief under Kahnawà:ke law in the 1850s at the age of twenty and who remained in this position until 1889, published a letter in the Montreal Daily Witness in 1895. He wished to refute Daly's version of the Kahnawà:ke meeting and to inform the public of the majority's desire to return to the old system. He took particular issue with Daly's assertion that the Advancement Act would lead to the "enlightenment" of his people and that reviving the old system would be a step backward. Shatekaienton argued that it would be better to "draw back, even as far back as one hundred and fifty years, to save our reserve from ruin, for the new system, the Indian Advancement act, has created nothing but divisions, enmity and separation among us, it has degraded us rather than promoted."[58] Daly and Reed's visit took place in the same month as the lot 205 inquiry, the subject of the second part of this chapter. The bitter and ironic responses of Kahnawa'kehró:non, including band councillors two years later at the conclusion of the lot 205 case, can be better understood in light of this deep grief and frustration.

In 1897, eighty-eight Kahnawà:ke women petitioned for a return to traditional governance, stating that the band council system had increased sorrows, eliminated advantages, and caused disputes. With little hope of success, Kahnawa'kehró:non continued petitioning to have the *Advancement Act* revoked. A clause in its 1886 version allowed the governor-in-council to declare that the *Advancement Act* no longer applied to a band if the desired impact were not being achieved.[59] Although this provision may have given some Kahnawa'kehró:non hope for a revocation, there is no indication that the DIA ever considered it for Kahnawà:ke. The community continued to petition against the band council system throughout the first decade of the twentieth century, and the DIA continued to ignore or reject its requests.[60] Opposition never disappeared, but Kahnawa'kehró:non understood that the DIA had never intended to listen to them if they disagreed with its agenda. Although more can and should be written about the *Indian Advancement Act* and the band council system in Kahnawà:ke, the short history given here should suffice to show that their purpose was to disrupt Kahnawà:ke sovereignty and to consolidate DIA control. The following case study, however, reveals that the DIA continued to struggle to impose itself while Kahnawa'kehró:non continued to assert their nationhood and lived according to their laws.

THE LOT 205 CASE

The Walbank Survey (Chapter 6) was launched in part to facilitate land expropriations for the construction of a CPR bridge and railway line in Kahnawà:ke, but the survey was not yet complete when construction began in 1886. Nevertheless, Walbank's map and valuations were used to determine compensation for expropriated land. Without obtaining a permit from anyone, CPR engineers simply began construction, leaving the DIA with the job of determining who should receive compensation.[61]

FIGURE 7.4   *First Lachine Bridge – Canadian Pacific Railway,* 1886. This was replaced by the present structure in 1913. | Dominion Bridge Company fonds, MIKAN no. 3703504, Accession no. 1987-161 NPC, LAC.

The bridge connecting Lachine to Kahnawà:ke was completed in August 1887, allowing CPR trains to cross the continent without the use of ferries (Figure 7.4).[62] Some Kahnawa'kehró:non took jobs and perceived other benefits related to the bridge and rail line, but they were the cause of much trouble for others.[63] During construction, the CPR trespassed on the lands of many Kahnawa'kehró:non, stored materials on certain lots against the wishes of their owners, and built waterlines and windmills without permission.[64] After the line was finished, landowners complained of flooded fields due to poorly maintained railway ditches, fires ignited by sparks from train engines, and valuable animals killed on the tracks due to poor CPR fencing.[65] The bridge approach crossed – and blocked – an important Kahnawà:ke road, and it cut off access for village cattle to graze on a seasonal island and wetland.[66]

Then, in 1893, the CPR informed the DIA that it intended to use a hill on a lot in Kahnawà:ke as a borrow pit. The bridge approach on the Kahnawà:ke side consisted of wooden trestles, and now the company wanted to make it more permanent by replacing it with an approach made of earth (see Figure 7.5 for a view of the village from the bridge approach). The hill on the lot would supply the necessary soil.[67] It is unclear if the company ever received formal departmental approval for this work, but regardless, in the fall of 1893 it began excavating a hill on what Walbank had labelled lot 205 (Figure 7.6).

FIGURE 7.5   *View West from the Rail Bridge Approach toward the Village of Kahnawake, ca 1910,* Joseph-Amédée Dumas | MP-0000.115.1, McCord Museum.

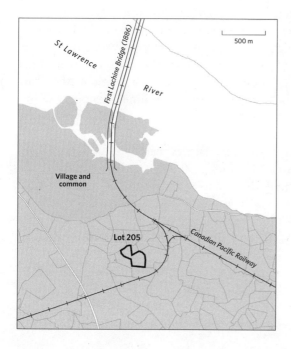

FIGURE 7.6   Map of Kahnawà:ke, showing location of lot 205 in relation to the CPR bridge, c. 1885. | Map by Eric Leinberger.

In some CPR-related expropriations, DIA officials were able to follow Walbank's lot lines to determine compensation, but this case confounded them. They simply could not determine who owned lot 205 and who should therefore receive the compensation money. A year after the excavation, the CPR paid the DIA $558 in compensation for the lot, leaving Indian Agent Brosseau the task of deciding who should receive it. Initially, there were two claimants, Tanekorens (Jacques Lachaudière) and Sakorewata (Peter Parquis), who agreed to split the money.[68] However, before it was paid out a third claimant came forward: Sakotion (William Meloche).[69] Curiously, Agent Brosseau went ahead and paid the two original claimants, but he withheld fifty dollars from each "to protect himself in case the Department should decide that Meloche's claim was a good one."[70] The DIA then decided to hold an inquiry to find the true owner of the lot and who was entitled to the remaining hundred dollars.[71]

According to Walbank, "lot 205" consisted of 9.4 acres, 7.1 of which were hay land and 2.3 were bush. He valued it at seventy-three dollars, a low figure that was typical of his approach if a property did not feature cultivated land, sugarbush, or buildings.[72] He listed the owner as Saio-nesakeren (Peter Montour Jr.),[73] but this man died soon after the Walbank tribunal collected its information. The previous owner had been his father, Peter Montour Sr. (known as Grey Horse), who was also father of the claimant Tanekorens's wife.[74] According to Agent Brosseau, a man named Peter Lachaudière had inherited the lot on the death of Saionesa-keren.[75] In an internal departmental memo, however, W.A. Austin stated that the lot was claimed by the widow of Saionesakeren (her name is not known).[76] For unknown reasons, the DIA inquiry accepted neither Peter Lachaudière nor the widow of Saionesakeren as legitimate claimants. When the department asked Brosseau what exactly the problem was, he explained that "there was no dispute respecting this land before the C.P.R. intended taking land at this site; that it was then that unknown owners began to make claims to lot No. 205."[77] This statement contradicted the DIA truism that intrinsically dysfunctional and irrational "Indians" fought chronic battles over land and that only outside intervention could end the eternal squabbles. Clearly, the multiple users and "owners" of lot 205 had operated side-by-side without difficulty under Kahnawà:ke law; conflict arose only when an outside entity interfered.

All parties agreed that Sakorewata's claim was legitimate and that he was entitled to half of the hundred dollars, so he did not participate in the inquiry. Documents provide few clues as to his claim, but the idea that more than one person had a legitimate claim to the lot appears to have been widely accepted, and the dispute eventually centred on whether Sakotion or Tanekorens should receive the remaining fifty dollars. I can find no explanation as to why Brosseau paid out $458 of the original $558 before the inquiry was held. The point of the inquiry was to determine who should receive the remaining hundred dollars, half of which was already earmarked for Sakorewata. The two claimants for the fifty dollars were Sakotion and Tanekorens.

Aged thirty-three, Sakotion (William Meloche) was married to Leontine Meloche, who was twenty-six. The 1901 census lists him as a foreman. His parents were members of the Meloche and Giasson families, both widely disliked in Kahnawà:ke and perceived as white. There was an ongoing effort to have both of these families evicted. In 1868, for example, chiefs pressured the DIA to evict white men, including Sakotion's father, Osias Meloche, and his maternal grandfather, Charles Gideon Giasson. The DIA initially issued an eviction order for Meloche and Giasson but then rescinded it on the basis that they had married "Indian" women before Canadian law specified that white men could not gain Indian status through marriage.[78] In 1878, Osias Meloche died in a barn fire that was deliberately set (see page 137). In 1885, Walbank listed Sakotion as a "half-breed" who owned no land (even though his family had extensive holdings). When Walbank asked him whether he was recognized as a member of the Kahnawà:ke band, he replied, "I think so." However, the four chiefs on the Walbank tribunal unanimously voted against him "because he does not belong to this Band and his father was a French-Canadian."[79]

Sakotion stated that lot 205 had belonged to his family for twenty-five years, ever since his father, Osias Meloche, had purchased it from Saionesakeren. When asked why he had not included it as part of his 1885 Walbank tribunal claim, he said that he and his family were so hated in Kahnawà:ke that he had not dared to attempt it. Before the inquiry, Tanekorens, Sakorewata, and their witnesses had declared to Agent Brosseau that Sakotion had never held land at the lot 205 site. They argued that Sakorewata's father had owned the land, but that several years before Saionesakeren took possession "by right of the improvements which he had made on the land."[80] This appears to be a case where Saionesakeren was able to make use of land that was not being used and that he thus gained a right to it in the customary way. The details of the arrangement are not divulged in the records, but Sakorewata's father and Saionesakeren apparently maintained their simultaneous ownership without any obvious conflict.

The other main claimant, Tanekorens (James Lachaudière), was fifty-one in 1895. Ten years earlier, Walbank had listed him as a sub-chief, yet his Kahnawà:ke membership was disputed by two of the four tribunal chiefs because he was born out of wedlock, and the identity of his father was unknown. Considering the matrilineal norms of Rotinonhsión:ni, their stance is significant. Tanekorens was a prominent leader, and even the lot 205 inquiry showed that he had support from those who held to Kahnawà:ke law. In 1885, he signed his claimant form with an X, which indicates that he was probably illiterate.[81] In 1895, he had a nine-year-old son who lived with him and his wife, and the 1901 census records him as a voyageur (river pilot).

The Inquiry

The DIA inquiry into the lot 205 compensation question began in February 1895, after the hill on it had been destroyed and was now a hole in the ground. None of the claimants had a clear idea of where lot 205 began and ended, and none of them had seen it as a piece of real estate to be bought and sold. It was only with the destruction of the hill and the subsequent inquiry that anyone attempted to frame the land in this way. Thus, this inquiry included much confusing testimony as to the extent of lot 205. Testimony suggests that the lot included the hill, but there is also discussion of land below the hill without providing any clarity as to where the boundary lay that Walbank had drawn.

As neither Sakotion nor Tanekorens had a deed for the lot, they brought witnesses to vouch for them under oath, but the DIA file includes few details on how the inquiry was run. Ten people testified on behalf of Sakotion and six for Tanekorens. Each claimant was also represented by a prominent person who spoke on his behalf and cross-examined the other claimant's witnesses. Sakotion was represented by Georges Cherrier, the former Indian agent who was also his uncle, and Tanekorens was represented by Waniente (John Jocks),[82] a thirty-year-old band councillor and owner of a major Kahnawà:ke quarry. Many of the testimonies were delivered in Kanien'kéha and subsequently translated into French and English, but the Kanien'kéha original is not in the DIA file. The file includes translations of some testimonials in English, of others in French, and of some in both languages. Below I summarize the highlights of the testimony, beginning with those who spoke on behalf of Sakotion on February 15, 1895.

The first witness for Sakotion was Ononsihata (Frank Hill).[83] As he explained, a certain François Beaudette had told him that he had recently purchased hay grown on lot 205 from Tanekorens. However, Sakotion had mown and taken the hay before Tanekorens could do it himself. On multiple occasions, Beaudette asked Tanekorens for his money back, only to be told that Tanekorens planned to sue Sakotion for compensation and would then reimburse him. But Tanekorens never followed through on this plan. The suggestion here is that Tanekorens's claim to the hay on lot 205 was weak because he would have fought for compensation had it been otherwise. The inference is that Tanekorens had no legal recourse when Sakotion removed the hay.[84]

Charles Xavier Giasson,[85] Sakotion's sixty-two-year-old uncle, spoke next. He owned lot 207, just northeast of lot 205. He claimed that for at least the last thirty years his neighbour on lot 205 had been Osias Meloche, Sakotion's father. He thought that Osias Meloche had purchased the lot from Peter Montour Jr. but admitted that his knowledge of the sale was based on hearsay. He had a good view of the lot from his own haying lands, and he had never seen or heard of anyone except Osias Meloche working it before Meloche's death. Meloche's activities on the land included planting crops, cutting branches, and removing stones. Giasson related a version of the story told by Ononsihata that Sakotion had appropriated Beaudette's hay in 1893.[86] Overall, Giasson had no direct knowledge of Osias Meloche's supposed purchase of the lot, but he bolstered Sakotion's case by showing that Meloche had farmed and gathered there.

The subsequent witness, Anatakarias (Thomas Hill),[87] also testified that the late Peter Montour Jr. had sold the lot to Osias Meloche. He then specified that it had actually belonged not to Montour but to Skasenhate (Marianne),[88] the widow of Peter Montour Sr., who was living in the house of Montour Jr. at the time. Because she was sick and very poor, she decided to sell the land to support herself and to pay for her eventual funeral. Anatakarias had heard Montour Jr. say that the land was his because he had looked after the woman who owned it.[89] The main contribution of this witness to Sakotion's case was to give a credible, detailed story of how, even though Skasenhate had apparently sold the lot to Osias Meloche, many believed that Peter Montour Jr. had owned the lot before he sold it to Osias Meloche.

Similarly, the next witness, Sarakwa,[90] testified that Peter Montour Jr. sold the land in question and that he had the right to it because he took care of Skasenhate. Sarakwa said he had been afraid to appear at the inquiry because he heard that whoever testified in favour of Sakotion would be branded a troublemaker, and he was worried about his health since he had heart problems. Under cross-examination, he was unwilling to reveal the source of his information.[91] His testimony confirmed some aspects of the way in which Peter Montour Jr. came to possess the lot by way of his relationship with Skasenhate. It also reveals the high stakes of the case, to the extent that Sarakwa feared retribution for taking the side of a family that was widely seen as harmful and illegitimate.

Satekarenhes (Mattias Hill),[92] a fifty-six-year-old agricultural labourer with no farmland of his own, testified that lot 205 had belonged to Osias Meloche and ought therefore to belong to his son Sakotion. Several times during the last twenty years, he himself had planted peas on the lot, and he knew of no one who had made a claim to it during that period. When cross-examined about its boundaries, he stated emphatically, "I do not know the boundaries of this land, but I know the land which I worked."[93] For at least eight years, he had been employed by Leon Giasson, Sakotion's uncle, during which he had worked on the lot three times. His testimony indicates that Leon Giasson had Osias Meloche's permission to work the land or had an arrangement to share it with him.[94]

The next five witnesses gave shorter statements. The first was Tahahente (Edward McComber),[95] a thirty-nine-year-old cousin of Sakotion's mother, who testified that Sakotion had hired him eight years previously to work the land. "Before I worked there," he recounted, "I did not know that he had land on the high ground; I knew that he had land below; but I did not know that he had it there."[96] This admission from a relative – that he did not know Sakotion owned land on the hill – may have hurt Sakotion's case. The next witness, Joseph Reed,[97] age thirty-eight, said that he had worked for Sakotion on the lot in about 1883. At the time, it had never occurred to him that the land might not belong to Sakotion. Like most other witnesses, he did not know where its boundaries lay, but he had cut hay on both its high and low land.[98] The next witness was Sakotion's fifty-year-old uncle Leon Giasson,[99] who said that he himself had paid people to work the land. He asserted that the Meloche family had owned it for over thirty years and that no one questioned their ownership before the CPR appropriated it. He could say very little about its size and location.[100] Delvida Meloche,[101] Sakotion's thirty-five-year-old brother, spoke next. He claimed that he knew the boundaries of the lot because his father, Osias Meloche, had showed them to him.[102]

Sakotion's final witness was his mother, Charlotte L. Giasson. She testified that she herself had purchased lot 205 some twenty-five to twenty-eight years previously from Peter Montour (it's unclear if it was the younger or the older) and that the sale had been notarized by Notary Defoy in the presence of two men. She had acquired the land to be nearer to her father but had told her son Sakotion that it was his. When asked about its extent, she said, "I bought all the high land in question, that is to say the flat land the length of my father's land up to another small piece of flat land behind; but I cannot say that this is all the high land."[103] She could not find the deeds to the lot and could not remember how much she had paid for it; in fact, she did not recall whether she had bought it with cash or in exchange for a horse. She had not visited it since the date of purchase, but she insisted that her husband, Osias Meloche, had showed her the boundary at the time.[104] Charlotte Giasson was the only one of these witnesses to claim that she had purchased the land and given it to her son.

Sakotion's witnesses thus largely agreed that the late Osias Meloche had owned lot 205 and that his ownership was uncontested until the CPR expropriation, with the notable exception of Charlotte Giasson, who portrayed herself as the owner rather than her husband. Some remembered that Osias Meloche had the authority to permit people to work on the lot and others recalled working for him there. Only Sakotion's brother and mother claimed to know its boundaries, and only the latter mentioned a notarized deed, which she said she had lost. Much of the testimony was vague, some was contradictory, and some even seemed to go against Sakotion's case. The witnesses for Tanekorens made their statements a week later, on February 22, 1895.

The first witness was Kanawaienton (Michel Jacob),[105] aged sixty-four, one of the largest landowners in Kahnawà:ke. In 1885, Walbank had recorded that he possessed seven lots totalling 112 acres, valued at $2,359. One was lot 210, which nearly bordered lot 205. According to Kanawaienton, lot 205 had belonged to Peter Montour Jr. about twenty years earlier, and he had seen Montour working there over the course of two summers. As he explained: "When I saw Montour working there, I believed that it was his."[106] Thus, he felt that Montour owned the land because he worked it. Various people had asked Montour for permission to cut hay on the land and had been allowed to do so. According to Kanawaienton, the land Montour owned was about four acres of high land, whereas Osias Meloche owned some land below the hill. When asked if Meloche could have purchased the land on the hill without his knowledge, Kanawaienton admitted that it was possible but added, "I know all the lands that he bought by having seen him working on those lands."[107] He had passed by nearly every year for forty-two years and never saw anyone planting a crop there before Montour. Kanawaienton's testimony reveals that he was familiar with the history of the land and of the lands worked by Osias Meloche. He had not seen Meloche working on lot 205 and thus was confident that it did not belong to him. By contrast, he had seen Montour farming there.[108]

Atiataronne (Thomas Jacob),[109] aged fifty-five, testified that in about 1873, Peter Montour Jr. had put him in charge of the wood he had cut on the hill. He and Montour encountered Osias Meloche there, who was loading their wood onto his cart. A fight ensued after Montour questioned Meloche and began to throw the wood out of the cart. Meloche got the worst of it and left. "The wood in question," stated Atiataronne, "had been cut where Montour was working on the land, he was master there; he was not afraid to go there; he had worked there and he was the master." Asked if Montour possessed a deed for the land, Atiataronne emphasized that his ownership flowed from the work he had done there: "He did not tell me that he had a document; but he told me that it was he who had worked on the land." Asked if Osias Meloche had been stealing the wood, he answered: "He must have meant to do so, as the late Montour took the wood in question away from him, because it was he who had worked the land."[110] The legal principles articulated by Atiataronne are in line with those expressed by Kahnawà:ke chiefs throughout the nineteenth century and embodied in the 1801 Code (Chapter 2). According to him, Montour had the right to the land because he worked it, and he had a right to the wood because he had cut it. Meloche was in the wrong because he was attempting to take wood that he had not cut.

The next two witnesses presented shorter statements. Thirty-eight-year-old Teharenions (François Beaudette or Frank Leclere) testified that he had known the land for twenty-six years and had never heard anyone say that it belonged to Osias Meloche.[111] He said that he had cut hay there with the permission of Tanekorens, whom he saw as the present owner, and that Meloche had never interfered with his haying, because the land was not his.[112] Teharenions thus emphasized that Tanekorens, not Meloche, gave permission to others who wanted to cut hay on the lot, that Meloche had nothing to do with it, and could not stop it. Fifty-four-year-old Aientonni (Raiontonnis or Jean-Baptiste Canadien or Big John),[113] a famous lacrosse player and river pilot, spoke next. He had known the parties and the land for thirty years and had heard that Peter Montour and his son were its recognized owners.[114] He appears to have offered no further details, which suggests that he was present because he was a well-known and trusted member of the community.

Next was François Daillebout,[115] aged forty-six, who said he first worked on lot 205 with Peter Montour Jr. some twenty-two years earlier "breaking up the land." "The first time I went there," he stated, "I went to cut underbrush. I worked on this land for the late Montour every spring for five consecutive years, and at other times in the autumn." He helped Montour quite often but was not paid for his labour. Also, he had observed Osias Meloche cutting wood below the hill, apparently with the blessing of Peter Montour. According to Daillebout, Osias Meloche "took possession of it [the low land] in order to work it in accordance with the custom at the time." The higher land, however, belonged to Peter Montour, "as it was he who worked the land."[116] In noting that both Meloche and Montour took possession of their respective areas by working them, Daillebout thus clearly references Kahnawà:ke legal principles.

The final witness for Tanekorens was Louis Norton,[117] aged eighty-two, who gave a slightly different perspective on who first claimed the land but also focused on Kahnawà:ke legal principles. He never saw Peter Montour Sr. on the lot and had never heard anyone say that it belonged to him. In fact, he said it was Peter Montour Jr. "took possession according to custom to work it." Norton had seen Montour Jr. working on the land in about 1880, which is how he knew he had rights to it. Because Norton passed by there nearly every day, he could confidently say that he had never seen anyone else working on the hill; nor had he noticed that the land was sown or cleared of stones. He then summarized the legal principle: "it has been the custom here that whoever worked a piece of land became the owner of it and was recognized as such by the tribe." Before Peter Montour Jr. worked the land, Norton argued, "this land did not belong to any one: no one could buy it, as no one had the right to sell it."[118] In his mind, Kahnawà:ke law was the only legitimate law, which meant that anyone who claimed to have owned, purchased, sold, or inherited the land without working it was wrong. He had never seen Osias Meloche working there, and therefore Meloche could not have been the owner.

There are some important differences between the testimonies of the two sides. Sakotion's witnesses tended think about landownership in colonial legal terms and thus focused on the supposedly uncontested nature of Osias Meloche's ownership of the lot. They saw landownership as passed down from father to son via inheritance. This was a relatively new, colonial way of viewing landownership in Kahnawà:ke and a departure from the legal principles expressed by Kahnawa'kehró:non throughout the century. Two of Sakotion's witnesses believed that Skasenhate had been the original owner and that Sakotion had inherited her claim to the land by way of Osias Meloche's purchase. Although it would seem to disrupt the patriarchal logic for a woman to be the first in this chain of ownership, the fact that she was a widow before her title was transferred to a man adds legitimacy in a colonial legal context.[119] Several witnesses said that Sakotion and his relatives had paid them to work the land, which they felt bolstered his case. Again, this logic is consistent with colonial legal principles, but it goes against Kahnawà:ke law, which focused on the extent of land a person could work unaided. For many people, the fact that Sakotion required hired help proved that he owned too much, and this would have been especially true of his family, widely seen as white interlopers who had no right to live in Kahnawà:ke.

Tanekorens's witnesses, on the other hand, interpreted landownership through the lens of Kahnawà:ke law. Nearly all of them insisted that a claim to land was legitimate only if the claimant worked the land. In fact, they suggested that claiming land without working it was ludicrous. Two witnesses mentioned having worked for or with Montour, but none were paid for their work. It is important to note, however, that Kanawaienton, one of the largest property owners in Kahnawà:ke, possessed much more land than he could possibly have worked without assistance, which suggests that Tanekorens's side may have had a double standard on this matter depending on who was being discussed. But overall, the witnesses who spoke for Tanekorens concentrated on how and when each claimant used the land. One of them, François Daillebout, even thought that Osias Meloche had gained his claim to the low land by following Kahnawà:ke law, working a piece of unclaimed land. Some of Sakotion's witnesses also referred to this basis for claiming land, but they tended to be more focused on deeds and inheritance, which never came up during the questioning of Tanekorens's witnesses.

Very few witnesses had any clue as to where lot 205 began and ended, even though its boundaries are so clearly marked on the Walbank map. Many spoke of it as an area with high and low ground, but few thought of it as a bounded lot that could be bought and sold. Witnesses on both sides were chosen for their deep knowledge of the place and for their memories of what had happened there, yet most could not answer questions about ownership in a way that would have made sense to DIA officials. The testimony of Atiataronne, who spoke for Tanekorens, was particularly revealing on this front. Even as he was being asked about the ownership of lot 205, he immediately pivoted to talking about wood rather than bounded territory. The wood belonged to the person who cut it, he asserted in response to questions about who owned the land. Even a decade after the Walbank Survey, these witnesses were still speaking about land in terms of its relationships with specific people – what people did there, rather than how it was bounded and who held the deed.

Former Kahnawà:ke Indian agent Georges Cherrier represented his nephew Sakotion at the inquiry and wrote a letter in support of his claim.

Grounding his argument in his interpretation of the past fifty years of Kahnawà:ke history, he stated that Kahnawa'kehró:non had typically allied themselves with the English and against the French. Aversion to the French according to Cherrier, was "traditional with them" and seemed to be "transmitted from father to son."[120] This explained their long-standing campaign to evict French Canadians. His narrative began with the attempted eviction of George Delorimier and the 1834 Supreme Court of Montreal decision that recognized his right to live in Kahnawà:ke (against the wishes of the chiefs). Then, in 1865, two barns belonging to "métis" farmers were set on fire after the harvest, and someone set fire to the barn of Osias Meloche in 1878, in which he died trying to save his animals. The following year, another five barns and sugar shacks went up in flames, and Cherrier cited other examples from more recent years. His point was to show the challenging position of the Meloche family and the difficulty of maintaining their lands and properties in the face of constant attacks. According to Cherrier, the DIA supported the "métis" only half-heartedly, and he was concerned that their rights as members of the Kahnawà:ke band had never been fully recognized. He portrayed the Meloches as among the few civilized people in Kahnawà:ke, surrounded by hateful "sauvages" (one of the most common racist tropes evoked to delegitimize Kahnawà:ke law and those who wished to live according to it). Cherrier also suggested that Osias Meloche's deed to lot 205 had been lost in the 1878 fire, although it seems unlikely that anyone would store legal documents in a barn.[121]

Waniente, Tanekorens's spokesperson, blasted Cherrier's "insinuations and wild statements," which merely demonstrated that the claims of the Meloches "are not founded on any other fact than upon their hatred and distrust of the Indians of Caughnawaga." In addition, Waniente found Sakotion's witnesses unreliable, especially Charlotte Giasson, whose testimony was contradictory and nonsensical. It was widely acknowledged, stated Waniente, that Sakotion owned land near lot 205 but not lot 205 itself.[122] Unlike Sakotion, who made his claim only after the CPR asked for the right to the lot, Tanekorens "always was the possessor," a fact that he proved with "fair and respectable" witnesses. He had acquired his title from the estate of Peter Montour, who had taken "hold of the property and improved the same which according to the Indian custom of old became his real and valid title."[123] A young quarry owner and band councillor, Waniente was familiar with colonial language around landownership, but he was also versed in Kahnawà:ke law even though he was only a teenager during the Walbank Survey. Thus, he noted that Peter Montour's claim to lot 205 was based on Kahnawà:ke "custom" or law, but unlike the witnesses for his client, Waniente also spoke the colonial language of improvement, property, and title.

Controversy and Conclusion of the Case

After hearing all the witnesses, Agent Brosseau was still unsure of how to proceed but obviously wanted to find in favour of Sakotion because of his close relationships with the Meloche family. He stated that a number of testimonies were "rather contradictory despite the fact that the witnesses were worthy of belief," and he emphasized that lot 205 was of poor quality, used by the claimants primarily for cutting wood and hay. Nevertheless, Brosseau thought that Sakotion was probably the real owner even though it was odd that he could not produce a title, given that his relatives were normally so scrupulous about acquiring such documents. Brosseau concluded that Tanekorens and his father-in-law, Peter Montour Sr., had cleared the land at one point but then "ceased to do any more work on this land" and "contented [themselves] with cutting the hay thereon or causing it to be cut." Although it seems absurd not to see haying as work, Brosseau was using every possible rhetorical tool to shore up the case for Sakotion. As for Sakorewata, the claimant who did not participate in the inquiry, Brosseau believed that he had intended to clear a piece of lot 205, but "while he was getting ready another Indian stepped in and took possession of it." Again, this point seems unjustified in light of the evidence presented and can be understood as further proof of Brosseau's preference for Sakotion.[124]

Unlike Brosseau, whose conclusions can be explained by his local relationships and loyalties, DIA officials had other motives. Secretary J.D. McLean thought that the widow of Peter Montour Sr., Skasenhate, should be seen as the true owner of the lot, because "otherwise the expense involved in Mr. Walbank's Survey ... would be of little value."[125] In making this comment, McLean admitted just how little relevance the Walbank Survey had for the reality of Kahnawà:ke landowners, so much so that he decided to ignore a great part of the witness testimony. DIA officials had no interest in Kahnawà:ke law, and since much of the testimony turned on its legal principles, the easiest course was simply to disregard what the most knowledgeable people had to say. Instead, the department turned to its own "experts," who would ensure that the Walbank Survey would indeed have value. Assigned the task of reading through the evidence in the case, Samuel Bray of the Surveys Branch declared that Peter Montour's widow Skasenhate was the rightful claimant, and since Tanekorens was her heir, the compensation money should go to him. Nevertheless, Bray gave Sakotion three months to produce further evidence that his family had purchased lot 205.

All three claimants contacted the department in the months following the inquiry to demand settlement in their favour. Tanekorens felt that he had proven his case and should now be paid the additional fifty dollars.[126] Sakotion's lawyer, on the other hand, suggested that since neither his client nor Tanekorens could prove his right to the lot, and since "they have actually occupied and worked it in turns," they should split the money.[127] For his part, Sakorewata wondered why he had not yet received his fifty dollars, since no one disputed his right.[128] Deputy Superintendent General Hayter Reed liked the suggestion of Sakotion's lawyer and asked Brosseau for his opinion.[129] Although Brosseau had shown favouritism toward Sakotion, and though Cherrier had advocated so strongly for Sakotion during the inquiry, Brosseau thought that granting him any compensation money was far too dangerous:

It is not possible to give any compensation to Meloche [Sakotion] without there being considerable discontent among the Indians, unless a new investigation is given to Meloche and he can prove his case with new facts. The difference between the two claimants is that the Meloche family has always been contested by the Indians and that they have always had contracts for the land they bought from the Indians, which they do not have in the sole case in dispute here. They have contracts in all other cases. There are a great number of cases among the Indians who have no other title than the appropriation of land with the verbal or written evaluation of the chiefs of the time.[130]

Since the Meloche family often possessed deeds of sale or other notarized documents for their lots, whereas most Kahnawa'kehró:non did not, the Meloches had a history of winning land disputes. The lot 205 case was unusual in that they could not produce the requisite paperwork to confirm their ownership. Hayter Reed acknowledged Brosseau's warning but insisted that the department would do what was "just and fair" and would not be "restrained from such course through any fear of the Indians being dissatisfied with its judgment."[131] Given Reed's career, which was very much focused on destroying Indigenous nations,[132] he was probably sincere on this point, but DIA officials also knew that Kahnawà:ke politics could not entirely be ignored. In August 1895, the department issued its decision that the lot had belonged to Skasenhate. Peter Montour Jr. had cared for her and had sold her land to Osias Meloche.[133] Reed admitted that the DIA based its assessment entirely on Sakotion's witnesses, whom it saw as more credible than Tanekorens's. He believed that the statements of Sakotion's witnesses "are direct positive ones" that "bear an air of truthfulness which carries conviction, and are free from any appearance of connivance between the witnesses or attempt on the part of any individual to prove too much."[134] As for Tanekorens's witnesses, Reed believed they contradicted each other in stating that both Peter Montour and Sakorewata had owned and used the land for three decades. It is indeed telling that Reed could not entertain the possibility of shared possession when in fact credible witnesses had clearly stated that multiple people were sharing the land and that the arrangement had not been seen as problematic until the CPR and DIA got involved. It should be mentioned that Reed seemed unaware that there was a third, undisputed claimant who had already been compensated. He also suspected that Tanekorens's witnesses were lying and coordinating their stories beforehand. Although the DIA had a close relationship with the Montour family, Reed was also influenced by the fact that Tanekorens's witnesses referred more often to Kahnawà:ke law and practice, whereas Sakotion's witnesses tended to focus on sales and transfers of legal title. Considering Reed's career focused on destroying Indigenous nationhood, is not surprising that here too he came down against anything unfamiliar or threatening, namely Indigenous ways of engaging with the land. He was so eager to believe Sakotion's case that he even found it "not unreasonable to suppose that the Deed may have been destroyed by the fire in which Osias Meloche lost his life." In the end, however, he did acknowledge that Sakotion's claim was rather weak since he did not have a title document and had not registered his claim with Walbank in 1885. Thus, Reed decided that the fairest thing under the circumstances was to divide the fifty dollars between Sakotion and Tanekorens.[135]

When this verdict was announced, Sakotion was content but Tanekorens angrily rejected it.[136] The DIA responded by threatening to give the entire amount to Sakotion.[137] But the department had botched the inquiry so badly that now Sakorewata demanded to have the case reopened so he could have a hearing as well. Although he and Tanekorens had received most of the compensation ($229 each), and he had not participated in the inquiry, he was furious about its outcome. He claimed to have acted on poor advice from the agent in absenting himself from the inquiry.[138] Months went by before the DIA finally decided in January 1896 to send one of its officers, James Campbell, to Kahnawà:ke to investigate. When

Campbell arrived, Sakorewata explained that he had nothing to say about the dispute between the other two claimants, Sakotion and Tanekorens. His contention was simply, in Campbell's words, that "the whole lot originally belonged to him, and that while he would not dispute the title which others might have acquired to parts of the lot, through having entered upon and improved such parts thereof, he claims that all of the lot not so improved belongs to him."[139] Sakorewata said that he only wanted the fifty dollars he had been promised, but Campbell now thought the easiest and fairest solution would be to divide the hundred dollars equally among the three claimants. Sakorewata understandably refused to take less than the sum originally promised, and Campbell concluded that neither Sakorewata nor Tanekorens would accept any decision that recognized even part of Sakotion's claim.[140] This is false since Campbell himself recorded Sakorewata as saying that it was none of his business whether the remaining fifty dollars be given to Tanekorens or to Meloche as long as he received what he had been promised. Sakorewata did not care about the other claims; he just wanted his half of the compensation money. Nevertheless, Campbell returned to Ottawa and advised the department to split the money three ways. He feared that the number of reversed decisions in the case reflected poorly on the department and suggested being more consistent in the future.[141] In the end, Tanekorens accepted the payment, but both Sakotion and Sakorewata refused it.[142] The sixty-seven unclaimed dollars remained with the department.

A year later, in the spring of 1897, Waniente wrote to DIA Superintendent General Clifford Sifton on behalf of Sakorewata. In light of the fact that the department had given "a decision, not one decision, but three decisions, each one worse than the preceding one," he asked that Sakorewata be paid the sixty-seven dollars in order to extinguish his claims for two lots, including lot 205.[143] The department declined to cooperate, so Waniente brought Sakorewata's case before the band council, which unanimously passed a resolution recognizing Sakorewata as the owner of lot 205 and authorizing the department to pay him sixty-seven dollars.[144] The DIA insisted on giving Sakotion a chance to defend himself before the council, with witnesses, even though Brosseau knew that the councillors would not be swayed.[145] In any case, Sakotion had already received his thirty-three dollars, so it is unclear why the department insisted on this course.

Sakotion presented his case before the band council on September 24, 1897, along with a number of witnesses who spoke on his behalf. As Brosseau had predicted, the council (dominated by opponents to the DIA) found in favour of Sakorewata.[146] With the help of the council,

Sakorewata had produced a document to prove his title, whereas Sakotion still had no such document. The councillors rejected the veracity of Sakotion's witnesses, saying that they "would not listen to witnesses against documentary evidence."[147] Driving the point home, they noted "that the force of writing could not be affected by witnesses."[148] This apparently sarcastic comment regarding the superiority of the written word was almost certainly a biting reference to the many instances in which the Meloches had used title documents to triumph over other Kahnawà:ke families. It was also probably a reference to the cavalier way in which Hayter Reed decided which witnesses had spoken truthfully at the inquiry.

After protracted consultation, and with obvious discomfort, the DIA finally approved the council resolution and paid Sakorewata his sixty-seven dollars in December 1897. He and his allies had won a resounding victory. This case, however, was not simply a battle between certain individuals. It was one of many clashes over differing understandings of landownership. Although the Indian agent was deeply entwined in these debates and often took sides, he was constrained by the dynamic political realities of Kahnawà:ke in ways that the department did not always understand. The case was also a site of contestation over the governance of Kahnawà:ke itself. The department repeatedly attempted to solve the lot 205 problem itself but eventually had to resort to the band council to get a final decision. Although it wanted to protect its allies in the community, in the end it proved unable to do so.

The case of lot 205 shows that ten years after it had been conducted, the Walbank Survey was still not very relevant to ordinary people. Walbank had drawn an elaborate map of all existing lots and had completed the Herculean task of determining an owner for each, but witnesses at the inquiry never once mentioned his map and only rarely referred to lots by number. There was a great deal of confusion about lot boundaries, suggesting that Walbank had not placed markers around lot 205 or that they had been lost.[149] What Walbank thought he was doing was to map the existing lots, but even the supposedly existing lots did not yet exist in the way he depicted them (bounded lots owned according to colonial norms). And in an attempt to show the relevance of his expensive survey, the DIA tried hard to match its decisions to Walbank's findings. Although its own reports criticized his work as unreliable and unfinished, it nevertheless insisted on the value and accuracy of his survey. In fact, it pursued this course so doggedly that, as one can argue, landownership in Kahnawà:ke eventually had to become what Walbank had envisioned.

Another key point revealed by the lot 205 case is that many Kahn-awa'kehró:non in the 1890s still thought about land and relationships in terms of Kahnawà:ke law. The *Indian Act* had been on the books for two decades, yet it seemed to have had little impact on what they believed and remembered about the hill that became lot 205. Even Agent Brosseau had to refer to the "custom of the reserve" in describing the situation to his DIA superiors.[150] Clearly, some Kahnawa'kehró:non still claimed land and cut wood according to Kahnawà:ke law. Many lots were still owned without documentary titles, ownership was still in flux from year to year, and people's relationships to land still did not match the colonial model envisioned in the *Indian Act*. The clash over lot 205 provides a dramatic glimpse into the great antipathy felt by many Kahnawa'kehró:non for deeds and other documents that were intended to prove ownership, as well as for those who relied on them to prevent others from accessing land and wood. Between the lines and behind the pragmatic arguments, however, there was a seething anger at repeated territorial and political incursions, and at their collective inability to stop them. Kahnawa'kehró:non could resist and refuse the colonial invasion, but it would continue regardless.

Another key takeaway from the lot 205 case is that the DIA, in a typical moment of inconsistency and weakness, attempted to protect its allies while making decisions that it hoped would have the appearance of lawfulness and fairness. My insistence here on the weakness of the DIA may seem to diminish the seriousness of the colonial invasion itself, but I contend that DIA inconsistency and incompetence wrought great harm. For those who suffered at its hands, the department would have seemed neither weak nor harmless, but it was widely known to be underfunded and understaffed. It was able to impose its will on the most devastated and vulnerable Indigenous people in ways that have been well documented,[151] but in Kahnawà:ke it encountered a type of resistance that it was poorly equipped to handle. Its goal in imposing the band council was to gain control, yet the lot 205 case shows that it still struggled to achieve its objectives, whereas Kahnawa'kehró:non continued their struggle to govern themselves as they wished.

CONCLUSION

Even most of those who supported a band council government structure in principle disliked the way in which the DIA ignored the will of

Kahnawa'kehró:non at every turn, sometimes breaking its own laws to do so. Very few in Kahnawà:ke wished for the department to undermine their own laws, voices, and sovereignty through the imposition of the *Indian Advancement Act,* and even after it was put in place many tried to have the decision reversed. The Indian agent regularly misrepresented Kahnawà:ke public opinion to his superiors in Ottawa, using any convenient stereotype to slander those who opposed the DIA and trying to remove uncooperative band councillors. After the *Advancement Act* had already disenfranchised Kahnawà:ke women, the DIA set up electoral districts in a way that gave its own supporters massively disproportionate power, effectively disenfranchising Kahnawà:ke men who lived in the village. At every turn, the department showed itself to be uninterested in what Kahnawa'kehró:non wanted and deeply invested in imposing its own agenda.

In the context of a 1900 land dispute, Brosseau expressed his frustration thus: "The question is one of the most difficult to settle, as it is necessary to follow the custom of the reserve, which is contrary to law."[152] He juxtaposed Kahnawà:ke "custom" with *Indian Act* "law," even though Kahnawà:ke law held sway for many. Some twenty-five years after the first *Indian Act* and more than a decade after the imposition of the *Advancement Act,* the DIA was still unable to ignore Kahnawà:ke law. The lot 205 case shows that many Kahnawa'kehró:non framed conflicts over land in their own terms, and the history of the imposition of the band council system shows their refusal of the DIA and settler colonialism in general.[153]

Part of the DIA's mandate was to protect Indigenous peoples and their lands, but the way in which it understood and practised this responsibility constantly undercut Indigenous self-determination and self-governance. Kahnawa'kehró:non did not ask for what they received. In some instances, DIA officials were undoubtedly genuine in claiming that they wanted what was best for Indigenous communities, but their good intentions often involved disregarding or overriding Indigenous laws and perspectives. At other times, their goal was obviously not the good of the community but that of the department, its allies, companies, and neighbouring settlers – in which cases the department responded promptly and enthusiastically. The problem of lot 205 sprang from just such a moment, when the DIA facilitated railroad incursions that were opposed by Kahnawà:ke leaders. But when Kahnawa'kehró:non asked the DIA to address their grievances, the department responded slowly and grudgingly (if it responded at all). However, the government documents of the day do not adequately capture the frustration and anger generated by departmental collusion in the degradation of Kahnawà:ke lands. Anyone who visits Kahnawà:ke today,

FIGURE 7.7   Lot 205 in 2011. Once a fertile hill, it was turned into a borrow pit and later filled in. Today, it is a maintenance area for the Kanawaki Golf Club.

cut up and criss-crossed as it is by canals, high-voltage power lines, highways, bridges, and railroads, might gain some idea of the emotion felt by those who lived on and loved this land. Figure 7.7 shows a place that remains rich in meaning long after its original character was lost.

The lot 205 inquiry reveals the ways in which Kahnawa'kehró:non understood landownership and remembered a cultivated and wooded hill that, by the time of the inquiry, had become an open pit (see Figure 7.7). It also brings to light the powerful antipathy between those Kahnawa'kehró:non who held lots based on title documents and those who had no such documents, and between those who wished to be governed under colonial law and those who wished to govern themselves according to Kahnawà:ke law. The case also shows just how little power the department had when an inquiry was held in a more public way and when band councillors were allowed a decision-making role. Although the band council was politically weaker than the council of chiefs had been, both in terms of perceived legitimacy within the community and in its ability to stand against the department, the lot 205 case reveals that it could still win small victories defending nationhood and slowing the colonial invasion. However, the case also shows how by the end of the nineteenth century, the patriarchal systems and assumptions of the settler colonial society had marginalized and invisibilized Kahnawà:ke women, their leadership, and their relationships with each other and the land.

After the Walbank Survey was completed, Kahnawa'kehró:non continued to buy and sell land: some provided themselves with notarized deeds, whereas others still claimed and used land according to the old ways. We cannot know how much land fell into each category, because Kahnawà:ke did not have a comprehensive land registry, and many of the relevant records were lost in a 1943 fire at the agency office.[154] Furthermore, lands held without legal documents left no paper trail unless a disagreement arose. Although the Kahnawà:ke land laws of the nineteenth century seem not to have been asserted in the same ways in the twentieth century, the issue of landownership was far from resolved. Thanks to the unfinished nature of the Walbank Survey, departmental inattention to land transactions, and the legislated inability of Kahnawà:ke leaders to properly govern their own territory, a high percentage of Kahnawà:ke lots are now classed as "undivided estates." Owned by multiple people, sometimes hundreds, they make up a large portion of Kahnawà:ke territory. Some who favour the preservation of undeveloped land can see this situation as a blessing, as getting several hundred people to agree on selling or developing a lot is virtually impossible, but others see it as an impediment to development and a root cause of widespread environmental contamination.[155] Another important problem is that many lots are not accessible by road for reasons closely related to the incomplete Walbank Survey. Some parcels are still held without any documentary title.[156] The current problematic landholding regime is the result of the history related in this book: While the DIA interfered in Kahnawà:ke affairs and undermined the ability of Kahnawà:ke leaders to govern, it also failed to implement a functional land management regime.

Conclusion

This book does not have a very satisfying ending, and for a reason. The story of Kahnawà:ke did not end in 1900. The settler invasion was not complete and did not conclude at that time. Neither did Kahnawà:ke capitulate and disappear at that moment. Nor did the story end with the 1951 overhaul of the *Indian Act*, the 1969 federal attempt to abolish it, or the 1985 effort to eliminate gender discrimination in it. The story did not end in 1959, with the catastrophic construction of the St. Lawrence Seaway through Kahnawà:ke, or with the military siege and invasion of Kahnawà:ke during the 1990 Kanehsatà:ke Resistance (Oka Crisis). It also did not end in the year 2000 or in 2021, when this book was published. The story of *The Laws and the Land* is ongoing. Canadian efforts to destabilize and eliminate Indigenous nationhoods persist, as do the daily actions of Indigenous peoples to build their lives and nations.

Using material from the DIA archives, this book shows the very specific ways in which the people of Kahnawà:ke maintained laws that prioritized economic equality within the community and ensured that those with the least wealth had access to agricultural land and firewood. These laws were designed to limit both the individual accumulation of land as property and the exploitation of wood for commercial gain. The territory was collectively owned, and only within that framework did individuals have rights to land and resources. The values reflected in these laws were the patrimony of Rotinonhsión:ni understandings of territories as spaces that must be shared between peoples, like a Dish with One Spoon. Unlike those who built the Canadian nation, who concentrated primarily on the property rights of certain individuals, Kahnawà:ke laws emphasized the good of the poorest and the common good. In practice, Kahnawà:ke and Rotinonhsión:ni law surely had its own problems, but it is clear that the goals of Rotinonhsión:ni lawmakers were peace and good relationships, whereas the goals of colonial lawmakers tended to focus on protecting the rights of property holders (employing the rhetoric of freedom and equality).[1]

Although colonial invasions and occupations always involve violence of some kind, the colonial invasion in this book was not accomplished with weapons and soldiers. Nevertheless, this invasion had the genocidal goal of eliminating an Indigenous nation, and the "slow violence" chronicled in these pages resulted in untold harm.[2] Thus, *The Laws and the Land* is a micro-history that tells the larger story of the Canadian project to install settler governments and settler law as the only legitimate authority while simultaneously weakening and destroying Indigenous nations and their laws. For DIA officials, this campaign necessitated a level of hubris and chauvinism that would allow them to ignore and discount the humanity of Indigenous people. They frequently repeated racist stereotypes in their correspondence and could not be seen as listening to, or respecting, the Indigenous people with whom they came in contact. Some were more sympathetic and kind than others, but none could stray too far from colonial dogma without damaging their own careers. The DIA never took responsibility for the harms it caused – instead, it always blamed Kahnawa'kehró:non – and its agents took care to blame "Indians" when something did not live up to expectations.

To accomplish the genocidal goals of enfranchising all Kahnawa'kehró:non and breaking up the community, DIA officials believed they must first gain political control. To do so, the department sowed political and social division, and took control of finances, education, membership, and economic development. It also undermined Kahnawà:ke leaders and frequently passed legislation that empowered both itself and its agent. Its "civilizing" project was to transform Indigenous people into Christian farmers and their lands into an agricultural landscape – it did not matter that Rotinonhsión:ni woman had always been proud farmers or that their landscape was already an agricultural one. Deeply unsympathetic to Kahnawà:ke's vernacular landscape of irregular lot shapes, shifting boundaries, gendered agricultural norms, and overlapping use rights, DIA officials intended to erase it all so that a new order could be built from scratch. The desired landscape, a grid of rectangular lots, would allow for the enfranchisement of everyone, the end of Kahnawà:ke law, the creation of a commercial land market, and the breakup of the nation – a model that could be applied elsewhere.

The DIA's imperial hubris and liberal ambitions, however, came up against Kahnawà:ke resistance. Although many Kahnawa'kehró:non appeared to be dissatisfied with their own government during the 1870s and 1880s (especially since the DIA intentionally undermined the authority of the chiefs and Kahnawà:ke law), almost everyone opposed the heavy-handed interference of the DIA, and almost no one wanted their landscape and society to be reorganized along the lines envisioned by the department. Many felt they had no choice except to cooperate, but some, such as Ohionkoton, simply refused (Chapter 6). Others burned and removed survey stakes, sent petitions, and lied and withheld information, all of which led to cost overruns and delays. They also wrote editorials in Montreal newspapers to counter DIA rhetoric and used political connections to raise their concerns and embarrass the government in the House of Commons. Many of these courageous people probably paid a high price for their principled stands. Due to their geography and history, Kahnawa'kehró:non may have had more capacity for resistance than many other Indigenous people at the time, but their options were still very limited.

The DIA was also beset by internal problems that impeded its ability to accomplish its grand plans and yet allowed it to do other kinds of damage. Its actions were poorly planned, subject to multiple agendas, and riddled with contradictions. Furthermore, it was vulnerable to shifts in public opinion and changes in federal government that could scuttle large projects or generate policy changes that could greatly affect Indigenous peoples. To visualize Canadian expansionist goals – to understand what elites wished the country to become – we need look no farther than the Dominion Lands Survey on the Prairies, where the government's ambitions were largely realized: a massive grid of privatized agricultural properties owned almost entirely by white men. In Kahnawà:ke, dogged opposition from Kahnawa'kehró:non prevented the Canadian government from achieving its most ambitious goals, but it did manage to attain significant political control. The conflicted, disorganized, and constrained nature of the DIA also played an important role in determining the outcomes of its actions. This is not to say that their inconsistent and ad hoc nature tended to benefit Indigenous communities; quite the opposite. Because the DIA operated without real public scrutiny in relation to a constituency that was legally disenfranchised, its officials could often act outside the law without facing consequences. Departmental indecision

GENERAL VIEW OF THE IROQUOIS INDIAN VILLAGE OF CAUGHNAWAGA, NEAR MONTREAL.

FIGURE 8.1 *General View of the Iroquois Indian Village of Caughnawaga, near Montreal,* early-twentieth-century postcard. View of the village of Kahnawà:ke from the church steeple. The CPR bridge is in the background. | CP 926, BANQ.

and incompetence meant that Kahnawà:ke leaders could not take action on important local issues, and Kahnawa'kehró:non were often left in limbo. The department asserted itself just enough to undermine Indigenous leaders but not enough to protect the land and people from the effects of the leadership vacuum. In like manner, although the most radical elements of the Walbank Survey were not realized, it still facilitated the imposition of private property and the compilation of a membership list. Long-term outcomes include a complicated and unequal property regime that reflects neither the ideals of the *Indian Act* nor those of Kahnawà:ke, the thorny issue of membership that continues to simmer and periodically explodes, and the unsettled question of leadership in which multiple forms of government (including band council and longhouses) vie for the support of the people.

Though bloodied and bruised after generations of DIA interference, and with a badly damaged territory, Kahnawa'kehró:non are still here.[3] They could not prevent the invasion and its damage to their people and lands, but they did not assimilate and disappear as the DIA had planned. From the outside, Kahnawà:ke could have the appearance of an ordinary Canadian or Quebec town (Figures 8.1 and 8.2), but it is anything but. Viewed from the air, the shape of the heavily forested Kahnawà:ke territory

167 MONTREAL. — The Indian Iroquois Village of Caughnawaga
MONTRÉAL. — Le Village d'Indiens Iroquois de Caughnawaga. — ND Phot.

FIGURE 8.2 *Montreal – The Indian Iroquois Village of Caughnawaga,* early-twentieth-century postcard. | CP 5221, BANQ.

contrasts sharply with the farms and suburbs of neighbouring areas, mirroring the contrasting cultural and legal realities inside and outside the reserve. Similarly, the enclosure of Indigenous lands and the destruction of collective Indigenous identities across North America remain incomplete due to the steadfast resistance and refusal of Indigenous peoples.[4]

As I wrote this book, I was increasingly struck by the similarity between what I was reading in the colonial archives and what I read in the news. As I conducted archival research and learned with Kahnawa'kehró:non, I was shaken out of my unexamined core belief that settler colonialism is somehow a thing of the past and that conditions are now much better than they used to be. In fact, Indigenous lands are still being unjustly taken, pillaged, and polluted, Indigenous families are still torn apart in ways that are unimaginable to most settlers, treaties are still broken, racism is still rampant, and even federal governments that seem friendly to Indigenous peoples are unable or unwilling to provide basic services that settlers take for granted. Of course, not everything is the same as it was, but it is clear to me that we are not living in a post-colonial era.

Another insight I gained was that settler colonialism is not just something that happened in Kahnawà:ke and other places "out there." It is tempting as a scholar to pretend that I am merely an observer instead of an active participant in the historical process, but that's simply not true. The settler colonial "frontier" isn't just somewhere else – it is in my home, my family, my classroom, and in my own heart. Thus, as I think carefully about what it might take to decolonize Canada's relationship with Indigenous peoples, I believe it begins with myself. I could write the best books and articles on the topic, but if I continue to live out settler colonial values in my daily life at home or at work, I continue to do harm. Rather than treating my daughter as my "civilizing project," I can work toward respecting and nurturing her authentic self. Rather than coercing and manipulating my spouse, I can find ways to communicate my needs without fear. Rather than approaching my students from a place of knowing better, I can learn to hear their wisdom and experience. Rather than disrespecting other-than-human creatures and forgetting about my relationship to my surroundings, I can pay attention and develop reciprocal connections with them. And finally, rather than speaking to myself in a punishing and hateful way (very much in the spirit of colonial communications discussed in this book), I can learn to be gentler and kinder toward myself. As many wise teachers have tried to teach me, everything is in relation to everything else, and the meaning of life is to strive for right relationships. This brings me full circle to the opening of this book, with its story about my relationship with Tionerahtoken A. Brian Deer. He taught me that the most important thing is not to get everything right, but to be continually learning with an open heart and mind. My agenda as a scholar is to be more like that every day and to make my scholarship and my daily actions flow from there.

Indigenous diplomacy has for centuries focused on building right relationships between peoples. Perhaps the most famous example is the Two Row Wampum, a record of one of the oldest treaties between Rotinonhsión:ni and Europeans. The two rows – the parallel lines of purple wampum beads – represent two boats, the Rotinonhsión:ni canoe and the European ship, each embodying the laws and customs of its respective people. The boats travel down the same river, represented by a background of white beads, but they do not interfere with each other's course.[5] It was this principle of non-interference and mutual respect, a long-standing feature of Indigenous-settler relations before Confederation, that the Canadian nation abandoned in the nineteenth century. Similarly, the Dish with One Spoon principle focuses on ways that peoples can live peacefully on the same land without harming each other. *The Laws and the Land* details the breakdown of this relationship, the uneven establishment of an asymmetrical power dynamic, and some of its cultural, political, and environmental consequences. Getting back to right relationships will not be easy, but I believe that settlers and settler governments need to become better listeners. We can put aside our agendas and learn how to speak with Indigenous people from our own ship, without feeling the need to criticize, build, improve, cross over to, or sink theirs.

Notes

Epigraphs: Tracey Banivanua Mar and Penelope Edmonds, "Making Space in Settler Colonies," in *Making Settler Colonial Space: Perspectives on Race, Place and Identity,* ed. Tracey Banivanua Mar and Penelope Edmonds (New York: Palgrave Macmillan, 2010), 2; Linda Tuhiwai Smith, *Decolonizing Methodologies: Research and Indigenous Peoples* (Dunedin: University of Otago Press, 2006 [1999]), 1.

1 For more on this use of the word "settler," see Emma Battell Lowman and Adam J. Barker, *Settler: Identity and Colonialism in 21st Century Canada* (Winnipeg: Fernwood, 2015).

2 A. Brian Deer, "The Iroquois Condolence," *Ecumenism* 159 (2005): 4–10; A. Brian Deer, "The Water and Sewer System in Kahnawake and St. Lawrence Seaway" (Mohawk Council of Kahnawake, Kahnawà:ke, 1982).

3 Chris Curtis, "Mapping Kahnawake History without an Agenda," *Eastern Door,* June 15, 2012.

4 The Department of Indian Affairs (DIA) changed its name several times over the nineteenth and twentieth centuries, and continues to do so periodically. This book generally refers to it as the "Indian Department" before Confederation and as the Department of Indian Affairs for the decades following Confederation. Contemporary documents continue to use "Indian Department" after it had been renamed, and I also sometimes use the names interchangeably.

5 The response of Kahrhó:wane Cory McComber to this statement was, "The end result of the invasion is always the same to us; when we do not comply we face violence at the hands of the Crown and/or its citizens." Pers. comm., January 10, 2020.

6 Patrick Wolfe, "Against the Intentional Fallacy: Legocentrism and Continuity in the Rhetoric of Indian Dispossession," *American Indian Culture and Research Journal* 36, 1 (2012): 3–45.

7 Paige Raibmon, "Unmaking Native Space: A Genealogy of Indian Policy, Settler Practice, and the Microtechniques of Dispossession," in *The Power of Promises: Rethinking Indian*

Treaties in the Pacific Northwest, ed. A. Harmon (Seattle: University of Washington Press, 2008), 56–85.

8 Frederick Jackson Turner, "The Significance of the Frontier in American History," *Proceedings of the Forty-First Annual Meeting of the State Historical Society of Wisconsin* (1894): 1–34.

9 Patrick Wolfe, "Settler Colonialism and the Elimination of the Native," *Journal of Genocide Research* 8, 4 (2006): 399.

10 Ibid.

11 Ibid., 393–95.

12 Ann Laura Stoler, *Duress: Imperial Durabilities in Our Times* (Durham: Duke University Press, 2016), 61.

13 Many of the best works published in the field of settler colonial studies (and related fields) emphasize the efforts of resurgent Indigenous peoples to assert their sovereignty and cast doubt on the legitimacy of the settler colonial state.

14 For works in the North American context that describe the "closing of the frontier" in terms of colonial appropriation of Indigenous lands, see Gregory H. Nobles, *American Frontiers: Cultural Encounters and Continental Conquest* (New York: Hill and Wang, 1997); Nicholas Blomley, "Law, Property, and the Geography of Violence: The Frontier, the Survey, and the Grid," *Annals of the Association of American Geographers* 93, 1 (2003): 121–41.

15 Tiffany Lethabo King, *The Black Shoals: Offshore Formations of Black and Native Studies* (Durham: Duke University Press, 2019), 49.

16 Haunani-Kay Trask, *From a Native Daughter: Colonialism and Sovereignty in Hawai'i* (Honolulu: University of Hawai'i Press, 1999 [1993]).

17 King, *The Black Shoals,* 57; Haunani-Kay Trask, "The Color of Violence," in *Color of Violence: The Incite! Anthology,* ed. INCITE! Women of Color against Violence (Durham: Duke University Press, 2016), 81–87.

18 For an overview of the subject and review of the literature, see Andrew Woolford and Jeff Benvenuto, "Canada and Colonial Genocide," *Journal of Genocide Research* 17, 4 (2015): 373–90; Matthew Wildcat, "Fearing Social and Cultural Death: Genocide and Elimination in Settler Colonial Canada – An Indigenous Perspective," *Journal of Genocide Research* 17, 4 (2015): 391–409.

19 United Nations, Office on Genocide Prevention and the Responsibility to Protect, "The Genocide Convention," https://www.un.org/en/genocideprevention/genocide-convention.shtml.

20 For "genocide" and its variants, see Karen Stote, *An Act of Genocide: Colonialism and the Sterilization of Aboriginal Women* (Winnipeg: Fernwood, 2015); Woolford and Benvenuto, "Canada and Colonial Genocide"; Truth and Reconciliation Commission of Canada, *The Final Report of the Truth and Reconciliation Commission of Canada* (Montreal and Kingston: McGill-Queen's University Press, 2015); National Inquiry into Missing and Murdered Indigenous Women and Girls, "Supplementary Report of the National Inquiry into Missing and Murdered Indigenous Women and Girls: A Legal Analysis of Genocide," https://www.mmiwg-ffada.ca/final-report/. For "ethnic cleansing," see James Daschuk, *Clearing the Plains: Disease, Politics of Starvation and the Loss of Aboriginal Life* (Regina: University of Regina Press, 2013). And for "elimination," see Wolfe, "Settler Colonialism and the Elimination of the Native"; Lorenzo Veracini, *Settler Colonialism: A Theoretical Overview* (Houndmills, UK: Palgrave Macmillan, 2010).

21 Audra Simpson, *Mohawk Interruptus: Political Life across the Borders of Settler States* (Durham: Duke University Press, 2014), 2.

22 Ibid., 7.

23 Ibid., 3.

24 Susan M. Hill, *The Clay We Are Made Of: Haudenosaunee Land Tenure on the Grand River* (Winnipeg: University of Manitoba Press, 2017).

25 Mar and Edmonds, "Making Space," 2.

26 For an accessible and wide-ranging formulation of Indigenous relationships with other-than-human creatures, see Robin Wall Kimmerer, *Braiding Sweetgrass: Indigenous Wisdom, Scientific Knowledge, and the Teachings of Plants* (Minneapolis: Milkweed Editions, 2013).

27 William Cronon, "The Trouble with Wilderness; or, Getting Back to the Wrong Nature," in *Uncommon Ground: Toward Reinventing Nature,* ed. William Cronon (New York: W.W. Norton, 1995), 69–90; Theodore Binnema and Melanie Niemi, "'Let the Line Be Drawn Now': Wilderness, Conservation, and the Exclusion of Aboriginal People from Banff National Park in Canada," *Environmental History* 11 (October 2006): 724–50.

28 John Borrows, "Indigenous Legal Traditions in Canada," *Washington University Journal of Law and Policy* 19 (2005): 175.

29 Richard White, *The Middle Ground: Indians, Empires, and Republics in the Great Lakes Region, 1650–1815* (Cambridge: Cambridge University Press, 1991); Jon Parmenter, *The Edge of the Woods: Iroquoia, 1534–1701* (East Lansing: Michigan State University Press, 2010); Timothy J. Shannon, *Iroquois Diplomacy on the Early American Frontier* (New York: Viking, 2008).

30 Michael Asch, *On Being Here to Stay: Treaties and Aboriginal Rights in Canada* (Toronto: University of Toronto Press, 2014); Aimée Craft, *Breathing Life into the Stone Fort Treaty: An Anishinabe Understanding of Treaty One* (Saskatoon: Purich, 2013).

31 Val Napoleon, "Thinking about Indigenous Legal Orders" (Research paper for the National Centre for First Nations Governance, June 2007), http://fngovernance.org/ncfng_research/val_napoleon.pdf; John Borrows, "Wampum at Niagara: The Royal Proclamation, Canadian Legal History, and Self-Government," in *Aboriginal and Treaty Rights in Canada,* ed. Michael Asch (Vancouver: UBC Press, 1997), 155–72.

32 Napoleon, "Thinking about Indigenous Legal Orders," 2.

33 Ibid., 3–4.

34 Val Napoleon, "The Role of the Sacred in Indigenous Law and Reconciliation" (paper presented at Ideafest, University of Victoria, March 20, 2018), https://www.youtube.com/watch?v=PEIoHsT2pag.

35 Hill, *The Clay We Are Made Of,* 27–46; Darren Bonaparte, *Creation and Confederation: The Living History of the Iroquois* (Ahkwesáhsne: Wampum Chronicles, 2006); Doug George-Kanentiio, *Iroquois Culture and Commentary* (Santa Fe: Clear Light, 2000), 112–41.

36 Gail D. MacLeitch, *Imperial Entanglements: Iroquois Change and Persistence on the Frontiers of Empire* (Philadelphia: University of Pennsylvania Press, 2011); Jean-François Lozier, *Flesh Reborn: The St. Lawrence Valley Mission Settlements through the Seventeenth Century* (Montreal and Kingston: McGill-Queen's University Press, 2018), Chapters 6 and 8.

37 Simpson, *Mohawk Interruptus,* 2.

38 Wolfe, "Settler Colonialism and the Elimination of the Native."

39 Yael Berda, *Living Emergency: Israel's Permit Regime in the Occupied West Bank* (Redwood City, CA: Stanford Briefs, 2017), 111.

40 Ibid., 112.

41 Keith D. Smith, *Liberalism, Surveillance, and Resistance: Indigenous Communities in Western Canada, 1877–1927* (Edmonton: Athabasca University Press, 2009), 127.

42 John L. Tobias, "Protection, Civilisation, Assimilation: An Outline History of Canada's Indian Policy," in *As Long as the Sun Shines and the Water Flows: A Reader in Canadian Native Studies,* ed. Ian A.L. Getty and Antoine S. Lucier (Vancouver: UBC Press, 1983), 39–55.

43 Smith, *Liberalism, Surveillance, and Resistance,* 93.

44 Sarah Carter, *Lost Harvests: Prairie Indian Reserve Farmers and Government Policy* (Montreal and Kingston: McGill-Queen's University Press, 1990), 16–22.

45 Sarah Carter, "Agriculture and Agitation on the Oak River Reserve, 1875–1895," *Manitoba History* 6 (Fall 1983): 2–9.

46 For more on education and literacy, see Thomas Peace, "Borderlands, Primary Sources, and the Longue Durée: Contextualizing Colonial Schooling at Odanak, Lorette, and Kahnawake, 1600–1850," *Historical Studies in Education/Revue d'histoire de l'éducation* 29, 1 (2017): 8–31. Even many Indigenous peoples who had not practised agriculture before European contact widely adapted certain agricultural practices long before the Indian Department became involved. D. Wayne Moodie and Barry Kaye, "Indian Agriculture in the Fur Trade Northwest," *Prairie Forum* 11, 2 (1986): 171–83.

47 Boyd Cothran, *Remembering the Modoc War: Redemptive Violence and the Making of American Innocence* (Chapel Hill: University of North Carolina Press, 2014); Thomas King, *The Inconvenient Indian: A Curious Account of Native People in North America* (Toronto: Doubleday, 2012).

48 An example of this is Weisinger's *Dreaming of Sheep in Navajo Country,* where the author argues that both the US government and Navajo leaders were to blame for environmental problems, rather than pointing out the colonial power dynamics that limited Navajo agency. Marsha L. Weisinger, *Dreaming of Sheep in Navajo Country* (Seattle: University of Washington Press, 2009).

49 Historian Shannon Stunden Bower defines the ecological commons as an area where "the private property landscape is overlaid by elements of the natural world that are of common concern to all landowners." Shannon Stunden Bower, *Wet Prairie: People, Land, and Water in Agricultural Manitoba* (Vancouver: UBC Press, 2011), 13.

50 For example, Melvin Tekahonwen:sere Diabo, "Comprehensive Land Report: Restoring Kanien'kehaka Approach to Land Holding and Land Use" (Report submitted to the Office of the Council of Chiefs, Kahnawà:ke, 2004); *Old Kahnawake; An Oral History of Kahnawake* (Kahnawà:ke: Kanien'kehaka Raotitiokwa Cultural Center, 1991).

51 Kahente Horn-Miller, "How Did Adoption Become a Dirty Word? Indigenous Citizenship Orders as Irreconcilable Spaces of Aboriginality," *AlterNative* 14, 4 (2018): 356.

CHAPTER 1: KAHNAWÀ:KE AND CANADA

Epigraphs: Arthur C. Parker, *The Constitution of the Five Nations,* New York State Museum Bulletin 184 (Albany: University of the State of New York, 1916): 103; William B. Newell, *Crime and Justice among the Iroquois Nations* (Montreal: Caughnawaga Historical Society, 1965), 38–39.

1 Deborah Doxtator, "What Happened to the Iroquois Clans? A Study of Clans in Three Nineteenth Century Rotinonhsyonni Communities" (PhD diss., University of Western Ontario, 1996), 336.

2 Hill, *The Clay We Are Made Of,* 42–43.

3 Kahrhó:wane Cory McComber, pers. comm., May 9, 2020.

4 Some key works on this subject are Stuart Banner, *Possessing the Pacific: Land, Settlers, and Indigenous People from Australia to Alaska* (Cambridge, MA: Harvard University Press, 2007); Kenneth H. Bobroff, "Retelling Allotment: Indian Property Rights and the Myth of Common Ownership," *Vanderbilt Law Review* 54 (2001): 1559–1623; Allan Greer, *Property and Dispossession: Natives, Empires and Land in Early Modern North America* (Cambridge: Cambridge University Press, 2018).

5 For a good overview of the diversity of Indigenous land tenure systems in North America, see Linda S. Parker, *Native American Estate: The Struggle over Indian and Hawaiian Lands* (Honolulu: University of Hawai'i Press, 1996), 15–23.

6 For a critical examination of the way in which recent environmental interpretations of the Dish with One Spoon have undermined Indigenous nationhoods, see Dean M. Jacobs and Victor P. Lytwyn, "Naagan Ge Bezhig Emkwaan: A Dish with One Spoon Reconsidered," *Ontario History* 112, 2 (2020): 191–210.

7 Speech of the Seven Nations of Lower Canada, Ottawas of Michilimackinac, Micmacs and Muskrats to Robert Prescott, August 13, 1796, RG8, vol. 249, pt. 2, pp. 301–4, reel C-2849, Library and Archives Canada (LAC).

8 Allan Greer, *Mohawk Saint: Catherine Tekakwitha and the Jesuits* (New York: Oxford University Press, 2005), 89–100; Kathryn Magee Labelle, *Dispersed but Not Destroyed: A History of the Seventeenth-Century Wendat People* (Vancouver: UBC Press, 2013), 133–35; Lozier, *Flesh Reborn,* Chapters 6 and 8.

9 Although there was a Kanien'kehá:ka village named Kahnawà:ke along the Mohawk River that predated the Kahnawà:ke on the St. Lawrence, migrants from the original Kahnawà:ke made up only a portion of the residents of the new Kahnawà:ke in the late seventeenth century.

10 Douglas W. Boyce, "A Glimpse of Iroquois Culture History through the Eyes of Joseph Brant and John Norton," *Proceedings of the American Philosophical Society* 117, 4 (1973): 286–94.

11 For example, see E.J. Devine, *Historic Caughnawaga* (Montreal: Messenger Press, 1922).

12 Gerald Reid, *Kahnawà:ke: Factionalism, Traditionalism, and Nationalism in a Mohawk Community* (Lincoln: University of Nebraska Press, 2004), 5–9; Greer, *Mohawk Saint,* 89–100.

13 There is evidence that before the fifteenth century, Iroquoian villages occupied sites for up to fifty years, but by the time of contact with Europeans the maximum was about twenty-five years. Matthew Dennis, *Cultivating a Landscape of Peace: Iroquois-European Encounters in Seventeenth-Century America* (Ithaca: Cornell University Press, 1993), 26, 77.

14 In this section, I have included evidence from a number of non-Rotinonhsión:ni Iroquoian peoples since Iroquoian peoples in the entire Great Lakes region followed similar land practices and land laws. For more on Iroquoian and Algonquian land practices, see Parmenter, *The Edge of the Woods,* xxxvii–xxxix; William Engelbrecht, *Iroquoia: The Development of a Native World* (Syracuse: Syracuse University Press, 2003), 88–91; William Cronon, *Changes in the Land: Indians, Colonists, and the Ecology of New England* (New York: Hill and Wang, 1983); Gordon M. Day, "The Indian as an Ecological Factor in the Northeastern Forest," *Ecology* 34, 2 (1953): 329–46; Deborah Doxtator, "What Happened to the Iroquois Clans? A Study of Clans in Three Nineteenth Century Rotinonhsyonni Communities" (PhD diss., University of Western Ontario, 1996); Hill, *The Clay We Are*

Made Of; Conrad Heidenreich, *Huronia: A History and Geography of the Huron Indians, 1600–1650* (Toronto: McClelland and Stewart, 1971).

15 Heidenreich, *Huronia,* 67, 110–11.

16 Doxtator, "What Happened to the Iroquois Clans?" 52–53; Parmenter, *The Edge of the Woods.*

17 Jane Mt. Pleasant, "The Paradox of Plows and Productivity: An Agronomic Comparison of Cereal Grain Production under Iroquois Hoe Culture and European Plow Culture in the Seventeenth and Eighteenth Centuries," *Agricultural History* 85, 4 (2011): 460–92.

18 Dennis, *Cultivating a Landscape,* 27.

19 Harmen Meyndertsz van den Bogaert, *A Journey into Mohawk and Oneida Country, 1634–1635: The Journal of Harmen Meyndertsz Van Den Bogaert,* ed. and trans. Charles T. Gehring and William A. Starna (Syracuse: Syracuse University Press, 2013). For further evidence of the high productivity of Iroquoian horticulture, see Day, "The Indian as an Ecological Factor," 330–34.

20 Mt. Pleasant, "The Paradox of Plows." For more on swidden agriculture around the world, see Hugh Brody, *The Other Side of Eden: Hunters, Farmers and the Shaping of the World* (Vancouver: Douglas and McIntyre, 2000); Cronon, *Changes in the Land;* D.B. Grigg, *The Agricultural Systems of the World* (Cambridge: Cambridge University Press, 1984); David Henley, "Swidden Farming as an Agent of Environmental Change: Ecological Myth and Historical Reality in Indonesia," *Environment and History* 17 (2011): 525–54.

21 For more on women in Iroquoian societies and their involvement in agriculture, see F.W. Waugh, *Iroquois Foods and Food Preparation* (Ottawa: Government Printing Bureau, 1973 [1916]); Elizabeth Tooker, "Women in Iroquois Society," in *Extending the Rafters: Interdisciplinary Approaches to Iroquoian Studies,* ed. Michael K. Foster and Jack Campisi (Albany: State University of New York Press, 1984), 109–23; Judith K. Brown, "Economic Organization and the Position of Women among the Iroquois," *Ethnohistory* 17 (1970): 151–65; Arthur C. Parker, *Parker on the Iroquois,* ed. William Fenton (Syracuse: Syracuse University Press, 1968); Hill, *The Clay We Are Made Of,* Chapter 2.

22 Parker, *The Constitution of the Five Nations,* 42.

23 Adriaen van der Donck, *Description of the New Netherlands [in 1640],* trans. Jeremiah Johnson (New York: New York Historical Society, 1841), 209.

24 Parker, *Parker on the Iroquois,* 22.

25 Alan Taylor, *The Divided Ground: Indians, Settlers, and the Northern Borderland of the American Revolution* (New York: Alfred A. Knopf, 2006), 18.

26 For recent scholarship on Lafitau, see Christopher Parsons, "The Natural History of Colonial Science: Joseph-François Lafitau's Discovery of Ginseng and Its Afterlives," *William and Mary Quarterly* 73, 1 (2016): 37–72.

27 Joseph François Lafitau, *Customs of the American Indians Compared with the Customs of Primitive Times,* trans. William N. Fenton and Elizabeth L. Moore (Toronto: Champlain Society, 1977 [1724]), 2:54. The original French gives "font diverses bandes nombreuses, selon les differens quartiers où elles ont leurs Champs, et elles passent d'un Champ à l'autre, s'aidant ainsi toutes mutuellement." Joseph François Lafitau, *Moeurs des sauvages ameriquains comparées aux moeurs des premiers temps* (Paris: Chez Saugrain l'aîné et al., 1724), 2:77.

28 Lafitau, *Customs of the American Indians,* 2:55. Original French: "ne paroissent faire tous ensemble qu'une seule piece; sans que pour cela elles aïent des disputes pour leurs bornes, que chacune sçait fort bien reconnoître." Lafitau, *Moeurs des sauvages,* 2:77. Early anthropologist Lewis H. Morgan noted that lots belonging to various families would have been

bounded by uncultivated ridges. Lewis H. Morgan, *League of the Ho-De'-No-Sau-Nee or Iroquois* (North Dighton, MA: JG Press, 1995 [1851]).

29 Van der Donck, *Description of the New Netherlands,* 209–10.

30 Newell, *Crime and Justice,* 40.

31 William Johnson to Lords of Trade, October 30, 1764, in E.B. O'Callaghan, ed., *Documents Relative to the Colonial History of the State of New York,* 7:672, quoted in Taylor, *The Divided Ground,* 36.

32 Parker, *Parker on the Iroquois,* 22–23.

33 Ibid., 29.

34 Tooker, "Women in Iroquois Society," 114.

35 Ibid.

36 Ibid. Lewis Morgan claimed that it was traditional for Rotinonhsión:ni to own, sell, buy, transfer, and inherit land and improvements, but I believe this applies only to post-contact permanent Rotinonhsión:ni villages. Morgan, *League of the Ho-De'-No-Sau-Nee,* 317.

37 Morgan, *League of the Ho-De'-No-Sau-Nee,* 317. Note that patriarchal colonial norms – male pronouns – had entered into Morgan's interpretation and/or Rotinonhsión:ni practice at the time.

38 "Interview with Ernie Kaientaron:kwen Benedict, 28 Oct 2003," in Diabo, "Comprehensive Land Report," 19–20.

39 "Interview with Tom Shakokwanion:kwas Porter, Kahnatsohare:ke," [2002], translated from Kanien'kéha by Diabo, in Diabo, "Comprehensive Land Report," 59. For an overview of the general principles of land tenure and custodianship in Rotinonhsión:ni history, see George-Kanentiio, *Iroquois Culture and Commentary,* 36, 54–55, 79.

40 Greer, *Mohawk Saint,* 97–98.

41 Arnaud Decroix, "Le conflit juridique entre les Jésuites et les Iroquois au sujet de la seigneurie du Sault Saint-Louis: analyse de la décision de Thomas Gage (1762)," *Revue Juridique Thémis* 41 (2007): 280; Devine, *Historic Caughnawaga,* 20–27; Gretchen Green, "A New People in an Age of War: The Kahnawake Iroquois, 1667–1760" (PhD diss., College of William and Mary, 1991), 57–58.

42 In *Mohawk Interruptus,* Audra Simpson refers to a broad range of Kanien'kehá:ka responses to settler colonial pressures as "refusal."

43 Reid, *Kahnawà:ke,* 7–11; Devine, *Historic Caughnawaga,* 129.

44 R.B. Simison, "The Indian Lands of Dundee: An Historical Perspective," *Journal annuel de la Société historique de la vallée de la Châteauguay* 11 (1978): 7–10.

45 Green, "A New People," 285.

46 Kurt Jordan, *The Seneca Restoration, 1715–1754: An Iroquois Local Political Economy* (Gainesville: Society for Historical Archaeology and University Press of Florida, 2008), Chapter 9.

47 Franquet believed that Jesuit missionaries were encouraging Kahnawa'kehró:non to build permanent single-family dwellings in the hope that they themselves would inherit the valuable properties when Kahnawa'kehró:non abandoned the territory. Louis Franquet, *Voyages et mémoires sur le Canada par Franquet* (Quebec City: Institut Canadien de Québec, 1889), 38–39.

48 Jordan, *The Seneca Restoration,* Chapter 9.

49 Green, "A New People," 284–85.

50 John Long, *John Long's Voyages and Travels in the Years 1768–1788* (Chicago: Lakeside, 1922 [1791]), 9.

51 Green, "A New People," 284–85.

52 Morgan, *League of the Ho-De'-No-Sau-Nee,* 307. For more on Rotinonhsión:ni architecture in the seventeenth and eighteenth centuries, see Jordan, *The Seneca Restoration,* Chapter 9.

53 Carl Benn, *The Iroquois in the War of 1812* (Toronto: University of Toronto Press, 1998), 26.

54 For Indigenous people who practise swidden agriculture, increasing population densities can cause hardship due to growing distances to fields and can prompt farmers to cultivate fallows rather than old growth forest. This brings new problems such as weeds, pests, and declining soil productivity. For a twenty-first-century example, see Anders Henrik Sirén, "Population Growth and Land Use Intensification in a Subsistence-Based Indigenous Community in the Amazon," *Human Ecology* 35, 6 (2007): 669–80.

55 Lafitau, *Customs of the American Indians,* 2:69–70. Original French: "Comme les Sauvages ne fument point leurs terres, et ne les laissent pas même reposer, elles s'épuisent bientôt et s'énervent; ce qui les met dans la nécessité de transporter ailleurs leurs Villages, et de faire de nouveaux champs dans des terres neuves. Ils sont encore réduits à cette nécessité, au moins dans l'Amérique Septentrionale, et dans les Païsfroids, par une autre raison plus pressante; car comme il faut que tous les jours les femmes portent à leurs cabanes le bois de chauffage, plus leur Village reste dans le même endroit, plus le bois s'éloigne; de sorte qu'après un certain nombre d'années, elles ne peuvent plus tenir au travail de charroyer de si loin le bois sur leurs épaules." Lafitau, *Moeurs des sauvages,* 2:107–8.

56 Lafitau, *Customs of the American Indians,* 2:70. Original French: "Ceux qui sont au voisinage des Villes Françoises dans la Nouvelle France, ont voulu parer à cet inconvenient, et se sont mis depuis quelque temps en possession d'avoir des chevaux pour conduire à la cabane leur bois en traineau pendant l'hyver, et fur le dos des mêmes chevaux pendant l'Eté. Les jeunes gens, ravis d'avoir des chevaux à mener, prennent volontiers cette peine, et les femmes déchargées par ce moyen d'un fardeau très-onéreux n'en ont pas moins de plaisir qu'eux." Lafitau, *Moeurs des sauvages,* 2:108.

57 Lafitau, *Customs of the American Indians,* 2:70. Original French: "Ces chevaux, qui sont en grand nombre, se répandant par troupes dans leurs champs de bled d'Inde, où il n'y a point de hayes et de clôture pour les arrêter, les désolent entièrement, sans qu'on état de les nourrir dans ces écuries, tout ce qu'on peut faire c'est de les enfermer dans de mauvais parcs, que ces chevaux franchissent aisément; soit que ne trouvant pas assez de nourriture dans ces enclos, ils soient portés d'eux-mêmes à en aller chercher ailleurs dans les bleds d'Indes, qui les affriandent plus que l'avoine; soit que les enfans, qui sont sans cesse occupés à les animer pour les faire battre, les pressent, et les forcent de sauter par-dessus leurs barrieres." Lafitau, *Moeurs des sauvages,* 2:108.

58 For more on John Bernard, see Douglas S. Harvey, "Strolling Players in Albany, Montreal, and Quebec City, 1797 and 1810: Performance, Class, and Empire," *Studies in Eighteenth Century Culture* 38 (2009): 237–60.

59 John Bernard, *Retrospections of America, 1797–1811* (New York: Harper and Brothers, 1887), 355–56.

60 Regarding fishing, see the extract of a speech made by Sir John Johnson to the Indian tribes, June 5, 1797, RG10, vol. 10, pp. 9236–40, reel C-11000, LAC. Regarding hunting, Alan Taylor mentions conflicts in the 1760s and 1770s between Kahnawa'kehró:non and southern Kanien'kehá:ka related to hunting in the Adirondacks. Taylor, *The Divided Ground,* 36–37.

61 Van den Bogaert, *A Journey into Mohawk;* Devine, *Historic Caughnawaga,* 404.

62 The concept of raising animals for food had not been unknown to Kanien'kehá:ka. Some hunters brought back young animals whose mothers they had killed, raising them for future slaughter. Van den Bogaert, for example, mentioned several bears that were kept in enclosures in Kanien'kehá:ka villages. Van den Bogaert, *A Journey into Mohawk*, 6, 10.

63 Long, *John Long's Voyages*, 6–7.

64 Green, "A New People," 290. Several articles in the 1801 Code concern livestock. "Règlements," February 26, 1801, LAC.

65 This was particularly vexing to Kanesatakeró:non, who did not derive revenues from their lands in the way that Kahnawa'kehró:non did. Devine, *Historic Caughnawaga*, 335–36.

66 Memorandum by John Lees based on information from M. Stacey, June 15, 1796, RG8, vol. 248, pp. 172–75, reel C-2848, LAC. Kahnawa'kehró:non had already been experimenting with wheat growing in 1678. Ibid., 48–49. At the beginning of the nineteenth century, Rotinonhsión:ni of the Grand River were growing corn, squash, beans, tobacco, pumpkins, wheat, rye, oats, peas, potatoes, turnips, flax, and orchard fruits, and the same was probably true in Kahnawà:ke. Benn, *The Iroquois in the War of 1812*, 26. Matthew Dennis explains that they retained traditional crops and techniques not because they lacked "a spirit of innovation but because they had found a practical and efficient long-term solution to their subsistence needs, one that made sense to them intellectually, morally, and religiously." Dennis, *Cultivating a Landscape*, 31.

67 Newell, *Crime and Justice*, 40.

68 Parmenter, *The Edge of the Woods*, 3.

69 Newell, *Crime and Justice*, 41.

70 Green, "A New People"; Parmenter, *The Edge of the Woods*; Dennis, *Cultivating a Landscape*; Daniel K. Richter, *The Ordeal of the Longhouse: The Peoples of the Iroquois League in the Era of European Colonization* (Chapel Hill: Institute of Early American History and Culture and University of North Carolina Press, 1992); Alain Beaulieu and Jean-Pierre Sawaya, "Qui sont les Sept-Nations du Canada? Quelques observations sur une appellation ambiguë," *Recherches amérindiennes au Québec* 27, 2 (1997): 43–51; Darren Bonaparte, "The Seven Nations of Canada: The Other Iroquois Confederacy," http://www.wampum chronicles.com/sevennations.html; Lozier, *Flesh Reborn*.

71 After prolonged resistance from Kahnawa'kehró:non and the Jesuit missionaries, the French colonial government gave up on the idea of placing a garrison in Kahnawà:ke in 1724. Green, "A New People," 186.

72 Decroix, "Le conflit juridique," 292.

73 Franquet, *Voyages et mémoires*, 119.

74 Isabelle Bouchard, "Des systèmes politiques en quête de légitimité: terres 'seigneuriales,' pouvoirs et enjeux locaux dans les communautés autochtones de la vallée du Saint-Laurent (1760–1860)" (PhD diss., Université du Québec à Montréal, 2017), 92.

75 Joseph Chew, "Indians of Lower Canada," October 12, 1795, RG8, vol. 248, p. 326, reel C-2848, LAC.

76 Joseph Doutre, "Les sauvages du Canada en 1852," in *Institut-Canadien en 1855*, ed. J.L. Lafontaine (Montreal: Sénécal and Daniel, 1855), 203. For a discussion of external recognition of elected chiefs, see Bouchard, "Des systèmes politiques," 101–9.

77 Bouchard, "Des systèmes politiques," 91.

78 Ibid., 108–16.

79 Ibid., 94.

80 In his comprehensive study of Indigenous petitioning practices during the British regime, Gohier observes the silencing of Indigenous women's political voices. Maxime Gohier, "La pratique pétitionnaire des Amérindiens de la vallée du Saint-Laurent sous le régime Britannique: pouvoir, représentation et légitimité (1760–1860)" (PhD diss., Université du Québec à Montréal, 2014), 375–79.

81 Louis XIV and Jean-Baptiste Colbert, *Titre du Sault Saint-Louis aux Jésuites,* May 29, 1680, RG10, vol. 121, pp. 5222–24, reel C-11480, LAC; Concession par Frontenac et Jacques Duchesnau du Sault Saint-Louis aux Jésuites, October 31, 1680 (Copie du 29 août 1828 de la concession du Sault-Saint-Louis aux Jésuites du 31 octobre 1680), MG11, CO42, vol. 227, pp. 458-59, reel B-170, LAC.

82 Military engineer Louis Franquet was told in 1752–53, possibly by the missionaries themselves, that the missionaries were the "seigneurs de l'endroit et des environs." Franquet, *Voyages et mémoires,* 37.

83 Carmen Lambert, "History of Kahnawake Land Claims, Seigneury of Sault-Saint-Louis" (paper prepared for the Confederation of Indians of Quebec, 1980), 17; Joan Holmes, "Kahnawake Mohawk Territory: From Seigneury to Indian Reserve" (paper presented at the National Claims Research Workshop, Ottawa, November 9, 2006).

84 Michel Morin, *L'usurpation de la souveraineté autochtone: Le cas des peuples de la Nouvelle-France et des colonies anglaises de l'Amérique du Nord* (Montreal: Boréal, 1997), 251. For more on the seigneurial system, see R. Cole Harris, *The Seigneurial System in Early Canada: A Geographical Study* (Quebec City: Presses de l'Université Laval, 1966); William Bennett Munro, *The Seigniorial System in Canada: A Study in French Colonial Policy* (New York: Longmans Green, 1907); Fernand Ouellet, "Le régime seigneurial dans le Québec: 1760–1854," in *France et Canada français du XVIe au XXe siècle,* ed. Claude Galarneau and Elzéar Lavoie (Quebec City: Presses de l'université Laval, 1966), 159–76; Marcel Trudel, *Le régime seigneurial* (Ottawa: Société historique du Canada, 1956).

85 Bouchard, "Des systèmes politiques."

86 Morin's original reads, "de terres appartenant aux autochtones." Morin, *L'usurpation,* 251.

87 Lambert, "History of Kahnawake Land Claims," 18.

88 Morin, *L'usurpation,* 351; Bouchard, "Des systèmes politiques," 146–205; Holmes, "Kahnawake Mohawk Territory."

89 Déposition de Thomas Arakwenté, April 7, 1800, TL19, S4, SS1, case 40, no. 3, dossier 155, Bibliothèque et Archives nationales du Québec (BANQ).

90 Bouchard, "Des systèmes politiques," 158–60; Holmes, "Kahnawake Mohawk Territory," iii–iv.

91 Holmes, "Kahnawake Mohawk Territory," iv.

92 There was probably no written text spelling out the Treaty of Oswegatchie, and if minutes were taken they were later lost. The negotiations ended with an exchange of wampum belts. Subsequent correspondence and speeches contain consistent references to the treaty so that its main points are well known. The Treaty of Oswegatchie was ratified in September of 1760 with the Treaty of Kahnawà:ke. See Alain Beaulieu, "La question des terres autochtones au Québec, 1760–1860" (Rapport de recherche déposé au Ministère de la Justice et au Ministère des Ressources naturelles du Québec, 2002); Alain Beaulieu, "Les pièges de la judiciarisation de l'histoire autochtone," *Revue d'histoire de l'Amerique français* 53, 4 (2000): 541–51; Holmes, "Kahnawake Mohawk Territory," iv.

93 Bouchard, "Des systèmes politiques," 76.

94 Borrows, "Wampum at Niagara," 155–72.

95 Daniel Francis, *A History of the Native Peoples of Quebec, 1760–1867* (Ottawa: Department of Indian Affairs and Northern Development, 1985), 9–25.

96 Decroix, "Le conflit juridique." At this time, the Jesuit Order in Canada was in steep decline, with only twenty-five ageing priests remaining, forbidden to recruit new members and suppressed by the Catholic Church itself in 1763. Marcel Trudel, "Le destin de l'Église sous le régime militaire," *Revue d'histoire de l'Amerique français* 11, 1 (1957): 21–22.

97 Bouchard, "Des systèmes politiques," 161; Decroix, "Le conflit juridique"; Holmes, "Kahnawake Mohawk Territory," iv–v; Lambert, "History of Kahnawake Land Claims," 25–26.

98 Lawrence Vankoughnet to C.E. Schiller, Clerk of the Crown (Secretary of the State), September 29, 1879, RG10, vol. 2093, file 15676, LAC.

99 Holmes, "Kahnawake Mohawk Territory," iv; Bouchard, "Des systèmes politiques," 169–70. Bouchard discusses some Kahnawà:ke political battles over the right to concede lands after the Gage Decision of 1762. Ibid., 199–203. It was reported that in 1796 Kahnawa'kehró:non "do not give any new Grants, preferring to keep the Lands for their own use." Memorandum by John Lees, June 15, 1796, LAC. Some documents refer to the receiver as an agent.

100 The situation was so dire in July 1771 that twenty-two Kahnawà:ke deputies visited Sir William Johnson to ask him to stop French families from settling on their common land. William Johnson, *The Papers of Sir William Johnson,* ed. Alexander C. Flick (Albany: University of the State of New York, 1933), 8:188–89.

101 Gohier, "La pratique pétitionnaire," 452–57.

102 Bouchard, "Des systèmes politiques," 209.

103 As late as 1810, Kahnawa'kehró:non had voting rights in Lower Canada on the basis of their status as owners of the seigneury. Petition of Augustin Cuviller to the Legislative Assembly of Lower Canada, February 9, 1810, *Journaux de la Chambre d'Assemblée du Bas-Canada* (29 January–26 February 1810): 89–101.

104 In 1858, the Pennefather Commission Report claimed that when the land was taken from the management of the Jesuits, "the interest of the Tribe only under the supervision of the Indian Department was recognized, the fee simple being retained by the Crown." "Report of the Special Commissioners to Investigate Indian Affairs in Canada," Appendix 21 in Province of Canada, *Sessional Papers* (Toronto, 1858), 16, A21-19.

105 Holmes, "Kahnawake Mohawk Territory," v.

106 Lambert, "History of Kahnawake Land Claims," 32–33.

107 Denys Delâge and Étienne Gilbert, "La justice coloniale britannique et les Amérindiens au Québec, 1760–1820. I – En terres amérindiennes," *Recherches amérindiennes au Québec* 32, 1 (2002): 70.

108 Jeremiah McCarthy, "Minutes concerning Seigniories of Sault St. Lewis and the Adjoining Seigniories," March 31, 1794, RG10, vol. 9, pp. 8976–78, reel C-10999, LAC; Alexander McKee to James Green, July 28, 1795, RG8, vol. 248, pp. 233–36, reel C-2848, LAC; Extract of a speech made by Sir John Johnson, June 5, 1797, LAC; Memorandum by John Lees, June 15, 1796, LAC; Speech of the Iroquois of Lake of Two Mountains and Caughnawaga to John Johnson, December 23, 1807, MG11, CO 42, vol. 136, pp. 267–72, reel B-122, LAC.

109 Lambert, "History of Kahnawake Land Claims," 33.

110 Devine, *Historic Caughnawaga,* 339; Lambert, "History of Kahnawake Land Claims," 33.

111 Devine, *Historic Caughnawaga,* 339; Matthieu Sossoyan, "The Kahnawake Iroquois and the Lower-Canadian Rebellions, 1837–1838" (master's thesis, McGill University, 1999), 77–78.

112   Memorandum signed by chiefs and warriors of the Iroquois of Sault St. Louis, October 15, 1829, annexed to Joseph Marcoux to Johann L. Tiarks, December 15, 1829, MG24, H64, vol. 1, file 2, pp. 15–17, reel H-1209, LAC.

113   McKee to Green, July 28, 1795, LAC; Extract of a speech made by Sir John Johnson, June 5, 1797, LAC; Memorandum by John Lees, June 15, 1796, LAC; Speech of the Iroquois of Lake of Two Mountains, December 23, 1807, LAC.

114   Lambert, "History of Kahnawake Land Claims," 35.

115   Pétition des Iroquois de Sault Saint-Louis à Charles Murray Cathcart, January 3, 1846, RG10, vol. 602, pp. 48642–46, reel C-13381, LAC; Petition from Louis Eustache Mackay to James Bruce Elgin, July 24, 1848, RG10, vol. 605, pp. 50483–88, reel C-13382, LAC.

116   Speech of the Iroquois of Lake of Two Mountains, December 23, 1807, LAC.

117   Devine, *Historic Caughnawaga*, 339; Decroix, "Le conflit juridique"; Holmes, "Kahnawake Mohawk Territory," v–vi; Lambert, "History of Kahnawake Land Claims," 33–35; McKee to Green, July 28, 1795, pp. 222–24, 233–36, LAC; Jonathan Sewell to James Henry Craig, June 22, 1808, MG11-CO42, vol. 136, pp. 277–78, reel 4M00-2849A, LAC.

118   Joseph Fleury Deschambault and Archibald Kennedy Johnson to John Johnson, March 10, 1821, RG10, vol. 14, pp. 11603–5, reel C-11002, LAC. Deschambault and Johnson also noted that Kahnawà:ke chiefs desired to "Reserve to themselves exclusively the management of their Mill, and the Profits arising therefrom," so this would not be included in the responsibilities of the agent.

119   Sossoyan, "The Kahnawake Iroquois," 27; Henry C. Darling to John Johnson, June 4, 1821, MG11-CO42, vol. 373, p. 206, reel B-306, LAC. Doucet wrote a long text on the law of Quebec in which he seems to treat Indigenous law as one of the three founding legal traditions of Canada. Girard, Phillips, and Brown recognize this as highly unusual for its time. Philip Girard, Jim Phillips, and R. Blake Brown, *A History of Law in Canada* (Toronto: University of Toronto Press for the Osgoode Society for Canadian Legal History, 2018), 1:482. Nicolas-Benjamin Doucet, *Fundamental Principles of the Laws of Canada as They Existed under the Natives, as They Were Changed under the French Kings, and as They Were Modified and Altered under the Domination of England* (Montreal: John Lovell, 1841).

120   Holmes, "Kahnawake Mohawk Territory," vi.

121   Original French: "que nous ne connessions pas, éloigné de nous, ne connoissant pas lui même les censitaires qui nous payent rentes, combien chacun d'eux doive payer non plus que l'étendue et la situation de leurs terres, ne nous donne ni bled ni argents pour soulager les maux de nos pauvres." Kahnawà:ke chiefs to Sir John Johnson Baronet, February 14, 1824, RG10, vol. 16, pp. 12470–71, reel C-11003, LAC.

122   Sossoyan, "The Kahnawake Iroquois," 24.

123   Report of Henry C. Darling on Indian Affairs, July 24, 1828, MG24-A12, vol. 9, reel A-535, LAC.

124   "Report of the Special Commissioners," A21-19.

125   Ibid., A21-19, A21-21.

126   For example, in 1820 over £1,000 were owed Kahnawà:ke from a number of sources, but since colonial law prevented it from suing debtors the sum could not be collected through legal channels. Devine, *Historic Caughnawaga*, 339–443; Lambert, "History of Kahnawake Land Claims," 32–33. For background in how colonial law came to treat Indigenous communities in this way, see Girard, Phillips, and Brown, *A History of Law*, 1:455–58.

127   Brian Gettler, *Colonialism's Currency: Money, State, and First Nations in Canada, 1820–1950* (Montreal and Kingston: McGill-Queen's University Press, 2020), 144.
128   Lambert, "History of Kahnawake Land Claims," 29.
129   Decroix, "Le conflit juridique," 294–95; Holmes, "Kahnawake Mohawk Territory," vi.
130   Holmes, "Kahnawake Mohawk Territory," vi.
131   Lambert, "History of Kahnawake Land Claims," 29–30, 42–43; Holmes, "Kahnawake Mohawk Territory," vi.
132   Lambert, "History of Kahnawake Land Claims," 42.
133   Vankoughnet, "Memo on Letter of the 28th Inst. from the Caughnawaga Chiefs Complaining of Their Agent," April 30, 1874, RG10, vol. 1924, file 3055, LAC.
134   Lambert, "History of Kahnawake Land Claims," 42; Holmes, "Kahnawake Mohawk Territory," vii.
135   Holmes, "Kahnawake Mohawk Territory," vii; Caughnawaga Agency – Claim of the Caughnawaga Indians to Devil Island and St. Nicholas Island, RG10, C-22399, vol. 2925, file 190,255, LAC.
136   Holmes, "Kahnawake Mohawk Territory," vii–viii.
137   Kahnawà:ke Claims, http://kahnawakeclaims.com/.
138   Holmes, "Kahnawake Mohawk Territory," vi–vii.
139   For an example from Six Nations of the Grand River, see the efforts of its leaders to lease lands to white settlers in order to provide an income for the community. Hill, *The Clay We Are Made Of,* Chapter 4.

Chapter 2: "Seigniory of Sault St. Louis"

Epigraph: Petition by eight Kahnawà:ke chiefs to Robert Prescott Esquire, Governor General, March 8, 1799, MG23-GII17, vol. 12, pp. 122–25, reel H-2532, LAC.

1   White, *The Middle Ground.*
2   Trudy Nicks, "The Iroquois and the Fur Trade in Western Canada," in *Old Trails and New Directions: Papers of the Third North American Fur Trade Conference,* ed. Carol M. Judd and Arthur J. Ray (Toronto: University of Toronto Press, 1980), 85–101; Jean Barman, *Iroquois in the West* (Montreal and Kingston: McGill-Queen's University Press, 2019); Nicole St-Onge, "'He Was Neither a Soldier nor a Slave: He Was under the Control of No Man': Kahnawake Mohawks in the Northwest Fur Trade, 1790–1850," *Canadian Journal of History* 51, 1 (2016): 1–32; Jack A. Frisch, "The Iroquois Indians and the 1855 Franklin Search Expedition in the Arctic," *Indian Historian* 8, 1 (1975): 27–30; Carl Benn, *Mohawks on the Nile: Natives among the Canadian Voyageurs in Egypt, 1884–1885* (Toronto: Natural Heritage Books, 2009).
3   Girard, Phillips, and Brown, *A History of Law,* 1:309–10.
4   Jan Grabowski, "The Common Ground: Settled Natives and French in Montreal, 1667–1760" (PhD diss., Université de Montréal, 1994); Jan Grabowski, "French Criminal Justice and Indians in Montreal, 1670–1760," *Ethnohistory* 43, 3 (1996): 405–29; Helen Stone, "Les Indiens et le système judiciaire criminel de la province de Québec: Les politiques de l'administration sous le régime britannique," *Recherches amérindiennes au Québec* 30, 3 (2000): 65–78. It was also common for Indigenous people to hand over non-Indigenous suspects to colonial authorities for trial. An example from Upper Canada comes from an 1814 incident where several Delaware men from Six Nations of the Grand River were

murdered. Six Nations warriors subsequently captured the suspects, who were sent to the provincial capital for trial. Benn, *The Iroquois in the War of 1812,* 135.

5 Donald Fyson, *Magistrates, Police and People: Everyday Criminal Justice in Quebec and Lower Canada* (Toronto: University of Toronto Press, 2006), 303.

6 Petition by eight Kahnawà:ke chiefs to Robert Prescott, 8 March 1799, LAC.

7 Ibid.

8 Ibid.

9 Ibid.

10 Delâge and Gilbert, "La justice coloniale," 64–65.

11 Evelyn Kolish, "Some Aspects of Civil Litigation in Lower Canada, 1785–1825: Towards the Use of Court Records for Canadian Social History," *Canadian Historical Review* 70, 3 (1989): 343–44.

12 Delâge and Gilbert, "La justice coloniale," 64.

13 Isaac Weld, *Travels through the States of North America and the Provinces of Upper and Lower Canada* (London: John Stockdale, 1800), 213–14.

14 I chose not to quote this passage because it included a dehumanizing epithet for Indigenous women. Ibid.

15 Ibid., 214.

16 Registre des procès-verbaux d'audiences, March 12, 1789–August 31, 1791, TL16, S4, BANQ; Denys Delâge and Alexandre Lefrançois, "Thomas Arakwenté: promoteur de la modernité dans la communauté iroquoise du Sault Saint-Louis (1791–1820)," in *Gouvernance autochtone: aspects juridiques, économiques et sociaux,* ed. Andrée Lajoie (Montreal: Les éditions Thémis, 2007), 72–76.

17 Delâge and Gilbert, "La justice coloniale," 65.

18 Joseph Chew to Thomas A. Coffin, January 28, 1796, RG8, vol. 249, pt. 1, p. 8, reel C-2849, LAC.

19 Joseph Chew to Thomas A. Coffin, February 18, 1796, RG8, vol. 249, pt. 1, pp. 30–31, reel C-2849, LAC.

20 Bouchard, "Des systèmes politiques," 220.

21 Girard, Phillips, and Brown, *A History of Law,* 1:310; Delâge and Gilbert, "La justice coloniale," 65.

22 Girard, Phillips, and Brown, *A History of Law,* 1:310–11.

23 Affidavit of Jacob Joseph Hill, August 1, 1798, TL32, S1, SS1, BANQ.

24 Deposition of Thomas Arakwente, April 1, 1800, TL19, S4, SS1, file 155, BANQ.

25 Testimony of Claude Duranseau, April 16, 1800, TL19, S4, SS1, file 155, BANQ.

26 Delâge and Gilbert, "La justice coloniale," 65; Girard, Phillips, and Brown, *A History of Law,* 1:311.

27 Original French: "n'avaient rien à voir avec la loi de Montréal." Alexandre Lefrançois, "Thomas Arakwenté: Promoteur de la modernité dans la communauté iroquoise du Sault Saint-Louis (1791–1820)," *Revue d'éthique et de théologie morale "Le Supplément"* 226 (2003): 364.

28 Girard, Phillips, and Brown, *A History of Law,* 1:311.

29 Declaration of Arakwente, June 15, 1807, TL19, S4, SS1, file 89, BANQ.

30 Ibid.

31 Execution of the sentence, August 10, 1807, Executions issued out of the Court of King's Bench at Montreal, TL19, S4, SS15, 1804–1811, BANQ.

32   Girard, Phillips, and Brown, *A History of Law,* 1:311.

33   Jean-Philippe Garneau, "Appartenance ethnique, culture juridique et représentation devant la justice civile de Québec à la fin du XVIIIe siècle," in *Entre justice et justiciables: Les auxiliaires de la justice du Moyen Âge au XXe siècle,* ed. Claire Dolan (Quebec City: Les presses de l'Université Laval, 2005), 405–42.

34   Fyson, *Magistrates, Police and People,* 303–4.

35   Kolish, "Some Aspects of Civil Litigation," 348.

36   Ibid., 350–51.

37   Ibid., 362.

38   Ibid., 365.

39   Ibid., 350–51.

40   Allan Greer, *Peasant, Lord, and Merchant: Rural Society in Three Quebec Parishes, 1740–1840* (Toronto: University of Toronto Press, 1985), 175.

41   John M. Duncan, *Travels through Part of the United States and Canada in 1818 and 1819* (Glasgow: University Press, 1823), 2:155.

42   His family name is spelled in a variety of ways, and I have chosen to standardize it as Delorimier. For his memoir of his war experiences, see Claude Nicolas-Guillaume de Lorimier, "Mes services pendant la guerre américaine," in *Invasion du Canada,* ed. M. L'abbé Verreau (Montreal: Eusèbe Senécal, 1873), 245–98, published in English as *At War with the Americans,* trans. and ed. Peter Aichinger (Victoria, n.d.).

43   Douglas Leighton, "Lorimier, Claude-Nicolas-Guillaume de," *Dictionary of Canadian Biography Online,* http://www.biographi.ca/en/bio/lorimier_claude_nicolas_guillaume_de_6E.html.

44   Contract between Guillaume Chevalier de Lorimier and the Iroquois Chiefs of Sault Saint-Louis, March 1, 1790, RG8, vol. 265, pp. 69–70, reel C-2855, LAC.

45   Rapport du procureur général adjoint sur certaines plaintes des Iroquois du Sault St-Louis pour Guy Carleton Dorchester, March 1794, RG10, vol. 625, pp. 182269–77, reel C-13395, LAC.

46   Pétition des chefs iroquois du Sault-Saint-Louis à James Henry Craig, July 15, 1809, RG10, vol. 625, pp. 182379–83, reel C-11002, LAC. Original French: "de Blancs qui tantôt veulent être sauvages, pour leurs avantages, tantôt Blancs pour nous humilier, nous écraser."

47   Sossoyan, "The Kahnawake Iroquois," 85–86.

48   Deposition of Thomas Arakouanté, March 22, 1803, TL19, S4, SS1, file 48, BANQ.

49   Plea of Guillaume Chevalier de Lorimier, April 5, 1803, TL19, S4, SS1, file 48, BANQ.

50   Lefrançois, "Thomas Arakwenté," 374–75.

51   Report of the Arbitrators, February 19, 1806, TL19, S4, SS1, file 48, BANQ.

52   In my earlier work, I refer to this document as "The Twenty-One Laws," but here I follow Girard, Phillips, and Brown in calling it the "1801 Code." More than a list, it is a cohesive and focused set of laws, the type often referred to as a code. Girard, Phillips, and Brown, *A History of Law,* 1:312.

53   "Règlements et conditions accordés et convenus par les chefs des Iroquois du Sault St. Louis Assemblés et convoqués a cette effet dans la Chambre du Conseil au village du Sault St. Louis," February 26, 1801, RG10, vol. 10, pp. 9446–54, reel C-11000, LAC.

54   Delâge and Gilbert, "La justice coloniale," 66. Delâge and Gilbert say that the rules were drawn up in 1808, but close examination shows that they appear to have been passed in 1801 and rescinded in 1808.

55 The original archival document is in French, and there is also an English translation that is extremely difficult to read due to the poor quality of the microfilm. My translation mostly adheres to the latter, but I also consulted and translated the French version where necessary. I removed the male gender from references to individuals, since the code was almost certainly first written in Kanien'kéha, in which an unknown individual is not automatically gendered male. "Règlements," February 26, 1801, LAC.

56 James Anaya, "Indigenous Peoples' Participatory Rights in Relation to Decisions about Natural Resource Extraction: The More Fundamental Issue of What Rights Indigenous Peoples Have in Lands and Resources," *Arizona Journal of International and Comparative Law* 22, 1 (2005): 7–18; Jo M. Pasqualucci, "International Indigenous Land Rights: A Critique of the Jurisprudence of the Inter-American Court of Human Rights in Light of the United Nations Declaration on the Rights of Indigenous Peoples," *Wisconsin International Law Journal* 27, 1 (2009): 51–98.

57 Hill, *The Clay We Are Made Of,* 42.

58 Ibid.

59 Bouchard, "Des systèmes politiques," 233.

60 Ibid., 232–33.

61 Ibid., 233–34. Original French: "La reconnaissance de leurs règlements par la législation coloniale permettrait notamment aux chefs de recourir à l'autorité coercitive des tribunaux coloniaux pour la résolution des conflits intracommunautaires."

62 Ibid., 234.

63 Sossoyan, "The Kahnawake Iroquois," 84.

64 Rapport du procureur général, March 1794, LAC.

65 Sossoyan, "The Kahnawake Iroquois," 85–86.

66 Ibid., 86.

CHAPTER 3: "OUT OF THE BEATEN TRACK"

Epigraph: Joseph Bouchette, *A Topographical Description of the Province of Lower Canada* (St-Lambert, QC: Payette and Simms, 1973 [1815]), 124, 125.

1 Benn, *The Iroquois in the War of 1812,* 174.

2 James Belich, *Replenishing the Earth: The Settler Revolution and the Rise of the Anglo-World, 1783–1939* (Oxford: Oxford University Press, 2009); John C. Weaver, *The Great Land Rush and the Making of the Modern World, 1650–1900* (Montreal and Kingston: McGill-Queen's University Press, 2003).

3 For accounts of the involvement of Kahnawa'kehró:non in the fur trade, see Barman, *Iroquois in the West;* St-Onge, "'He Was Neither a Soldier nor a Slave'"; Nicks, "The Iroquois and the Fur Trade."

4 Francis, *A History of the Native Peoples,* 1–20; Carter, *Lost Harvests,* 23–24.

5 Nathan Ince, "As Long as That Fire Burned: Indigenous Warriors and Political Order in Upper Canada, 1837–1842," essay submitted for publication, 2021. A relevant work for Lower Canada is Sossoyan, "The Kahnawake Iroquois."

6 Report of Henry C. Darling on Indian Affairs, July 24, 1828, LAC.

7 Tobias, "Protection, Civilisation, Assimilation"; Duncan Campbell Scott, "Indian Affairs, 1763–1841," in *Canada and Its Provinces,* ed. Adam Shortt and Arthur G. Doughty (Toronto: Glasgow, Brook, 1914), vol. 2, section 2, part 2; Duncan Campbell Scott, "Indian Affairs,

1840–1867," in *Canada and Its Provinces,* ed. Adam Shortt and Arthur G. Doughty (Toronto: Glasgow, Brook, 1914), vol. 5, section 3.

8 "Indian Education – Historic Sketch," file 114, General Synod Archives, Anglican Church of Canada.

9 Benn, *The Iroquois in the War of 1812,* 182–83.

10 Theodore Binnema and Kevin Hutchings, "The Emigrant and the Noble Savage: Sir Francis Bond Head's Romantic Approach to Aboriginal Policy in Upper Canada, 1836–1838," *Journal of Canadian Studies/Revue d'études canadiennes* 39, 1 (2005): 115–38.

11 Benn, *The Iroquois in the War of 1812,* 189.

12 Hill, *The Clay We Are Made Of,* 182.

13 Speech by Sawenoenne on behalf of the chiefs and members of the council to Duncan C. Napier, June 1, 1839, RG10, vol. 97, pp. 40204–5, reel C-11470, LAC.

14 Pétition des Iroquois de Sault Saint-Louis, January 3, 1846, LAC.

15 Petition of Michel Perthuis to George Ramsay Dalhousie, n.d., attached to Duncan C. Napier to Henry C. Darling, January 31, 1827, RG10, vol. 496, pp. 31402–3, reel C-13341, LAC. Original French: "Qu'à l'imitation des habitants Canadiens, votre suppliant désire s'etablir d'une manière stable et permanente, en se procurant un lot de terre qui repondroit par son travail et son industrie, aux besoins et maintien de sa famille, non seulement de son vivant, mais après sa mort."

16 Ibid.

17 Napier to Darling, January 31, 1827, pp. 31402–3, LAC.

18 Ibid.

19 Petition of Michel Perthuis to George Ramsay Dalhousie, n.d., pp. 31402–3, LAC. Original French: "Que dans les limites du fief Le Sault St Louis, il y a une grande étendu de terre vacante et inculte, laquelle, dans son etat actuel, n'est d'aucune utilité et ne donne aucun profit à cette tribu ny à aucune autre personne qu'il paroit à votre suppliant, qu'il seroit pour le profit commun de cette tribu et l'avantage individuel de ses membres, d'en conceder une partie pour être mise en culture plutot que de la laisser dans son etat naturel inculte."

20 Napier to Darling, January 31, 1827, pp. 31402–3, LAC.

21 As quoted in Devine, *Historic Caughnawaga,* 379. Devine took this to mean that though Kahnawa'kehró:non had had 160 years to make use of the land, they still used only a fraction of it.

22 For a powerful analysis of the colonial rhetoric of "improvement" in the Palestinian context, see Brenna Bhandar, *Colonial Lives of Property: Law, Land, and Racial Regimes of Ownership* (Durham: Duke University Press, 2018), Chapter 3.

23 Report of the Superintendent of Indian Affairs, Duncan C. Napier, 1845, Department of Lands and Forests, D-3 359-44, sec. 2, BANQ, quoted in Lambert, "History of Kahnawake Land Claims," 56.

24 Devine, *Historic Caughnawaga,* 379.

25 T. Eug. Antoine report to R.T. Pennefather, February 27, 1857, in "Report of the Special Commissioners."

26 Reid, *Kahnawà:ke,* 18.

27 "Report of the Special Commissioners."

28 Ibid.

29 Antoine report to Pennefather, February 27, 1857, in ibid.

30 Devine, *Historic Caughnawaga,* 379–80.
31 Quoted in ibid., 380 (emphasis in original).
32 St-Onge, "'He Was Neither a Soldier nor a Slave,'" 20.
33 Ibid.
34 Serge Courville, "La crise agricole du Bas-Canada, éléments d'une réflexion géographique
     (1e partie)," *Cahiers de géographie du Québec* 24, 62 (1980): 197. Courville's calculations for
     the average Quebec farmer are for the years 1844 and 1851, and are converted from arpents
     to acres.
35 Sossoyan, "The Kahnawake Iroquois," 19.
36 Ibid., 20.
37 Ibid., 19.
38 Solomon Y. Chesley to James Hughes, January 18, 1834, RG10, vol. 88, pp. 35006–8, reel
     C-11466, LAC.
39 Arthur C. Parker, *The Code of Handsome Lake, the Seneca Prophet* (Albany: New York State
     Museum, 1913). Written versions of the Karihwí:io often give the impression that it stipu-
     lated a change in gender roles to replicate colonial ones, but oral recitations are clearer in
     showing that it simply gave permission (or divine sanction) for men to get involved in
     agriculture if they wished, as long as this did not lead them to become vain. Kahrhó:wane
     Cory McComber, pers. comm., January 23, 2021.
40 Hill, *The Clay We Are Made Of,* 73–76.
41 Bouchette, *A Topographical Description,* 125.
42 See Chapter 2 on parts of the 1801 Code that required people to keep their animals away
     from gardens and fields at certain times of the year.
43 Joseph Marcoux, "Notes Explicatives du memoire pour les Sauvages du Sault St Louis,"
     January 25, 1830, RG10, vol. 24, pp. 25759–69, reel C-11006, LAC. This practice was con-
     tinued into the twentieth century. Kahrhó:wane Cory McComber, pers. comm., January
     10, 2021.
44 "Report of the Special Commissioners."
45 Ibid.
46 For more on Rotinonhsión:ni adoption and naturalization, see James Axtell, "The White
     Indians of Colonial America," *William and Mary Quarterly* 32, 1 (1975): 55–88; E. Jane
     Dickson-Gilmore, "'More Mohawk Than My Blood': Citizenship, Membership and
     the Struggle over Identity in Kahnawake," *Canadian Issues* 21 (1999): 44–62; Horn-Miller,
     "How Did Adoption Become a Dirty Word?"; Evan Haefeli and Kevin Sweeney, *Captors
     and Captives: The 1704 French and Indian Raid on Deerfield* (Boston: University of
     Massachusetts Press, 2003).
47 Kahrhó:wane Cory McComber, pers. comm., January 10, 2021.
48 "White man" remains one of the worst things one can call another Kahnawa'kehró:non,
     even today. In contrast with the word "Onkwehón:we" ("true person, meaning within the
     culture bounds our ancestors have laid down for us"), "white man" implies that a person
     is "acting in a way that is completely divorced from the right way of conducting one's self
     as an Indigenous person in North America." Ibid.
49 Pamela D. Palmater, *Beyond Blood: Rethinking Indigenous Identity* (Saskatoon: Purich,
     2011).
50 Quoted in Sossoyan, "The Kahnawake Iroquois," 88–89.
51 Ibid.

52 Ibid., 83–84. In 1804, the chiefs expressed that both they and the missionary had the authority to remove men from the church and to prevent them from entering. This was probably aimed at preventing certain white men from marrying Kahnawà:ke women and thus gaining access to land and privileges. Bouchard, "Des systèmes politiques," 233.

53 Report of Henry C. Darling on Indian affairs, July 24, 1828, LAC.

54 Devine, *Historic Caughnawaga*, 353–54.

55 For broader colonial context on issues of Indian status, race, and property, see Bhandar, *Colonial Lives of Property*, Chapter 4.

56 George Delorimier was the son of Claude Delorimier, who appears in the previous chapter as a leading dissident in the early nineteenth century. He married Marie-Louise McComber, a daughter of Jarvis McComber.

57 Joseph Marcoux, "Mémoire pour le Missionnaire du Sault St-Louis," September 28, 1835, file 3A, document 170, Archives du Diocèse de Saint-Jean-de-Québec-à-Longueuil.

58 Sossoyan, "The Kahnawake Iroquois," 93.

59 Duncan C. Napier to Thomas W.C. Murdoch, November 20, 1840, RG10, vol. 100, pp. 41805–8, reel C-11471, LAC.

60 Sossoyan, "The Kahnawake Iroquois," 82–100.

61 James Hughes to Duncan C. Napier, March 20, 1836, Collection Baby, P0058U05881, Université de Montréal, division des archives.

62 Sossoyan, "The Kahnawake Iroquois," 94.

63 Ibid., 93.

64 Ibid., 95–103.

65 Ibid., 101.

66 Ibid., 105; Pétition des chefs et guerriers de Caughnawaga à Charles Poulet Thompson, Gouverneur Général, May 29, 1840, file 3A, document 210, Archives du Diocèse de Saint-Jean-de-Québec-à-Longueuil.

67 Sossoyan, "The Kahnawake Iroquois," 103–5.

68 Superintendent of Indian Affairs Duncan C. Napier initially believed there was enough unconceded land to allow each Kahnawà:ke family a hundred-acre farm but appears to have been corrected by a local surveyor. Napier to Lieutenant Colonel Couper, April 14, 1830, RG8-I, C Series, vol. 269, pp. 347–50, reel C-2857, LAC.

69 Iroquois of Caughnawaga to Duncan C. Napier, June 1, 1839, LAC.

70 Devine, *Historic Caughnawaga*, 390.

71 John H. Hanson, *The Lost Prince: Facts Tending to Prove the Identity of Louis the Seventeenth, of France, and the Rev. Eleazar Williams, Missionary among the Indians of North America* (New York: G.P. Putnam, 1854), 355.

72 Doutre, "Les sauvages du Canada," 212–15.

73 Elizabeth Elbourne, "Broken Alliance: Debating Six Nations Land Claims in 1822," *Cultural and Social History* 9, 4 (2012): 497–525; Sidney L. Harring, "'A Condescension Lost on Those People': The Six Nations' Grand River Lands, 1784–1860," in Sidney L. Harring, *White Man's Law: Native People in Nineteenth-Century Canadian Jurisprudence* (Toronto: University of Toronto Press for the Osgoode Society for Canadian Legal History, 1998), 35–61.

74 Elsbeth Heaman, "Space, Race, and Violence: The Beginnings of 'Civilization' in Canada," in *Violence, Order, and Unrest: A History of British North America, 1749–1876*, ed. Elizabeth Mancke et al. (Toronto: University of Toronto Press, 2019), 146–49.

75 Ibid.

CHAPTER 4: "QUESTIONS OF PROPERTY"

Epigraph: Doutre, "Les sauvages du Canada," 202–3. Original French: "Le chemin de fer qui traverse maintenant toute la profondeur de la seigneurie, va être inévitablement l'occasion de nombreuses difficultés. Déjà les blancs attirés par le commerce que vient d'y créer le chemin de fer, se sont répandu dans le village et sur la route; – et l'on verra, par l'exposé de l'existence politique des sauvages, dans quelle anarchie légale vont bientôt se trouver les questions de propriété, dans un endroit où tout le monde est propriétaire et où personne ne l'est."

1   The passage reads, "des observations assez frivolement recueillies dans le cours de deux ou trois ans et cousues ensemble par une étude de vingt-quatre heures, faite sur les lieux et gravée d'après nature." Ibid., 194.
2   Ibid., 203. Original French: "ne résulteront aucunement de leur forme de gouvernement mais uniquement du mélange de races hétérogènes, soumises à une législation essentielle-ment différente."
3   For a comparative legal history of Indigenous dispossession, see Banner, *Possessing the Pacific.* One important Canadian example is Carter, *Lost Harvests.* For the United States and Australia, see Lisa Ford, *Settler Sovereignty: Jurisdiction and Indigenous People in America and Australia, 1788–1836* (Cambridge, MA: Harvard University Press, 2010).
4   Also along these lines, historian R. Cole Harris dedicated his book *Making Native Space* to Gilbert Malcolm Sproat, "a colonizer who eventually listened." R. Cole Harris, *Making Native Space: Colonialism, Resistance, and Reserves in British Columbia* (Vancouver: UBC Press, 2002).
5   Doutre, "Les sauvages du Canada," 201.
6   Newell, *Crime and Justice,* 18–20; Parmenter, *The Edge of the Woods,* xlii.
7   Newell, *Crime and Justice,* 22–25.
8   Ibid., 31. Note the problematic masculine pronouns and patriarchal assumptions in this passage. See also historian Arthur Parker, who emphasized that Rotinonhsión:ni social cohesion was preserved through ostracism, informal social pressure, and the elimination of members who were seen as antisocial. Arthur C. Parker, *An Analytical History of the Seneca Indians* (N.p.: Kraus Reprint, 1970 [1926]), 6:65.
9   Doutre, "Les sauvages du Canada," 204–5.
10 Ibid., 205, 217.
11 Ibid., 205. Original French: "Ils tiennent pour maxime, que l'enfant appartient à la mère, et que le père n'en est, comme disait Balzac, que l'éditeur responsable. Alors pour opérer une transmission légitime des insignes de l'autorité, du chef mort à son successeur, ils ont voulu que la mère et son estoc et ligne en fussent les dépositaires, jusqu'à l'élection du successeur. Le père du chef n'est considéré que comme un étranger à cet effet."
12 Ibid., 202. Original French: "Au Sault St.-Louis, les Iroquois jouissent collectivement, mais non individuellement, d'une manière incontestée d'une seigneurie de trois lieues de front, sur deux lieues de profondeur entre Châteauguay et Laprairie. Les blancs cultivent une partie, à titre de censitaires et le reste se compose de bois debout ou haute futaie, d'une partie cultivée par les sauvages, d'une prairie commune et du village de Caughnawaga."
13 Ibid., 203. Original French: "Ceux qui ont considéré le phalanstère, le communisme et le socialisme, comme des rêveries irréalisables, seraient bien étonnés, s'ils voyaient fonctionner un système presque analogue, avec une parfaite régularité, et s'ils savaient que cette espèce de communisme existe ici depuis des siècles et s'y trouve encore en plaine opération. Car

le gouvernement actuel des Iroquois est le gouvernement traditionel des Indiens d'Amerique, et la civilisation européenne n'en a rien changé." Conceived by utopian socialist
Charles Fourier, a "phalanstère" is a building designed for communal living.

14 Ibid., 206. Original French: "Depuis longtemps, ils ont chacun un morceau de terre à
cultiver, une sucrerie et une terre à bois, et tout cela compose un patrimoine que se transmet,
sans l'intervention de la commune. Mais comme la commune est obligée de concéder les
terres incultes à ceux des sauvages qui en exigent, on conçoit que de ce mélange de communisme et de la propriété individuelle auraient surgi de grandes difficultés, si la population
en était arrivée à épuiser toutes les terres non concédées."

15 Ibid.

16 Jean-Claude Robert, *Atlas Historique de Montréal* ([Montreal]: Art Global/Libre Expression, 1994), 58, 78–79, 92.

17 G.R. Stevens, *Canadian National Railways,* vol. 1, *Sixty Years of Trial and Error (1836–1896)*
(Toronto: Clarke, Irwin, 1960), 30, 38.

18 Gerald Tulchinsky, *The River Barons: Montreal Businessmen and the Growth of Industry and
Transportation, 1837–53* (Toronto: University of Toronto Press, 1977), 188.

19 Stevens, *Canadian National Railways,* 31–33.

20 "Caughnawaga Agency – Correspondence regarding the Grand Trunk Railway's Interests
on the Caughnawaga Reserve," RG10, vol. 7661, file 22005-1, LAC.

21 Devine, *Historic Caughnawaga,* 390–92.

22 Canada similarly made business deals for (and without the knowledge of) Six Nations
of the Grand River that resulted in the loss of large swaths of prime agricultural land. The
Crown held hundreds of thousands of dollars of the nation's money in trust and then
proceeded to lose most of it to poor investments. Hill, *The Clay We Are Made Of,*
178–79.

23 Thomas Henry Clark, *Rapport Géologique: Région de Montréal/Geological Report: Montreal
Area* (Quebec City: Ministère des richesses naturelles, Direction générale des mines, Service de l'exploration géologique, 1972), 54, 60, 63.

24 Gerald Tulchinsky, "The Construction of the First Lachine Canal, 1815–1826" (master's
thesis, McGill University, 1960), 104.

25 Department of Railways and Canals – Moneys due Indians for stone quarried at Caughnawaga for works on the Cornwall Canal, RG13-A-2, file 1890-149, LAC; Jim Rasenberger,
High Steel: The Daring Men Who Built the World's Greatest Skyline (New York: HarperCollins,
2004), 136.

26 Report by J.A. Macrae, Inspector of Indian Agencies, February 14, 1906, RG10, vol. 3076,
file 261,942-1, LAC.

27 Canada, "Survey of a Projected Canal between the St. Lawrence and Lake Champlain," in
"Annual Report of the Commissioner of Public Works," June 30, 1867, *Sessional Papers*
5 (1867–68), 68–69.

28 "Ship-Canal from the St. Lawrence to Lake Champlain Proposed," *New York Times,* August
19, 1870.

29 Kahnawà:ke Chiefs to Edmund Walker Head (narrated by unknown person), September
13, 1855, RG10, pp. 130264–70, reel C-11528, LAC.

30 John A. Macdonald to H. Allan, January 26, 1871, MG26-A, LAC.

31 Omar Z. Ghobashy, *The Caughnawaga Indians and the St. Lawrence Seaway* (New York:
Devin-Adair, 1961).

32 For more on Indigenous mobility and colonial law, see John Borrows, *Freedom and Indigenous Constitutionalism* (Toronto: University of Toronto Press, 2016).

33 Francis, *A History of the Native Peoples,* 21; Tobias, "Protection, Civilisation, Assimilation," 40.

34 Francis, *A History of the Native Peoples,* 20–24.

35 Robert J. Surtees, "The Development of an Indian Reserve Policy in Canada," *Ontario History* 61, 2 (1969): 87–98; Binnema and Hutchings, "The Emigrant and the Noble Savage."

36 Girard, Phillips, and Brown, *A History of Law,* 1:460–61.

37 This act is the legal origin of the Tioweró:ton territory, also known as Doncaster or St-Lucie, in the Laurentian Mountains, which serves as a hunting and fishing territory for Kahnawà:ke and Kanehsatà:ke. Richard H. Bartlett, *Indian Reserves in Quebec* (Saskatoon: University of Saskatchewan Native Law Centre, 1984), 5; Carter, *Lost Harvests,* 25; Scott, "Indian Affairs, 1763–1841," 593; Francis, *A History of the Native Peoples,* 35. For more on the origin of reserves in Lower Canada outside the St. Lawrence Valley, see Gérard L. Fortin and Jacques Frenette, "L'acte de 1851 et la création de nouvelles réserves indiennes au Bas-Canada en 1853," *Recherches amérindiennes au Québec* 19, 1 (1989): 31–77.

38 Francis, *A History of the Native Peoples,* 32; Tobias, "Protection, Civilisation, Assimilation," 40; Theodore Binnema, "Protecting Indian Lands by Defining Indian: 1850–76," *Journal of Canadian Studies/Revue d'études canadiennes* 48, 2 (2014): 11–12.

39 Binnema, "Protecting Indian Lands," 11–13.

40 Simpson, *Mohawk Interruptus,* 60 (emphasis in original).

41 Ibid.

42 Doxtator, "What Happened to the Iroquois Clans?" 217–18; Hill, *The Clay We Are Made Of,* 186–211.

43 Speech of the Grand Chiefs of the Seven Fires to Edmund Walker Head, August 8, 1856, RG10, vol. 232, pt. 2, pp. 138229–32, reel C-11541, LAC.

44 This probably refers to the practice of leasing a field in exchange for half of the harvest.

45 Speech of the Grand Chiefs of the Seven Fires, August 8, 1856, pp. 138229–32, LAC.

46 Petition of fifteen Iroquois of Sault Saint Louis to Edmund Walker Head, May 3, 1856, RG10, vol. 231, pp. 137028–31, reel C-11540, LAC. Original French: "les recommandations, avis et conseils."

47 Ibid. Original French: "détruit, pillé et incendié leurs demeures."

48 Ibid. Original French: "Que leur Tribu s'élevant actuellement au nombre de treize cents, et dans le but d'éviter a l'avenir toute difficulté entre ses membres au sujet de l'occupation des terres communes et de venir en aide à ceux de ses membres qui veulent s'adonner à la culture vos Pétitionnaires croient qu'il serait grandement avantageux de faire le partage de ces terres."

49 Ibid.

50 Édouard-Narcisse de Lorimier to Duncan C. Napier, July 30, 1856, RG10, vol. 227, pp. 135212–14, reel C-11539, LAC. Delorimier wrote "15–20 louis," which was probably a colloquial term for dollars. The Louis d'argent was a coin that circulated in New France and during the period immediately after the conquest. Raewyn Passmore, assistant curator, National Currency Collection, Bank of Canada, pers. comm., August 3, 2011.

51 Édouard-Narcisse de Lorimier to Duncan C. Napier, July 30, 1856, LAC. Original French: "la population c'est levés en masse, contre les dix vendeurs de bois, qui sont au nombre de quinze à vingt qui s'approprie le bois appartenant à Treize a Quatorze cents."

52 Ibid. Original French: "un grand malheur pour cette tribu."
53 S.C., 20 Vict., c. 26; Francis, *A History of the Native Peoples,* 36.
54 Because the act allowed for the alienation of Indigenous land to individuals without the consent of the Indigenous nation, it was in violation of the Royal Proclamation of 1763.
55 Tobias, "Protection, Civilisation, Assimilation," 42.
56 Ibid., 43.
57 Scott, "Indian Affairs, 1763–1841," 593.
58 Tobias, "Protection, Civilisation, Assimilation," 43; Gerald Reid, "'To Renew Our Fire': Political Activism, Nationalism, and Identity in Three Rotinonhsionni Communities," in *Tribal Worlds: Critical Studies in American Indian Nation Building,* ed. Brian Hosmer and Larry Nesper (Albany: State University of New York Press, 2013), 40–41.
59 Binnema, "Protecting Indian Lands."
60 Reid, "'To Renew Our Fire,'" 41–42.
61 Theodore Binnema and Kevin Hutchings have written on some aspects of early attempts to move Indigenous communities from southern Ontario. Binnema and Hutchings, "The Emigrant and the Noble Savage."
62 Devine, *Historic Caughnawaga,* 393.
63 "Report of the Special Commissioners," A21-78.
64 Reid, *Kahnawà:ke,* 22; Devine, *Historic Caughnawaga,* 393.
65 Chiefs to DIA, March 21, 1870, RG10, vol. 328, reel C-9580, LAC.
66 Petition from Chiefs to the Superintendent of Indian Affairs, June 17, 1875, RG10, vol. 1963, file 5029, LAC.
67 Chiefs to DIA, March 21, 1870, LAC.
68 Complaint of Chiefs Francis Atorahishon and Joseph Taioroniote, March 10, 1870, RG10, vol. 328, reel C-9580, LAC.
69 Petition from Chiefs to the Superintendent of Indian Affairs, June 17, 1875, LAC.
70 Ibid.
71 Chiefs to E.A. Meredith, May 14, 1875, RG10, vol. 1917, file 2764, LAC.
72 If the May and June petitions are viewed together, it becomes apparent that at least five of the seven chiefs agreed with the initiative.
73 Vankoughnet, "Memo on a Petition from Four of the Chiefs of the Iroquois of Caughnawaga," July 7, 1875, RG10, vol. 1963, file 5029, LAC.
74 As detailed in Chapter 6, the DIA declined to spend $50,000 from its own budget, even though it anticipated a healthy return on the investment.
75 Joseph Pinsonneault to David Laird, September 15, 1875, RG10, vol. 1969, file 5348, LAC.
76 Girard, Phillips, and Brown, *A History of Law,* 1:455–58.
77 Doutre, "Les sauvages du Canada," 203.

CHAPTER 5: "PROMISCUOUS OWNERSHIP"

Epigraph: Kahnawà:ke Chiefs to Edmund Walker Head, September 13, 1855, LAC.
1 Daniel Rueck, "Imposing a Mindless Geometry: Surveyors versus the Canadian Plains, 1869–1885" (master's thesis, McGill University, 2004).
2 Richard Price, ed., *The Spirit of the Alberta Indian Treaties* (Montreal: Institute for Research on Public Policy, 1979); Paul W. DePasquale, *Natives and Settlers, Now and Then: Historical Issues and Current Perspectives on Treaties and Land Claims in Canada* (Edmonton: University of Alberta Press, 2007); Walter Hildebrandt, Dorothy First Rider, and Sarah Carter, *The*

True Spirit and Original Intent of Treaty 7, McGill-Queen's Native and Northern Series 14 (Montreal and Kingston: McGill-Queen's University Press, 1996); Arthur J. Ray, J.R. Miller, and Frank Tough, *Bounty and Benevolence: A History of Saskatchewan Treaties*, McGill-Queen's Native and Northern Series 23 (Montreal and Kingston: McGill-Queen's University Press, 2000); D.N. Sprague, *Canada's Treaties with Aboriginal People* (Winnipeg: Canadian Legal History Project, Faculty of Law, University of Manitoba, 1991); Alexander Morris, *The Treaties of Canada with the Indians of Manitoba and the North-West Territories* (Toronto: Willing and Williamson, 1880).

3   For some examples of such scholarship, see Helen Buckley, *From Wooden Ploughs to Welfare: Why Indian Policy Failed in the Prairie Provinces* (Montreal and Kingston: McGill-Queen's University Press, 1992); Carter, *Lost Harvests;* Sarah Carter, *Aboriginal People and Colonizers of Western Canada to 1900* (Toronto: University of Toronto Press, 1999); Maureen K. Lux, *Medicine That Walks: Disease, Medicine, and Canadian Plains Native People, 1880–1940* (Toronto: University of Toronto Press, 2001); D.N. Sprague, *Canada and the Métis, 1869–1885* (Waterloo: Wilfrid Laurier University Press, 1988); Ray, Miller, and Tough, *Bounty and Benevolence*.

4   Reid, *Kahnawà:ke*, 61; Tobias, "Protection, Civilisation, Assimilation," 43.

5   Tobias, "Protection, Civilisation, Assimilation," 44–45.

6   *An Act to amend and consolidate the laws respecting Indians,* S.C. 1880, c. 28.

7   *An Act to amend "The Indian Act, 1880,"* S.C. 1881, c. 17; *An Act to further amend "The Indian Act, 1880,"* S.C. 1882, c. 30.

8   *An Act for conferring certain privileges on the more advanced Bands of the Indians of Canada, with the view of training them for the exercise of municipal powers,* S.C. 1884, c. 28 *(Indian Advancement Act, 1884).*

9   Tobias, "Protection, Civilisation, Assimilation," 47. For more on Canadian "betterment discourses" regarding Indigenous people, see C. Drew Bednasek and Anne M.C. Godlewska, "The Influence of Betterment Discourses on Canadian Aboriginal Peoples in the Late Nineteenth and Early Twentieth Centuries," *Canadian Geographer/Le Géographe canadien* 53, 4 (2009): 444–61.

10 For example, in Six Nations of the Grand River, there were 4 cases of enfranchisement in the council records from 1880 to 1924, but Susan Hill notes that a preliminary review of Indian Affairs files from that period produced 197 cases. However, LAC classifies nearly all of those cases as "restricted" under the *Privacy Act,* so historians appear to lack data about enfranchisement applications. Hill, *The Clay We Are Made Of,* 203.

11 Tobias, "Protection, Civilisation, Assimilation," 44–47.

12 Pamela D. Palmater, "Genocide, Indian Policy, and Legislated Elimination of Indians in Canada," *Aboriginal Policy Studies* 3, 3 (2014): 27–54.

13 Tobias, "Protection, Civilisation, Assimilation," 45.

14 Ibid., 45.

15 Because white decision makers considered western First Nations not adequately civilized to be governed by the *Indian Act,* most of its sections did not initially apply to them. Ibid.

16 Carter, *Lost Harvests,* 51–52.

17 Berda, *Living Emergency,* 111.

18 For an examination of similar issues related to wood in nineteenth-century Wendake, see Gettler, *Colonialism's Currency,* Chapter 5.

19 Copy of a report by the Crown Privy Council, May 19, 1873, RG10, C-11107, file 1802, LAC.

20 E.A. Meredith, Deputy Minister of Interior, to Chiefs, March 12, 1874, RG10, vol. 1924, file 3055, LAC.
21 Chiefs Sose Thaioronhiote and Francis Otonharishon to David Laird, Minister of Interior, March 11, 1874, RG10, vol. 1924, file 3055, LAC.
22 Meredith to Chiefs, March 12, 1874, LAC.
23 DIA to Joseph Pinsonneault (English-language draft for translation into French), May 2, 1874, RG10, vol. 1924, file 3055, LAC.
24 J.M. Neeson, *Commoners: Common Right, Enclosure and Social Change in England, 1700–1820* (Cambridge: Cambridge University Press, 1993); E.P. Thompson, *Customs in Common* (New York: New Press, 1991).
25 An Order-in-Council is primary legislation issued by the Queen's Privy Council.
26 Petition from Marie-Louise McComber, Roren Teokhasion, Saksarie Anetenre, Saksarie Aroniente, and Ennias Atonnonien to David Laird, Minister of Interior, December 20, 1873, RG10, vol. 1917, file 2764, LAC.
27 M. MacIver to David Laird, December 23, 1873, RG10, vol. 1917, file 2764, LAC.
28 Ibid.
29 For more on a nineteenth-century understanding of "improvement," see Daniel Samson, *The Spirit of Industry and Improvement: Liberal Government and Rural-Industrial Society, Nova Scotia, 1790–1862* (Montreal and Kingston: McGill-Queen's University Press, 2008).
30 Sean Carleton, "Colonizing Minds: Public Education, the 'Textbook Indian,' and Settler Colonialism in British Columbia, 1920–1970," *BC Studies* 169 (Spring 2011): 101–30; Michael Taussig, *Shamanism, Colonialism, and the Wild Man: A Study in Terror and Healing* (Chicago: University of Chicago Press, 1991); Philip J. Deloria, *Indians in Unexpected Places* (Lawrence: University of Kansas Press, 2004); Marianna Torgovnick, *Gone Primitive: Savage Intellects, Modern Lives* (Chicago: University of Chicago Press, 1990).
31 MacIver to Laird, December 23, 1873, LAC.
32 Cronon, "The Trouble with Wilderness," 69–90; Tracey Banivanua Mar, "Carving Wilderness: Queensland's National Parks and the Unsettling of Emptied Lands, 1890–1910," in Mar and Edmonds, *Making Settler Colonial Space,* 73–94.
33 MacIver to Laird, December 23, 1873, LAC.
34 *An Act providing for the organisation of the Department of the Secretary of State of Canada, and for the management of Indian and Ordinance Lands,* S.C. 1868, 31 Vict., c. 42, s. 37.
35 Order-in-Council, May 5, 1862.
36 DIA to petitioners, December 31, 1873, RG10, vol. 1917, file 2764, LAC.
37 Nineteen petitioners to DIA, February 28, 1874, RG10, vol. 1917, file 2764, LAC.
38 MacIver to Laird, March 10, 1874, RG10, vol. 1917, file 2764, LAC.
39 Pinsonneault to DIA, May 17, 1875, RG10, vol. 1917, file 2764, LAC.
40 Pinsonneault to DIA, April 22, 1875, RG10, vol. 1917, file 2764, LAC.
41 Chiefs Jarvis A. Dione, Joseph K. Delisle, Joseph T. Skey, Thomas Asennase to Meredith, May 14, 1875, LAC.
42 Ibid.
43 Ibid.
44 Ibid.
45 Since this document is handwritten in non-standard English, I am not certain what is meant by "parpied." Perhaps the word should be "par pied," meaning that the territory would be cut up into small morsels against the interest of the community.

46 Chiefs Jarvis A. Dione, Joseph K. Delisle, Joseph T. Skey, Thomas Asennase to Meredith, May 14, 1875, LAC.
47 Ibid.
48 Reid, *Kahnawà:ke,* 64–66.
49 Ibid., 61–68.
50 Chiefs Jarvis A. Dione, Joseph K. Delisle, Joseph T. Skey, Thomas Asennase to Meredith, May 14, 1875, LAC.
51 Meredith to Chiefs, March 12, 1874, LAC.
52 Chiefs Sose Taioweniote (Thaioronhiote), Atonwa Asennase (Haton8a Hasennase or Thomas Deer), 8o8i Taio8akri8on, Francis Atoharishon (or Otonharishon) to Joseph Howe, n.d. [1873], RG10, vol. 1880, file 1081, LAC.
53 J.V. de Boucherville to Joseph Howe, February 9, 1873, RG10, vol. 1880, file 1081, LAC.
54 Vankoughnet to Pinsonneault, June 20, 1874, RG10, vol. 1934, file 3552, LAC.
55 Vankoughnet, "Memo on Letter of the 28th Inst.," April 30, 1874, LAC.
56 Georges Cherrier to Alexander Brosseau, February 22, 1895, RG10, vol. 2774, file 155,133, LAC.
57 "Fatal Fire at Caughnawaga: Animosities between Indians and French-Canadians," *Montreal Daily Witness,* May 13, 1878.
58 Tekanonnowehon (Alexander Delorimier), Walbank reference no. 471, was born in 1841, was unmarried in 1885, and owned about eighty-five acres in that year, including sixteen acres of sugarbush, all of it valued at $1,940, not including quarry lands that were not valued by William Walbank. Chapter 6 gives context for the Walbank data. Caughnawaga Reference Books, 1885, RG10-B-8-aj, vols. 8968–72, LAC.
59 Alexander de Lorimier to David Laird, November 4, 1875, RG10, vol. 1972, file 5555, LAC.
60 Ibid.
61 Pinsonneault to David Laird, November 17, 1875, RG10, vol. 1972, file 5555, LAC. Original French: "Veuillez pour le bonheur des Sauvage donner une protection aux erables."
62 Two chiefs to David Laird, March 11, 1874, RG10, vol. 1924, file 3055, LAC.
63 Extant copies of the grants do not include such a provision.
64 Vankoughnet memo, April 25, 1876, RG10, vol. 1972, file 5555, LAC.
65 Canada, Order-in-Council "for the protection from pillage of Timber on lands occupied by Indians on the Indian Reserve at Caughnawaga," January 1, 1876.
66 Vankoughnet to Pinsonneault, January [5], 1876, RG10, vol. 1972, file 5555, LAC.
67 Vankoughnet to Pinsonneault, January 19, 1876, RG10, vol. 1972, file 5555, LAC.
68 Pinsonneault to Vankoughnet, January 22, 1876, RG10, vol. 1972, file 5555, LAC.
69 Thomas A. Dawes to E.A. Meredith, January 21, 1876, RG10, vol. 1972, file 5555, LAC.
70 Ibid.
71 Vankoughnet to Dawes, January 27, 1876, RG10, vol. 1972, file 5555, LAC.
72 Petition from Chiefs [SoSe taironiote], SoSe [Shentareontie], Francis [Athearishon], Louis [Tiovakaron], and Thomas [Asennouse] (and others) to David Laird, February 7, 1876, RG10, vol. 1972, file 5555, LAC. Repeated words and spelling left as in original document.
73 Ibid.
74 Thaioronhiote (Joseph Skye), Walbank reference no. 347. Born in 1819, he was listed as owning about a hundred acres in 1885. Shatekaienton (Louis Beauvais), Walbank reference no. 423. He was born in 1833 and was listed as owning 10.5 acres in 1885. Caughnawaga Reference Books, 1885, LAC.

75   Vankoughnet to Pinsonneault, February 12, 1876, RG10, vol. 1972, file 5555, LAC.
76   Thomas A. Dawes to E.A. Meredith, January 21, 1876, RG10, vol. 1972, file 5555, LAC.
77   Thomas A. Dawes to DIA, February 14, 1876, RG10, vol. 1972, file 5555, LAC.
78   Thomas A. Dawes to DIA, February 2, 1877, RG10, vol. 1972, file 5555, LAC.
79   Vankoughnet to Dawes, February 6, 1877, RG10, vol. 1972, file 5555, LAC.
80   Chiefs to DIA, March 16, 1881, RG10, vol. 1972, file 5555, LAC.
81   Canada, "Annual Report of the Department of Indian Affairs," *Sessional Papers* 11 (1877), 9; Pinsonneault to DIA, May 30, 1876, RG10, vol. 1987, file 6411, LAC.
82   Ohionkoton (Angus Jacob), Walbank reference no. 582, owned about one acre in 1885. At that time, he refused to cooperate with Walbank, saying that he liked things the way they were. See Chapter 6.
83   Pinsonneault to David Laird, April 29, 1876, RG10, vol. 1987, file 6411, LAC. Departmental translation. Original French: "il a fait des travaux sur ce terrin pour une valeur de $20 à 25 piastres, il a semé l'an dernier du blé d'inde dans une grandeur de environ ¼ d'arpent, en différentes parties de la dite carrière et il reclame la somme de $50.00 pour une étendu de 4 arpents dont les travaux de la carrière en ont pri une partie de son terrin qui n'a pas encore été cultivé."
84   Pinsonneault to DIA, May 30, 1876, LAC.
85   Pinsonneault to Laird, April 29, 1876, LAC. Departmental translation. Original French: "il serait peut être bon qu'il serait indemniser, pour [éviter] tout trouble avec lui."
86   Vankoughnet to Pinsonneault, May 16, 1876, RG10, vol. 1987, file 6411, LAC.
87   Law Suit by Ignace Onniakoton brought by Doutre, Doutre, Robidoux &c&c, Advocates for Ig. Onniakoton, May 19, 1876, RG10, vol. 1987, file 6411, LAC.
88   Taiorakaron (or Louis Tehorakaron) is mentioned by Reid as having died in 1886. Little else is known of him. He does not appear in the Walbank reference books. Reid, *Kahnawà:ke,* 60.
89   Pinsonneault to DIA, May 30, 1876, LAC. Full quote in original French: "Je suis certain que ce Sauvage veux faire du trouble oú avoir de l'argent pour rien."
90   Ibid.
91   Vankoughnet to Pinsonneault, June 7, 1876, RG10, vol. 1987, file 6411, LAC.
92   Chiefs Joseph [Taioroniohte], Joseph [Kentarontie], Thomas Asennase, and Louis Taiorakaron to Laird, September 9, 1876, RG10, vol. 1987, file 6411, LAC.
93   Zebulon A. Lash to E.A. Meredith, October 1, 1877, and Lash memo, August 7, 1878, RG10, vol. 1987, file 6411, LAC
94   Chiefs Sose [Kentrouitie], Sose [Taionkniote], Sose [Taioakrwen], [Sak Hasenserse], Louis Shatekaienton to DIA, n.d., RG10, vol. 1998, file 7153, LAC. A sworn statement by two Kahnawa'kehró:non indicated that they had seen Pinsonneault that summer in the village, completely drunk and asking for a woman. Sworn statement by Ennias [Kanonsarionwe] and Sose [Anerarotonkwas], October 14, 1876, RG10, vol. 1998, file 7153, LAC.
95   DIA to Pinsonneault, May 2, 1874, LAC.
96   Pinsonneault believed that his dismissal was politically motivated and related to the political leanings of his father, A. Pinsonneault, MP for La Prairie.
97   DIA to Georges Cherrier, March 8, 1877, RG10, vol. 2004, file 7600, LAC.
98   Ibid. The other nine points of Cherrier's instructions can be summarized as follows: prevent liquor traffic; encourage agriculture or industrial pursuits; collect seigneurial dues and other rents; measure stone and regulate quarries; forward money to the department every month; maintain roads by Indian statute labour, or band funds if necessary; inspect schools;

write annual updates; and also be responsible for Kanehsatà:ke, as well as for the sick and infirm.

99 Georges Cherrier to DIA, March 5, 1877, RG10, vol. 2004, file 7600, LAC.

100 Petition from 87 Kahnawa'kehró:non, n.d. [winter 1877–78], RG10, vol. 1972, file 5555, LAC.

101 Ibid.

102 Taretane (Tom Jacob), Walbank reference no. 417. Born in 1830, he was listed as owning four lots totalling about sixty-seven acres in 1885. Walbank estimated their value at $1,563. Tewenitasen (Tom 20Months), Walbank reference no. 184. Born in 1829, he owned 8.5 acres in 1885 (2.75 acres cultivated, 5.75 acres bush). Walbank estimated the value at $56. Caughnawaga Reference Books, 1885, LAC.

103 Georges Cherrier to DIA, April 26, 1878, and Vankoughnet to Cherrier, May 6, 1878, RG10, vol. 2057, file 9698, LAC.

104 Cherrier to DIA, January 24, 1878, RG10, vol. 1972, file 5555, LAC.

105 Cherrier to DIA, March 15, 1879, RG10, vol. 1972, file 5555, LAC. Karhaienton (Matthew Jocks), Walbank reference no. 457, was born in 1845 and was listed in 1885 as owning eight acres valued at $209. Caughnawaga Reference Books, 1885, LAC.

106 DIA to Cherrier, March 24, 1879, RG10, vol. 1972, file 5555, LAC.

107 Sakoraiatakwa (Martin Parquis), Walbank reference no. 536, was born in 1819. In 1885, he was listed as owning a forty-eight-acre lot, valued at $1,078. Caughnawaga Reference Books, 1885, LAC.

108 Cherrier to DIA, October 17, 1878, RG10, vol. 2070, file 10,556, LAC.

109 DIA to Cherrier, November 5, 1878, RG10, vol. 2070, file 10,556, LAC.

110 Correspondence from a few years later reveals that Agent Cherrier was involved in grazing cattle on the territory and thus opposed the fencing of individual lots. See correspondence from July and August 1883, RG10, vol. 2162, file 33,790, LAC.

111 The documents refer to Pierre Guillaume, but this was almost certainly Thiretha (Peter Diome), Walbank reference no. 577, owner of four lots totalling 194 acres of all land-use categories, valued at $1,473. In 1887, Walbank also identified Thiretha as one of the people who obstructed his survey. Walbank to Vankoughnet, September 13, 1887, RG10, vol. 7749, file 27005-1, LAC. Tekaonwake (Louis Canot), Walbank reference no. 4, was born in 1828 and owned sixteen acres in 1885. Caughnawaga Reference Books, 1885, LAC.

112 Cherrier to DIA, April 17, 1879, and Vankoughnet to Cherrier, April 28, 1879, RG10, vol. 2084, file 12,817, LAC.

113 Chiefs Thomas Asennase, Louis Shatekaienton, Louis Taiorakaron Council Resolution, July 10, 1880, RG10, vol. 2084, file 12,817, LAC.

114 Cherrier to DIA, July 18, 1879, RG10, vol. 2084, file 12,817, LAC.

115 Chief Joseph Onasakenra to John A. Macdonald, April 23, 1879, RG10, vol. 2084, file 12,817, LAC.

116 DIA to Cherrier, August 19, 1881, RG10, vol. 2084, file 12,817, LAC.

117 Alternative spellings are Shorio 8a ne and Sariowani. Walbank reference no. 77, Rowi Shorihowane (Louis Leclerc) was born in 1830 and married his second wife, Onwari Katsitsaronk[wa], in 1880. Caughnawaga Reference Books, 1885, LAC.

118 Louis Shorihowane to L. Vankoughnet, November 10, 1881, RG10, vol. 2162, file 33,840, LAC.

119 In 1885, four years later, Walbank listed him as owning three lots outside of the village totalling about thirty acres, of which thirteen were sugarbush and nearly six were cultivated.

They were valued at $605. Walbank reference no. 77, Caughnawaga Reference Books, 1885, LAC.

120 Council Resolution, December 29, 1881, RG10, vol. 2162, file 33,840, LAC.

121 Vankoughnet to Cherrier, January 9, 1882, RG10, vol. 2162, file 33,840, LAC.

122 Article 6 of the 1801 Code. "Règlements," February 26, 1801, LAC.

123 According to article 3 of the 1801 Code, individuals could not possess more land than they could cultivate without having someone work in their place. See Chapter 2 for details.

124 Atianota (Michel Thomas), Walbank reference no. 155, was born in 1856, was married to Rowis Josephine in 1881, and owned no land in 1885. Caughnawaga Reference Books, 1885, LAC.

125 Cherrier to Vankoughnet, March 9, 1883, LAC, RG10, vol. 2208, file 41,900. For a judge to solicit information in this way is irregular, but the LAC file provides nothing further on the subject.

126 Council Resolution, March 27, 1883, LAC, RG10, vol. 2208, file 41,900.

127 DIA to Cherrier, April 30, 1883, LAC, RG10, vol. 2208, file 41,900.

128 Caughnawaga Reference Books, 1885, LAC.

129 The Walbank reference books list several men named Michel Delisle but none with the Kanien'kéha name Tehowenkarakwen. Edouard DeBlois, Walbank reference no. 525, was born in 1833. Caughnawaga Reference Books, 1885, LAC. He had a permit of occupation "until a further order" dating from June 3, 1874. Cherrier to DIA, December 26, 1879, RG10, vol. 2100, file 17,475, LAC. In 1885, DeBlois was postmaster and was listed as owning two lots totalling about thirty-eight acres (mostly "bush") valued at $192.

130 Cherrier to DIA, January 9, 1880, RG10, vol. 2100, file 17,475, LAC.

131 Ibid.

132 Akwirotonkwas, also spelled Kakwiratokwas or Ak8rhotonk8as (Tom Phillips), Walbank reference no. 307, was born in 1845. In 1885, he owned five lots totalling 152 acres, which were valued at $2,668. Caughnawaga Reference Books, 1885, LAC.

133 Cherrier to DIA, May 21, 1877, RG10, vol. 2016, file 8139, LAC.

134 Department of Justice opinion, July 4, 1877, RG10, vol. 2016, file 8139, LAC.

135 DeBlois statement, January 8, 1880, RG10, vol. 2100, file 17,475, LAC.

136 Vankoughnet to Cherrier, January 28, 1880, RG10, vol. 2100, file 17,475, LAC.

137 Cherrier to DIA, January 30, 1880, RG10, vol. 2100, file 17,475, LAC.

138 Michel Teho8enkarak8en statement, April 12, 1880, and Vankoughnet to Cherrier, May 21, 1880, RG10, vol. 2100, file 17,475, LAC.

139 Charles Léon Giasson, Walbank claimant no. 276, was born in 1859 and married Lumina Mallette in 1881. He had died by 1885, but the Walbank reference books give no details regarding his death. Caughnawaga Reference Books, 1885, LAC.

140 Léon Giasson to DIA, December 22, 1881, RG10, vol. 2132, file 26,397, LAC.

141 Cherrier to DIA, January 19, 1881, RG10, vol. 2132, file 26,397, LAC.

142 Cherrier to DIA, January 28, 1881, RG10, vol. 1972, file 5555, LAC. This was probably Louis Beauvais (Shatekaienton), Walbank reference no. 423, who was born in 1833 and who owned 10.5 acres in 1885. Caughnawaga Reference Books, 1885, LAC.

143 Vankoughnet to Cherrier, February 3, 1881, RG10, vol. 2132, file 26,397, LAC.

144 Canada, Order-in-Council, July 14, 1881.

145 The well-documented racism of the department also helps to explain many counter-intuitive and contradictory policies and actions.

146 Cherrier to DIA, November 28, 1881, RG10, vol. 2132, file 26,397, LAC.

147 Court of Queen's Bench ruling, November 11, 1881, RG10, vol. 2132, file 26,397, LAC.

148 Léon Giasson to DIA, December 22, 1881, RG10, vol. 2132, file 26,397, LAC.

149 Vankoughnet to Zebulon A. Lash, Deputy Minister of Justice, December 30, 1881; Lash to Vankoughnet, January 19, 1882, RG10, vol. 2132, file 26,397, LAC.

150 Giasson to DIA, December 22, 1881, LAC.

151 Ibid.

152 The DIA investigated the Indian status of the Giasson family in the following years, with typically unclear results. "Correspondence regarding Whites on the Caughnawaga Reserve," 1884–94, RG10, vol. 2693, file 139,964, LAC.

153 Cherrier to DIA, November 28, 1881, LAC.

154 Jean-Baptiste Jacques alias [Karonhiaktatie] statement, November 28, 1881, and Thomas Kanatsohare statement, November 28, 1881, RG10, vol. 2132, file 26,397, LAC. Karonhiaktatie does not appear in the Walbank reference books. Kanatsohare (Thomas Patton), Walbank reference no. 63, was born in 1832. In 1885, he owned 135 acres worth $3,717. Caughnawaga Reference Books, 1885, LAC.

155 Cherrier to DIA, November 28, 1881, LAC.

156 Otseroniaton (Peter Jacob), Walbank reference no. 443. Born in 1840, he owned about ten acres, including orchards, that were valued at $670. Thohenton does not appear to be included in the Walbank reference books. Harhontonkwas (Angus Deer), Walbank reference no. 56. Born in 1851, he owned about seven acres valued at $62 in 1885.

157 Chiefs Jos. Williams, Louis Shatekaienta, P. Murray, Thomas Jocks, Thomas [Ascenan] and [no si to sa go yon] to Cherrier, July 16, 1878, RG10, vol. 2092, file 14,827, LAC.

158 DIA to Cherrier, August 9, 1878, RG10, vol. 2092, file 14,827, LAC.

159 Michel Martin was probably Wishe Otsitsatakon, Walbank reference no. 378, born in 1842. His wife died around 1880. He was listed in 1885 as owning three lots that totalled about forty-five acres and were valued at $485. Caughnawaga Reference Books, 1885, LAC.

160 Vankoughnet to Cherrier, November 9, 1881, RG10, vol. 2162, file 33,644, LAC.

161 Cherrier to Vankoughnet, November 14, 1881, RG10, vol. 2162, file 33,644, LAC.

162 See correspondence from July and August, 1883, RG10, vol. 2162, file 33,790, LAC.

163 Cherrier to Vankoughnet, November 14, 1881, LAC.

164 Cherrier to DIA, October 16, 1878, RG10, vol. 2070, file 10,526, LAC. Departmental translation. Original French: "il existe des abus parmi les Indiens dans leurs transactions entr'eux qui ont de funestes conséquences."

165 Ibid. Departmental translation. Original French: "plusieurs indiens sont les victimes, soit par leur ignorance ou à défaut de sages avis."

166 Chief Joseph Onasakenra to Macdonald, April 23, 1879, LAC.

167 Sonowonhesse does not appear in the Walbank reference books. Kanonwatase (Louis Beauvais), Walbank reference no. 79, was born in 1835. In 1885, he owned a 3.26-acre lot valued at $28. Caughnawaga Reference Books, 1885, LAC.

168 Cherrier to DIA, October 16, 1878, LAC.

169 DIA to Cherrier, November 7, 1878, RG10, vol. 2070, file 10,526, LAC.

170 Chiefs DIA, March 16, 1881, LAC.

171 Ibid.

172 Cherrier to DIA, March 30, 1881, RG10, vol. 1972, file 5555, LAC.

173 DIA to Cherrier, April 13, 1881, RG10, vol. 1972, file 5555, LAC.

174 Taiorakaron (or Louis Tarorakaron) does not appear in the Walbank Survey. Chief Asennase (Thomas Deer), Walbank reference no. 430, was born in 1813. Walbank noted that he had

been grand chief for thirty years in 1885. Walbank listed him as owning two lots totalling thirty-one acres and valued at $782. Thiretha (Peter Diome), Walbank reference no. 577, had holdings of nearly two hundred acres, according to Walbank in 1885, but refused to provide him with information. Caughnawaga Reference Books, 1885, LAC.

175 Because lots were not registered and numbered before 1885, we don't know which one was chosen by Cherrier, Taiorakaron, and Asennase. No lot description is included in the file.

176 Shatekaronhies does not appear in the Walbank reference books.

177 Resolution of the council of chiefs (Mic. Shakohentinetha, Thomas Asennase, Louis Shatekaienton, Louis Tairakaron), January 14, 1884, RG10, vol. 1972, file 5555, LAC. Satekaronies (Arene Daillebout), Walbank reference no. 121, was born in 1817. In 1885, Walbank noted that he owned two lots totalling 23.5 acres valued at $647. Caughnawaga Reference Books, 1885, LAC.

178 Gerald Reid, "Kahnawake's Council of Chiefs: 1840–1889," Mohawk Nation at Kahnawake, http://www.kahnawakelonghouse.com/index.php?mid=2&p=2.

179 *An Act to amend and consolidate the laws respecting Indians*, 1880, s. 16.

CHAPTER 6: "EQUAL TO AN ORDNANCE MAP OF THE OLD COUNTRY"

Epigraph: Caughnawaga Reference Books, 1885, LAC.

1 Leanne Simpson, "Looking after Gdoo-Naaganinaa: Precolonial Nishnaabeg Diplomatic and Treaty Relationships," *Wicazo Sa Review* 23, 2 (2008): 29–42; Hill, *The Clay We Are Made Of,* 34.

2 The legacy of this transfer is that white people currently own almost all the agricultural land in Canada. Sarah Rotz, "'They Took Our Beads, It Was a Fair Trade, Get over It': Settler Colonial Logics, Racial Hierarchies and Material Dominance in Canadian Agriculture," *Geoforum* 82 (2017): 158–69. Historical geographer Cole Harris links enclosure and the process of confining First Nations to reserves. He specifically makes a comparison with the evictions of tenants in Scotland's western highlands toward the end of the eighteenth century, which were characterized by a "reorientation of land away from custom and towards the market." He points out that in both cases dispossessed people were confined to small spaces (crofts, Indian reserves) where survival (cultural and often physical) was next to impossible and that similar language was used in both cases to disparage those being dispossessed. Harris, *Making Native Space,* 266–67.

3 Irene M. Spry, "The Great Transformation: The Disappearance of the Commons in Western Canada," in *Canadian Plains Studies 6: Man and Nature on the Prairies,* ed. Richard Allen (Regina: Canadian Plains Research Centre, University of Regina, 1976), 41.

4 The most prominent text promoting the association of common property with inevitable environmental degradation is Garrett Hardin, "The Tragedy of the Commons," *Science* 162, 3859 (1968): 1243–48. For studies on the management of commons, see Daniel W. Bromley and Michael M. Cernea, *The Management of Common Property Natural Resources: Some Conceptual and Operational Fallacies,* World Bank Discussion Papers 57 (Washington, DC: World Bank, 1989); Elinor Ostrom, *Governing the Commons: The Evolution of Institutions for Collective Action, Political Economy of Institutions and Decisions* (Cambridge: Cambridge University Press, 1990); Thompson, *Customs in Common.*

5 Legal historian Sidney Harring shows how the North-West Mounted Police and the application of Canadian law on the Prairies contributed to the enclosure of Indigenous

lands. Harring also points to evidence suggesting that the Canadian government, though it had no policy promoting bison extermination, deliberately refrained from protecting the herds because it knew their reduction would force Indigenous peoples onto reserves. Sidney L. Harring, "'There Seemed to Be No Recognized Law': Canadian Law and the Prairie First Nations," in *Laws and Societies in the Canadian Prairie West, 1670–1940,* ed. Louis A. Knafla and Jonathan Swainger (Vancouver: UBC Press, 2005), 92–126. On the US side of the border, the influx of settlers was accompanied by a purposeful effort to eradicate the bison so as to destroy Indigenous peoples who relied on them, and of course the impacts were felt on both sides of the line. Andrew Isenberg, *The Destruction of the Bison: An Environmental History, 1750–1920* (Cambridge: Cambridge University Press, 2000).

6 *The Great Law of Peace of the Longhouse People – Kaianerekowa Hotinonsionne* (Mohawk Nation via Rooseveltown, NY: Akwesasne Notes, 1975), laws 72–73; William Fenton, *The Great Law and the Longhouse: A Political History of the Iroquois Confederacy* (Norman: University of Oklahoma Press, 1998); Parker, *The Constitution of the Five Nations;* Kayanesenh Paul Williams, *Kayanerenkó:Wa: The Great Law of Peace* (Winnipeg: University of Manitoba Press, 2018).

7 Aileen Moreton-Robinson, *The White Possessive: Property, Power, and Indigenous Sovereignty* (Minneapolis: University of Minnesota Press, 2015).

8 Although the Kahnawà:ke case is quite unlike those studied by anthropologist James Scott in his influential book *Seeing Like a State,* it could be seen as a smaller-scale, less successful example of a similar trend in the modernist ambitions of nation-states. James C. Scott, *Seeing Like a State: How Certain Schemes to Improve the Human Condition Have Failed* (New Haven: Yale University Press, 1998).

9 Thompson, *Customs in Common,* 102.

10 Ibid., 106.

11 Neeson, *Commoners,* 17.

12 Ibid., 30–42.

13 In *Property and Dispossession,* historian Allan Greer argues that the greatest part of Indigenous dispossession in North America was accomplished by the establishment of a colonial commons that competed with or replaced Indigenous commons, which were later enclosed.

14 Canada, "Annual Report of G.E. Cherrier, Indian Agent, Caughnawaga Agency," *Sessional Papers* 6 (1882), 12–13.

15 This boundary dispute remains unresolved and is of great importance to Kahnawa'kehró:non today. For more on the history of the boundary and land claim, see Decroix, "Le conflit juridique"; Gerald R. Alfred, "To Right Certain Wrongs: A Report on Research into Lands Known as the Seigniory of Sault St. Louis" (Kahnawake Seigneury Office, 1995); Lambert, "History of Kahnawake Land Claims." See also the website Kahnawà:ke Claims, http://kahnawakeclaims.com/.

16 Pinsonneault to E.A. Meredith, May 13, 1874, RG10, vol. 1933, file 3407, LAC. Departmental translation. Original French: "Permettez-moi d'attiré votre attention sur la ligne entre la reserve des sauvages de Caughnawaga et les blancs. Plusieurs sauvages qui ont des terres voisin des blancs se plaignes qu'ils empiète sur leurs terres, et comme il ne peuvent pas trouvée de bornes afin que les blancs n'empiète pas sur leurs terrain."

17 Council Resolution signed by Joseph Williams, April 12, 1880, RG10, vol. 2109, file 20,131, LAC.

18　Decroix, "Le conflit juridique," 291.

19　Cherrier to Vankoughnet, May 25, 1880, RG10, vol. 2109, file 20,131, LAC.

20　William Walbank, "Report on the Caughnawaga Reserve Survey," December 31, 1880, RG10, vol. 2109, file 20,131, LAC.

21　Joseph Roberts Smallwood and Robert D.W. Pitt, "Walbank, Matthew William," in *Encyclopedia of Newfoundland and Labrador*, vol. 5 (St. John's: Newfoundland Book Publishers, 1981); "William McLea Walbank," 1856–1909, accession no. 20, Canadian Architecture Collection, McGill University Rare Books and Special Collections; "William McLea Walbank," 1883–93, CA601, S139, BANQ; Larry S. McNally "Pringle, Thomas," *Dictionary of Canadian Biography Online*. http://www.biographi.ca/en/bio/pringle_thomas_14E.html.

22　Walbank, "Report on the Caughnawaga Reserve Survey," December 31, 1880, LAC.

23　Ibid. Walbank's complaints ultimately bore fruit, as the department paid him more than three times his original bid. Even a year later, farmers whose land bordered the reserve were protesting that Walbank's survey had deprived them of land and conflicted with previous surveys. The DIA response was simply that it considered Walbank's survey to be correct. Vankoughnet to Cherrier, May 6, 1881, RG10, vol. 2140, file 28,880, LAC.

24　W.A. Austin to Hayter Reed, September 26, 1895, Carnet I022, William-Auguste Austin, 1894-07-27, E21, S60, SS3, PI22, BANQ.

25　Correspondence between Walbank and the DIA, 1880–81, RG10, vol. 2109, file 20,131, LAC.

26　Sawenoenne to Napier, June 1, 1839, pp. 40204-5, LAC.

27　Petition of fifteen Iroquois of Sault Saint Louis to Head, May 3, 1856, LAC; Édouard-Narcisse de Lorimier to Duncan C. Napier, July 30, 1856, RG10, vol. 227, pp. 135212–14, reel C-11539, LAC.

28　Two chiefs to Laird, March 11, 1874, LAC.

29　"Remarks by Deputy Superintendent General of Indian Affairs" and "Substance of Statement of Caughnawaga Chiefs," March 11, 1874, RG10, vol. 1924, file 3055, LAC.

30　Meredith to Chiefs, March 12, 1874, LAC.

31　Chiefs Jarvis A. Dione, Joseph K. Delisle, Joseph T. Skey, and Thomas Asennase to Meredith, May 14, 1875, LAC.

32　Cherrier to David Mills, Minister of the Interior, February 5, 1878, RG10, vol. 2018, file 8268, LAC.

33　James P. Dawes to Lawrence Vankoughnet, June 3, 1880, RG10, vol. 2113, file 21,156, LAC.

34　Walbank to Vankoughnet, September 7, 1880, RG10, vol. 2109, file 20,131, LAC.

35　Zebulon A. Lash to James P. Dawes, June 16, 1880, RG10, vol. 2113, file 21,156, LAC.

36　For examples from southeast Asia, see Scott, *Seeing Like a State*, 188, 273–78; John F. Richards, *The Unending Frontier: An Environmental History of the Early Modern World* (Berkeley: University of California Press, 2003), 103–4. Peasants and small-scale farmers have often been subject to similar criticism. For examples from England, see Neeson, *Commoners*. The same was true for French Canadian farmers. Travel writer George Sala serves as a good example here. Describing farmland near Montreal, he wrote that "to the European eye it looks shiftless and slovenly. The fields are too large (which would scarcely be a fault in the eye of a farmer); there are ugly posts and rails in lieu of hedges, and the trees are few." George Augustus Sala, *Under the Sun: Essays Mainly Written in Hot Countries* (London: Vizetelly, 1886), 214–15.

37　For more on the tropes of the indolent and improvident Indian, see John S. Lutz, *Makúk: A New History of Aboriginal-White Relations* (Vancouver: UBC Press, 2008); Robin Jarvis

Brownlie, *A Fatherly Eye: Indian Agents, Government Power, and Aboriginal Resistance in Ontario, 1918–1939* (Don Mills: Oxford University Press, 2003); Gettler, *Colonialism's Currency.* Similar tropes exist for Indigenous peoples and minorities around the world. For an example from Asia, see Emily T. Yeh, "Tropes of Indolence and the Cultural Politics of Development in Lhasa, Tibet," *Annals of the Association of American Geographers* 97, 3 (2007): 593–612.

38 Dawes to Vankoughnet, June 3, 1880, LAC.

39 Colonizers often asserted their self-serving axiom that Indigenous people did not practise agriculture, or practised it incorrectly – a good example here comes from Francis Bond Head, lieutenant governor of Upper Canada, who declared to Ontario First Nations in 1836, "If you would cultivate your land it would be considered your property, in the same way as your dogs are considered among yourselves to belong to those who have reared them; but uncultivated land is like wild animals." Francis Bond Head, *The Emigrant* (London: John Murray, 1846), 145. In Six Nations of the Grand River, the colonial government eventually gave legal title to many white squatters in the 1840s, employing the argument that the Indigenous owners had not improved the land, whereas the squatters had. Doxtator, "What Happened to the Iroquois Clans?" 225–30.

40 Ian McKay, "The Liberal Order Framework: A Prospectus for a Reconnaissance of Canadian History," *Canadian Historical Review* 81, 4 (December 2000): 617–45.

41 Austin Sarat and Thomas R. Kearns, "Introduction," in *Law's Violence,* ed. Austin Sarat and Thomas R. Kearns (Ann Arbor: University of Michigan Press, 1993), 5.

42 Blomley, "Law, Property, and the Geography of Violence," 124. For more on how law in a liberal society acts to create and enforce borders such as these, see Michael Walzer, "Liberalism and the Art of Separation," *Political Theory* 12, 3 (1994): 315–30; Cornelia Vismann, "Starting from Scratch: Concepts of Order in No-Man's-Land," in *War, Violence, and the Modern Condition,* ed. Bernd Hüppauf (Berlin: Walter de Gruyter, 1997), 46–65.

43 For examples, see Canada, Order-in-Council, July 14, 1881; *An Act to amend "The Indian Act, 1880,"* S.C. 1881, c. 17.

44 Vankoughnet to Mayne Daly, April 14, 1893, RG10, vol. 7749, file 27005-1, LAC

45 "The Caughnawaga Ejectments: The Catechism on Which Residents Established Their Claims to Be Indians," *Montreal Daily Witness,* July 13, 1886, 6.

46 Vankoughnet to Mayne Daly, April 14, 1893, LAC.

47 Canada, House of Commons, *Debates* (March 18, 1890), 2158.

48 Rueck, "Imposing a Mindless Geometry."

49 Vankoughnet to J.V. de Boucherville, February 7, 1882, RG10, vol. 7749, file 27005-1, LAC; De Boucherville to DIA, March 11, 1882, RG10, vol. 7749, file 27005-1, LAC.

50 Vankoughnet to Mayne Daly, April 14, 1893, LAC.

51 For example, the federal police on the Prairies prevented First Nations from keeping intruders out of their country by force. Government policies heavily favoured Euro-Canadian access to resources and criminalized Indigenous access. Spry, "The Great Transformation," 29–31.

52 Ibid., 26.

53 Carter, *Lost Harvests,* 81–83.

54 Canada, House of Commons, *Debates* (March 18, 1890), 2158.

55 Gerald Tulchinsky, "Across the Rivers with Steel: The First Decade of Dominion Bridge: 1882–1892" (unpublished manuscript, 1976), MG28 III 100, Dominion Bridge, vol. 21, file 6, pp. 50–52, LAC.

56 Walbank to Vankoughnet, July 28, 1882, and Vankoughnet to Walbank, August 11, 1882, RG10, vol. 7749, file 27005-1, LAC.

57 Gerald Tulchinsky, "The Second Decade of Dominion Bridge: 1882–1892" (unpublished manuscript, 1976), MG28 III 100, Dominion Bridge, vol. 21, file 7, pp. 10–11, LAC.

58 "Brevities," *Winnipeg Daily Sun,* December 4, 1884, 2.

59 For another example, see Raymond Craib's excellent study on the role of surveying and cartography in Mexican nation building. Raymond B. Craib, *Cartographic Mexico: A History of State Fixations and Fugitive Landscapes* (Durham: Duke University Press, 2004), 91.

60 "Report of the Special Commissioners," A21-21.

61 Christine Zachary Deom, "Chronology of Political Events Relative to Kahnawake" (Mohawk Council of Kahnawake Draft Document, 2010).

62 Lambert doubts that this figure is related to the indemnity because the indemnity had been fixed at an amount nearly ten times as much in 1860. Lambert, "History of Kahnawake Land Claims," 30.

63 Since bands had only limited control over their own funds, money was sometimes invested in ways that did not reflect their needs and desires. Something similar happened at Grand River, where almost $160,000 of Six Nations funds were used, without Six Nations permission, to purchase stock in a steamship company that failed. The money has not yet been recovered. E. Brian Titley, *A Narrow Vision: Duncan Campbell Scott and the Administration of Indian Affairs in Canada* (Vancouver: UBC Press, 1992), 124; Hill, *The Clay We Are Made Of,* 178–80.

64 J.V. de Boucherville to DIA, March 11, 1882, RG10, vol. 7749, file 27005-1, LAC.

65 Ibid.

66 Canada, "Annual Report of the Department of Indian Affairs," *Sessional Papers* 5 (1883), xxxiv–xxxv.

67 Robert M. Cover, "Violence and the Word," *Yale Law Journal* 95, 8 (1986): 1607; Blomley, "Law, Property, and the Geography of Violence," 130.

68 "Indian Work," *Montreal Gazette,* November 1, 1879.

69 "City Items," *Montreal Daily Witness,* May 1, 1878.

70 Correspondence between Cherrier, Joseph Williams, and the DIA, Caughnawaga Agency – Resignation of Joseph Williams as Grand Chief, 1880–1883, RG10, vol. 2124, file 23,685, LAC.

71 Joseph Williams to J.V. de Boucherville, February 28, 1882, RG10, vol. 7749, file 27005-1, LAC.

72 Joseph Williams Sose Skatsenhati, Walbank reference no. 407, was born in 1846, married Anen Katsitsarokwas in 1869, and owned two barns and four lots totalling 103.65 acres: 27.83 acres cultivated ($529), 14.5 acres hay ($149), 51 acres bush ($159), and 10.32 acres sugarbush ($290). The total assessed value was $1,127. He died on May 15, 1885. Caughnawaga Reference Books, 1885, LAC; "At Caughnawaga, P.Q.," *Catholic World* 37, 221 (August 1883): 610–12.

73 Vankoughnet to John A. Macdonald, April 19, 1882, RG10, vol. 7749, file 27005-1, LAC.

74 Ibid.

75 Vankoughnet to Walbank, April 24, 1882, RG10, vol. 7749, file 27005-1, LAC.

76 Walbank to Vankoughnet, June 22 and September 27, 1882, RG10, vol. 7749, file 27005-1, LAC.

77 Walbank to Vankoughnet, November 20, 1882, RG10, vol. 7749, file 27005-1, LAC.

78 W.A. Austin report to Deputy Minister of Indian Affairs, February 25, 1887, and Walbank to DIA, March 7, 1887, RG10, vol. 7749, file 27005-1, LAC.

79 "The Indian Exhibition," *Montreal Daily Witness,* September 29, 1883, reprinted in Canada, *Sessional Papers* 4 (1884), 152–58.

80 "Annual Report of G.E. Cherrier, Indian Agent, Caughnawaga Agency," in *Annual Report of the Department of Indian Affairs for the Year ended 31st December, 1883* (Ottawa: MacLean, Roger, 1884).

81 Ibid.

82 Ibid.

83 Canada, "Annual Report of the Department of Indian Affairs," *Sessional Papers* 5 (1883), xxxiv–xxxv.

84 "At Caughnawaga, P.Q.," *Catholic World.*

85 Canada, "Annual Report of the Department of Indian Affairs," xxxiv–xxxv.

86 Vankoughnet to Walbank, July 28, 1884, RG10, vol. 7749, file 27005-1, LAC.

87 Austin report to Deputy Minister, February 25, 1887, LAC.

88 "Public Notice: Subdivision of the Caughnawaga Reserve," January 15, 1885, RG10, vol. 2693, file 139,964, pt. 1, LAC.

89 Caughnawaga Reference Books, 1885, LAC.

90 "The Caughnawaga Ejectments," *Montreal Daily Witness,* July 13, 1886, 6.

91 Walbank to Vankoughnet, February 28, 1885, RG10, vol. 7749, file 27005-1, LAC.

92 Walbank to Vankoughnet, February 19, 1885, and Vankoughnet to Walbank, February 21, 1885, RG10, vol. 7749, file 27005-1, LAC.

93 Benn, *Mohawks on the Nile,* 65, 225–27; James D. Deer, *The Canadian Voyageurs in Egypt* (Montreal: John Lovell, 1885); Louis Jackson, *Our Caughnawagas in Egypt* (Montreal: Wm. Drysdale, 1885).

94 Reid, *Kahnawà:ke,* 40–45.

95 Chiefs Thomas Asennase, Wishe Shakoentinetha, Louis Shatekaienton, Thomas Jocks to DIA, August 3, 1885, RG10, vol. 2310, file 61,693, LAC.

96 Palmater, *Beyond Blood;* Kim TallBear, *Native American DNA: Tribal Belonging and the False Promise of Genetic Science* (Minneapolis: University of Minnesota Press, 2013).

97 Reid, *Kahnawà:ke,* 27–28.

98 W.A. Austin report to Deputy Minister, February 25, 1887, LAC.

99 Reid, *Kahnawà:ke,* 40–45.

100 Sprague, *Canada and the Métis.*

101 Petition from about fifty Kahnawa'kehró:non (in general council) to Vankoughnet, July 7, 1885, RG10, vol. 7749, file 27005-1, LAC

102 Walbank to Vankoughnet, July 27, 1885, RG10, vol. 7749, file 27005-1, LAC.

103 Walbank to Vankoughnet, October 19, 1885, RG10, vol. 7749, file 27005-1, LAC.

104 Ibid.

105 Petition from several Kahnawa'kehró:non to Vankoughnet, June 15, 1886, RG10, vol. 7749, file 27005-1, LAC.

106 Walbank to Vankoughnet, [July 26], 1886, RG10, vol. 7749, file 27005-1, LAC.

107 Vankoughnet to Walbank, July 30, 1886, RG10, vol. 7749, file 27005-1, LAC.

108 Caughnawaga Reference Books, 1885, LAC. Official translation, probably by Owakenhen (Peter Stacey). Free interpretation/translation by Kahrhó:wane Cory McComber: "Gentlemen: I've already answered. I like the way I have (it/s.t.), my land is not for sale." Kahrhó:wane also provided the Kanien'kéha transcription above and rendered the statement

in modern orthography: "Ó:nen sewenhsiónshon wa'tkerihwa'sera:ko,' Kenón:we's nì:'I tsi ní:io wákien, iah tekatenhní:nons nakonhwéntsia." Pers. comm., November 26, 2020.

109 Caughnawaga Reference Books, 1885, LAC. The reference books give no personal information for Ohionkoton (Walbank reference no. 582, lot 237).

110 Not included in the area of these lots were 550 acres for the village and common (a community managed pasture), 30 acres for quarrying, and 60 acres for roads.

111 Walbank to Vankoughnet, September 10, 1886, RG10, vol. 7749, file 27005-1, LAC.

112 W.A. Austin memo to Deputy Minister, September 21, 1886, RG10, vol. 7749, file 27005-1, LAC.

113 W.A. Austin report to Deputy Minister, February 25, 1887, LAC.

114 W.A. Austin memo to Deputy Minister, March 11, 1887, RG10, vol. 7749, file 27005-1, LAC.

115 Walbank to Vankoughnet, September 13, 1887, LAC.

116 Thiretha (Peter Diome) was Walbank claimant 577, and Katarariron (Joseph Jacob), was claimant 210. Caughnawaga Reference Books, 1885, LAC.

117 Walbank to Vankoughnet, September 13, 1887, LAC.

118 Vankoughnet to Walbank, May 21, 1887, vol. 7749, file 27005-1, RG10, LAC.

119 Walbank to Vankoughnet, May 18, 1887, RG10, vol. 7749, file 27005-1, LAC; Vankoughnet to Walbank, May 21, 1887, LAC.

120 Ohonwakerha (Louis Jocko), Walbank reference no. 143, was born in 1841. He was very active in purchasing land around the time of the survey, so it is hard to specify which lots were his. He is also listed as a disputed owner of lot 143. Caughnawaga Reference Books, 1885, LAC.

121 Walbank to DIA, July 4, 1887, and R. Sinclair to Walbank, July 13, 1887, RG10, vol. 7749, file 27005-1, LAC.

122 Vankoughnet to Walbank, December 31, 1887, and Walbank to Vankoughnet, January 2, 1888, RG10, vol. 7749, file 27005-1, LAC.

123 Walbank to DIA, January 2, 1888, RG10, vol. 7749, file 27005-1, LAC.

124 Walbank report to John A. Macdonald, June 14, 1888, RG10, vol. 7749, file 27005-1, LAC.

125 Alexander Brosseau to Superintendent General of Indian Affairs, November 18, 1887, RG10, vol. 2394, C-11213, file 81,361, LAC.

126 Brosseau to R. Sinclair, July 12, 1889, RG10, vol. 7749, file 27005-1, LAC.

127 Brosseau to DIA, March 19, 1890, and DIA to Brosseau, April 11, 1890, RG10, vol. 2102, file 18,571, LAC.

128 Phrases taken from Berda, *Living Emergency,* Chapter 4.

129 For example, his map did not include astronomical bearings or specify the length of boundaries for each lot. Thus, if a fire chanced to obliterate the lines that Walbank had marked on the ground, his map would provide no help in retracing them, as DIA surveyor W.A. Austin pointed out. Austin to Acting Deputy Minister, September 7, 1888, RG10, vol. 7749, file 27005-1, LAC.

130 Another example of Walbank's problematic work came to light in September 1889, when DIA surveyor Samuel Bray discovered that the planned roads should have been much wider. Bray to Deputy Minister, September 18, 1889, RG10, vol. 7749, file 27005-1, LAC.

131 Canada, House of Commons, *Debates* (June 15, 1887; March 28, 1888; May 21, 1888; March 7 and 8, 1889).

132 Ibid. (March 18, 1890), 2158.

133 E. Brian Titley, "Dewdney, Edgar," *Dictionary of Canadian Biography Online,* http://www.biographi.ca/en/bio/dewdney_edgar_14E.html.

134 House of Commons, *Debates* (March 18, 1890) 2158 (emphasis added).

135 Tim Owen and Elaine Pilbeam, *Ordnance Survey: Map Makers to Britain since 1791* (London: HMSO, 1992); W.A. Seymour, *A History of the Ordnance Survey* (Folkestone, UK: Dawson, 1980); Whitworth Porter, *History of the Corps of Royal Engineers* (London: Longmans, Green, 1889), 1:167–68.

136 Internal DIA memo, February 5, 1890, RG10, vol. 7749, file 27005-1, LAC.

137 R. Sinclair memo to Deputy Minister, January 30, 1891, RG10, vol. 7749, file 27005-1, LAC.

138 W.A. Austin memo to Deputy Minister, September 29, 1890, RG10, vol. 7749, file 27005-1, LAC.

139 W.A. Austin memo to Hayter Reed, n.d. [1894], RG10, vol. 2181, file 36,622-3A, LAC.

140 For more on this trope, see Philip J. Deloria, *Playing Indian* (New Haven: Yale University Press, 1998); Lutz, *Makúk;* Torgovnick, *Gone Primitive.*

141 Douglas Leighton, "A Victorian Civil Servant at Work: Lawrence Vankoughnet and the Canadian Indian Department, 1874–1893," in *As Long as the Sun Shines and the Water Flows: A Reader in Canadian Native Studies,* ed. Ian L. Getty and Antoine S. Lussier (Vancouver: UBC Press, 1983), 104–19.

142 Vankoughnet to Mayne Daly, April 14, 1893, LAC.

143 Hayter Reed to Chief J.W. Jocks, January 18, 1894, RG10, vol. 7749, file 27005-1, LAC.

144 Craib, *Cartographic Mexico,* 93; see also Scott, *Seeing Like a State.*

145 Canada, House of Commons, *Debates* (May 5, 1880), 1994.

146 For more on this topic, see Neeson, *Commoners,* Chapter 6.

147 It is also worth noting that Rotinonhsión:ni had a historic antipathy for English conceptions of property and territory, which many associated with anti-Indigenous violence. A number of authors cite Rotinonhsión:ni preference for feudal land tenure systems such as the seigneurial one in New France. See Anthony Hall, *The Bowl with One Spoon,* vol. 1 of *The American Empire and the Fourth World,* McGill-Queen's Native and Northern Series 34 (Montreal and Kingston: McGill-Queen's University Press, 2003), 10–15.

148 Neeson, *Commoners,* 30.

149 Ibid., 30–34.

150 Chiefs Jarvis A. Dione, Joseph K. Delisle, Joseph T. Skey, and Thomas Asennase to Meredith, May 14, 1875, LAC.

151 D.S. Otis, *The Dawes Act and the Allotment of Indian Lands* (Norman: University of Oklahoma Press, 1973 [1934]); Leonard A. Carlson, *Indians, Bureaucrats and Land: The Dawes Act and the Decline of Indian Farming* (Westport: Greenwood Press, 1981); C. Joseph Genetin-Pilawa, *Crooked Paths to Allotment: The Fight over Federal Indian Policy after the Civil War* (Chapel Hill: University of North Carolina Press, 2012); Stuart Banner, *How the Indians Lost Their Land: Law and Power on the Frontier* (Cambridge, MA: Belknap Press of Harvard University Press, 2005).

152 H. Reed to Eugène-Étienne Taché, February 12, 1894, RG10, vol. 2109, file 20,131, LAC.

CHAPTER 7: "FOLLOW THE CUSTOM OF THE RESERVE"

Epigraphs: Statement of Thomas Jacob, February 22, 1895, and Statement of Louis Norton, February 22, 1895, RG10, vol. 2774, file 155,133, LAC; "Caughnawaga Heard From," *Montreal Daily Witness,* March 7, 1895.

1 This shift from customary modes of legal interaction toward formalized state practices (associated with the emergence of modernity) occurred more generally in Canada and

elsewhere during this period. For more on the topic, see James G. Snell, *In the Shadow of the Law: Divorce in Canada, 1900–1939* (Toronto: University of Toronto Press, 1991).

2 Alexander Brosseau to J.D. McLean, October 15, 1900, RG10, vol. 3022, file 224,850, LAC.

3 Reid, "Kahnawake's Council of Chiefs."

4 Brosseau to DIA, January 18, 1888, RG10, vol. 7921, file 32-5, pt. 1, LAC.

5 Reid, *Kahnawà:ke,* 70.

6 Ibid., 70–73.

7 Brosseau to DIA, January 18, 1888, LAC.

8 Brosseau to Vankoughnet, April 10, 1888, RG10, vol. 7921, file 32-5, pt. 1, LAC.

9 Caughnawaga Indians to DIA, received January 25, 1888, RG10, vol. 7921, file 32-5, pt. 1, LAC.

10 Reid, *Kahnawà:ke,* 71–74.

11 Brosseau to DIA, February 14, 1888, RG10, vol. 7921, file 32-5, pt. 1, LAC.

12 Brosseau to Vankoughnet, May 1, 1888, RG10, vol. 7921, file 32-5, pt. 1, LAC. Departmental translation. Original French: "qu'il est encore préférable pour la Tribu d'avoir des conseillers malgré tout ces inconvénients, que de réélire des Chefs, qui dans mon opinion serait livré la partie saine de la Tribu à la mercie des turbulents et des hommes de l'intempérance qui veulent se protéger entre eux sur ce point, et ramener ainsi le trouble et le désordre dans le village."

13 Vankoughnet to Brosseau, April 28, 1889, RG10, vol. 7921, file 32-5, pt. 1, LAC.

14 Brosseau to Vankoughnet, January 9, 1889, RG10, vol. 7921, file 32-5, pt. 1, LAC. Departmental translation. Original French: "j'ai la visite de délégués deux ou trois fois par semaines pour avoir des informations, précises et immédiates à ce sujet, ce qui m'est impossible de leur donner" and "il est impossible d'administrer les affaires de la Tribu plus longtemps sans cela."

15 Petitions, January 13, 1889, RG10, vol. 7921, file 32-5, LAC; Reid, *Kahnawà:ke,* 74. The clans mentioned included Turtle, Deer, Big Bear, Stone, and Small Bear. The two others were not specified.

16 Atonwa Taiawensere (Thomas Leclerc), Walbank reference no. 80, was born in 1847 and married Sisir Kaeonwenta in 1867. In 1885, he owned lot 424; of its 45.36 acres, 20.09 were cultivated, 7.34 were pasture, 2.5 hay, and 15.43 bush. The lot also included an orchard. Walbank valued the property at $1,031. Ennias Ohahakete (George Wood), Walbank reference no. 333, was born in 1843 and married Onwari Konwawennaronken in 1866. In 1885, he owned lot 426; of its 30.40 acres, 11.06 were cultivated, 1.25 pasture, and 18.09 bush. It included a barn valued at $100. Walbank valued the property at $402. Mais Anatahes (Moise Mailloux), Walbank reference no. 296, was born in 1846 and married Sesir Kaianenta in 1872. In 1885, he owned lot 153, which was 2.35 acres, all classified as bush and valued by Walbank at $12. He also owned half of lot 151; of its 50.18 acres, 19.89 were cultivated, 13.06 hay, and 17.23 bush. The lot included an orchard and several buildings. Walbank valued it at $1,266. Teatenhawita (Jacques Montour), Walbank reference no. 224, was born in 1851 and married Teres Tsotneariio in 1874. In 1885, he owned four lots totalling 87.9 acres of which 12.22 were cultivated, 4.83 were hay, 53.81 were bush, and 17.04 were sugarbush. Walbank valued the lots at $1,132. Sak Katsitsiio (Jacques Daillebout), Walbank reference no. 545, was born in 1845 and married Teres Kwarasenni (Betsy Mandeau) in 1880. In 1885, he owned one-third of lot 518; of its 12.2 acres, 2.95 were hay, 2.36 bush, and 6.89 sugarbush. Walbank valued it at $184. Caughnawaga Reference Books, 1885, LAC.

17 Petition from Taiawensere, Ohahakete, Anatahes, Teatenhawita, and Katsitsiio, February 26, 1889, RG10, vol. 7921, file 32-5, LAC. Departmental translation. Original French (parts illegible): "Comptant sur la promesse que vous nous avez faite [?] nous donner une bonne loi qui soit à [l'avantage des] cultivateurs de la Réserve de Caughnawaga nous prenons la liberté [?] de nous [?] adresser à vous pour vous faire savoir [?] qui nous faudrait, ce serait d'avoir des Conseillers qui aient les pouvoirs exprimés dans l'acte concernant les Sauvages et l'avancement des Sauvages. Ce serait, nous le pensons, le meilleur moyen de régler les difficultés et de pourvoir au bien général de la tribu."

18 Vankoughnet to Thomas Leclerc, George Wood, and the Iroquois of Caughnawaga, March 5, 1889, RG10, vol. 7921, file 32-5, LAC.

19 Order-in-Council, March 5, 1889, RG10, vol. 7921, file 32-5, LAC.

20 *Indian Advancement Act, 1884,* s. 4.

21 Brosseau to Vankoughnet, May 1, 1888, LAC.

22 Brosseau to DIA, January 18, 1888, LAC.

23 The *Indian Advancement Act* specified that electors must reside in the section where they voted, but the candidates were not required to live in the section where they ran. Vankoughnet to Brosseau, April 28, 1888, RG10, vol. 7921, file 32-5, LAC.

24 Rowi Tawehiakenra (Louis Jackson), Walbank reference no. 503, was born in 1843, married Honorine Lafleur at an unspecified date, and owned no land outside the village in 1885. Caughnawaga Reference Books, 1885, LAC.

25 Élection des Conseillers du Conseil de bande de Caughnawaga, March 26, 1889, RG10, vol. 7921, file 32-5, LAC.

26 Reid, *Kahnawà:ke,* 76–77.

27 Kanenharoton (Thomas B. Jocks), Walbank reference no. 151, was born in 1859, married Lydia Smith in 1879, and owned no land outside of the village in 1885. Caughnawaga Reference Books, 1885, LAC.

28 Declaration of Louis F. Jackons, alias Rewi [?] Taweiakenra, March 27, 1889, RG10, vol. 7921, file 32-5, LAC; Department of Justice to Lawrence Vankoughnet, April 9, 1889, RG10, vol. 7921, file 32-5, LAC.

29 Iroquois of Caughnawaga (five pages of signatures) to the Superintendent of Indian Affairs, April 8, 1889, RG10, vol. 7921, file 32-5, LAC.

30 Michael Sokienton Bourdeau et al. to the Superintendent General of Indian Affairs, April 22, 1889, RG10, vol. 7921, file 32-5, LAC. The petition was transmitted by Cyrille Doyon, Liberal MP for La Prairie, who was often active on behalf of Kahnawa'kehró:non. C. Doyon to the Minister of the Interior, April 24, 1889, RG10, vol. 7921, file 32-5, LAC.

31 Vankoughnet to Michael Sokienton Bourdeau et al., April 29, 1889, RG10, vol. 7921, file 32-5, LAC.

32 Reid, *Kahnawà:ke,* 76–80.

33 Superintendent of Indian Affairs to Privy Council, February 7, 1890, RG10, vol. 7921, file 32-5, LAC; *Indian Act,* 1886, s. 75.

34 Department of Interior to Vankoughnet, March [23], 1890, RG10, vol. 7921, file 32-5, LAC.

35 They also asked the DIA to limit the franchise to educated property owners. Petition from about 50 Kahnawa'kehró:non, March 3, 1890, RG10, vol. 7921, file 32-5, LAC.

36 Vankoughnet to Dewdney, February 3, 1890, RG10, vol. 2523, file 107,382, LAC.

37 Reid, *Kahnawà:ke,* 81–88. Reid offers a detailed analysis of this debate and the related petitions.

38 Ibid., 90.

39 Brosseau to Vankoughnet, May 4, 1891, RG10, vol. 7921, file 32-5, LAC.

40 Brosseau to Superintendent General, February 3, 1892, RG10, vol. 7921, file 32-5, LAC.

41 Reid, *Kahnawà:ke*, 102.

42 Brosseau to Vankoughnet, February 2, 1892, RG10, vol. 7921, file 32-5, LAC. Original French: "des hommes qui veulent vivre qu'aux dépens du gouvernement." This is an example of the tendency of DIA officials (at all levels) to attempt to make and enforce rules that had no basis in law. See Harring, "'There Seemed to Be No Recognized Law.'"

43 DIA to Brosseau, February 16, 1892, RG10, vol. 7921, file 32-5, LAC.

44 Objections aux voteurs des différentes Sections de la Réserve de Caughnawaga, March 26, 1892, RG10, vol. 7921, file 32-5, LAC.

45 "Caughnawaga Elections," *Montreal Gazette,* April 25, 1892, RG10, vol. 7921, file 32-5, LAC.

46 Élection du Conseiller en Chef, délibérations et résolutions du Conseil de bande de Caughnawaga, April 20, 1892, RG10, vol. 7921, file 32-5, LAC.

47 Vankoughnet to Brosseau, June 30, 1892, RG10, vol. 7921, file 32-5, LAC.

48 Brosseau to DIA, December 12, 1896, RG10, vol. 7921, file 32-5, LAC.

49 Wishe Thasennonstie et al. to Clifford Sifton, February 1, 1897, and Brosseau to DIA, February 2, 1897, RG10, vol. 7921, file 32-5, LAC.

50 Reid, *Kahnawà:ke*, 102. It was found in 1934 that the 1906 Order-in-Council replacing the six-district system with a single district had not been legal and was thus null and void. However, all actions taken under that Order-in-Council since 1906 were declared valid and lawfully made. *Caughnawaga Indian Reserve Act,* S.C. 1934, c. 29. The *Indian Advancement Act* required a minimum of two electoral districts. *Indian Advancement Act,* R.S.C. 1886, c. 44, s. 4.

51 Gohier, "La pratique pétitionnaire."

52 Reid, *Kahnawà:ke*, 97.

53 "Indians in Council," *Daily Nor'Wester,* February 21, 1895, 4.

54 For more on the Seven Nations, see Bonaparte, "The Seven Nations of Canada"; Alain Beaulieu and Jean-Pierre Sawaya, "L'importance stratégique des Sept-Nations du Canada (1650–1860)," *Bulletin d'histoire politique* 8, 2-3 (Winter–Spring 2000): 87–107; Beaulieu and Sawaya, "Qui sont les Sept-Nations du Canada?."

55 "Indians in Council," *Daily Nor'Wester,* 4.

56 "Looking at 'Bothsidesing': When Equal Coverage Leads to Uneven Results," https://www.merriam-webster.com/words-at-play/bothsidesing-bothsidesism-new-words-were-watching.

57 "Indians in Council," *Daily Nor'Wester,* 4.

58 As quoted in Reid, *Kahnawà:ke*, 100.

59 *Indian Advancement Act, 1886,* s.2(2).

60 Reid, *Kahnawà:ke*, 103–4.

61 Walbank to Vankoughnet, June 29, 1887, RG10, vol. 7661, file 22005, LAC.

62 Tulchinsky, "Across the Rivers with Steel," LAC.

63 Daniel Rueck, "When Bridges Become Barriers: Montreal and Kahnawake Mohawk Territory," in *Metropolitan Natures: Urban Environmental Histories of Montreal,* ed. Stéphane Castonguay and Michèle Dagenais (Pittsburgh: University of Pittsburgh Press, 2011), 228–44.

64 Michel Sharenhes to DIA, October 14, 1886; Brosseau to DIA, November 9, 1886; R.J. Heucker to Vankoughnet, January 4, 1888, all in RG10, vol. 7661, file 22005, LAC.

65 Brosseau to DIA, August 30, 1889; Brosseau to Vankoughnet, May 30, 1891, and August 13, 1892; Brosseau to Vankoughnet, October 30, 1892, all in RG10, vol. 7661, file 22005, LAC.

66 Brosseau to DIA, September 26, 1890, RG10, vol. 2532, file 110,237, LAC. The peninsula/island was destroyed by the construction of the St. Lawrence Seaway in the 1950s, but in 2009 the elder Eddie Diabo recalled the days when the cows went to the island in the morning and would have to be brought back at night. Pers. comm., spring 2009.

67 Brosseau to DIA, August 31, 1893, RG10, vol. 2697, file 141,258, LAC.

68 Tanekorens (Jacques Lachandiere or Lachiere), Walbank reference no. 89, was born in 1844 and married Warisose Karonianoron in 1868. The 1901 census lists him as married to a woman named Josephine (born 1861). In 1885, Walbank recorded that he owned a seventeen-acre lot valued at $124. Sakorewata (Peter Parquis), Walbank reference no. 48, was born in 1840 and married Warisose Kaentawaks in 1861. In 1885, he owned two lots totalling seven acres, which were valued at $93. He signed his own name in Kanien'kéha on the claim form, indicating some level of literacy. Sakorewata was the son of Kateri Kaonwentha (Widow C. Parquis, claimant 565), who died shortly after the 1885 tribunal. She was born in 1815, and her husband died around 1855. Walbank noted that she had given all her land outside the village to her sons by 1885. She signed her claim form with an X. Sakorewata was fifty-five in 1895, when the DIA launched an inquiry into the ownership of lot 205. Caughnawaga Reference Books, 1885, LAC.

69 Sakotion (William Simon Meloche), Walbank reference no. 303, was born in 1862. Caughnawaga Reference Books, 1885, LAC.

70 James J. Campbell to H. Reed, January 26, 1896, RG10, vol. 2774, file 155133, LAC.

71 Brosseau to DIA, October 22, 1894, RG10, vol. 2774, file 155,133, LAC.

72 Caughnawaga Reference Books, 1885, LAC.

73 Tier Saionesakeren (Peter Montour), Walbank reference no. 314, was born in 1832. Ibid.

74 Confusingly, a number of witnesses in the DIA inquiry referred to Peter Montour without specifying whether it was the older or the younger.

75 Brosseau to DIA, October 22, 1894, LAC. It is likely that Peter Lachaudière was the man whom Walbank listed as Sakokennie (Peter Lachiere), then eighty-seven years old. Sakokennie (claimant 140) was born in 1798 and had been married to a woman named Kawennaere since 1820. He was recorded as the owner of lot 176; of its thirty-four acres, twenty-one were cultivated, and it was valued at $608. Caughnawaga Reference Books, 1885, LAC.

76 W.A. Austin memo, November 4, 1894, RG10, vol. 2774, file 155,133, LAC. Walbank refers to her as "Indian woman." Caughnawaga Reference Books, 1885, LAC.

77 Brosseau to DIA, November 3, 1894, RG10, vol. 2774, file 155,133, LAC. Departmental translation. Original French: "il n'y a eu aucunes disputes pour ce terrain avant que la compagnie du C.P.R. ait eu l'intention de prendre du terrain à cet endroit, que les propriétaires inconnus jusqu' alors ont commencés a faire leurs réclamations."

78 Reid, Kahnawà:ke, 28.

79 Sakotion was the son of Charlotte Meloche, reference no. 287, who was born in 1836. In 1885, Charlotte Meloche was listed as owning three lots outside the village totalling forty acres and valued at $376. The Walbank claim form identifies her as Charlotte Louise Giasson. The chiefs voted unanimously to reject the claims of both Charlotte and her son Sakotion, in her case because "her father is a French-Canadian and her husband was also a French-Canadian." Caughnawaga Reference Books, 1885, LAC.

80 Brosseau to DIA, November 3, 1894, RG10, vol. 2774, file 155,133, LAC. Department translation. Original French: "par les améliorations qu'il a fait sur ce terrain."
81 Caughnawaga Reference Books, 1885, LAC.
82 John Waniente Jocks (1865–1917), the owner of a Kahnawà:ke quarry, is not listed in the Caughnawaga Reference Books, because he was too young to be a candidate for the land redistribution. According to the 1901 census, John W. Jocks was born in 1866 and was married to Marie-Anne Jocks (born 1877), with a son named John born 1894 and a daughter named Maggie born 1896. In the early twentieth century, Waniente served as interpreter for the band council. Caughnawaga Council Resolution, November 4, 1904, RG10, vol. 3085, file 278,440, LAC. For more on Waniente Jocks, see Johnny Beauvais, *Kahnawake: A Mohawk Look at Canada and Adventures of Big John Canadian, 1840–1919* (Kahnawà:ke: Khanata Industries, 1985), 41–46.
83 Saksarie Ononsihata (Frank Hill), Walbank reference no. 321, was born in 1847 and had been married to Edawith Katsitsaronkwas since 1882. He had some level of literacy because he signed his own name, "SaK sa rie a non si ata," below his inquiry statement. Caughnawaga Reference Books, 1885, LAC.
84 Statement of Frank Hill, February 15, 1895, RG10, vol. 2774, file 155,133, LAC.
85 Charles Xavier Giasson or Saro Awennaratie, Walbank reference no. 284, was born in 1832 and married Catherine Perrat in 1855. Caughnawaga Reference Books, 1885, LAC. He signed his own name as "Charles X. Giasson," indicating a level of literacy and also that he self-identified using his French name. I have followed his preference.
86 Statement of Charles X. Giasson, February 15, 1895, RG10, vol. 2774, file 155,133, LAC.
87 Anatakarias (Tom Hill), Walbank reference no. 290, was born in 1840 and married Konwakiri Karakwas in 1864. Caughnawaga Reference Books, 1885, LAC.
88 A possible alternative spelling of her name is Skanahote. She seems to have died before the Walbank Survey, since she is not included in it.
89 Anatakarias signed his statement with an X. Statement of Thomas Hill, February 15, 1895, RG10, vol. 2774, file 155,133, LAC.
90 Sarakwa does not appear in the Caughnawaga Reference Books, and as the lot 205 inquiry did not record a European surname for him, he could not be identified in any census.
91 Sarakwa signed his statement with an X. Statement of Jean Sarakwa, February 15, 1895, RG10, vol. 2774, file 155,133, LAC.
92 Satekarenhes (Mattias Hill), Walbank reference no. 320, was born in 1837 and married Wariianen Kaiatienens in 1862. In 1885, he possessed no land outside the village. Caughnawaga Reference Books, 1885, LAC. In 1889, the first Kahnawà:ke band council appointed him to the position of commons gatekeeper. Paid twenty-four dollars annually, he was allowed to live in the gatehouse, but it is not known whether he still held this job in 1895. Council Resolutions, May 18, 1889, RG10, vol. 2465, file 96,069, LAC.
93 Statement of Satekarenhas, February 15, 1895, RG10, vol. 2774, file 155,133, LAC. Departmental translation. Original French: "Je ne connais pas les lignes de ce terrain mais je connais le terrain que j'ai travaillé."
94 Ibid. He signed his statement "mathias Satekarenhas," indicating a level of literacy.
95 Etwar Tahahente (Edward McComber), Walbank reference no. 295, was born in 1855 and married Anies Kwanatontion in 1877. Caughnawaga Reference Books, 1885, LAC. He signed his statement with an X. Statement of Edouard McComber, February 15, 1895, RG10, vol. 2774, file 155,133, LAC.

96 Statement of Edouard McComber, February 15, 1895, LAC. Departmental translation. Original French: "Avant que j'ai été travaillé la, je ne savais pas qu'il avait un terrain sur la butte, je savais qu'il avait un terrain en bas, mais la je ne le savais pas."

97 Joseph Reed does not appear in the Walbank record books or the 1901 census.

98 Statement of Joseph Reed, February 15, 1895, RG10, vol. 2774, file 155,133, LAC. Reed signed his statement with an X.

99 Leon Giasson does not appear in the Walbank books. According to the 1901 census, T. Leon Giasson, born in 1844, was a farmer. His wife was Agnes Giasson (born 1857). The couple had three children, who were born before 1895.

100 Statement of Leon Giasson, February 15, 1895, RG10, vol. 2774, file 155,133, LAC.

101 Jean Baptiste Delvida Meloche, Walbank reference no. 302, was born in 1860 and married Excillia Lefebvre in 1883. In 1885, when Meloche was twenty-five, Walbank listed him as owning no land but stated that he had a share in his mother's land. The four tribunal chiefs unanimously rejected him as a band member, as they did other members of his family, "because he does not belong to this Band and his father was a French-Canadian." His 1885 claimant form includes the note "This claimant does not speak Indian." Caughnawaga Reference Books, 1885, LAC. The 1901 census lists him as Dalvide Meloche, born in 1861, a stonemason, married to Zelia Meloche (born 1865) with three children who were born between 1886 and 1892.

102 Delvida Meloche signed his Walbank claimant form with an X, but signed his name for his 1895 statement. Statement of Delvida Meloche, February 15, 1895, RG10, vol. 2774, file 155,133, LAC.

103 Statement of Charlotte L. Giasson, February 15, 1895, RG10, vol. 2774, file 155,133, LAC. Departmental translation. Original French: "J'ai acheté toute la butte en question, c'est à dire la prairie le long du terrain de papa jusqu'à un autre petite prairie en arrière, mais je puis pas dire que c'est toute la butte."

104 Ibid. She signed her name in her own hand.

105 Wishe Kanawaienton (Michel Jacob), Walbank reference no. 15, was born in 1831 and married Agat Watawennenta in 1853. He signed his name on both the Walbank claim form and below his 1895 statement as "8ih She Ka na 8aien ton" and was listed as possessing deeds for most of his lots. Caughnawaga Reference Books, 1885, LAC. The 1901 census lists him as a merchant, still married to Agat, and with two adopted teenage children who lived with them.

106 Statement of Michel Jacob, February 22, 1895, RG10, vol. 2774, file 155,133, LAC. Departmental translation. Original French: "lorsque j'ai vu travaillé Montour j'ai cru que c'était à lui."

107 Ibid. Departmental translation. Original French: "je connais tout les terrains qu'il a acheté par l'avoir vu travailler sur ces terrrains."

108 Ibid.

109 Atiataronne (Tom Jacob), Walbank reference no. 45, was born in 1839 and married Konwakeri Kaententa in 1866. In 1885, he owned three lots totalling nineteen acres and valued at $236. He signed his 1885 claim form and his 1895 statement with an X. He was the son of Widow Teres Kakenseronkwas (claimant 60), who was born in 1823. She too signed her claim form with an X. Caughnawaga Reference Books, 1885, LAC. Atiataronne is not included in the 1901 census.

110 Statement of Thomas Jacob, February 22, 1895, LAC.

111 François Beaudette is probably the man listed by Walbank as Teharenions (Frank Leclere), Walbank reference no. 277, who was born in 1857 and who married Tsiniis Kasennote in 1877. At the time of the Walbank Survey, he owned no land. His father is given as "Frank Burdette or Leclere Saksarie Katarakenra," Walbank reference no. 97, son of an "Indian" man and a "French" woman. Teharenions signed his inquiry statement as "SaK sarie te ho re nions," indicating that he self-identified with his Kanien'kéha name. At the time of the Walbank Survey, the four chiefs on the tribunal unanimously voted to reject him because "he does not belong to the Band." Caughnawaga Reference Books, 1885, LAC. Teharenions appears in the 1901 census as François Leclair, born in 1856, a "French" carpenter whose wife, Hertemise Leclair, was born in 1859. They had at least two children at the time of the lot 205 inquiry.

112 Statement of François Beaudette, February 22, 1895, RG10, vol. 2774, file 155,133, LAC.

113 Sawatis Aientonni (Big John Canadien), Walbank reference no. 115, was born in 1840 and married Malvina McComber in 1863. Walbank listed him as the disputed owner of a tiny and not-very-valuable lot. Caughnawaga Reference Books, 1885, LAC. In the 1901 census, Baptiste Canadien (Aientonni) is recorded as "Indian," whereas Malvina is given as Scottish. He signed his statement and Walbank claim form with an X. For more on Aientonni, see Beauvais, *Kahnawake*.

114 Statement of Jean-Baptiste Canadien, February 22, 1895, RG10, vol. 2774, file 155,133, LAC.

115 The Walbank books list two men named Frank Daillebout, whose birthdays are given as 1849 and 1850, so I cannot know with certainty which one testified on behalf of Tanekorens. However, the François Daillebout who testified signed his own name, whereas only one of the two Frank Daillebouts in the Walbank Survey did so. This was Thanonsokota. The other marked his claim form with an X. Therefore, the witness in the case was probably Saksarie Thanonsokota (Frank Daillebout), Walbank reference no. 256, who was born in 1850 and married Wiriia Tiorhathe in 1873. Walbank listed him as owning a 10.5-acre lot valued at $77. Caughnawaga Reference Books, 1885, LAC. It is not possible to determine whether Thanonsokota appears in the 1901 census.

116 Statement of François Daillebout, February 22, 1895, RG10, vol. 2774, file 155,133, LAC.

117 Louis Norton cannot be positively identified in the Walbank reference books. The 1901 census lists Louis Norton (born 1813) as widowed and living with Alex and Maria D'Ailleboust, his daughter. The household is described as "Indian" and as Kanien'kéha speakers. Louis Norton signed his statement with an X.

118 Statement of Louis Norton, February 22, 1895, LAC.

119 Bettina Bradbury, *Wife to Widow: Lives, Laws, and Politics in Nineteenth-Century Montreal* (Vancouver: UBC Press, 2012).

120 Cherrier to Brosseau, February 22, 1895, LAC. Original French: "traditionnelle chez eux et semble s'être transmise de père en fils."

121 Ibid.

122 J. Waniente Jocks to H. Reed, March 16, 1895, RG10, vol. 2774, file 155,133, LAC.

123 Ibid.

124 Brosseau to Hayter Reed, March 19, 1895, RG10, vol. 2774, file 155,133, LAC.

125 J.D. McLean to Deputy Minister, April 9, 1895, RG10, vol. 2774, file 155,133, LAC.

126 James La Chaiere to Hayter Reed, April [23], 1895, RG10, vol. 2774, file 155,133, LAC.

127 L.C. Pelletier to Hayter Reed, July 17, 1895, RG10, vol. 2774, file 155,133, LAC.

128 Sako are watha to Brosseau, July 18, 1895, RG10, vol. 2774, file 155,133, LAC.

129 Reed to Brosseau, July 22, 1895, RG10, vol. 2774, file 155,133, LAC.
130 Brosseau to DIA, August 5, 1895, RG10, vol. 2774, file 155,133, LAC. Original French: "il n'est pas possible d'accorder aucune compensation à Meloche sans qu'il y ait un mécontentement considérable parmi les Sauvages, à mois qu'une nouvelle enquête serait accordée à Meloche et qu'il pourrait prouver de nouveaux faits, la différence qui existe entre les deux réclamants est que la famille Meloche a toujours été contestée par les Sauvages et qu'ils ont toujours eu des contrats des individus pour les terrains qu'ils ont achetés des Sauvages, ce qu'ils n'ont pas dans le seul cas en litige, ils en ont dans tous les autres cas; et qu'il y a un grand nombre de cas parmi les Sauvages qui n'ont d'autres titres que l'appropriation de terrain avec l'approbation verbal ou par écrit des chefs du temps."
131 Reed to Brosseau, August 19, 1895, RG10, vol. 2774, file 155,133, LAC.
132 Carter, Lost Harvests; Carter, "Agriculture and Agitation"; Brian Titley, "Isoler et embrigader: la tendance coercitive des politiques d'éducation pour enfants autochtones (1870–1932)," Recherches amérindiennes au Québec 41, 1 (2011): 3–15.
133 Reed to Brosseau, August 19, 1895, LAC.
134 Ibid.
135 Ibid.
136 Brosseau to DIA, September 12, 1895, RG10, vol. 2774, file 155,133, LAC.
137 DIA to Brosseau, September 14, 1895, RG10, vol. 2774, file 155,133, LAC.
138 Louis F. Jackson to Reed, October 12, 1895, RG10, vol. 2774, file 155,133, LAC.
139 Campbell to Reed, January 26, 1896, LAC.
140 Ibid.
141 Ibid.
142 Brosseau to DIA, February 24, 1896, RG10, vol. 2774, file 155133, LAC.
143 J. Waniente Jocks to Clifford Sifton, May 31, 1897, RG10, vol. 2774, file 155,133, LAC.
144 McLean to J.W. Jocks, June 5, 1897, and J.W. Jocks to McLean, July 23, 1897, RG10, vol. 2774, file 155,133, LAC.
145 Brosseau to DIA, August 9 and 20, 1897, RG10, vol. 2774, file 155,133, LAC.
146 Council Resolution, September 24, 1897, RG10, vol. 2774, file 155,133, LAC.
147 Brosseau to DIA, December 6, 1897, RG10, vol. 2774, file 155,133, LAC.
148 Brosseau to DIA, September 25, 1897, RG10, vol. 2774, file 155,133, LAC.
149 Walbank picketed only some of the new rectangular lots, which were never actualized.
150 Brosseau to DIA, October 22, 1895, RG10, vol. 2774, file 155133, LAC. Departmental translation. French original missing from file.
151 Carter, Lost Harvests; F. Laurie Barron, "The Indian Pass System in the Canadian West, 1882–1935," Prairie Forum 13, 1 (1988): 25–42; Daschuk, Clearing the Plains.
152 Brosseau to McLean, October 15, 1900, LAC.
153 Simpson, Mohawk Interruptus.
154 C.H. Taggart to Harold W. McGill, June 14, 1944, Appendix G, in C.H. Taggart, Caughnawaga Indian Reserve: Report, General and Final (Ottawa: Department of Mines and Resources, 1948).
155 Pers. comms. with several Kahnawa'kehró:non, including A. Brian Deer, on a number of occasions; Martha Montour, July 20, 2012; and Kakwirakeron Ross Montour, June 2, 2021. See also "This Is Indian Land: An Exhibit on the State of Kahnawake Lands" (report for the Socio-Economic Development Program of the Mohawk Council of Kahnawake, [1982]).
156 Martha Montour, pers. comm., July 20, 2012.

CONCLUSION

1 For more on Haudenosaunee legal and political values, see Williams, *Kayanerenkó:wa*. For Canadian legal and political values, see McKay, "The Liberal Order Framework."

2 Geographer Madeline Whetung and Rob Nixon use the term "slow violence" to describe impacts that accumulate gradually and unseen over time. Whetung specifically refers to "slow gendered violence." Madeline Whetung, "(En)Gendering Shoreline Law: Nishnaabeg Relational Politics along the Trent Severn Waterway," *Global Environmental Politics* 19, 3 (2019): 16–32. Rob Nixon, *Slow Violence and the Environmentalism of the Poor* (Cambridge, MA: Harvard University Press, 2013).

3 The construction of the St. Lawrence Seaway through the village in the 1950s is remembered as one of the greatest environmental and cultural tragedies in the history of the community. See Stephanie Phillips, "The Kahnawake Mohawks and the St. Lawrence Seaway" (master's thesis, McGill University, 2000); Kakwiranó:ron Cook, *Kahnawà:ke Revisited: The St. Lawrence Seaway* (N.p.: Kakari:io Pictures, 2009).

4 Sarah Carter points out the irony that laws intended to assimilate First Nations gave them a separate legal status and kept them apart from settler populations. Carter, *Lost Harvests*, 25.

5 Kathryn V. Muller, "The Two 'Mystery' Belts of Grand River: A Biography of the Two Row Wampum and the Friendship Belt," *American Indian Quarterly* 31, 1 (2007): 129–64; Jon Parmenter, "The Meaning of Kaswentha and the Two Row Wampum Belt in Haudenosaunee (Iroquois) History: Can Indigenous Oral Tradition Be Reconciled with the Documentary Record?" *Journal of Early American History* 3 (2013): 82–109.

Bibliography

PRIMARY SOURCES

Bibliothèque et Archives nationales du Québec (BANQ)
CA601   Fonds Cour supérieure. District judiciaire de Montréal. Greffes d'arpenteurs
E21   Fonds Ministère des Terres et Forêts
TL16   Fonds Cour des plaidoyers communs du district de Montréal
TL19   Fonds Cour du banc du roi/de la reine du district de Montréal
TL32   Fonds Cour des sessions générales de la paix du district de Montréal
Collection numérique: images, cartes et plans

General Synod Archives, Anglican Church of Canada

Library and Archives Canada (LAC)
MG1   Fonds des Colonies
MG11   Colonial Office fonds
MG23-GII17   Robert Prescott fonds
MG24-A12   George Ramsay, 9th Earl of Dalhousie fonds
MG26-A   Fonds Sir John A. Macdonald
MG28   Dominion Bridge Company fonds
MG29-B1, R7666-0-8-E   Sandford Fleming fonds
R3908-0-0-E W.H. Coverdale collection of Canadiana
RG8   British Military and Naval Records
RG10   Indian Affairs
RG13   Department of Justice

McCord Museum – Paintings, photographs, postcards
McGill University Rare Books and Special Collections
Canadian Architecture Collection

Université de Montréal, division des archives
CA-UDEM01 P0058, Collection Louis-François-George Baby

Government Publications

Canada, House of Commons, *Debates*
Canada, House of Commons, *Sessional Papers*
Censuses
Journaux de la Chambre d'Assemblée du Bas-Canada
Province of Canada, *Journals of the Legislative Assembly*
Statutes of Canada

Newspapers and Journals

Catholic World
Daily Nor'Wester
Eastern Door
Montreal Daily Witness
Montreal Gazette
New York Times
Winnipeg Daily Sun

Published and Recent Sources

Alfred, Gerald R. "To Right Certain Wrongs: A Report on Research into Lands Known as the Seigniory of Sault St. Louis." Kahnawake Seigneury Office, 1995.
Anaya, James. "Indigenous Peoples' Participatory Rights in Relation to Decisions about Natural Resource Extraction: The More Fundamental Issue of What Rights Indigenous Peoples Have in Lands and Resources." *Arizona Journal of International and Comparative Law* 22, 1 (2005): 7–18.
Asch, Michael. *On Being Here to Stay: Treaties and Aboriginal Rights in Canada.* Toronto: University of Toronto Press, 2014.
"At Caughnawaga, P.Q." *Catholic World* 37, 221 (August 1883): 607–16.
Axtell, James. "The White Indians of Colonial America." *William and Mary Quarterly* 32, 1 (1975): 55–88.
Banner, Stuart. *How the Indians Lost Their Land: Law and Power on the Frontier.* Cambridge, MA: Belknap Press of Harvard University Press, 2005.
–. *Possessing the Pacific: Land, Settlers, and Indigenous People from Australia to Alaska.* Cambridge, MA: Harvard University Press, 2007.
Barman, Jean. *Iroquois in the West.* Montreal and Kingston: McGill-Queen's University Press, 2019.
Barron, F. Laurie. "The Indian Pass System in the Canadian West, 1882–1935." *Prairie Forum* 13, 1 (1988): 25–42.
Bartlett, Richard H. *Indian Reserves in Quebec.* Saskatoon: University of Saskatchewan Native Law Centre, 1984.
Beaulieu, Alain. "Les pièges de la judiciarisation de l'histoire autochtone." *Revue d'histoire de l'Amerique français* 53, 4 (2000): 541–51.

–. "La question des terres autochtones au Québec, 1760–1860." Rapport de recherche déposé au Ministère de la Justice et au Ministère des Ressources naturelles du Québec, 2002.

Beaulieu, Alain, and Jean-Pierre Sawaya. "L'importance stratégique des Sept-Nations du Canada (1650–1860)." *Bulletin d'histoire politique* 8, 2–3 (Winter–Spring 2000): 87–107.

–. "Qui sont les Sept-Nations du Canada? Quelques observations sur une appellation ambiguë." *Recherches amérindiennes au Québec* 27, 2 (1997): 43–51.

Beauvais, Johnny. *Kahnawake: A Mohawk Look at Canada and Adventures of Big John Canadian, 1840–1919*. Kahnawà:ke: Khanata Industries, 1985.

Bednasek, C. Drew, and Anne M.C. Godlewska. "The Influence of Betterment Discourses on Canadian Aboriginal Peoples in the Late Nineteenth and Early Twentieth Centuries." *Canadian Geographer/Le Géographe canadien* 53, 4 (2009): 444–61.

Belich, James. *Replenishing the Earth: The Settler Revolution and the Rise of the Anglo-World, 1783–1939*. Oxford: Oxford University Press, 2009.

Benn, Carl. *The Iroquois in the War of 1812*. Toronto: University of Toronto Press, 1998.

–. *Mohawks on the Nile: Natives among the Canadian Voyageurs in Egypt, 1884–1885*. Toronto: Natural Heritage Books, 2009.

Berda, Yael. *Living Emergency: Israel's Permit Regime in the Occupied West Bank*. Redwood City, CA: Stanford Briefs, 2017.

Bernard, John. *Retrospections of America, 1797–1811*. New York: Harper and Brothers, 1887.

Bhandar, Brenna. *Colonial Lives of Property: Law, Land, and Racial Regimes of Ownership*. Durham: Duke University Press, 2018.

Binnema, Theodore. "Protecting Indian Lands by Defining Indian: 1850–76." *Journal of Canadian Studies/Revue d'études canadiennes* 48, 2 (2014): 5–39.

Binnema, Theodore, and Kevin Hutchings. "The Emigrant and the Noble Savage: Sir Francis Bond Head's Romantic Approach to Aboriginal Policy in Upper Canada, 1836–1838." *Journal of Canadian Studies/Revue d'études canadiennes* 39, 1 (2005): 115–38.

Binnema, Theodore, and Melanie Niemi. "'Let the Line Be Drawn Now': Wilderness, Conservation, and the Exclusion of Aboriginal People from Banff National Park in Canada." *Environmental History* 11 (October 2006): 724–50.

Blomley, Nicholas. "Law, Property, and the Geography of Violence: The Frontier, the Survey, and the Grid." *Annals of the Association of American Geographers* 93, 1 (2003): 121–41.

Bobroff, Kenneth H. "Retelling Allotment: Indian Property Rights and the Myth of Common Ownership." *Vanderbilt Law Review* 54 (2001): 1559–623.

Bonaparte, Darren. *Creation and Confederation: The Living History of the Iroquois*. Akwesáhsne: Wampum Chronicles, 2006.

–. "The Seven Nations of Canada: The Other Iroquois Confederacy." http://www.wampumchronicles.com/sevennations.html.

Borrows, John. *Freedom and Indigenous Constitutionalism*. Toronto: University of Toronto Press, 2016.

–. "Indigenous Legal Traditions in Canada." *Washington University Journal of Law and Policy* 19 (2005): 167–223.

–. "Wampum at Niagara: The Royal Proclamation, Canadian Legal History, and Self-Government." In *Aboriginal and Treaty Rights in Canada*, ed. Michael Asch, 155–72. Vancouver: UBC Press, 1997.

Bouchard, Isabelle. "Des systèmes politiques en quête de légimité: terres 'seigneuriales,' pouvoirs et enjeux locaux dans les communautés autochtones de la vallée du Saint-Laurent (1760–1860)." PhD diss., Université du Québec à Montréal, 2017.

Bouchette, Joseph. *A Topographical Description of the Province of Lower Canada.* St-Lambert, QC: Payette and Simms, 1973 [1815].

Boyce, Douglas W. "A Glimpse of Iroquois Culture History through the Eyes of Joseph Brant and John Norton." *Proceedings of the American Philosophical Society* 117, 4 (1973): 286–94.

Bradbury, Bettina. *Wife to Widow: Lives, Laws, and Politics in Nineteenth-Century Montreal.* Vancouver: UBC Press, 2012.

Brody, Hugh. *The Other Side of Eden: Hunters, Farmers and the Shaping of the World.* Vancouver: Douglas and McIntyre, 2000.

Bromley, Daniel W., and Michael M. Cernea. *The Management of Common Property Natural Resources: Some Conceptual and Operational Fallacies.* World Bank Discussion Papers 57. Washington, DC: World Bank, 1989.

Brown, Judith K. "Economic Organization and the Position of Women among the Iroquois." *Ethnohistory* 17 (1970): 151–65.

Brownlie, Robin Jarvis. *A Fatherly Eye: Indian Agents, Government Power, and Aboriginal Resistance in Ontario, 1918–1939.* Don Mills: Oxford University Press, 2003.

Buckley, Helen. *From Wooden Ploughs to Welfare: Why Indian Policy Failed in the Prairie Provinces.* Montreal and Kingston: McGill-Queen's University Press, 1992.

Carleton, Sean. "Colonizing Minds: Public Education, the 'Textbook Indian,' and Settler Colonialism in British Columbia, 1920–1970." *BC Studies* 169 (Spring 2011): 101–30.

Carlson, Leonard A. *Indians, Bureaucrats and Land: The Dawes Act and the Decline of Indian Farming.* Westport: Greenwood Press, 1981.

Carter, Sarah. *Aboriginal People and Colonizers of Western Canada to 1900.* Toronto: University of Toronto Press, 1999.

–. "Agriculture and Agitation on the Oak River Reserve, 1875–1895." *Manitoba History* 6 (Fall 1983): 2–9.

–. *Lost Harvests: Prairie Indian Reserve Farmers and Government Policy.* Montreal and Kingston: McGill-Queen's University Press, 1990.

Clark, Thomas Henry. *Rapport Géologique: Région de Montréal/Geological Report: Montreal Area.* Quebec City: Ministère des richesses naturelles, Direction générale des mines, Service de l'exploration géologique, 1972.

Cook, Kakwiranó:ron. *Kahnawà:ke Revisited: The St. Lawrence Seaway.* N.p.: Kakari:io Pictures, 2009.

Cothran, Boyd. *Remembering the Modoc War: Redemptive Violence and the Making of American Innocence.* Chapel Hill: University of North Carolina Press, 2014.

Courville, Serge. "La crise agricole du Bas-Canada, éléments d'une réflexion géographique (1e partie)." *Cahiers de géographie du Québec* 24, 62 (1980): 193–224.

Cover, Robert M. "Violence and the Word." *Yale Law Journal* 95, 8 (1986): 1601–29.

Craft, Aimée. *Breathing Life into the Stone Fort Treaty: An Anishinabe Understanding of Treaty One.* Saskatoon: Purich, 2013.

Craib, Raymond B. *Cartographic Mexico: A History of State Fixations and Fugitive Landscapes.* Durham: Duke University Press, 2004.

Cronon, William. *Changes in the Land: Indians, Colonists, and the Ecology of New England.* New York: Hill and Wang, 1983.

–. "The Trouble with Wilderness; or, Getting Back to the Wrong Nature." In *Uncommon Ground: Toward Reinventing Nature,* ed. William Cronon, 69–90. New York: W.W. Norton, 1995.

Curtis, Chris. "Mapping Kahnawake History without an Agenda." *Eastern Door,* June 15, 2012.

Daschuk, James. *Clearing the Plains: Disease, Politics of Starvation and the Loss of Aboriginal Life.* Regina: University of Regina Press, 2013.

Day, Gordon M. "The Indian as an Ecological Factor in the Northeastern Forest." *Ecology* 34, 2 (1953): 329–46.

Decroix, Arnaud. "Le conflit juridique entre les Jésuites et les Iroquois au sujet de la seigneurie du Sault Saint-Louis: analyse de la décision de Thomas Gage (1762)." *Revue Juridique Thémis* 41 (2007): 279–97.

Deer, A. Brian. "The Iroquois Condolence." *Ecumenism* 159 (2005): 4–10.

–. "The Water and Sewer System in Kahnawake and St. Lawrence Seaway." Mohawk Council of Kahnawake, Kahnawà:ke, 1982.

Deer, James D. *The Canadian Voyageurs in Egypt.* Montreal: John Lovell, 1885.

Delâge, Denys, and Alexandre Lefrançois. "Thomas Arakwenté: promoteur de la modernité dans la communauté iroquoise du Sault Saint-Louis (1791–1820)." In *Gouvernance autochtone: aspects juridiques, économiques et sociaux,* ed. Andrée Lajoie, 72–76. Montreal: Les éditions Thémis, 2007.

Delâge, Denys, and Étienne Gilbert. "La justice coloniale britannique et les Amérindiens au Québec, 1760–1820 – I. En terres amérindiennes." *Recherches amérindiennes au Québec* 32, 1 (2002): 63–82.

–. "La justice coloniale britannique et les Amérindiens au Québec, 1760–1820. II – En territoire coloniale." *Recherches amérindiennes au Québec* 32, 2 (2002): 107–17.

Deloria, Philip J. *Indians in Unexpected Places.* Lawrence: University of Kansas Press, 2004.

–. *Playing Indian.* New Haven: Yale University Press, 1998.

Dennis, Matthew. *Cultivating a Landscape of Peace: Iroquois-European Encounters in Seventeenth-Century America.* Ithaca: Cornell University Press, 1993.

DePasquale, Paul W. *Natives and Settlers, Now and Then: Historical Issues and Current Perspectives on Treaties and Land Claims in Canada.* Edmonton: University of Alberta Press, 2007.

Devine, E.J. *Historic Caughnawaga.* Montreal: Messenger Press, 1922.

Diabo, Melvin Tekahonwen:sere. "Comprehensive Land Report: Restoring Kanien'kehaka Approach to Land Holding and Land Use." Report submitted to the Office of the Council of Chiefs, Kahnawà:ke, 2004.

Dickson-Gilmore, E. Jane. "'More Mohawk Than My Blood': Citizenship, Membership and the Struggle over Identity in Kahnawake." *Canadian Issues* 21 (1999): 44–62.

Doucet, Nicolas-Benjamin. *Fundamental Principles of the Laws of Canada as They Existed under the Natives, as They Were Changed under the French Kings, and as They Were Modified and Altered under the Domination of England.* Montreal: John Lovell, 1841.

Doutre, Joseph. "Les sauvages du Canada en 1852." In *Institut-Canadien en 1855,* ed. J.L. Lafontaine, 190–225. Montreal: Sénécal and Daniel, 1855.

Doxtator, Deborah. "What Happened to the Iroquois Clans? A Study of Clans in Three Nineteenth Century Rotinonhsyonni Communities." PhD diss., University of Western Ontario, 1996.

Duncan, John M. *Travels through Part of the United States and Canada in 1818 and 1819.* Vol. 2. Glasgow: University Press, 1823.

Elbourne, Elizabeth. "Broken Alliance: Debating Six Nations Land Claims in 1822." *Cultural and Social History* 9, 4 (2012): 497–525.

Engelbrecht, William. *Iroquoia: The Development of a Native World.* Syracuse: Syracuse University Press, 2003.

Fenton, William. *The Great Law and the Longhouse: A Political History of the Iroquois Confederacy.* Norman: University of Oklahoma Press, 1998.

Ford, Lisa. *Settler Sovereignty: Jurisdiction and Indigenous People in America and Australia, 1788–1836.* Cambridge, MA: Harvard University Press, 2010.

Fortin, Gérard L., and Jacques Frenette. "L'acte de 1851 et la création de nouvelles réserves indiennes au Bas-Canada en 1853." *Recherches amérindiennes au Québec* 19, 1 (1989): 31–37.

Francis, Daniel. *A History of the Native Peoples of Quebec, 1760–1867.* Ottawa: Department of Indian Affairs and Northern Development, 1985.

Franquet, Louis. *Voyages et mémoires sur le Canada par Franquet.* Quebec City: Institut Canadien de Québec, 1889.

Frisch, Jack A. "The Iroquois Indians and the 1855 Franklin Search Expedition in the Arctic." *Indian Historian* 8, 1 (1975): 27–30.

Fyson, Donald. *Magistrates, Police and People: Everyday Criminal Justice in Quebec and Lower Canada.* Toronto: University of Toronto Press, 2006.

Garneau, Jean-Philippe. "Appartenance ethnique, culture juridique et représentation devant la justice civile de Québec à la fin du XVIIIe siècle." In *Entre justice et justiciables: Les auxiliaires de la justice du Moyen Âge au XXe siècle,* ed. Claire Dolan, 405–42. Quebec City: Les presses de l'Université Laval, 2005.

Genetin-Pilawa, C. Joseph. *Crooked Paths to Allotment: The Fight over Federal Indian Policy after the Civil War.* Chapel Hill: University of North Carolina Press, 2012.

George-Kanentiio, Doug. *Iroquois Culture and Commentary.* Santa Fe: Clear Light, 2000.

Gettler, Brian. *Colonialism's Currency: Money, State, and First Nations in Canada, 1820–1950.* Montreal and Kingston: McGill-Queen's University Press, 2020.

Ghobashy, Omar Z. *The Caughnawaga Indians and the St. Lawrence Seaway.* New York: Devin-Adair, 1961.

Girard, Philip, Jim Phillips, and R. Blake Brown. *A History of Law in Canada.* Vol. 1. Toronto: University of Toronto Press for the Osgoode Society for Canadian Legal History, 2018.

Gohier, Maxime. "La pratique pétitionnaire des Amérindiens de la vallée du Saint-Laurent sous le régime Britannique: pouvoir, représentation et légitimité (1760–1860)." PhD diss., Université du Québec à Montréal, 2014.

Grabowski, Jan. "The Common Ground: Settled Natives and French in Montreal, 1667–1760." PhD diss., Université de Montréal, 1994.

–. "French Criminal Justice and Indians in Montreal, 1670–1760." *Ethnohistory* 43, 3 (1996): 405–29.

The Great Law of Peace of the Longhouse People – Kaianerekowa Hotinonsionne. Mohawk Nation via Rooseveltown, NY: Akwesasne Notes, 1975.

Green, Gretchen. "A New People in an Age of War: The Kahnawake Iroquois, 1667–1760." PhD diss., College of William and Mary, 1991.

Greer, Allan. *Mohawk Saint: Catherine Tekakwitha and the Jesuits.* New York: Oxford University Press, 2005.

–. *Peasant, Lord, and Merchant: Rural Society in Three Quebec Parishes, 1740–1840.* Toronto: University of Toronto Press, 1985.

–. *Property and Dispossession: Natives, Empires and Land in Early Modern North America.* Cambridge: Cambridge University Press, 2018.

Grigg, D.B. *The Agricultural Systems of the World.* Cambridge: Cambridge University Press, 1984.

Haefeli, Evan, and Kevin Sweeney. *Captors and Captives: The 1704 French and Indian Raid on Deerfield.* Boston: University of Massachusetts Press, 2003.

Hall, Anthony. *The Bowl with One Spoon.* Vol. 1 of *The American Empire and the Fourth World.* Montreal and Kingston: McGill-Queen's University Press, 2003.

Hanson, John H. *The Lost Prince: Facts Tending to Prove the Identity of Louis the Seventeenth, of France, and the Rev. Eleazar Williams, Missionary among the Indians of North America.* New York: G.P. Putnam, 1854.

Hardin, Garrett. "The Tragedy of the Commons." *Science* 162, 3859 (1968): 1243–48.

Harring, Sidney L. "'A Condescension Lost on Those People': The Six Nations' Grand River Lands, 1784–1860." In Sidney L. Harring, *White Man's Law: Native People in Nineteenth-Century Canadian Jurisprudence,* 35–61. Toronto: University of Toronto Press for the Osgoode Society for Canadian Legal History, 1998.

–. "'There Seemed to Be No Recognized Law': Canadian Law and the Prairie First Nations." In *Laws and Societies in the Canadian Prairie West, 1670–1940,* ed. Louis A. Knafla and Jonathan Swainger, 92–126. Vancouver: UBC Press, 2005.

Harris, R. Cole. *Making Native Space: Colonialism, Resistance, and Reserves in British Columbia.* Vancouver: UBC Press, 2002.

–. *The Seigneurial System in Early Canada: A Geographical Study.* Quebec City: Presses de l'Université Laval, 1966.

Harvey, Douglas S. "Strolling Players in Albany, Montreal, and Quebec City, 1797 and 1810: Performance, Class, and Empire." *Studies in Eighteenth Century Culture* 38 (2009): 237–60.

Head, Francis Bond. *The Emigrant.* London: John Murray, 1846.

Heaman, Elsbeth. "Space, Race, and Violence: The Beginnings of 'Civilization' in Canada." In *Violence, Order, and Unrest: A History of British North America, 1749–1876,* ed. Elizabeth Mancke, Jerry Bannister, Denis McKim, and Scott W. See, 135–58. Toronto: University of Toronto Press, 2019.

Heidenreich, Conrad. *Huronia: A History and Geography of the Huron Indians, 1600–1650.* Toronto: McClelland and Stewart, 1971.

Henley, David. "Swidden Farming as an Agent of Environmental Change: Ecological Myth and Historical Reality in Indonesia." *Environment and History* 17 (2011): 525–54.

Hildebrandt, Walter, Dorothy First Rider, and Sarah Carter. *The True Spirit and Original Intent of Treaty 7.* Montreal and Kingston: McGill-Queen's University Press, 1996.

Hill, Susan M. *The Clay We Are Made Of: Haudenosaunee Land Tenure on the Grand River.* Winnipeg: University of Manitoba Press, 2017.

Holmes, Joan. "Kahnawake Mohawk Territory: From Seigneury to Indian Reserve." Paper presented at the National Claims Research Workshop, Ottawa, November 9, 2006.

Horn-Miller, Kahente. "How Did Adoption Become a Dirty Word? Indigenous Citizenship Orders as Irreconcilable Spaces of Aboriginality." *AlterNative* 14, 4 (2018): 354–64.

Isenberg, Andrew. *The Destruction of the Bison: An Environmental History, 1750–1920.* Cambridge: Cambridge University Press, 2000.

Jackson, Louis. *Our Caughnawagas in Egypt.* Montreal: Wm. Drysdale, 1885.

Jacobs, Dean M., and Victor P. Lytwyn. "Naagan Ge Bezhig Emkwaan: A Dish with One Spoon Reconsidered." *Ontario History* 112, 2 (2020): 191–210.

Johnson, William. *The Papers of Sir William Johnson.* Edited by Alexander C. Flick. Vol. 8. Albany: University of the State of New York, 1933.

Jordan, Kurt. *The Seneca Restoration, 1715–1754: An Iroquois Local Political Economy.* Gainesville: Society for Historical Archaeology and University Press of Florida, 2008.

Kimmerer, Robin Wall. *Braiding Sweetgrass: Indigenous Wisdom, Scientific Knowledge, and the Teachings of Plants.* Minneapolis: Milkweed Editions, 2013.

King, Thomas. *The Inconvenient Indian: A Curious Account of Native People in North America.* Toronto: Doubleday, 2012.

King, Tiffany Lethabo. *The Black Shoals: Offshore Formations of Black and Native Studies.* Durham: Duke University Press, 2019.

Kolish, Evelyn. "Some Aspects of Civil Litigation in Lower Canada, 1785–1825: Towards the Use of Court Records for Canadian Social History." *Canadian Historical Review* 70, 3 (1989): 337–65.

Labelle, Kathryn Magee. *Dispersed but Not Destroyed: A History of the Seventeenth-Century Wendat People.* Vancouver: UBC Press, 2013.

Lafitau, Joseph François. *Customs of the American Indians Compared with the Customs of Primitive Times.* Translated by William N. Fenton and Elizabeth L. Moore. Vol. 2. Toronto: Champlain Society, 1977 [1724].

–. *Moeurs des sauvages ameriquains comparées aux moeurs des premiers temps.* Vol. 2. Paris: Chez Saugrain l'aîné et al., 1724.

Lambert, Carmen. "History of Kahnawake Land Claims, Seigneury of Sault-Saint-Louis." Paper prepared for the Confederation of Indians of Quebec, 1980.

Lefrançois, Alexandre. "Thomas Arakwenté: Promoteur de la modernité dans la communauté iroquoise du Sault Saint-Louis (1791–1820)." *Revue d'éthique et de théologie morale "Le Supplément"* 226 (2003): 357–78.

Leighton, Douglas. "A Victorian Civil Servant at Work: Lawrence Vankoughnet and the Canadian Indian Department, 1874–1893." In *As Long as the Sun Shines and the Water Flows: A Reader in Canadian Native Studies,* ed. Ian L. Getty and Antoine S. Lussier, 104–19. Vancouver: UBC Press, 1983.

Long, John. *John Long's Voyages and Travels in the Years 1768–1788.* Chicago: Lakeside, 1922 [1791].

Lorimier, Claude Nicolas-Guillaume de. "Mes services pendant la guerre américaine." In *Invasion du Canada,* ed. M. L'abbé Verreau, 245–98. Montreal: Eusèbe Senécal, 1873.

Lowman, Emma Battell, and Adam J. Barker. *Settler: Identity and Colonialism in 21st Century Canada.* Winnipeg: Fernwood, 2015.

Lozier, Jean-François. *Flesh Reborn: The St. Lawrence Valley Mission Settlements through the Seventeenth Century.* Montreal and Kingston: McGill-Queen's University Press, 2018.

Lutz, John S. *Makúk: A New History of Aboriginal-White Relations.* Vancouver: UBC Press, 2008.

Lux, Maureen K. *Medicine That Walks: Disease, Medicine, and Canadian Plains Native People, 1880–1940*. Toronto: University of Toronto Press, 2001.

MacLeitch, Gail D. *Imperial Entanglements: Iroquois Change and Persistence on the Frontiers of Empire*. Philadelphia: University of Pennsylvania Press, 2011.

Mar, Tracey Banivanua, and Penelope Edmonds. "Making Space in Settler Colonies." In *Making Settler Colonial Space: Perspectives on Race, Place and Identity*, ed. Tracey Banivanua Mar and Penelope Edmonds, 1–24. New York: Palgrave Macmillan, 2010.

McKay, Ian. "The Liberal Order Framework: A Prospectus for a Reconnaissance of Canadian History." *Canadian Historical Review* 81, 4 (December 2000): 617–45.

Moodie, D. Wayne, and Barry Kaye. "Indian Agriculture in the Fur Trade Northwest." *Prairie Forum* 11, 2 (1986): 171–83.

Moreton-Robinson, Aileen. *The White Possessive: Property, Power, and Indigenous Sovereignty*. Minneapolis: University of Minnesota Press, 2015.

Morgan, Lewis H. *League of the Ho-De'-No-Sau-Nee or Iroquois*. North Dighton, MA: JG Press, 1995 [1851].

Morin, Michel. *L'usurpation de la souveraineté autochtone: Le cas des peuples de la Nouvelle-France et des colonies anglaises de l'Amérique du Nord*. Montreal: Boréal, 1997.

Morris, Alexander. *The Treaties of Canada with the Indians of Manitoba and the North-West Territories*. Toronto: Willing and Williamson, 1880.

Mt. Pleasant, Jane. "The Paradox of Plows and Productivity: An Agronomic Comparison of Cereal Grain Production under Iroquois Hoe Culture and European Plow Culture in the Seventeenth and Eighteenth Centuries." *Agricultural History* 85, 4 (2011): 460–92.

Muller, Kathryn V. "The Two 'Mystery' Belts of Grand River: A Biography of the Two Row Wampum and the Friendship Belt." *American Indian Quarterly* 31, 1 (2007): 129–64.

Munro, William Bennett. *The Seigniorial System in Canada: A Study in French Colonial Policy*. New York: Longmans Green, 1907.

Napoleon, Val. "The Role of the Sacred in Indigenous Law and Reconciliation." Paper presented at Ideafest, University of Victoria, March 20, 2018. https://www.youtube.com/watch?v=PEIoHsT2pag.

–. "Thinking about Indigenous Legal Orders." Research paper for the National Centre for First Nations Governance, June 2007. http://fngovernance.org/ncfng_research/val_napoleon.pdf.

National Inquiry into Missing and Murdered Indigenous Women and Girls. "Supplementary Report of the National Inquiry into Missing and Murdered Indigenous Women and Girls: A Legal Analysis of Genocide." https://www.mmiwg-ffada.ca/wp-content/uploads/2019/06/Supplementary-Report_Genocide.pdf.

Neeson, J.M. *Commoners: Common Right, Enclosure and Social Change in England, 1700–1820*. Cambridge: Cambridge University Press, 1993.

Newell, William B. *Crime and Justice among the Iroquois Nations*. Montreal: Caughnawaga Historical Society, 1965.

Nicks, Trudy. "The Iroquois and the Fur Trade in Western Canada." In *Old Trails and New Directions: Papers of the Third North American Fur Trade Conference*, ed. Carol M. Judd and Arthur J. Ray, 85–101. Toronto: University of Toronto Press, 1980.

Nixon, Rob. *Slow Violence and the Environmentalism of the Poor*. Cambridge: Harvard University Press, 2013.

Nobles, Gregory H. *American Frontiers: Cultural Encounters and Continental Conquest.* New York: Hill and Wang, 1997.

Old Kahnawake; An Oral History of Kahnawake. Kahnawà:ke: Kanien'kehaka Raotitiokwa Cultural Center, 1991.

Ostrom, Elinor. *Governing the Commons: The Evolution of Institutions for Collective Action.* Political Economy of Institutions and Decisions. Cambridge: Cambridge University Press, 1990.

Otis, D.S. *The Dawes Act and the Allotment of Indian Lands.* Norman: University of Oklahoma Press, 1973 [1934].

Ouellet, Fernand. "Le régime seigneurial dans le Québec: 1760–1854." In *France et Canada français du XVIe au XXe siècle,* ed. Claude Galarneau and Elzéar Lavoie, 159–76. Quebec City: Presses de l'université Laval, 1966.

Owen, Tim, and Elaine Pilbeam. *Ordnance Survey: Map Makers to Britain since 1791.* London: HMSO, 1992.

Palmater, Pamela D. *Beyond Blood: Rethinking Indigenous Identity.* Saskatoon: Purich, 2011.

–. "Genocide, Indian Policy, and Legislated Elimination of Indians in Canada." *Aboriginal Policy Studies* 3, 3 (2014): 27–54.

Parker, Arthur C. *An Analytical History of the Seneca Indians.* Vol. 6. N.p.: Kraus Reprint, 1970 [1926].

–. *The Code of Handsome Lake, the Seneca Prophet.* Albany: New York State Museum, 1913.

–. *The Constitution of the Five Nations.* New York State Museum Bulletin 184. Albany: University of the State of New York, 1916.

–. *Parker on the Iroquois.* Edited by William Fenton. Syracuse: Syracuse University Press, 1968.

Parker, Linda S. *Native American Estate: The Struggle over Indian and Hawaiian Lands.* Honolulu: University of Hawai'i Press, 1996.

Parmenter, Jon. *The Edge of the Woods: Iroquoia, 1534–1701.* East Lansing: Michigan State University Press, 2010.

–. "The Meaning of Kaswentha and the Two Row Wampum Belt in Haudenosaunee (Iroquois) History: Can Indigenous Oral Tradition Be Reconciled with the Documentary Record?" *Journal of Early American History* 3 (2013): 82–109.

Parsons, Christopher. "The Natural History of Colonial Science: Joseph-François Lafitau's Discovery of Ginseng and Its Afterlives." *William and Mary Quarterly* 73, 1 (2016): 37–72.

Pasqualucci, Jo M. "International Indigenous Land Rights: A Critique of the Jurisprudence of the Inter-American Court of Human Rights in Light of the United Nations Declaration on the Rights of Indigenous Peoples." *Wisconsin International Law Journal* 27, 1 (2009): 51–98.

Peace, Thomas. "Borderlands, Primary Sources, and the Longue Durée: Contextualizing Colonial Schooling at Odanak, Lorette, and Kahnawake, 1600–1850." *Historical Studies in Education/Revue d'histoire de l'éducation* 29, 1 (2017): 8–31.

Phillips, Stephanie. "The Kahnawake Mohawks and the St. Lawrence Seaway." Master's thesis, McGill University, 2000.

Porter, Whitworth. *History of the Corps of Royal Engineers.* Vol. 1. London: Longmans, Green, 1889.

Price, Richard, ed. *The Spirit of the Alberta Indian Treaties.* Montreal: Institute for Research on Public Policy, 1979.

Raibmon, Paige. "Unmaking Native Space: A Genealogy of Indian Policy, Settler Practice, and the Microtechniques of Dispossession." In *The Power of Promises: Rethinking Indian Treaties in the Pacific Northwest*, ed. A. Harmon, 56–85. Seattle: University of Washington Press, 2008.

Rasenberger, Jim. *High Steel: The Daring Men Who Built the World's Greatest Skyline*. New York: HarperCollins, 2004.

Ray, Arthur J., J.R. Miller, and Frank Tough. *Bounty and Benevolence: A History of Saskatchewan Treaties*. Montreal and Kingston: McGill-Queen's University Press, 2000.

Reid, Gerald. *Kahnawà:ke: Factionalism, Traditionalism, and Nationalism in a Mohawk Community*. Lincoln: University of Nebraska Press, 2004.

–. "Kahnawake's Council of Chiefs: 1840–1889." Mohawk Nation at Kahnawake. http://www.kahnawakelonghouse.com/index.php?mid=2&p=2.

–. "'To Renew Our Fire': Political Activism, Nationalism, and Identity in Three Rotinonhsionni Communities." In *Tribal Worlds: Critical Studies in American Indian Nation Building*, ed. Brian Hosmer and Larry Nesper, 37–64. Albany: State University of New York Press, 2013.

Richards, John F. *The Unending Frontier: An Environmental History of the Early Modern World*. Berkeley: University of California Press, 2003.

Richter, Daniel K. *The Ordeal of the Longhouse: The Peoples of the Iroquois League in the Era of European Colonization*. Chapel Hill: Institute of Early American History and Culture and University of North Carolina Press, 1992.

Robert, Jean-Claude. *Atlas historique de Montréal*. [Montreal]: Art Global/Libre Expression, 1994.

Rotz, Sarah. "'They Took Our Beads, It Was a Fair Trade, Get over It': Settler Colonial Logics, Racial Hierarchies and Material Dominance in Canadian Agriculture." *Geoforum* 82 (2017): 158–69.

Rueck, Daniel. "Imposing a Mindless Geometry: Surveyors versus the Canadian Plains, 1869–1885." Master's thesis, McGill University, 2004.

–. "When Bridges Become Barriers: Montreal and Kahnawake Mohawk Territory." In *Metropolitan Natures: Urban Environmental Histories of Montreal*, ed. Stéphane Castonguay and Michèle Dagenais, 228–44. Pittsburgh: University of Pittsburgh Press, 2011.

Sala, George Augustus. *Under the Sun: Essays Mainly Written in Hot Countries*. London: Vizetelly, 1886.

Samson, Daniel. *The Spirit of Industry and Improvement: Liberal Government and Rural-Industrial Society, Nova Scotia, 1790–1862*. Montreal and Kingston: McGill-Queen's University Press, 2008.

Sarat, Austin, and Thomas R. Kearns. "Introduction." In *Law's Violence*, ed. Austin Sarat and Thomas R. Kearns, 1–21. Ann Arbor: University of Michigan Press, 1993.

Scott, Duncan Campbell. "Indian Affairs, 1763–1841." In *Canada and Its Provinces*, ed. Adam Shortt and Arthur G. Doughty, vol. 2, section 2, part 2. Toronto: Glasgow, Brook, 1914.

–. "Indian Affairs, 1840–1867." In *Canada and Its Provinces*, ed. Adam Shortt and Arthur G. Doughty, vol. 5, section 3. Toronto: Glasgow, Brook, 1914.

Scott, James C. *Seeing Like a State: How Certain Schemes to Improve the Human Condition Have Failed*. New Haven: Yale University Press, 1998.

Seymour, W.A. *A History of the Ordnance Survey*. Folkestone, UK: Dawson, 1980.

Shannon, Timothy J. *Iroquois Diplomacy on the Early American Frontier.* New York: Viking, 2008.

Simison, R.B. "The Indian Lands of Dundee: An Historical Perspective." *Journal annuel de la Société historique de la vallée de la Châteauguay* 11 (1978): 7–10.

Simpson, Audra. *Mohawk Interruptus: Political Life across the Borders of Settler States.* Durham: Duke University Press, 2014.

Simpson, Leanne. "Looking after Gdoo-Naaganinaa: Precolonial Nishnaabeg Diplomatic and Treaty Relationships." *Wicazo Sa Review* 23, 2 (2008): 29–42.

Sirén, Anders Henrik. "Population Growth and Land Use Intensification in a Subsistence-Based Indigenous Community in the Amazon." *Human Ecology* 35, 6 (2007): 669–80.

Smallwood, Joseph Roberts, and Robert D.W. Pitt. "Walbank, Matthew William." In *Encyclopedia of Newfoundland and Labrador.* Vol. 5. St. John's: Newfoundland Book Publishers, 1981.

Smith, Keith D. *Liberalism, Surveillance, and Resistance: Indigenous Communities in Western Canada, 1877–1927.* Edmonton: Athabasca University Press, 2009.

Smith, Linda Tuhiwai. *Decolonizing Methodologies: Research and Indigenous Peoples.* Dunedin: University of Otago Press, 2006 [1999].

Snell, James G. *In the Shadow of the Law: Divorce in Canada, 1900–1939.* Toronto: University of Toronto Press, 1991.

Sossoyan, Matthieu. "The Kahnawake Iroquois and the Lower-Canadian Rebellions, 1837–1838." Master's thesis, McGill University, 1999.

Sprague, D.N. *Canada and the Métis, 1869–1885.* Waterloo: Wilfrid Laurier University Press, 1988.

–. *Canada's Treaties with Aboriginal People.* Winnipeg: Canadian Legal History Project, Faculty of Law, University of Manitoba, 1991.

Spry, Irene M. "The Great Transformation: The Disappearance of the Commons in Western Canada." In *Canadian Plains Studies 6: Man and Nature on the Prairies,* ed. Richard Allen, 21–75. Regina: Canadian Plains Research Centre, University of Regina, 1976.

Stevens, G.R. *Canadian National Railways.* Vol. 1, *Sixty Years of Trial and Error (1836–1896).* Toronto: Clarke, Irwin, 1960.

Stoler, Ann Laura. *Duress: Imperial Durabilities in Our Times.* Durham: Duke University Press, 2016.

Stone, Helen. "Les Indiens et le système judiciaire criminel de la province de Québec: Les politiques de l'administration sous le régime britannique." *Recherches amérindiennes au Québec* 30, 3 (2000): 65–78.

St-Onge, Nicole. "'He Was Neither a Soldier nor a Slave: He Was under the Control of No Man': Kahnawake Mohawks in the Northwest Fur Trade, 1790–1850." *Canadian Journal of History* 51, 1 (2016): 1–32.

Stote, Karen. *An Act of Genocide: Colonialism and the Sterilization of Aboriginal Women.* Winnipeg: Fernwood, 2015.

Stunden Bower, Shannon. *Wet Prairie: People, Land, and Water in Agricultural Manitoba.* Vancouver: UBC Press, 2011.

Surtees, Robert J. "The Development of an Indian Reserve Policy in Canada." *Ontario History* 61, 2 (1969): 87–98.

Taggart, C.H. *Caughnawaga Indian Reserve: Report, General and Final.* Ottawa: Department of Mines and Resources, 1948.

TallBear, Kim. *Native American DNA: Tribal Belonging and the False Promise of Genetic Science*. Minneapolis: University of Minnesota Press, 2013.

Taussig, Michael. *Shamanism, Colonialism, and the Wild Man: A Study in Terror and Healing*. Chicago: University of Chicago Press, 1991.

Taylor, Alan. *The Divided Ground: Indians, Settlers, and the Northern Borderland of the American Revolution*. New York: Alfred A. Knopf, 2006.

"This Is Indian Land: An Exhibit on the State of Kahnawake Lands." Report for the Socio-Economic Development Program of the Mohawk Council of Kahnawake, [1982].

Thompson, E.P. *Customs in Common*. New York: New Press, 1991.

Titley, Brian. "Isoler et embrigader: la tendance coercitive des politiques d'éducation pour enfants autochtones (1870–1932)." *Recherches amérindiennes au Québec* 41, 1 (2011): 3–15.

Titley, E. Brian. *A Narrow Vision: Duncan Campbell Scott and the Administration of Indian Affairs in Canada*. Vancouver: UBC Press, 1992.

Tobias, John L. "Protection, Civilisation, Assimilation: An Outline History of Canada's Indian Policy." In *As Long as the Sun Shines and the Water Flows: A Reader in Canadian Native Studies*, ed. Ian A.L. Getty and Antoine S. Lucier, 39-55. Vancouver: UBC Press, 1983.

Tooker, Elizabeth. "Women in Iroquois Society." In *Extending the Rafters: Interdisciplinary Approaches to Iroquoian Studies*, ed. Michael K. Foster and Jack Campisi, 109–23. Albany: State University of New York Press, 1984.

Torgovnick, Marianna. *Gone Primitive: Savage Intellects, Modern Lives*. Chicago: University of Chicago Press, 1990.

Trask, Haunani-Kay. "The Color of Violence." In *Color of Violence: The Incite! Anthology*, ed. INCITE! Women of Color against Violence, 81–87. Durham: Duke University Press, 2016.

–. *From a Native Daughter: Colonialism and Sovereignty in Hawai'i*. Honolulu: University of Hawai'i Press, 1999 [1993].

Trudel, Marcel. "Le destin de l'Église sous le régime militaire." *Revue d'histoire de l'Amerique français* 11, 1 (1957): 10–41.

–. *Le régime seigneurial*. Ottawa: Société historique du Canada, 1956.

Truth and Reconciliation Commission of Canada. *The Final Report of the Truth and Reconciliation Commission of Canada*. Montreal and Kingston: McGill-Queen's University Press, 2015.

Tulchinsky, Gerald. "The Construction of the First Lachine Canal, 1815–1826." Master's thesis, McGill University, 1960.

–. *The River Barons: Montreal Businessmen and the Growth of Industry and Transportation, 1837-53*. Toronto: University of Toronto Press, 1977.

Turner, Frederick Jackson. "The Significance of the Frontier in American History." *Proceedings of the Forty-First Annual Meeting of the State Historical Society of Wisconsin* (1894): 1–34.

United Nations, Office on Genocide Prevention and the Responsibility to Protect. "The Genocide Convention." https://www.un.org/en/genocideprevention/genocide-convention.shtml.

Van den Bogaert, Harmen Meyndertsz. *A Journey into Mohawk and Oneida Country, 1634–1635: The Journal of Harmen Meyndertsz Van Den Bogaert*. Edited and translated by Charles T. Gehring and William A. Starna. Syracuse: Syracuse University Press, 2013.

Van der Donck, Adriaen. *Description of the New Netherlands [in 1640]*. Translated by Jeremiah Johnson. New York: New York Historical Society, 1841.

Veracini, Lorenzo. *Settler Colonialism: A Theoretical Overview.* Houndmills, UK: Palgrave Macmillan, 2010.

Vismann, Cornelia. "Starting from Scratch: Concepts of Order in No-Man's-Land." In *War, Violence, and the Modern Condition,* ed. Bernd Hüppauf, 46–65. Berlin: Walter de Gruyter, 1997.

Walzer, Michael. "Liberalism and the Art of Separation." *Political Theory* 12, 3 (1994): 315–30.

Waugh, F.W. *Iroquois Foods and Food Preparation.* Ottawa: Government Printing Bureau, 1973 [1916].

Weaver, John C. *The Great Land Rush and the Making of the Modern World, 1650–1900.* Montreal and Kingston: McGill-Queen's University Press, 2003.

Weisinger, Marsha L. *Dreaming of Sheep in Navajo Country.* Seattle: University of Washington Press, 2009.

Weld, Isaac. *Travels through the States of North America and the Provinces of Upper and Lower Canada.* London: John Stockdale, 1800.

Whetung, Madeline. "(En)Gendering Shoreline Law: Nishnaabeg Relational Politics along the Trent Severn Waterway." *Global Environmental Politics* 19, 3 (2019): 16–32.

White, Richard. *The Middle Ground: Indians, Empires, and Republics in the Great Lakes Region, 1650–1815.* Cambridge: Cambridge University Press, 1991.

Wildcat, Matthew. "Fearing Social and Cultural Death: Genocide and Elimination in Settler Colonial Canada – An Indigenous Perspective." *Journal of Genocide Research* 17, 4 (2015): 391–409.

Williams, Kayanesenh Paul. *Kayanerenkó:wa: The Great Law of Peace.* Winnipeg: University of Manitoba Press, 2018.

Wolfe, Patrick. "Against the Intentional Fallacy: Legocentrism and Continuity in the Rhetoric of Indian Dispossession." *American Indian Culture and Research Journal* 36, 1 (2012): 3–45.

–. "Settler Colonialism and the Elimination of the Native." *Journal of Genocide Research* 8, 4 (2006): 387–409.

Woolford, Andrew, and Jeff Benvenuto. "Canada and Colonial Genocide." *Journal of Genocide Research* 17, 4 (2015): 373–90.

Worster, Donald. *A River Running West: The Life of John Wesley Powell.* Oxford: Oxford University Press, 2001.

Yeh, Emily T. "Tropes of Indolence and the Cultural Politics of Development in Lhasa, Tibet." *Annals of the Association of American Geographers* 97, 3 (2007): 593–612.

Zachary Deom, Christine. "Chronology of Political Events Relative to Kahnawake." Mohawk Council of Kahnawake Draft Document, 2010.

Index

Note: "(f)" after a page number indicates an illustration or map

Index

PUBLICATIONS OF THE OSGOODE SOCIETY FOR CANADIAN LEGAL HISTORY

2021   LYNDSAY CAMPBELL, *Truth and Privilege: Libel Law in Massachusetts and Nova Scotia, 1820–1840*

COLIN CAMPBELL and ROBERT RAIZENNE, *Income Tax in Canada: Laying the Foundations 1917–1948*

MARTINE VALOIS, IAN GREENE, CRAIG FORCESE, and PETER McCORMICK, eds., *The Federal Court of Appeal and the Federal Court: 50 Years of History*

2020   HEIDI BOHAKER, *Doodem and Council Fire Anishinaabe Governance through Alliance*

CAROLYN STRANGE, *The Death Penalty and Sex Murder in Canadian History*

2019   HARRY ARTHURS, *Connecting the Dots: The Life of an Academic Lawyer*

ERIC H. REITER, *Wounded Feelings: Litigating Emotions in Quebec, 1870–1950*

2018   PHILIP GIRARD, JIM PHILLIPS, and BLAKE BROWN, *A History of Law in Canada: Volume 1, Beginnings to 1866*

SUZANNE CHIODO, *The Class Actions Controversy: The Origins and Development of the Ontario Class Proceedings Act*

2017   CONSTANCE BACKHOUSE, *Claire L'Heureux-Dubé: A Life*

DENNIS G. MOLINARO, *An Exceptional Law: Section 98 and the Emergency State, 1919–1936*

2016   LORI CHAMBERS, *A Legal History of Adoption in Ontario, 1921-2015*
BRADLEY MILLER, *Borderline Crime: Fugitive Criminals and the Challenge of the Border, 1819-1914*
JAMES MUIR, *Law, Debt, and Merchant Power: The Civil Courts of Eighteenth-Century Halifax*

2015   BARRY WRIGHT, ERIC TUCKER, and SUSAN BINNIE, eds., *Canadian State Trials, Volume IV: Security, Dissent and the Limits of Toleration in War and Peace, 1914-1939*
DAVID FRASER, *"Honorary Protestants": The Jewish School Question in Montreal, 1867-1997*
C. IAN KYER, *A Thirty Years War: The Failed Public /Private Partnership that Spurred the Creation of The Toronto Transit Commission, 1891-1921*

2014   CHRISTOPHER MOORE, *A History of the Ontario Court of Appeal*
DOMINIQUE CLÉMENT, *Equality Deferred: Sex Discrimination and British Columbia's Human Rights State, 1953-84*
PAUL CRAVEN, *Petty Justice: Low Law and the Sessions System in Charlotte County, New Brunswick, 1785-1867*
THOMAS TELFER, *Ruin and Redemption: The Struggle for a Canadian Bankruptcy Law, 1867-1919*

2013   ROY MCMURTRY, *Memoirs & Reflections*
CHARLOTTE GRAY, *The Massey Murder: A Maid, Her Master and the Trial that Shocked a Nation*
C. IAN KYER, *Lawyers, Families, and Businesses: The Shaping of a Bay Street Law Firm, Faskens 1863-1963*
G. BLAINE BAKER and DONALD FYSON, eds., *Essays in the History of Canadian Law. Volume 11: Quebec and the Canadas*

2012   R. BLAKE BROWN, *Arming and Disarming: A History of Gun Control in Canada*
ERIC TUCKER, JAMES MUIR, and BRUCE ZIFF, eds., *Property on Trial: Canadian Cases in Context*
SHELLEY A.M. GAVIGAN, *Hunger, Horses, and Government Men: Criminal Law on the Aboriginal Plains, 1870-1905*
BARRINGTON WALKER, ed., *The African-Canadian Legal Odyssey: Historical Essays*

2011   ROBERT J. SHARPE, *The Lazier Murder: Prince Edward County, 1884*
PHILIP GIRARD, *Lawyers and Legal Culture in British North America: Beamish Murdoch of Halifax*

JOHN MCLAREN, *Dewigged, Bothered and Bewildered: British Colonial Judges on Trial*

LESLEY ERICKSON, *Westward Bound: Sex, Violence, the Law, and the Making of a Settler Society*

2010 JUDY FUDGE and ERIC TUCKER, eds., *Work on Trial: Canadian Labour Law Struggles*

CHRISTOPHER MOORE, *The British Columbia Court of Appeal: The First Hundred Years*

FREDERICK VAUGHAN, *Viscount Haldane: The Wicked Step-father of the Canadian Constitution*

BARRINGTON WALKER, *Race on Trial: Black Defendants in Ontario's Criminal Courts, 1850-1950*

2009 WILLIAM KAPLAN, *Canadian Maverick: The Life and Times of Ivan C. Rand*

R. BLAKE BROWN, *A Trying Question: The Jury in Nineteenth-Century Canada*

BARRY WRIGHT and SUSAN BINNIE, eds., *Canadian State Trials. Volume 3: Political Trials and Security Measures, 1840-1914*

ROBERT J. SHARPE, *The Last Day, the Last Hour: The Currie Libel Trial*

2008 CONSTANCE BACKHOUSE, *Carnal Crimes: Sexual Assault Law in Canada, 1900-1975*

JIM PHILLIPS, R. ROY MCMURTRY, and JOHN SAYWELL, eds., *Essays in the History of Canadian Law. Volume 10: A Tribute to Peter N. Oliver*

GREGORY TAYLOR, *The Law of the Land: Canada's Receptions of the Torrens System*

HAMAR FOSTER, BENJAMIN BERGER, and A.R. BUCK, eds., *The Grand Experiment: Law and Legal Culture in British Settler Societies*

2007 ROBERT SHARPE and PATRICIA MCMAHON, *The Persons Case: The Origins and Legacy of the Fight for Legal Personhood*

LORI CHAMBERS, *Misconceptions: Unmarried Motherhood and the Ontario Children of Unmarried Parents Act, 1921-1969*

JONATHAN SWAINGER, ed., *The Alberta Supreme Court at 100: History and Authority*

MARTIN FRIEDLAND, *My Life in Crime and Other Academic Adventures*

2006 DONALD FYSON, *Magistrates, Police and People: Everyday Criminal Justice in Quebec and Lower Canada, 1764-1837*

DALE BRAWN, *The Court of Queen's Bench of Manitoba 1870-1950: A Biographical History*

R.C.B. Risk, *A History of Canadian Legal Thought: Collected Essays,* edited and introduced by G. Blaine Baker and Jim Phillips

2005 Philip Girard, *Bora Laskin: Bringing Law to Life*
Christopher English, ed., *Essays in the History of Canadian Law. Volume 9: Two Islands, Newfoundland and Prince Edward Island*
Fred Kaufman, *Searching for Justice: An Autobiography*

2004 John D. Honsberger, *Osgoode Hall: An Illustrated History*
Frederick Vaughan, *Aggressive in Pursuit: The Life of Justice Emmett Hall*
Constance Backhouse and Nancy Backhouse, *The Heiress versus the Establishment: Mrs. Campbell's Campaign for Legal Justice*
Philip Girard, Jim Phillips, and Barry Cahill, eds., *The Supreme Court of Nova Scotia, 1754-2004: From Imperial Bastion to Provincial Oracle*

2003 Robert Sharpe and Kent Roach, *Brian Dickson: A Judge's Journey*
George Finlayson, *John J. Robinette: Peerless Mentor*
Peter Oliver, *The Conventional Man: The Diaries of Ontario Chief Justice Robert A. Harrison, 1856-1878*
Jerry Bannister, *The Rule of the Admirals: Law, Custom and Naval Government in Newfoundland, 1699-1832*

2002 John T. Saywell, *The Law Makers: Judicial Power and the Shaping of Canadian Federalism*
David Murray, *Colonial Justice: Justice, Morality and Crime in the Niagara District, 1791-1849*
F. Murray Greenwood and Barry Wright, eds., *Canadian State Trials. Volume 2: Rebellion and Invasion in the Canadas, 1837-38*
Patrick Brode, *Courted and Abandoned: Seduction in Canadian Law*

2001 Ellen Anderson, *Judging Bertha Wilson: Law as Large as Life*
Judy Fudge and Eric Tucker, *Labour before the Law: Collective Action in Canada, 1900-1948*
Laurel Sefton MacDowell, *Renegade Lawyer: The Life of J.L. Cohen*

2000 Barry Cahill, *"The Thousandth Man": A Biography of James McGregor Stewart*
A.B. McKillop, *The Spinster and the Prophet: Florence Deeks, H.G. Wells, and the Mystery of the Purloined Past*
Beverley Boissery and F. Murray Greenwood, *Uncertain Justice: Canadian Women and Capital Punishment*
Bruce Ziff, *Unforeseen Legacies: Reuben Wells Leonard and the Leonard Foundation Trust*

1999   CONSTANCE BACKHOUSE, *Colour-Coded: A Legal History of Racism in Canada, 1900-1950*
      G. BLAINE BAKER and JIM PHILLIPS, eds., *Essays in the History of Canadian Law. Volume 8: In Honour of R.C.B. Risk*
      RICHARD W. POUND, *Chief Justice W.R. Jackett: By the Law of the Land*
      DAVID VANEK, *Fulfilment: Memoirs of a Criminal Court Judge*

1998   SIDNEY HARRING, *White Man's Law: Native People in Nineteenth-Century Canadian Jurisprudence*
      PETER OLIVER, *"Terror to Evil-Doers": Prisons and Punishments in Nineteenth-Century Ontario*

1997   JAMES W. ST. G. WALKER, *"Race," Rights and the Law in the Supreme Court of Canada: Historical Case Studies*
      LORI CHAMBERS, *Married Women and Property Law in Victorian Ontario*
      PATRICK BRODE, *Casual Slaughters and Accidental Judgments: Canadian War Crimes and Prosecutions, 1944-1948*
      IAN BUSHNELL, *The Federal Court of Canada: A History, 1875-1992*

1996   CAROL WILTON, ed., *Essays in the History of Canadian Law. Volume 7: Inside the Law – Canadian Law Firms in Historical Perspective*
      WILLIAM KAPLAN, *Bad Judgment: The Case of Mr. Justice Leo A. Landreville*
      MURRAY GREENWOOD and BARRY WRIGHT, eds., *Canadian State Trials. Volume 1: Law, Politics and Security Measures, 1608-1837*

1995   DAVID WILLIAMS, *Just Lawyers: Seven Portraits*
      HAMAR FOSTER and JOHN MCLAREN, eds., *Essays in the History of Canadian Law. Volume 6: British Columbia and the Yukon*
      W.H. MORROW, ed., *Northern Justice: The Memoirs of Mr. Justice William G. Morrow*
      BEVERLEY BOISSERY, *A Deep Sense of Wrong: The Treason, Trials and Transportation to New South Wales of Lower Canadian Rebels after the 1838 Rebellion*

1994   PATRICK BOYER, *A Passion for Justice: The Legacy of James Chalmers McRuer*
      CHARLES PULLEN, *The Life and Times of Arthur Maloney: The Last of the Tribunes*
      JIM PHILLIPS, TINA LOO, and SUSAN LEWTHWAITE, eds., *Essays in the History of Canadian Law. Volume 5: Crime and Criminal Justice*
      BRIAN YOUNG, *The Politics of Codification: The Lower Canadian Civil Code of 1866*

1993   GREG MARQUIS, *Policing Canada's Century: A History of the Canadian Association of Chiefs of Police*

MURRAY GREENWOOD, *Legacies of Fear: Law and Politics in Quebec in the Era of the French Revolution*

1992   BRENDAN O'BRIEN, *Speedy Justice: The Tragic Last Voyage of His Majesty's Vessel* Speedy
ROBERT FRASER, ed., *Provincial Justice: Upper Canadian Legal Portraits from the* Dictionary of Canadian Biography

1991   CONSTANCE BACKHOUSE, *Petticoats and Prejudice: Women and Law in Nineteenth-Century Canada*

1990   PHILIP GIRARD and JIM PHILLIPS, eds., *Essays in the History of Canadian Law. Volume 3: Nova Scotia*
CAROL WILTON, ed., *Essays in the History of Canadian Law. Volume 4: Beyond the Law – Lawyers and Business in Canada 1830-1930*

1989   DESMOND BROWN, *The Genesis of the Canadian Criminal Code of 1892*
PATRICK BRODE, *The Odyssey of John Anderson*

1988   ROBERT SHARPE, *The Last Day, the Last Hour: The Currie Libel Trial*
JOHN D. ARNUP, *Middleton: The Beloved Judge*

1987   C. IAN KYER and JEROME BICKENBACH, *The Fiercest Debate: Cecil A. Wright, the Benchers and Legal Education in Ontario, 1923-1957*

1986   PAUL ROMNEY, *Mr. Attorney: The Attorney General for Ontario in Court, Cabinet and Legislature, 1791-1899*
MARTIN FRIEDLAND, *The Case of Valentine Shortis: A True Story of Crime and Politics in Canada*

1985   JAMES SNELL and FREDERICK VAUGHAN, *The Supreme Court of Canada: History of the Institution*

1984   PATRICK BRODE, *Sir John Beverley Robinson: Bone and Sinew of the Compact*
DAVID WILLIAMS, *Duff: A Life in the Law*

1983   DAVID H. FLAHERTY, ed., *Essays in the History of Canadian Law. Volume 2*

1982   MARION MACRAE and ANTHONY ADAMSON, *Cornerstones of Order: Courthouses and Town Halls of Ontario, 1784-1914*

1981   DAVID H. FLAHERTY, ed., *Essays in the History of Canadian Law. Volume 1*

Printed and bound in Canada by Friesens
Set in Garamond by Artegraphica Design Co. Ltd.
Copy editor: Deborah Kerr
Proofreader: Alison Strobel
Indexer: Margaret de Boer
Cartographer: Eric Leinberger
Cover designer: Will Brown